Reflections on the life of United States Senator Daniel Baugh Brewster

"When the going was tough, and when the campaign was rough, Maryland produced a courageous and a valiant Senator to uphold my hand, and he stood in for me when I couldn't be here—my old and good and trusted and beloved friend, your great Senator Danny Brewster."

> — President Lyndon B. Johnson (following Brewster's 1964 presidential primary win against Alabama Governor George Wallace as a stand-in for LBJ)

"Daniel Brewster's legacy can be found in his commitment to civil rights, his ability to find strength through adversity, and his devotion to the state of Maryland and its people."

> — Speaker Nancy Pelosi

"We need to acknowledge the depths of his fall from privilege and victory to understand the courage and grace of his ascent to the gentle man of decency and principle that he had been and would remain."

> — Majority Leader Steny Hoyer

"This beautifully written and carefully researched biography portrays the fascinating life of Daniel B. Brewster, from his courageous fighting in the South Pacific, where he was wounded seven times but never relinquished command, to his rise in national politics, to a downward spiral that nearly destroyed him, followed by an amazing comeback."

— Ambassador Tyler Abell, President Lyndon Johnson's Advisor and Chief of Protocol

"Senator Daniel Brewster became caught in the vortex of American politics of the 1960s: the New Frontier, Great Society, Vietnam War, Civil Rights Movement, and conservative reaction. How he coped with these challenges, personally and politically, and the price he paid, makes a powerful story."

— Donald A. Ritchie, U.S. Senate Historian Emeritus

Self-Destruction

*The Rise, Fall, and Redemption
of U.S. Senator
Daniel B. Brewster*

John W. Frece

Apprentice
House Press
Loyola University Maryland

First Edition

Library of Congress Control Number: 2022950412

Hardcover ISBN: 978-1-62720-468-2
Paperback ISBN: 978-1-62720-469-9
Ebook ISBN: 978-1-62720-470-5

Design by Kamryn Spezzano
Editorial Development by Natalie Misyak

Cover photo credits:
Danny Brewster, commissioned as a Marine Corps Lieutenant at age 19, was reportedly the youngest Marine Corps combat officer in World War II. *United States Marine Corps Photo*

As World War II combat veterans, Danny Brewster and President John F. Kennedy developed a friendship as they served together in Congress – a partnership that continued until the President's assassination in November 1963. *Brewster Family Photo*

Nearing rock bottom, Danny Brewster and his son, Gerry, leave federal court on November 11, 1972, after the former U.S. Senator was found guilty of "accepting an unlawful gratuity." *Associated Press Photo*

Having rebuilt his shattered life, Danny Brewster, pictured in the horse barn on his Baltimore County farm, found happiness and contentment in a new family, a quiet lifestyle, and a renewed commitment to service. *Brewster Family Photo*

Published by Apprentice House Press

Loyola University Maryland
4501 N. Charles Street, Baltimore, MD 21210
410.617.5265
www.ApprenticeHouse.com
info@ApprenticeHouse.com

Contents

For Priscilla Cummings, William Frece, and Hannah Carroll
With a lifetime of love.
John W. Frece
June 2022

A Selected Geneaology of Daniel Baugh Brewster

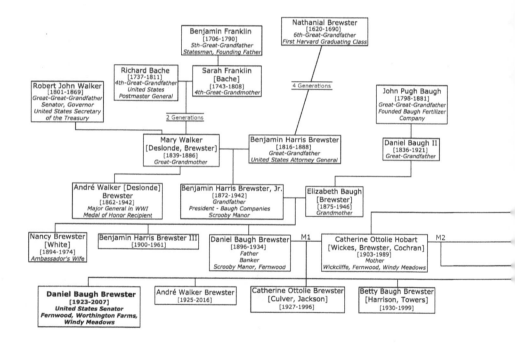

Brewster Marriages

M1 – 1954-1967 – Carol Helme Leiper de Havenon Brewster (Michael H. de Havenon, Andre V. de Havenon, Daniel Baugh Brewster Jr., Gerry Leiper Brewster)

M2 – 1967-1972 – Anne Moen Bullitt Townsend Biddle More O'Ferrall Brewster (daughter of Ambassador William C. Bullitt, first U.S. Ambassador to the Soviet Union and U.S. Ambassador to France during WWII)

M3 – 1976-2007 – Judy Lynn Beckham Aarsand Brewster (Krista A. Bedford, Kurt R. Aarsand, Danielle Brewster Oster, Jennilie Beckham Brewster, Dana Franklin Brewster)

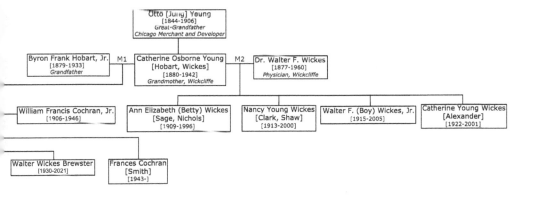

Otto [July] Young
[1844-1906]
Great-Grandfather
Chicago Merchant and Developer

Byron Frank Hobart, Jr.
[1879-1933]
Grandfather

M1

Catherine Osborne Young
[Hobart, Wickes]
[1880-1942]
Grandmother, Wickcliffe

M2

Dr. Walter F. Wickes
[1877-1960]
Physician, Wickcliffe

William Francis Cochran, Jr.
[1906-1946]

Ann Elizabeth (Betty) Wickes
[Sage, Nichols]
[1909-1996]

Nancy Young Wickes
[Clark, Shaw]
[1913-2000]

Walter F. (Boy) Wickes, Jr.
[1915-2005]

Catherine Young Wickes
[Alexander]
[1922-2001]

Walter Wickes Brewster
[1930-2021]

Frances Cochran
[Smith]
[1943-]

Family tree graphic designed by Shannon Sheetz.

ix

Speaker Nancy Pelosi

My personal roots are firmly planted in Baltimore, Maryland.

It was there where my father and mother first met, were married in a traffic-stopping celebration and started a family of their own. And it was there where my dear father, Tommy D'Alesandro, Jr., served for twelve years as Mayor: fighting for dignity and justice for all in our city. Later, my darling older brother, Tommy D'Alesandro III, would also follow in his footsteps.

Our family quickly developed a warm friendship with the family of an up-and-coming public servant, Danny Brewster. Our bonds were forged by our shared values – duty, service, faith, patriotism – as well as our undying love for the state of Maryland.

As fate would have it, my first job after graduating from Trinity University was on the staff of Maryland's newly elected United States Senator – none other than Danny Brewster.

Senator Brewster asked me to serve as a junior assistant, responding to constituent correspondence and answering phones. Working in his office, I saw firsthand how he embodied Maryland principles and priorities.

Coincidentally, also working in Senator Brewster's office was a young staffer by the name of Steny Hoyer. For decades, we have proudly served together in the House – and now, we serve together in Democratic Leadership: I as Speaker and Steny as Majority Leader.

While his biography – much like his life – is centered around his career in politics, it would be impossible to tell his story fully without examining his turbulent personal life.

All are in awe of his heroism: a courageous 20-year-old who answered his nation's call to serve by enlisting in the fight against fascism in the South Pacific. Enduring some of the most brutal combat of World War II, he was wounded multiple times in the battles for Guam and Okinawa. Returning home a decorated war hero, Danny continued to serve his beloved nation: first in the Maryland legislature, then in the House of Representatives and finally in the United States Senate.

Senator Brewster came to the Senate during an exciting time for our nation, under the leadership of a young, dynamic leader in President John Kennedy. His friendship with President Kennedy – and his subsequent friendship with President Johnson – gave him the opportunity to have a voice in national affairs at the highest level during a pivotal moment in history.

But he also grappled with personal demons, which damaged his stature and ultimately ended his political career. It is a testament to his strength of character and indomitable resilience that he could triumph over his challenges, rebuild his life and redeem his reputation.

Reexamining the life and legacy of Senator Brewster is particularly timely at this pivotal moment in our nation's history, in light of our renewed national struggle for racial justice. Danny showed notable political courage in helping pave the way for progress on civil rights. In the 1964 Maryland Presidential Primary, he fiercely opposed and ultimately defeated segregationist Governor George Wallace, serving as a stand-in for President Lyndon Johnson. He was the only Senator from south of the Mason-Dixon Line to co-sponsor both the 1964 Civil Rights Act and the 1965 Voting Rights Act. And he also supported open housing legislation at a time of great civil unrest.

At their best, political biographies are meant to illuminate the private lives of public figures – and deepen our understanding of the era in which they served. John W. Frece's honest, meticulous narrative for the first time shines a bright light on Senator Danny Brewster: a consequential leader whose two decades in public office helped shape the history of both my beloved home state and our entire nation.

In Self-Destruction: The Rise, Fall, and Redemption of U.S. Senator Daniel B. Brewster, we follow one man's journey navigating power and privilege, duty and devotion, horror and hardship. In the end, Danny led a life of meaning, purpose and service. He was a good man, who loved his family.

As his good friend, I am grateful that his story will finally, fully be told.

Prologue

SHOOT THE DAMNED DOG

The door to the second-floor bedroom of the old farmhouse banged open with a crash. Gerry's father, Danny Brewster, dressed only in his boxer shorts and a white V neck T-shirt, stood in the doorway waving a loaded Colt .45. It was the same sidearm he had carried as a Marine officer in the battles for Guam and Okinawa during World War II.

It was two or three in the morning and Gerry and his prep school friend, Chris Hutchins, had been sound asleep. The two sixteen-year-olds had driven up to the farm that Friday evening to go goose hunting with Gerry's dad in the morning. Still groggy with sleep but frightened, the boys jumped to their feet.

"Gerry, go shoot that damned dog," his father commanded. "Gerry, I can't sleep. The damned dog is barking. Go shoot that damned dog."

Startled, Gerry realized his father was probably still drunk from the night before. Chris thought he was either drunk or crazy. Or both.

"It was definitely an out-of-control human being, as scary as you could get," Hutchins recalled years later.[1]

Gerry considered the absurdity of his father's request. "I'm not going to shoot it," he protested.

"Gerry, go shoot that damned dog," his father demanded again in his loud, commanding voice and again menacingly swung the loaded handgun through the air.

Desperate, Gerry tried to gauge what to do. He tried to reason with his father, but Danny Brewster was having none of it. After a minute or so, Gerry said, "OK, Dad, I will take care of it. Give me the gun." To the boys' surprise and relief, Gerry's father calmly handed over the handgun.

Gerry turned to his friend. "Chris, come with me."

Dressed only in their T-shirts and underwear, the two teens descended the stairs and walked out into the cold winter night air. The nearest neighbor to Windy Meadows Farm—and the nearest dog—was about a mile away. The boys could hear a dog barking, but it was a long way off. Gerry walked across the lawn, took aim toward the lower meadow where he knew a shot would do no harm, and pulled the trigger once, then a second time. Miraculously, the dog in the distance stopped barking.

The boys returned to the house and climbed the stairs where Gerry's father waited.

"I got the dog, Dad," Gerry lied.

"Good, son."

With that, Daniel Baugh Brewster, decorated war hero, former United States Senator, and one-time candidate for President of the United States as a stand-in for Lyndon B. Johnson, went back to bed.

Part I

The Rise:
"The Golden Boy of Maryland Politics"

Chapter 1

AMBUSH

The sniper's bullet ripped through the back of the young Marine lieutenant's steel helmet, just above and behind his right ear, and exited the front on a downward trajectory, shaving a layer of skin off the scalp at the hairline above his left eye. The bullet left a small, neat, pencil-sized hole where it entered the back of the olive drab helmet but splintered an opening twice as large in the front circled by ragged, counter-clockwise tears in the metal. Had the bullet's path been an inch lower, it likely would have ended the privileged life of Daniel Baugh Brewster in a rice paddy at the bottom of a deep, nameless ravine on the Japanese island of Okinawa long before he could become a Maryland state legislator, congressman, United States senator, or presidential standard bearer.

The near miss happened before the Hollywood-handsome Brewster would marry three times, first to a cover girl model and accomplished steeplechase rider, then to a rich ambassador's daughter who owned her own stud farm in Ireland, and finally—and most happily—to a one-time cheerleader at a small West Virginia college whom he had met in rehab. It also happened long before Brewster's public drunkenness turned into a politically costly spectacle, before he would be accused by a once loyal aide of taking a bribe Brewster denied for the rest of his life ever accepting, and before the government he so faithfully once served came after him, forcing him to defend himself throughout a slow-moving public trial that nearly ruined him.

And it happened a long, long time before Daniel Baugh Brewster would find himself and remake his life.

Brewster's story is one of wealth and opportunity, of personal courage and political stardom. But it also is the saga of a tragic fall, of personal and political humiliation, and of a self-inflicted incapacitation that nearly proved fatal. The tale reveals the lifelong effects of trauma experienced by many World War II veterans—what you might call the dark side of the Greatest Generation—yet it also is a story of recovery, of new beginnings, of personal resurrection.

The force of the bullet that spring day in 1945 snapped Brewster's head forward, and blood streamed down his forehead into his eye. A second bullet slammed through his boot. A moment earlier, another shot felled Captain Nelson C. Dale Jr., the L Company commander, who was standing at Brewster's side. Dale dropped to the ground where, seconds later, he was struck again, this time fatally paralyzing him.

It had been Dale, confused and impatient, who had pressed the blind assault up the ravine northeast of the landing beaches, despite seeing signs that the Japanese had only recently vacated the area. He had directed Brewster to move his Second Platoon forward quickly without either of them taking time to check to see if anyone was in the caves that pockmarked the sides of the ravine. By this late stage of the war, veterans of the South Pacific fighting knew—or should have known—that the Japanese were no longer making reckless, suicidal banzai attacks. Instead, they were burrowing into caves that formed naturally in the coral islands, often connected by interlocking tunnels, and were protected by snipers on the high ground and camouflaged one-man spider holes on the approach. Some caves were so large they housed mobile artillery pieces.

For the Japanese on Okinawa, the goal wasn't victory as much as delay and attrition: slow down the relentless American advance toward mainland Japan by inflicting as many casualties as possible for as long as possible.

The jagged ravine quickly became known to other Marines as "that place where L Company got it" or "back there where Captain Dale was hit" or, as a Marine Corps combat correspondent reported at the time, "the scene of one of the most cunning ambushes the Jap ever has been able to pull."[2]

The ravine's ridges were heavily overgrown with brush and scrub pine, which camouflaged the Japanese lying in wait. High on the right ridge, Lieutenant Everett A. Hedahl, the Third Platoon leader, was almost immediately wounded by machine gun fire and evacuated, leaving his platoon sergeant in charge. On the opposite ridge, First Platoon, led by Lieutenant Marvin C. Plock, also was pinned down but managed to withdraw behind a shield of smoke grenades. Casualties were quickly mounting in all three platoons, but Brewster's men in the rice paddy below were beyond reach as the Japanese crisscrossed their area with fire.

"I completely failed to realize the danger of our situation," Brewster, who at age twenty was perhaps the youngest commissioned officer in the US Marine Corps at the time,[1] admitted five months later in an entry in his handwritten personal war diary. "Dale was also oblivious to our precarious situation, as he continued to press me to move faster."[3] None of Brewster's Marines realized until it was too late that there were as many as two hundred Japanese hidden in caves and pillboxes on the heavily vegetated high ground above them, some as close as fifty yards away. The Japanese ambushers were now pouring relentless fire down upon them.

The point man of Brewster's platoon was hit in the shoulder; a machine gun squad leader, in the arm; a third Marine was killed. In the confusion, the Marines struggled to find cover and couldn't tell where the shooting was coming from, in part because the Japanese were now using smokeless powder. Brewster had been in firefights in Guam while the Americans were retaking that island about nine months earlier, but he was hardly a combat veteran. By the time he could assess his platoon's situation, five men in his second squad were dead, including the squad leader, another was seriously wounded, and four others had somehow escaped to the rear. Second Squad was essentially no more.

"I did not know what to do," Brewster later confessed in his diary. "I

---

1. In a Senate floor speech in 1965 commemorating the 20th anniversary of the battle for Okinawa, Senator Paul Douglas, Democrat of Illinois, introduced remarks by fellow Senator Daniel B. Brewster, calling Brewster "the youngest commissioned officer in the entire Marine Corps in the earlier days of World War II. He commanded a company in battle before he was 21." Cong. Rec. S7737 (April 9, 1965).

could not help Dale but hated to leave him dying. He ordered me to go back. I answered, God knows why, 'Fuck you, Dale!' I left him a moment later [after I] realized where the Nips were."[4]

Diving for cover, Brewster found himself face down in a narrow irrigation ditch, his platoon, which probably numbered about forty to forty-five men, was split into five groups, each about twenty yards apart, all helplessly pinned down. "My walkie-talkie was hit and my runner was killed."[5] His machine gun unit was a prime target. "I hit the deck and ordered our machine gun unit to return fire on the caves above, but they were struck within seconds. I don't think they managed to get a shot off before all of the [six] men of the gun crew were killed."[6]

The only saving grace was that the Japanese on the high ground inexplicably failed to lob grenades at the Americans trapped and exposed on the floor of the ravine below.

"Mostly, the men could do nothing but hug the mud, get wounded and die," recorded Sergeant George R. Voigt, an official Marine correspondent who later reported on the ambush. Brewster managed to move some of his men into a small indentation on the side of the ravine where there was a tiny measure of cover. "The cove where the platoon was situated became sticky with blood. The ground was covered with it. Scarcely a dozen men of the platoon were still alive and unwounded," Voigt later wrote.[7]

"In moving about to keep his men organized and to look after the wounded, [Brewster] had drawn fire to himself numerous times," Voigt said, adding that the narrow neck of the ravine, not more than ten yards wide, was now "a wall of lead."[8]

"The slightest show of a head, or even a hand, over the top brought a spurt of enemy fire into the position," he said.[9]

"The situation was extremely bad," Brewster later wrote in what now seems like a gross understatement. "No contact with outside, several wounded lying about, and a strong force of Nips just above us."[10]

Brewster sent several men back for help, but each was killed or wounded, according to Voigt. Anthony Caso, a private first class from

Jersey City, New Jersey, asked permission to make yet another attempt to break out, but Brewster refused to allow it. After Caso insisted, Brewster relented but feared Caso would die trying. The young private rolled into a small muddy stream that skirted the rice paddy and snaked his way out, staying under water for a good portion of the dangerous journey.[11] Only when he arrived at the rear did Lieutenant Marvin D. Perskie, the L Company executive officer who had taken charge in place of the fatally wounded Dale, finally have bearings on the location of the caves from which the Japanese were pouring down fire on Brewster and his men. Perskie wanted to call in artillery but worried the shells would accidentally hit Brewster or his men.

Brewster's platoon repulsed two Japanese attacks designed to finish them off yet remained stranded from the rest of L Company for the next seven hours. Young Lieutenant Brewster could see the rest of the company in the distance behind his platoon's position, but the firing in the ravine was too intense for anyone to reach them. Six Marines were killed just trying to get close enough to Brewster and his men to see what could be done to help. Finally one sergeant managed to crawl within hailing distance.

Brewster surmised that he could not expect the Third Platoon under Hedahl—"a brilliant officer"[12]—to come to his rescue because Hedahl himself had been wounded. And Brewster figured that Plock, whose First Platoon had already been hard hit by the Japanese ambush, might not risk sending his men into such a dangerous situation a second time.

It fell to Perskie—whom Brewster had described early in his war diary as "a fighting Jew from New Jersey"[13]—to rescue what remained of Brewster's platoon. Perskie and Brewster were buddies. They had fought together on Guam and they shared the same political views. "They were both Democrats, they were both liberals in their day, they were both pro-Roosevelt," Perskie's son, Daniel Perskie, recalled his father telling him. "He was very fond of [Brewster]."[14]

The physically powerful, 6-foot 2-inch, 230-pound Perskie had already been through several dangerous South Pacific battles, including nasty fighting on the island of Bougainville in New Guinea. He had been trained to be a Marine Raider, a short-lived experiment in creating a Marine special forces team. Worried that it was beginning to get dark and afraid to leave Brewster's platoon stranded at the mercy of the skilled Japanese night attackers, Perskie led what Brewster later described as "a gung ho charge"[15] down the right side of the ravine that overwhelmed the enemy, reportedly killing more than 150 Japanese. Hedahl's platoon, led by First Sergeant Elmer P. Imus, and Plock and his platoon were right behind Perskie.

"It seemed almost suicide to charge into the face of such fire," said Voigt, the Marine Corps combat correspondent. "But there was nothing else left to do. The battle had been going on all day." Wounded Marines were dying from lack of care and several Navy corpsmen had been killed trying to treat those who had been hit. When Perskie organized the attack, "Not a man in the company flinched," Voigt reported.[16]

"He knew if they moved real quick, using flamethrowers and hand grenades—no rifles, just flamethrowers and hand grenades—that would do the job." Dan Perskie said his late father had recalled these details in the years after the war. "These grenades they had—your ears would pop. So they were throwing the grenades [into the caves] in front of them with the flamethrowers behind them." The younger Perskie said his father told him the counterattack was over in a matter of minutes.[17]

"The attack evidently had been too swift and unexpected for the Japs," Voigt wrote in his summary.[18]

"It was great—what a relief," Brewster later recorded in his diary.[19]

After the ambush was over, stretchers soon came up and the dead and wounded were carried out of the ravine. Brewster's platoon was nearly destroyed. According to the official Marine Corps history of the battle, "Only 10 men of Brewster's platoon walked out."[20]

"I felt then, as I do now, that the stupidity and inexperience of Dale and myself cost the lives of 12 Marines and caused several more to be seriously wounded," Brewster confided to his diary four months later when he finally had enough distance from the events to write about them. "We were surprised and ambushed. There is never an excuse for this."[21]

The trauma of this event may well have reminded Brewster of a quote from the Greek-Roman essayist Plutarch that appeared at the bottom of the program at his 1943 graduation from officer's training school at Quantico: "In war it is not permitted to make the same mistake twice."

Brewster's platoon was ambushed on April 2, 1945, just one day after American forces had landed on the beaches of Okinawa. While the invasion force had been warned to anticipate 80 to 85 percent casualties during the landing, to everyone's surprise and relief, the invasion itself was unopposed. But the Japanese were there. Waiting.

The fight for Okinawa would grind on for nearly three bloody, muddy, miserable months. It would become the biggest, most savage, and—as it turned out—final major battle of World War II. It was a kill or be killed struggle. Neither side took prisoners. The April 2 ambush was just the beginning.

The battle involved more troops (183,000 Army, Navy and Marine), more ships, and more supplies than the Allied landing on the beaches of Normandy one year before. By the time the carnage on Okinawa ended, more than 7,600 Americans had been killed and another 30,000 wounded. A third of the island's civilian population was dead. More than 1,000 ships under the command of Navy Vice Admiral Raymond A. Spruance made up the huge US Navy fleet offshore, which relentlessly pounded the island with their guns and airplanes, but 36 ships were lost, more than in any other battle of the war, and another 368 were damaged, many by as many as 1,500 kamikaze dive bombers.[22]

Starting in May and rolling into June, an almost constant rain turned the battlefield into mud so deep that the arrival of reinforcements, resupply of ammunition and food, or evacuation of dead and wounded became almost impossible. The two sides unleashed such a torrent of aerial bombs, ship bombardment, artillery shelling, mortars, machine guns, flamethrowers, tanks, hand grenades, rifle fire, and bayonet attacks that neither side could move. If a soldier were to stick his head up, he was likely to be hit. Dead bodies, Japanese and American alike (but mostly

Japanese), began to cover the fighting ground because no one dared try to retrieve or bury them. The Japanese routinely shot at the American wounded, at stretcher bearers, and at medics. The corpses soon began rotting in the rain and tropical humidity, attracting maggots and huge swarms of flies. The stench, combined with smells of excrement, smoke from weapons, and filthy bodies, was overwhelming and pervasive; the hellish scene, regularly illuminated at night by flares, unimaginable. It was all but unbearable, breaking men's spirit and often their minds.

The fight for Okinawa produced the most cases of US combat fatigue—what today is called post-traumatic stress disorder, or PTSD—ever recorded in a single battle.[23]

Defending their own soil for the first time, the Japanese refused to surrender. Of the 110,000 Japanese defenders, all but 10,000 were killed or committed suicide.[24]

E. B. Sledge, a mortar man with the First Marine Division who later wrote a best-selling participant's account of the grim battle for Okinawa, said of the Japanese, "They were no more likely to surrender to us than we would have been to them had we ever been confronted with the possibility of surrender. In fighting the Japanese, surrender was not one of our options."[25]

Few Americans knew much about this brutal battle as it raged on even in the months and years afterward. That may be because Okinawa was so quickly overshadowed by the dropping of the atomic bombs on Hiroshima and Nagasaki just two months later and the end of the war itself. While Americans were fighting and dying on Okinawa, many Americans were celebrating in the streets after the US and Allied forces in Europe finally secured surrender from the Nazis. Americans were also distracted by news from Warm Springs, Georgia, that Franklin Delano Roosevelt had died. For many Americans, including the young troops in the South Pacific, Roosevelt had been the only President in office during most of their lives.[2]

---

2. Even the death in Okinawa of the renowned war correspondent Ernie Pyle did not seem to draw much attention to the prolonged fight.

The Americans wanted to capture Okinawa to use it as a staging area for bombing industrial areas in southern Japan, roughly four hundred miles to the north, but all that carnage went for naught. The war was suddenly over.

Young Danny Brewster of Brooklandville, Maryland—and of L Company, Third Marine Battalion, Fourth Marine Regiment, Sixth Marine Division—would be wounded five more times on Okinawa before the fighting there ended and was later decorated for his service. The experience was life-changing, as it was for most of those who survived the fighting in World War II.

A little more than three weeks after the battle had finally, mercifully ended, the only words Brewster could initially record in his diary were these:

"Have lived through Okinawa. I feel as if I was saved for a purpose."[26]

Chapter 2

A LIFE OF PRIVILEGE

Although most of his fellow Marines surely never knew it, Lieutenant Daniel B. Brewster was a trust fund baby.

He was hardly your typical fresh-faced twenty-year-old Marine officer in the thick of things on a South Pacific coral island. Brewster came from inherited wealth on both sides of his family, a family of privilege and connections, of accomplishments and lineage.

Brewster's family included cabinet secretaries and business tycoons and decorated war heroes. Family members lived on expansive Maryland farms, in large and often opulent houses, even in a replica English castle. There were butlers and cooks, upstairs maids and outside gardeners, stablemen, chauffeurs, and live-in nurses and governesses. The families collected fine artwork and the nicest silver, carpets, and furnishings. They indulged in hunting trips to rural England, regularly took the sun in southern climes, or leisurely traveled through Europe.

"We didn't really have chores," Danny's youngest brother, Walter Wickes Brewster, recalled decades later. "Oh, we would hang up our clothes, but we didn't make the bed. Pearl made the bed. Her husband was the butler, Hawkins. We had a cook named Vera."[27]

Walter recounted that upstairs at Fernwood, the estate where he and Danny and their siblings grew up, near the bedrooms, was not only a pressing room where the ironing was done but a separate room dedicated to the household seamstress. But Walter also remembered that he and his twin sister, Betty Baugh, had bars on their windows, installed at the insistence of his grandmother as a safety precaution that wealthy families sometimes took after the twenty-month-old son of aviator Charles Lindbergh was kidnapped and murdered in 1932. "Our bedrooms were right over the front porch and someone could take a ladder and come up there," Walter said.[28]

Most of the young boys from these well-to-do families spent their summers away at the finest camps in Maine or elsewhere in New England and then were sent off to prestigious all-male schools like Gilman in Baltimore or boarding schools like the St. Paul's School in Concord, New Hampshire. From there, they were expected to attend Princeton or other elite colleges such as Harvard or Yale. Law school was usually next.

In some cases, the children were away from home so much they had infrequent interaction and distant relationships with their own parents. That was the way Danny was brought up, and that was the way he brought up his first two sons.

Danny Brewster's father went to Gilman and then to Princeton. Before Danny entered World War II, he went to Gilman, St. Paul's, and Princeton. Decades later, his son, Gerry L. Brewster, went to Gilman and Princeton. This path was not dictated; it was a tradition, a way of life.

In 1941, as senior class president at St. Paul's, then seventeen-year-old Brewster said in a speech to his fellow students, "Gentlemen, we have had every opportunity and advantage—we have never lacked anything—in fact, we have always had practically anything we wanted. Now we have a debt to pay to… society."[29]

Danny Brewster's family lineage is interwoven with the history of this country. It includes one of the first graduates of the oldest college in America, one of the country's most famous Founding Fathers, a pair of presidential cabinet secretaries, a Medal of Honor-winning military man, and influential bankers and businessmen.

The Brewster who found himself under fire in an Okinawan rice paddy in World War II was a direct descendant of the Founding Father, colonial statesman, and first postmaster general, Benjamin Franklin, Brewster's great-great-great-great-great-grandfather. Brewster's ancestors also included Benjamin Harris Brewster, a great-grandfather who was

US Attorney General under President Chester Arthur, and Robert John Walker, a great-great-grandfather who was a US Senator from Mississippi, the US Secretary of the Treasury under President Polk, and briefly the territorial Governor of Kansas.

In 1642, a full generation before Ben Franklin's time and more than a century before the American Revolution, Nathanial Brewster (Danny Brewster's grandfather six times removed) was a member of the very first graduating class at a new Boston area college named Harvard.

Danny's great uncle, Major General Andre Walker Brewster, was awarded the Medal of Honor for his actions during the anti-imperialist Boxer Rebellion in China in 1900. He later served as Inspector General of the US Expeditionary Force in France during World War I. Danny's father was also in WWI, during which he was decorated for his valiant fighting in eastern France and then finished the war as his Uncle Andre's aide-de-camp.

Families in the Brewster circle of friends were affluent enough to engage in serious philanthropy and extensive, permanent land preservation. Children were brought up to be educated, cultured, and polite, with nothing but the best manners.

"We were never allowed to pick up a drumstick or lamb chop with our fingers," Walter Brewster laughingly recalled. "And there was no cussing. [Danny] never swore. I don't even remember him telling a dirty joke. I think they taught them that at the St. Paul's School. They were taught that people who talked dirty weren't educated because they didn't have the right adjectives."[30]

Daughters were also sent to fine private schools—to Garrison Forest, Bryn Mawr, or the Roland Park Country School, among others. Some were sent to New England boarding schools, but the Foxcroft School in Middleburg, Virginia, was a particular favorite for many refined young Green Spring Valley girls because of its excellent horseback riding program.

Ah, the horses! Horses were—and still are—central to everything in the Green Spring Valley and also in the neighboring Worthington and

Western Run Valleys, all to the north of Baltimore. The horses were thoroughbreds, and most were steeplechase racers trained to jump the high timber fences at the My Lady's Manor, the Grand National, and the most prestigious steeplechase race of them all, the Maryland Hunt Cup, often billed as the world's toughest timber race.

For generations, the majority of the Maryland Hunt Cup has been run over the fields of the five hundred-plus acre Worthington Farms with a smaller portion of the race run on the neighboring Snow Hill farm across the road. The five-timber fence on the third of twenty-two jumps was so high and dangerous it became known as the "Union Memorial jump"—nicknamed after a nearby Baltimore hospital, Union Memorial, where too many unfortunate riders finished their race.

Both Danny's father and his grandfather had held the prestigious position of Master of Foxhounds for the Green Spring Valley Hounds. In the sport of foxhunting, it is all about the chase and it is the hounds that lead the horses and riders over and through the fields, fences, and tree lines until the fox finally "goes to ground." Brewster's father became an expert on the breeding of foxhounds, bringing English hounds to the States and crossing them with American hounds. He kept a handwritten record that included the family trees of various hounds as if they were aristocracy. Hunt clubs would typically keep more hounds than the several dozen that would join any given hunt, all watched over by a professional kennelman.

The whole Brewster family—males and females alike—was deeply enmeshed in the valley's horse culture. Brewsters, or their close relatives, have always been riders, owners, and occasionally winners of the Maryland Hunt Cup and have participated in almost every race from 1911 to the present.

After World War II ended, Worthington Farms was purchased by Danny Brewster and his first wife, Carol Leiper Brewster. Carol was from a prominent old-line Philadelphia family and was an accomplished horsewoman. Fate may have put their purchase of the farm in play years before when, in 1922, the year the Hunt Cup first ran at Worthington

Farms, Danny's father, Daniel B. Brewster Sr., competed in a field that included Carol's father, J. Gerry Leiper of Chestnut Hill, Pennsylvania.

This lifestyle was possible due to family wealth. The Brewster family fortune grew from two streams. The larger portion came from Danny's mother's side of the family (see family tree). Brewster's grandmother was Catherine Osborne Young, daughter of Otto Young, a fabulously rich Illinois businessman. Young—or Jung, as it was originally spelled in his native Prussia—immigrated to New York toward the end of the nineteenth century and made his way to Chicago. There he started as a jewelry merchant but later made a fortune by buying up and redeveloping downtown property devastated by the great Chicago fire of 1871. He became rich enough that, in 1886, he acquired half-interest in the famous Chicago World's Fair.

As a testament to his wealth, Otto Young owned a mansion in downtown Chicago and a country home—a huge stone edifice—on the shores of Wisconsin's Lake Geneva. Known as Younglands but sometimes referred to as "the Marble Palace," it is still the largest house on Lake Geneva, a posh retreat for Chicago's wealthy that was described at the time as the "Newport of the West." With fifty rooms, a 250-foot-wide veranda, gold-plated plumbing fixtures, parquet tile floors, an ornate pink marble fireplace, and the carved faces of Catherine and her three sisters on the exterior walls, Younglands was valued at $1 million at the time of Young's death from tuberculosis in 1906. His personal worth was said to be about $20 million—or $40 billion in today's dollars.

Four years before Young died, however, his daughter Catherine Osborne Young, then eighteen, eloped to California with Byron Frank Hobart Jr., a Midwest lumber manufacturer and coal company owner she had recently met while vacationing in Pasadena with her parents. Her father was not amused, and the marriage was quickly dissolved, allegedly after Otto Young paid young Hobart—possibly as much as $200,000, according to one Young family researcher—to quietly disappear. Before he did, however, Catherine and Byron produced a daughter, Catherine Ottolie Hobart. Decades later, Ottolie would become Danny Brewster's mother.

After her father's death and with Hobart long gone, Catherine Young Hobart remarried in 1908, this time to Dr. Walter F. Wickes, a thirty-one-year-old physician-turned-stockbroker she had met in Chicago. The Wickeses' ancestors had been early settlers along the Chester River in Kent County on Maryland's Eastern Shore. In 1912, the young couple moved from Chicago back to Maryland where they bought 182 acres in Brooklandville in the Green Spring Valley just north of Baltimore. The property had once been owned by Charles Carroll, a Marylander who was the only Catholic signer of the Declaration of Independence.

By then, the ridges of the Green Spring, Worthington, and Western Run valleys were dotted with mansions and large farms where verdant fields for horses and cattle were framed by forests and tree-lined fences. The Green Spring Valley Hunt was formed in 1892 and the first Maryland Hunt Cup was run two years later, so it was not unusual to see packs of hounds chasing foxes across the pastures followed by dozens of horse riders dressed in breeches and black Melton riding coats.

Dr. Wickes and his wife—now Catherine Osborne Young Hobart Wickes—hired an architect to design a suitable residence for their new Greenspring Valley Road property. Liberated by Catherine's plentiful inheritance, the Wickeses built a massive, Tudor-style structure modeled on England's medieval Warwick Castle, built in the twelfth century. They named it Wickcliffe. It had sixty-five rooms and seventeen bedrooms, each with its own bathroom (including bedrooms for some of the family's seventeen full-time servants). The stone fortress was rimmed at the top with battlements and embrasures as if an imminent attack with spears and arrows was expected. The castle, seemingly out of place if not out of time in the wooded hills of Baltimore County, featured turrets and a tall central tower, carved crimson chimneys, dark wood paneling on the inside, lead-paned and stained-glass windows, and a *porte cochere*, or carriage porch, that framed the front entrance. The grounds included a pool, lake, tennis court, stables, and more. [31]

As many as nine servants, all immigrants from Europe, lived on the premises. In the 1920s, these servants included an English nurse, an Italian butler, both Norwegian and Swedish cooks, and a German houseman; in the 1930s, a Swedish butler, a Polish cook, an Irish laundress, and an English governess, among others.[32] Other help was brought in for daytime duty. Dinners were served by servants attired in tuxedos.

Ottolie, their eldest daughter, was given the Wickes name and soon was joined by three half-sisters and a half-brother: Elizabeth, known as Betty; Nancy; Catherine, known as Kitty; and Walter Junior, who, with four sisters, was saddled with the lifelong nickname "Boy" Wickes.

The Wickeses were neighbors to the Brewsters.

On the other side of the family, it was fertilizer that grew the Brewster family wealth, just as it does with crops. This was the other stream of money that contributed to the Brewsters' fortune.

In 1817, Danny Brewster's great-great-grandfather, John Pugh Baugh, began manufacturing what later would become a well-regarded fertilizer made through the process of crushing cow bones together with other materials. His firm also imported guano—the excrement of seabirds and bats—from Peru to be processed and resold as fertilizer. Incorporated as Baugh & Sons Company in 1855, the firm moved to Philadelphia on the eve of the Civil War.

The fertilizer was widely sold to farmers growing wheat, corn, alfalfa, potatoes, string beans, rye, strawberries, tobacco, asparagus, oats, and other crops. It also was said to improve grazing pastures for cattle. In 1901, the firm—which was generally known as Baugh's, had split into two subsidiary companies, Baugh & Sons and the Baugh Chemical Company, both of which were incorporated in Maryland in the first years of the twentieth century. Over the next forty years, the firms opened factories in Baltimore; Philadelphia; New Bern, North Carolina; Norfolk, Virginia; and Oneida, New York. Brochures often showed aerial renderings of the plants with stacks belching smoke and three- and four-masted sailing ships and steamships docked at the company wharfs where they unloaded their cargoes of bones and guano and reloaded cargoes of fertilizer.

The well-known logo of the "House of Baugh" depicted a side view of a bull with horns. The front half of the bull looked normal, but the back half showed only the interior bone structure. "The Sign of the Bull is the connecting link between the Baugh bone piles and the full hay wagon," proclaimed a company advertising brochure in 1930. One principal type of fertilizer was pure, finely ground bone meal; another was sulphate of ammonia; and still another was called bone black or bone charcoal, sometimes used to remove colored impurities from liquids.[33]

A 1937 brochure pictured a workman standing next to a pile of animal bones, probably thirty feet high or higher, prior to processing. In the same brochure, the firm billed itself as the "world's largest importers and collectors of pure animal bones," and the fertilizer was regularly marketed as "the oldest brand in America."[3]

It was the Baugh fertilizer company that brought Danny's grandparents, Benjamin Harris Brewster Jr. and Elizabeth Baugh Brewster, from Philadelphia to the Green Spring Valley in 1912 where they bought an estate just west of Wickcliffe. Brewster was the wealthy president of the Baugh companies (and a former president of the Union Trust Company) and needed to be closer to the family's fertilizer business in Baltimore.

They quickly began calling their new property Scrooby Manor, a name that came from the English home of a passenger on the *Mayflower* named Elder Will Brewster. Although he was related, Danny Brewster was not a direct descendant of the *Mayflower* Brewster, but his grandparents liked the story enough to name their newly acquired Maryland estate after Will Brewster's native home.[4]

---

3. The Baugh Chemical Company's long run finally ended in August 1963 when the firm was purchased by Kerr-McGee Oil Industries, a company started in 1932 by Robert S. Kerr. Kerr would later become US Senator from Oklahoma from 1949 until his death in January 1963. At the time he died, he and Danny Brewster were serving in the Senate together.

4. Scrooby Manor was built in 1902 by Alexander Cassatt, president of the Pennsylvania Railroad, and originally named Gramercy Mansion. The Old English Tudor-style manor house featured twenty-five rooms, an eighteen-horse stall carriage house, an ice house, barn, and creamery. It was purchased by Benjamin H. Brewster Jr., the only child of former US Attorney General Benjamin H. Brewster, in 1912. The Brewster family called the estate Scrooby Manor and lived there for thirty years. In recent years, both the property and its original name have been restored, and it has become an eleven-room bed and breakfast and a site for weddings and receptions. Source: https://www.gramercymansion.com/blog/history-gramercy-mansion/

The Brewsters had three children: Daniel Baugh, who would become Danny's father and namesake; Benjamin Harris III, known to Danny as Uncle Benny; and Nancy Wills Baugh.

Families such as the Brewsters and other well-to-do families in the valleys north of Baltimore often married their offspring into similarly situated families, not unlike royalty intent on joining kingdoms.

In 1920, Danny's Aunt Nancy Brewster announced plans to marry the fast-rising young diplomat Francis White (later to become the US Minister to Czechoslovakia, US Ambassador to Mexico, and then US Ambassador to Sweden), the wedding to be followed by a reception at Scrooby Manor. The *Baltimore Evening Sun's* society column gushed, "The Brewster mansion and grounds are beautifully adapted for a large affair of this kind and practically everyone of importance has been invited."[34]

In 1937, Danny's Uncle Walter—"Boy" Wickes—married Aimee du Pont, a daughter of the famous du Pont family of Delaware. Their marriage came just a few months after they attended the wedding of Aimee's sister, Ethel, who married Franklin D. Roosevelt Jr., son of the President. When Walter and Aimee du Pont Wickes sailed from their honeymoon in Hawaii to the West Coast, their mere arrival in port was considered noteworthy enough to be featured in that day's *San Francisco Examiner.*[35]

After World War I ended, young Daniel Baugh Brewster returned home to Scrooby Manor and reconnected with his childhood neighbor, Ottolie Hobart Wickes. They saw each other at parties at Wickcliffe castle, which had become a dazzling center of social life in the Green Spring Valley. Among the guests attending at least one party there was F. Scott Fitzgerald, who had been a student with Brewster at Princeton. They both were members of an eating club known as the Cottage Club until Fitzgerald, who was a class ahead of Brewster, went off to war and then was soon followed into the military by Brewster.

After Prohibition began in 1920, the Wickes were said to throw parties at Wickcliffe during which alcoholic drinks were openly served. Family members recalled how the illicit booze was stashed away in secret cabinets later found in the paneled walls, behind a storage closet wall, and even in a drop ceiling in the parlor. There were rumors, never confirmed, of a tunnel under the castle through which the liquor was delivered.[5]

On February 5, 1923, Daniel Baugh Brewster married his neighbor, Ottolie Hobart Wickes. They moved to an estate named Fernwood located on the eastern side of Wickcliffe. Brewster and Ottolie were within walking distance of both sets of parents. The three homes—the elder Brewster's Scrooby Manor, the Wickcliffe castle, and the young Brewster's Fernwood—are still neighboring estates on Greenspring Valley Road.

Nine months after the marriage, on November 23, Daniel Baugh Brewster Jr. was born.[6] He was soon joined by a brother, Andre, a sister, Catherine, and then twins, Betty Baugh and Walter.

"One would assume with so many servants that the Brewster boys and I would have led a very pampered, sheltered life. It was to a certain extent," recalled Francis N. "Ike" Iglehart, who lived at Ivy Hill, another Greenspring Valley Road estate sandwiched between Wickcliffe and Scrooby Manor. "But we were allowed to roam pretty freely around the three properties, fishing, catching snapping turtles, squirrel hunting with .22s, and endangering ourselves and others near us as we approached the 4th of July." Ike, who was just a year or so younger than Danny and the same age as Danny's brother, Andre, recalled the boys hunting fox and rabbits together with a pack of beagles and riding horses as early as the age of eight.[36]

In 1933, Danny and Andre and their neighbor "Ikey" began the first of several summers at Kieve, a camp for boys in Maine, where they canoed, fished, camped overnight, and played baseball and tennis. They took Red Cross lifesaving courses in swimming on Lake Damariscotta, where the average summer water temperature was a frigid seventy-one degrees. They also participated in the camp's National Rifle Association-sponsored

---

5. After Mrs. Wickes' death, Dr. Wickes sold the property to the Sisters of Notre Dame de Namur in 1945 for $75,000. It was then converted into an independent Catholic school for girls in grades six through twelve called Maryvale Preparatory School.

6. Daniel Baugh Brewster Jr. shared the same name as his father, but after his father died, Danny dropped the suffix. In 1955, when his own first son was born, he named him exactly as he had been named himself: Daniel Baugh Brewster Jr.

Junior Rifle Corps, through which they were taught discipline, self-control, and the safe handling of guns and scored well in marksmanship.

Then, toward the end of the following school year, on May 14, 1934, an unexpected tragedy: Brewster's father, a vice president of the Fidelity Trust Company, officer of Baugh & Sons, and a trustee of the Gilman School, suddenly died at Fernwood of what newspapers described as a heart attack. He was thirty-seven and left a wife and five children.

What the newspapers did not report, but what family members believe, is that Danny's father's heart attack was caused by alcoholism and the injection of a drug called paraldehyde, which was sometimes used to treat the side effects of alcoholism. Paraldehyde was historically used to induce sleep in sufferers from delirium tremens (DTs), a severe form of alcohol withdrawal that can cause confusion or involve sudden and severe mental or nervous system changes. Paraldehyde was generally considered a safe drug, although an overdose could prove fatal.

Brewster's death certificate stated that the cause was "acute dilation of the heart occurring in the course of toxic myocarditis of a number of months standing." Myocarditis is an inflammation of the heart muscle that is sometimes caused by a viral infection, but it can also result as a reaction to a drug used either illicitly or as part of medical treatment. "Toxic myocarditis, even if recognized early in its course, may not be reversible," according to an article on the medical condition published in the Texas Heart Journal in 2003.[37]

"Bottom line, he drank himself to death with a possible assist from an agent given to him," Gerry L. Brewster wrote of his grandfather's death in a letter to his father, Danny, and to other family members in 2004.[38]

This would not be the only time the Brewster family in general—and Danny Brewster in particular—would be afflicted by the myriad problems associated with alcoholism. With his father's death, Danny Brewster, at age ten, suddenly became the man of the house.

Chapter 3

SUDDENLY CAME THE CHANGE

It is easy to believe that Danny Brewster's determination to drop out of Princeton and enlist in the Marine Corps at the outset of World War II was a familiar act of *noblesse oblige*: when those who are fortunate in life feel the moral obligation to give back to their nation. After all, Brewster's late father—whom he adored—had shown the way: Brewster Sr. had dropped out of Princeton to join the fighting in France during the First Great War.

That may be how it started, but another interpretation of Danny Brewster's almost reckless desire to immerse himself in the horrific South Pacific fighting is that his happy life had taken an unexpected turn and he suddenly didn't care what might happen to him. When he shipped out, he was young, lovesick, and in despair.

"You know, I went off to the war and I didn't care if I got killed or not," Brewster confided decades later to DeCourcy "Dick" McIntosh, who served on Brewster's US Senate staff.[39]

Brewster appeared to be having a routine first semester at Princeton, where he played on the freshman football squad, but on December 7, 1942, the one-year anniversary of the surprise Japanese attack on Pearl Harbor, he dropped out of school and enlisted in the US Marine Corps. This was not a sudden impulse. Brewster's interest in joining the military had been brewing for about two years, at least since his junior year at St. Paul's. In June 1941, the summer before he was to be a senior, Reverend

Norman B. Nash, the school's headmaster, wrote Danny's mother, Ottolie, to express his concern about "the desire of some of the boys to enter military service," including Danny.

"He asked me what my advice would be, and I told him that I thought the country did not need 18-year-old soldiers or sailors... and that my own military experience, including a year in France, led me to believe that men of 21 and upward were much better soldiers, especially as officers, since the immaturity of the younger men stood in their way in handling the men under their command," Nash wrote, adding that he advised Danny to stay at St. Paul's to finish his final year.[40]

St. Paul's was then, and still is, a prep school for America's aristocracy. Founded in 1856, "SPS" has produced a disproportionately long list of congressmen, senators, ambassadors, philanthropists, authors, historians, actors, church leaders, playwrights, television stars, and more. Among its many notable graduates have been the publisher William Randolph Hearst; New York Mayor John Lindsay; Watergate Special Prosecutor Archibald Cox; banker J. P. Morgan Jr.; the *Doonesbury* cartoonist Garry Trudeau; Kennedy administration Chief of Protocol (and later ambassador) Angie Biddle Duke; and US Senator and Secretary of State John Kerry.[7]

Approximately 1,900 St. Paul's graduates served during World War II and 104 died while on active duty.[41]

For Brewster, a suddenly fatherless teenager, the students at St. Paul's became his brothers, and the faculty members, who lived *in loco parentis* in the dormitories and were known as Masters, became his surrogate parents.

Brewster followed his headmaster's advice and finished his final year with honors, excelling in both sports and academics. For three years, he

_____

7. Other notable graduates have included Maxwell Perkins, the editor at Charles Scribner's Sons credited with discovering the writers F. Scott Fitzgerald, Ernest Hemingway, and Thomas Wolfe; and FBI Director Robert Mueller, who more recently served as the Special Counsel who investigated Russian interference in the 2016 US election. Brewster's brother, Andre, graduated one year after he did. One graduate, John Jacob Astor IV, perished when *HMS Titanic* went under; another, Archibald Gracie IV, survived the sinking and later wrote about the ordeal. Source: Notable alumni from St. Paul's School found at https://en.m.wikipedia.org/wiki/List_of_St._Paul%27s_School_alumni

played on the SPS football team, which in those days competed against freshmen teams from Harvard, Yale, and Princeton. As a member of the Isthmian Club, one of three clubs to which all SPS students were assigned, Brewster captained the club football team, skated ice hockey outside in the winter on what was then named Turkey Pond, and played baseball and ran track in the spring. He was in the dramatics club and the Cadmean Literary Society (the debate team).

The school headmaster took special notice of Brewster's honesty when, in his junior year, he turned in "one of his close friends" for smoking in violation of school rules. "He came through admirably, rightly deciding that the offense must be reported to me, even if it might involve the boy's expulsion. (It didn't.) I think this took a good deal of inner struggle, and I am sure he acted rightly," Nash, the headmaster and rector, wrote in a letter to Brewster's mother.[42]

By the time Brewster completed his senior year at the disciplined and demanding school, he had one of the highest grade point averages among the school's 426 students and was named winner of the Frazier Prize, awarded to the student with the greatest distinction in both scholarship and athletics. He also served as senior class president and leader of a student council that advised the headmaster on student issues, for which he was awarded the President's Medal "for maintaining a remarkably high academic standing… tireless in his leadership and service… and high courage and sound judgment whenever—and it has not been seldom—these have been called for."[43]

Upon Brewster's enlistment, he was sent to Parris Island, South Carolina, but like his time at Princeton, his stint there was to last only a few months. His education and abilities were soon noticed, and he was quickly transferred to Officer Candidate School at Quantico, Virginia. At that point in the war, the Japanese were fast chewing up young Marine lieutenants in the South Pacific.

"The need for second lieutenants to be used as 'cannon fodder' was so great they couldn't get them trained fast enough," wrote author Laura Homan Lacey in *Stay Off the Skyline*, her detailed book about the Sixth

Marine Division's deployment in Okinawa.[44]

In June 1943, at the age of nineteen, Brewster was commissioned a second lieutenant and assigned as an instructor at the Marine training base in Quantico, Virginia. He detested the job but later admitted he learned self-confidence by leading men. "The only hard part of my duties there was the flushing out of the unworthy candidates. However, regardless of the unpleasantries, I am glad I had to do it for it gave me a great deal of practice in judging men and character."[45]

By the time he arrived at Quantico, he had another serious interest, one that would have an outsized impact on his life: her name was Anne Moen Bullitt.

Like Brewster, Anne Bullitt had a famous pedigree. Her doting father was the wealthy William Christian Bullitt of Philadelphia, a Yale graduate, friend of President Franklin D. Roosevelt, and grandson of nineteenth century lawyer John C. Bullitt, whose statue stands in Philadelphia's City Hall Plaza.

In 1933, FDR appointed Anne's father as the first US Ambassador to the Soviet Union and later as US Ambassador to France in the years leading up to the Nazi invasion of Paris in June 1940. During those diplomatic postings, Bullitt, by then twice divorced, was accompanied by his only daughter, Anne, first in Moscow as a plump nine-year-old with braces on her teeth and later as a pretty and precocious teen in Paris who was described in the press as her father's "Assistant American Ambassador." Various feature stories described her swimming in the Moscow River, coping with the Soviet secret police, playing hostess to the international set at a 170-room mansion in Paris, and sitting in a checkered gingham dress helping to decode State Department dispatches at the American Embassy during the frantic summer of 1939, just before Germany invaded Poland.[46]

Anne's mother was Louise Bryant, the American journalist, feminist, and political activist who was probably best known not for her marriage to Bullitt but for her previous marriage to the socialist John Reed, whose support for Russia's 1917 Bolshevik revolution was captured in his first-hand account, "*Ten Days That Shook the World*." Reed and Bryant were later immortalized in the 1981 Warren Beatty movie *Reds*, in which actress Diane Keaton played Anne's mother. Reed died of typhus in Moscow in 1920 and is buried beside Russian luminaries in the Kremlin Wall Necropolis.

Bryant married Bullitt, who was an admirer of Reed's, in Paris four years later, not long after he divorced his wife of seven years, socialite Ernesta Drinker of Philadelphia. Anne was born about three months after the marriage. Before they were wed, Bullitt is said to have convinced Bryant to change her maiden name from Mohan to the more refined sounding Moen.[47] Bullitt divorced Bryant in 1930, allegedly after discovering she was having a lesbian affair with a Parisian sculptor, and from then on raised Anne himself. Bryant died in 1936.

Anne, who was lovingly called Duck by her father, became his constant companion and she simply adored him. "My father is God," she once was quoted as saying.[48] In early letters to her father, she often jotted a dozen or more small Xs inside circles next to her signature to signify kisses for her dad. In one missive from Florida, she sketched a little bug and explained, "This is a mosquito who also sends his love."[49]

When Anne was twelve, Bullitt took his daughter with him for a meeting with Roosevelt and others at Hyde Park, the President's estate along the Hudson River in New York. FDR, so the story goes, told the young girl, "I'll tell you what, let's have some fun. Why don't you hide behind the sofa—the one there in the corner—and you can listen in to what goes on at these meetings. You may find it very boring, but then again…"[50]

Anne Bullitt grew up worldly and sophisticated beyond her years. By seventeen, she was said to have already crossed the Atlantic numerous times. In Moscow, she attended the ballet, the theater, and the opera. She named her cat Revolutzia, and was politic enough not to criticize Christmas in Russia because it made no references to Santa Claus.[51]

Anne was fluent in French and, between years at Foxcroft, spent at least part of her teenage summers in Paris with her father. She was finally evacuated at age fifteen in 1939, the year before the Nazis reached the city. She was chaperoned on the voyage home by then Postmaster General James A. Farley and his wife. "When Mrs. Farley saw her talking to [Mrs. Farley's] two daughters, she asked what they were discussing. 'Oh,' explained Anne, 'we are concocting a plot to do away with Hitler.'"[52]

Back in the States, Anne graduated from the Foxcroft School in Middleburg, Virginia, as valedictorian with *cum laude* honors in June 1941. She was art editor of the school yearbook, was involved in drama, art, and writing, and received school awards for both her poetry and her prose. Her always devoted father delivered her class's commencement address.[53]

A couple weeks later, the new Foxcroft graduate was formally introduced to Philadelphia society at a lavish debutante party given by her father at his summer home, Meadow Farm, in Gwynedd Valley in nearby Pennlyn. Among the one thousand guests: President and Mrs. Roosevelt, the Duke and Duchess of Windsor (the Duchess had also been a Foxcroft graduate), House Speaker Sam Rayburn, Supreme Court Justice Felix Frankfurter, US Senator Millard Tydings, various Vanderbilts, Wanamakers, Biddles, Whitneys and Rockefellers, the governors of at least eight states, cabinet secretaries, members of the diplomatic corps, and scores of other celebrities. The crowd was so large that Anne's father had a pasture cleared to serve as a special airplane runway for guests.[54] Blue and white awnings covered two large dance pavilions, one with a swing band and the other with a Hungarian orchestra. The house was decorated with delphinium and Madonna lilies and waiters served Anne's favorite supper dish, lobster Parisienne.[55]

Society columnist Nancy Randolph gushed, "Bill Bullitt is one of the most devoted fathers in the country." She noted that Anne always danced the first dance with her father. For this event, Randolph said the orchestra leader was asked to write special lyrics to the tune "My Sister and I," to be renamed "My Daddy and I," and that Anne planned to sing it to her guests. She also mentioned that Bullitt had given his daughter the extravagant coming out party despite the fact that Europe was at war and the United States was edging close to joining the conflict. "It is refreshing," she told readers, "that Bill Bullitt is not making 'these times' an excuse for gypping his daughter of the bang-up parties debutantes of her standing get in peace times."[56]

Anne took a civilian job with the Navy in Washington but managed to break away for winter vacations in Hobe Sound or Palm Beach, Florida. In Palm Beach, Anne's friends included Nedenia "Deenie" Hutton, daughter of Marjorie Merriweather Post, perhaps the wealthiest woman of her era, and her husband, financier E. F. Hutton. Anne reported going everywhere in a huge Cadillac driven by Deenie's chauffeur. Deenie, who was raised, in part, at Mar-a-Lago, the palatial Palm Beach estate that Post built in 1927, grew up to become TV film and Broadway actress Dina Merrill.

"All Deenie's friends appear to be junior millionaires and are definitely unattractive," Anne complained to her father in one January 1943 letter written on the stationery of the Everglades Club in Palm Beach. "You were certainly right about this being a kind of life one should look at to be amused, but all the people who live it are so ghastly and everything is so overdone that it makes me a little ill. The opening of the Everglades Club on New Year's Eve in War Time was really shocking. Diamonds dripped and champagne ran and all the older generation became very raucous. I horrified Deenie by disagreeing with her when she said, 'Isn't this the most divine place?' It really isn't."[57]

It is not clear when or where Danny Brewster first met Anne Bullitt, but it likely was through mutual friends at the Foxcroft School, where Anne first enrolled in October 1937. One of Anne's classmates at Foxcroft was Catherine "Kitty" Wickes who was Danny Brewster's aunt, although she was only a year older than he.

The Brewster and Bullitt families moved in the same social circles, so they could have met elsewhere, such as during Ottolie Brewster's and the Bullitt family's regular winter vacations in Hobe Sound or at Ottolie's summer vacations in Northeast Harbor, Maine, where so many residents from eastern Pennsylvania visited that it was nicknamed "Philadelphia on the Rocks."

In late summer 1943, Danny drove the eighty-some miles from Quantico to Baltimore County to attend a party on his home turf at the Green Spring Valley Hunt Club. Kitty Wickes drove Anne to the party from Washington, and almost immediately Anne and Danny began seeing each other at every opportunity. With young men in uniform, with war raging in Europe and the Pacific, and with everyone's future uncertain, young romance could blossom almost overnight.

"On August 7th, I proposed most successfully," Danny later recorded. "Everything was perfect; we were very much in love and wanted to get married in the near future. I was happy—did not even regret being stationed at Quantico."[58]

Anne Bullitt and Danny Brewster made a good-looking couple. As a young girl abroad, she had often been described in the press as "little Anne Bullitt," but by their engagement she had grown into a gorgeous young woman with waves of long brown hair that fell to her shoulders, a thin waist, high forehead, and perfect smile. Danny was equally attractive: tall, trim, square shoulders, and a strong chin, with his light brown hair trimmed short on the sides in keeping with Marine protocol. People noticed he kept his hazel eyes focused on whomever he was conversing with. Anne and Danny were the polished offspring of the same well-to-do social set, who shared a love of horses and riding and whose youthful ages belied their cultivated, worldly outlook.

Their engagement was announced on October 12, 1943, and Danny only slightly exaggerated when he boasted that the announcement was "in every paper in the country."[59] [8] A notice even appeared in *Time* magazine, describing Anne as "fetching," he as a "peacetime Princetonian."[9] William Bullitt drove to Baltimore to meet with Ottolie and arrange for

---

8. Write-ups about the engagement appeared in at least forty-eight newspapers in all parts of the country, from Seattle to New Orleans, Cleveland to Boston, Washington to Birmingham.

9. "Anne Moen Bullitt, 19, fetching daughter of Philadelphia's socialite-Democratic candidate for mayor, William Christian Bullitt, ex-Ambassador to Russia, France; and Marine Corps Lieut. Daniel Baugh Brewster Jr., 19, peacetime Princetonian of Brooklandville, Md.; in Philadelphia. Her mother, the late Anne Moen Louise Bryant (widow of Soviet hero John Reed), became Bullitt's second wife in 1923, was divorced by him in 1930, died in France in 1936." *Time*, Oct. 25, 1943, http://www.time.com/time/magazine/article/0,9171,796206,00.html.

the marriage to be held less than two months later, on December 4.

"Then," as Danny glumly reported in the early pages of the handwritten diary he would carry with him to war, "suddenly came the change." In late October, Anne told him "she wasn't so sure."

"I was wild," Danny said of his emotions.[60]

He and Anne went together for a weekend in Philadelphia just before the November election to try to sort things out, but when the weekend was over, Brewster was resigned to the fact that he would never marry Anne Bullitt, at least not before the war was over. For her part, Anne seemed confused, alternately suggesting she still wanted to marry him, but then postponing any serious discussion until after she took a month-long vacation to Florida.

"It was difficult—she acted like a little kid," Brewster observed.[61] But he was hard on himself, too, saying he never showed "that force and determination that I believe is so essential. I begged; I let her do whatever she wanted and was content to hang on in the hopes that matters might turn out alright."[62]

In early November, with her son's engagement in doubt, Brewster's "heart sick" mother wrote him at Quantico to say how sorry she was to hear that "things still seem to be at sixes and sevens between you and Anne." She advised not to marry Anne "unless everything is all cleared up."

"Maybe it's Charlie Bartlett," she suggested, referring to a young Yale graduate who had dated Anne and who years later became famous as the man who introduced Jacqueline Bouvier (whom he also once dated) to John F. Kennedy. Brewster's mother also wondered whether Anne "has realized that you haven't enough money to keep her as she has been accustomed," an assertion that ignores that the Brewsters were wealthy in their own right, although perhaps on a different scale. "Maybe Anne is getting temperamental like her mother," she added, referring to the iconoclastic Louise Bryant. "You don't want to marry a neurotic. It would be hell for you."[63]

It all came to a head just before Christmas. On December 18,

Brewster took Anne out for dinner but neither of them discussed their engagement. He brought her back to her father's home on Kalorama Road in Washington, where, he later said, "I played the part of the hurt gentleman—I was hurt."[64] Anne gave back a ring, a pin, and his mother's watch, but Danny insisted she keep the pin to remember him.

The following day, Brewster had an urgent, private conversation with Anne's father to ask the former Ambassador to use his connections to get Brewster an immediate transfer to the fighting war in the South Pacific. "We understood each other completely," Brewster later said.[65] Ambassador Bullitt said he would personally speak to the Commandant of the Marine Corps on Brewster's behalf and, if that failed, would go directly to James Forrestal, then Under Secretary of the Navy, or to Navy Secretary Frank Knox. Brewster really admired Anne's father. "He is without a doubt the most interesting and intelligent man with whom I have ever had the privilege to talk to on even terms," the nineteen-year-old lieutenant wrote of the man he had hoped was going to be his father-in-law. "Bullitt was eager to help me," he said, "not only for my sake but also for his daughter's name."[66]

It took only three weeks for Brewster's transfer to come through, nine months ahead of when his tour at Quantico had been scheduled to end. "Mr. Bullitt was entirely responsible for getting it," he said.[67] He had a week before shoving off, so he went home to see his family, traveled up to Concord, New Hampshire, to visit friends and teachers at St. Paul's School, stopped by Princeton on the way home, and then paid one final visit to Anne and her father in Washington in late January 1944.

Arriving at six p.m., Brewster had drinks with Anne's father, and the Ambassador gave the young officer a small gold St. Christopher's medal for good luck—"a gallant gesture," Brewster said.[68] They discussed world affairs, but by seven p.m. Anne had not bothered to come downstairs, so Brewster prepared to leave. Bullitt asked if he wanted to see Anne before departing, and Brewster said it was up to Anne. Her father went upstairs and Anne finally came down.

"We talked; she cried and kept turning the subject to our engagement.

I acted the way I should have at the very beginning: There were no tears or soft words on my part—there wasn't even a depressed feeling. I was happy." He said Anne "made me go over the story we would give about our engagement being broken," saying they should say their marriage was being postponed "until after the war." "I scratched this out. I sincerely wanted to make a clean break of it—or did I?"[69]

By Brewster's count, he tried to leave the house five separate times, only to be pulled back each time by Anne. The last time, "I kissed her very roughly—she was more than willing. Now I had to leave [and] this I did. My last words were: 'I'll come back some day. I hope you're waiting.'"[70]

As he mulled over what had happened, Brewster concluded their marriage never would have worked if they had tried to live together at the Marine base in Quantico, nor would it have worked if they were separated by his inevitable departure for overseas.

"As far as the future is concerned, let it take care of itself," Brewster said after the relationship had ended. "I meant my last words to Anne—I will look her up again. I hope she is waiting, but I won't care if she isn't. I am not in love with her now— not even close to it; but there is something inside me that continually causes me to think of her. If I had to bet my life on it, one way or the other, I would say that someday I will marry that girl."[71]

Chapter 4

SUGAR LOAF HILL

Not long after Danny Brewster was born in 1923, his father presented his first-born son with an odd but uniquely personal gift: his Croix de Guerre with Bronze Palm,[10] the medal presented to Brewster Sr. by the French government for extraordinary heroism during World War I.

Because of the untimely death of Daniel Baugh Brewster Sr., young Danny would only know his father for ten years, yet he grew up to revere him and, in many ways, to imitate him. Father and son shared a love of horses, fox hunting, and the lifestyle of the gentleman farmer. They both attended Gilman and Princeton and both dropped out of Princeton to fight for their country in different world wars. Both had great pride in being a Marine, and when young Danny went off to war in the South Pacific, he went armed with the same Colt .45 his father had carried in France. Both men were wounded and both were decorated for unselfish gallantry in battle, yet both surely were affected by what they witnessed in combat. Both married well, but their relationships with their children were often distant. As they moved into adulthood, both relished the social life of the Green Spring Valley, and both became overly fond of drink.

As young Marine lieutenants anticipating the glories of war, both

---

10. The Croix de Guerre [or War Cross], adopted in 1915, is a bronze Florentine cross over a pair of crossed swords suspended from a forest green ribbon accented with seven bright red vertical stripes. In the center of the obverse is the profile of a woman's head and the words "Republique Francaise." A bronze palm frond, indicating the highest level of gallantry, angles slightly upward from the bottom left of the ribbon. Brewster's medal is in the family's collection of papers and other memorabilia.

father and son professed a naïve eagerness to engage in combat. When the fighting was over, and with the experience of carnage and death fresh in their memory, both admitted to being changed by it, perhaps permanently. Both wrote of their longing to return to the quiet and comfort of home.

"When I get back to the Green Spring Valley, the Statute of Liberty will have to do an 'about face' if she ever wants to see me again," Danny's father wrote to his mother in October 1918.[72]

In early 1944, just after Danny boarded the troop ship that was to transport him across the Pacific, he already was daydreaming of when he would come back home. "I'm looking forward to the day I return to Maryland—with its debutante parties, champagne, the MHC [Maryland Hunt Cup steeplechase race], my friends, the charming ladies, and all the things that I love."[73]

By contrast, Daniel Brewster Sr., who was a twenty-two-year-old Marine second lieutenant when he reached France in May 1918, seemed a happy warrior in his letters home, telling his parents he was eager to be sent up to the front lines. "The men work like hell, cheerfully and willingly, and come back singing and cheering like hell every night. I tell you I am mighty proud to be a Marine Officer," he said, adding that his quarters and food were "excellent," that the French had welcomed the American troops with open arms, and that he "could not possibly be happier."[74]

By that October, however, both his circumstances and his viewpoint had changed. The newly promoted first lieutenant was among several divisions of fresh American troops under the command of Major General John A. Lejeune who were thrown into the front lines near Saint-Etienne in southeastern France. Side by side with exhausted French troops, their task was to push back an entrenched line of Germans who had stubbornly repelled the French for four years. The resulting Battle of Mont Blanc lasted for more than three cold, wet weeks before the US Marines and Doughboys finally broke through, but at a cost of some 7,800 dead, wounded, and missing. It was for his role in this fighting between

October 3 and 10, 1918, that Brewster Sr. was personally awarded the Croix de Guerre, as well as two Croix de Guerre medals for his Marine unit, plus other American decorations. The accompanying citation stated that Brewster "exposed himself several times to artillery and machine-gun fire to ensure that his men were safely withdrawn, and his lines were fortified, and showed great skill in his section quickly bringing it into a parity against threats, during the enemy attack that was repulsed."[75]

"I have been 'over the top' twice and God willing I shall go over every time the Marines go over, but I don't like it, and you can take my word for it," a more sobered Brewster wrote to his mother after the battle. "Anybody that says he is fond of it is a damned liar." In the same letter home, Brewster concluded simply: "This thing changes a man."[76]

In early November—just a week, as it turned out, before the "war to end all wars" finally ended at the eleventh hour on the eleventh day of the eleventh month—Brewster was wounded, a shot through the left forearm that missed the bone but sent him almost giddily to the comfort of a field hospital where he was tended to by a bevy of nurses. "I can tell you," he wrote his mother, "it's pretty nice after laying around in a wet shell hole with Jerry throwing things the size of a kitchen stove at you."[77]

Compared with his father's almost gleeful arrival in a war zone in France, Danny's youthful foray into war some twenty-six years later seems driven, at least in part, by an urge to escape the collapse of his romance with Anne Bullitt. His admission to himself, through his own handwritten diary, that he was suffering through swings of depression.

"I am so darn moody that it just will not do for me," the twenty-year-old confided in the diary as he started his journey to the South Pacific. "At times, I can hardly restrain myself, and then at times I am depressed to a point of desperation."[78]

Brewster's first stop was Camp Elliott in San Diego, where Marine replacements were trained for combat in the Pacific. Housed in cream-colored, two-story barracks shaped like an H and with twenty-five double-decker metal bunks to a room, the recruits were taught how to engage in hand-to-hand combat and how to use the Ka-Bar knife, a lightweight, perfectly balanced, foot-long knife with a seven-inch blade that was widely known as the "Marine's foxhole companion."

Their instructors knew that lives depended on the effectiveness of their training and didn't sugarcoat the serious danger the young and inexperienced troops would face in battle. "Don't hesitate to fight Japs dirty," they would say. "Kick him in the balls before he kicks you in yours."[79] Sergeants routinely asked recruits to identify any scars, birthmarks, or other unusual features. When asked why, the recruits were told, "So they can identify you on some Pacific beach after the Japs blast off your dog tags."[80]

Not long after arriving in Southern California, Brewster and a friend found themselves, through wealthy acquaintances, at a weekend party in Los Angeles attended by a teenage starlet named Shirley Temple.

"She is young, pretty, attractive, but will come to no good end," Brewster prophesied. "At 15, she proceeded to get fairly tight. Not so good for a girl younger than [Brewster's sister] Catherine, but nevertheless, in spite of youth and liquor, she was damnably attractive and unaffected." But Brewster also complained, "I failed to make much of an impression on the girl as I was very moody and couldn't bring myself to make an effort."[81]

By early March 1944, Lieutenant Danny Brewster was at sea en route to the South Pacific aboard a ship named the *Santa Monica*. As if he needed yet another reason to go off to war, Anne Bullitt provided it. Just after his ship sailed, Brewster saw a notice in a newspaper that the nineteen-year-old woman who just two months earlier had briefly been his fiancée had suddenly married Army Staff Sergeant Caspar Wistar Barton Townsend, a twenty-three-year-old Yale graduate who was stationed at Fort George G. Meade in Maryland. Like Anne, Cappy Townsend was from a socially prominent Philadelphia family.

"Needless to say, this amazed me, but frankly I am very glad," Brewster recorded in his diary. "Now I no longer think of her. She was obviously not the one for me. However, I sincerely hope that I will see Mr. Bullitt again some day."[82]

As for Mr. Bullitt, when *Time* magazine asked him to comment on his daughter's surprise elopement, about which he knew nothing, his stunned reply was, "What?"[11]

"I am very glad I'm finally shoving off," Brewster wrote from shipboard in his diary. "I want very much to get in the thick of it." Yet he professed to feeling less excited going off to war than he felt leaving St. Paul's School on specially chartered trains for Christmas holidays. "It all seems very natural and even commonplace," he said. "I'm glad I have left. I hope I see all there is to see."[83]

First stop was Pearl Harbor, in Hawaii, where he raved about his sexual exploits, parties on Waikiki Beach and in various restaurants, and how, after one night of carousing, he "attempted to arrest the chief of the Honolulu police," a prank that he said nearly got him "locked up for the duration."[84]

Then it was off on another ten-day voyage aboard the *Typhoon,* a cruise that, for self-protection, zig-zagged 3,600 miles deep into the South Pacific to American-controlled Guadalcanal where the soldiers would receive more intensive training. There General Lemuel C. Shepherd was forming a new Marine Division, the Sixth, to which Lieutenant Brewster was about to be assigned.

Before the war, General Shepherd had known members of Brewster's family and when Brewster arrived on Guadalcanal, Shepherd summoned the young lieutenant to his headquarters and invited him to join his staff as commandant of his headquarters company. "I wasn't trying to take care of him, but his chances of surviving in division headquarters were a damn site better than they were as a platoon commander," Shepherd recalled in an oral history interview he did in 1966 for the Marine Corps.

According to Shepherd, Brewster replied, "General, that's a great compliment, and I'd appreciate it very much, but I want to remain with

---

11. "Married. Anne Moen Bullitt, 19, only child of Philadelphia's former US Ambassador to Russia and France William Christian Bullitt; and Army Staff Sergeant Caspar Wistar Barton Townsend, 23, of Philadelphia, a 1942 Yale graduate; in a surprise ceremony at Fort George G. Meade, Md. In October 1943, her father announced her engagement to Marine Lieut. Daniel Baugh Brewster Jr. of Brooklandville, Md. Mr. Bullitt's comment on the marriage: 'What?'" *Time,* Feb. 28, 1944, http://www.time.com/time/printout/0,8816,796476,00.html

my platoon and make the landing."

"Well, Danny," Shepherd recalled saying, "I never deny an officer an opportunity to fight for his country."[85]

In the third week of July 1944, Brewster was dispatched aboard the *President Polk*, a peacetime luxury liner now painted gray and topped with antiaircraft guns and life rafts, as part of the invasion force to retake the island of Guam. The Japanese had captured Guam the day after Pearl Harbor in December 1941.

"I saw my share of action," Brewster recorded after the successful invasion. "Went on several patrols; killed a half dozen Japs myself; and watched a few score more killed. Had several exciting experiences, but that is only part of the game."[86]

One of his "exciting experiences" came when he tried to get a little shut-eye on Guam but was awakened in the middle of the night by a knife-wielding Japanese infiltrator who jumped into Brewster's foxhole and tried to kill him.

"When night came, it was like another world," recalled E. B. Sledge, the Marine who wrote a book about his South Pacific war experiences. "Then the enemy came out of their caves, infiltrating or creeping up on our lines to raid all night, every night." Sometimes, he said, the nighttime raiders threw grenades, "but [they were] always swinging a saber, bayonet, or knife."[87]

For their own safety, the Marines always worked in pairs, with one on watch while the other tried to sleep. As the attacker tried to stab Brewster, his runner almost immediately shot the assailant dead, but not before Brewster, who had tried to push the attacker away, received lacerations that left three scars on his right forearm for the rest of his life.[88]

"Dangerous at times, but on the whole boring and uncomfortable," Brewster nonchalantly said of the fighting in Guam. Once the island was secured, his unit returned to Guadalcanal for months of additional training to prepare for, as he described it, "the next show."[89]

"I'm bored," he complained again. "Anything would be better than marking time here. Am looking forward to the next operation—wish we were shoving off tomorrow."[90] But when Brewster cavalierly said "anything would be better" than training on Guadalcanal, he could not have imagined the living hell he was about to enter on the island of Okinawa.

After his rifle platoon was ambushed on just his second day on Okinawa, after he was twice shot and almost killed, and after most of the men under his command were either killed or wounded, L Company was pulled back and placed in reserve.

"My platoon was badly shot up, but the men's spirits remained surprisingly high. They were really great," Brewster said.[91] During the company's third night in reserve, Brewster approached his veteran platoon sergeant, Paddy Doyle, to ask if he thought the men "still had any respect for me after what had happened that second day? I was very worried. I would not have blamed them if they all hated me."

"Paddy answered—'Everyone has the greatest respect in the world for you. They say you ran about the second day never once thinking of your own safety!'" After that exchange, Brewster admitted relief because he respected Doyle. "I felt much better. I believed Paddy—He never ear-banged, soft-soaped, or lied. At least I still had the remainder of my platoon behind me."[92]

A week or two later, Brewster had a chance encounter with General Shepherd on a wooded trail on the Motobu Peninsula in the northwestern part of Okinawa. "Danny, how are you doing?" the General asked. Brewster held out his helmet, which had bullet holes in the front and back, and said, "Well, General, I guess I'm doing all right."[93]

What Brewster, Shepherd, or any of the Marines could not possibly have known was that things were about to get much worse.

The Okinawa campaign began with the assembly of the US Tenth Army, as the combined American invasion force was called, consisted of 183,000 members of the Army, Navy, and Marines. They began landing on April 1, 1945, which was both Easter Sunday and April Fool's Day. The Americans were commanded by US Army General Simon Bolivar Buckner Jr.[12]

---

12. Lieutenant General Buckner was killed at a forward outpost on June 18, 1945, three days be-

In 1944, the year before the American invasion of Okinawa, the 110,000 Japanese under General Mitsuri Ushijimi began to dig spider holes, trenches, and tunnels, build pillboxes and artillery positions, outfit and connect a warren of caves, and lay out a welcome mat of minefields.[94] Ushijimi proved to be such a peerless defensive strategist he was nicknamed the "Demon General." The Japanese then just waited for the Americans, who arrived the following spring.

Okinawa is a long, narrow island, about seventy miles from north to south but only about seven miles wide. The Americans landed on the island's west coast about a third of the way up from the southern tip, but not until Navy ships offshore had announced the American arrival by firing 45,000 rounds of five-inch or larger shells plus 33,000 rockets and 22,500 mortar shells.[95] The general plan was to send the Marines north to conquer the upper two-thirds of the island, while the Army turned to the south. On April 19, the Marines reached the northernmost tip of the island, but by then the Army was already running into stiff opposition in the south. The Marines, Brewster among them, were sent south to help. (The cocky Marines claimed they were being sent in "to bail out the Army.")

The heart of General Ushijimi's plan was a defensive line that blocked American progress toward the southern end of the island. Called the Shuri-Yonaburu line, it began near the island's biggest city, Naha, on the west coast and stretched all the way across to Yonaburu on the island's east coast. At the center was the ancient and revered Shuri Castle, which served as Ushijimi's headquarters, but otherwise the line was a maze of small, heavily defended and often booby-trapped hills, interconnected with an estimated sixty miles of tunnels and set up so the Japanese could provide mutually supportive fire. Attack one hill, and the Japanese would respond with deadly crossfire from two or more adjoining hills. Each location along the Shuri line was almost perfectly defended by the others.

The Americans were pitted against Japanese machine gun nests,

fore the battle ended, when a Japanese artillery shell hit a coral rock outcropping and fragments pierced his chest. He was the highest-ranking US military officer killed by enemy fire during World War II. Source: https://en.wikipedia.org/wiki/Simon_Bolivar_Buckner_Jr.

snipers, and individual riflemen hidden in brush covered "spider holes," from which the Japanese would emerge to shoot passing soldiers in the back. The Japanese fired mortars and artillery from behind the hills and then scurried inside their caves and tunnels for protection. Even aerial bombs or blasts of artillery from ships offshore could not dislodge the defenders. General Buckner referred to the Okinawa campaign as "prairie dog warfare."[96]

By the beginning of May, about a month after the April 2 ambush, Buckner had lined up the Sixth and the First Marine Divisions and the Seventy-Seventh and Ninety-Sixth Army Infantry Divisions in four parallel columns from west to east. These units were to advance southward side by side and overwhelm the Shuri line. That was about the time, however, the incessant rains began and when all movement forward halted in an apocalyptic scene of mud, death and dismemberment, smoke, noise, explosions, fire, screams, putrid smells, filth, and hellish fear. Overnight, units routinely lost half their complement or more. In the constant rain, weapons jammed and even began to rust.

The westernmost column facing south along the coast was the Sixth Marines—Brewster's division. The Sixth drew the unlucky straw, the objective of taking an otherwise indistinct little hillock listed on the American maps as Sugar Loaf Hill. It was on the Shuri line's left flank and was the forward corner of an integrated triangle of low hills, the others called Horseshoe and Half-Moon. Each of the three hills was honeycombed with Japanese tunnels and each had its weapons zeroed in to protect the other two. The Marines began attacking Sugar Loaf on May 12 but were turned back ten times before they finally captured the otherwise meaningless hill on the eleventh try on May 18.

Time magazine reported, "There were 50 Marines on top of Sugar Loaf Hill. They had been ordered to hold the position all night, at any cost. By dawn, 46 of them had been killed or wounded. Then, into the foxhole where the remaining four huddled, the Japs dropped a white phosphorous shell, burning three men to death. The last survivor crawled to an aid station."[97]

"In the battle for Sugar Loaf Hill alone, the 6th [Marine Division] suffered 2,662 killed or wounded and there were 1,289 cases of combat fatigue," chronicled author Laura Homan Lacey. "Those 7 days in 1945 encapsulated all that was the worst of war.... It became more than the mind could bear."[98]

In the early days of that horrific assault, Brewster's L Company was held in reserve a little behind the line. To get a better view of the action, Brewster's battalion commander, Colonel B. A. Hochmuth, and about a dozen men—including Hochmuth's Marine orderly and runner, Bernard G. Passman—moved onto a forward observation hill, about one thousand yards behind Sugar Loaf. Suddenly around eight thirty or nine p.m., a force of some six hundred Japanese raced over the Sugar Loaf, attacked Hochmuth's group and the troops some yards behind them, and momentarily broke through.

Passman, in a letter written after the war describing the incident, said the battalion commander called in artillery strikes and brought up a regimental weapons company that finally repelled the attack. With star shells fired by the Navy offshore illuminating the night sky, "the place was lit up like the 4th of July," Passman wrote. The next morning, he said he accompanied Hochmuth to assess the condition of Brewster's company and found that during the previous night it had suffered 40 percent casualties. On their trip to that meeting, Passman reported having to shoot Japanese bodies lying along the way to make sure they were really dead, fearing they might jump up to ambush them as they walked by.[99]

While the meeting was going on, the Japanese launched a mortar barrage that hit the battalion's ammunition dump halfway down a hill behind where they stood. One case of mortar shells exploded and threatened to set fire to other crates of ammunition, grenades, mortar and bazooka shells, and flame thrower tanks.

"We all knew that if the ammo dump blew, it was curtains," Passman recalled.[100]

Lieutenant Marvin D. Perskie—the same officer who had led the attack that saved Brewster and his ambushed platoon a little more than a month earlier—"ran down the hill and picked up these eight burning crates and threw them further down into a gully at the bottom of the hill, where they later exploded. Lt. Brewster, the company exec[utive officer], also ran down and threw two burning crates to help [Perskie]."

"Thank God it was raining and helped delay the burning," Passman wrote, adding that Perskie's and Brewster's "quick thinking and bravery up and beyond saved our lives."[101]

By the time Brewster's company was thrown into the fray, it was May 19 and the Marines had finally captured Sugar Loaf Hill, although it remained under relentless fire. "This was the most bitterly contested hill of the entire campaign," Brewster recorded in his diary. "The hill was a small knot in the middle of an open valley. It was covered with dead and rotten Marines and Nips. Not one living tree or blade of grass remained. Thousands of rounds of mortar and artillery fire had been dropped on this one small but vital terrain feature."[102]

As Brewster and his platoon sergeant, Paddy Doyle, began discussing precisely how to deploy their unit, the Japanese opened a new mortar and artillery barrage. "Paddy and I were talking," Brewster recounted in an unemotional entry in his diary. "A mortar shell landed on his shoulder. One arm gone, his head and chest smashed. He died in a moment. I was knocked down, holes in right shin and left thigh. Several others were hit." Another Marine who was "Paddy's best friend, cracked up," he said, a mental breakdown caused by the stresses of war that were becoming commonplace among the troops slogging through the din of Okinawa.[103]

Brewster tried to describe the almost indescribable: living in the muck and mud during horrendous, seemingly endless artillery attacks, not knowing if the next shell has your name on it, plus platoon buddies being shot or blown apart, others with nasty face wounds, and still others becoming crazed by the constant concussion of exploding ammunition. They often could only watch as a single shell killed four and wounded a fifth. Or, as whole squads were wiped out, sometimes their bodies falling in a line just as they had stood. Or, the horror of seeing comrades whose arms, legs, or even heads were suddenly gone. There was often a feeling of utter helplessness. Some tough Marines screamed incoherently; others quietly sobbed in their foxholes. It was all too much.

"I'd already seen so many people killed—including my own men—that I had no feeling whatsoever for the Japanese," Brewster acknowledged years later. "We really didn't consider them human beings."[104]

With only seventeen men left in his platoon, Brewster advanced to the Asato River, just north of Naha, but the water was too deep to swim across with heavy packs. They tried instead a rickety footbridge, but halfway across the Japanese opened fire. A photographer was killed and at least two others wounded. A shell fragment sliced through the left side of Brewster's neck; another tore open his left index finger. Perskie ordered him to the rear where he got patched up. By the time he returned, his company had finally been relieved and sent back in reserve to rest and regain its strength.

By then, in addition to everything else, many of the Americans were simply sick from exhaustion and the horrible weather: pneumonia, respiratory problems, or fever from being drenched by rain day and night. For days and sometimes weeks, the Marines had no opportunity to take off their soaked boondockers—their boots—to put on a dry pair of socks, and many suffered from what was called "immersion foot," which back in World War I was known as "trench foot." Sores developed on their hands and fingers, caused in part by malnutrition.[105]

"We were all tired as hell—the company had little to no fight left in them," Brewster said. "Our replacements came. They were mostly kids— few if any were adequately trained. Several were to be killed because of this."[106]

There were so many American casualties on Okinawa that raw recruits, and equally inexperienced second lieutenants, were quickly brought up as replacements and were then just as quickly slaughtered. "They were wounded or killed with such regularity that we rarely knew anything about them other than a code name and saw them on their feet only once or twice.... Our officers got hit so soon and so often that it seemed to me the position of second lieutenant in a rifle company had been made obsolete by modern warfare," said First Marine Division mortar man E. B. Sledge, who was involved in the inch-by-inch fighting around Horseshoe Hill.[107]

When he returned to combat, Brewster's company took part in an amphibious landing on the Oroku Peninsula south of Naha that enabled the Americans to capture the left flank of the Japanese line. Once the Japanese were driven out of their caves and toward the southern tip of the island at the end of May, the Americans took command.

"We had the Nips disorganized and in the open. We killed several hundred each day. It was good—we had a score to settle," Brewster said.[108]

"It would go down in history as the bloodiest battle involving American forces since Gettysburg in 1863," wrote historian Blaine Taylor in an article about the Okinawa battle.[109]

The eighty-two-day battle of Okinawa finally ended on June 21, 1945. As a halt in the fighting drew near, Lieutenant General Ushijima and others in his high command committed suicide rather than be captured. American troops also came across the bodies of ordinary Japanese soldiers whose telltale missing hand and spilled entrails demonstrated in gory detail that they, too, chose to die by hand grenade to the belly rather than surrender.

Daniel Baugh Brewster Jr. had witnessed fighting that was every bit as horrific as anything his father had experienced during World War I, but for a far longer time. On Okinawa, Brewster was wounded seven times in all—on his forehead, his foot, his neck, his finger, and both his legs—yet he never missed a day when his platoon was in the field.

In the mid-1960s, Brewster, by then both a US Senator and a colonel in the US Marine Reserves, returned to Okinawa and visited Sugar Loaf Hill, only to discover a housing development had been built on the former battlefield. "There were no signs or memorials to remember all the Marines who fought and died on that very spot," he sadly reported.[110]

Contrary to complaints in his diary that the system for awarding military decorations unfairly favored high ranking officers rather than the fighting man in the foxhole, Brewster was decorated for his service in Okinawa with a Bronze Star for heroic achievement affixed with a "V Device" to indicate specific acts of valor; a Purple Heart for being wounded in action, affixed with a gold star in lieu of a second Purple Heart; and the Presidential Unit Citation, which was awarded to specific US Navy and Marine Corps units for extraordinary heroism in action.[111]

After Okinawa, he was sent back to Guam, likely to be trained for the big American invasion of mainland Japan that was already being planned for 1946. But within two months, President Harry S. Truman ordered the atomic bombs to be dropped and the war abruptly ended. Brewster said he turned down a chance to go home immediately and instead readily accepted an order to make one final "beachhead" in Tokyo so he could be there when the Japanese formally surrendered on September 2, 1945. "Would certainly hate to miss this initial landing on Japan," he wrote on his diary's last page.[112]

Danny Brewster's experiences on Okinawa—like those of so many survivors of both great wars—would haunt him for the rest of his life. A month after the Japanese on Okinawa were finally defeated, Brewster recounted throughout the final pages of his diary the long list of his Marine friends and comrades who had been killed or wounded. He said the overall experience "fried my mind in a way nothing else ever could have."[113]

Chapter 5

AMBITION

"Am in one hell of a big hurry to get out of the Marines," Lieutenant Daniel B. Brewster recorded on the final page of his war diary as he was about to return home from Japan in August 1945. "Restless as usual."[114]

Brewster had barely lived through some of the most savage, barbarous fighting that occurred on any battlefield on any continent during World War II. As mind-searing as those experiences were, however, they added up to only a small fraction of the total days he spent with the Marines in the South Pacific. Most of his time was spent waiting—in transit, in training, and in silent contemplation of what to do with the rest of his life.

"After much doubt, I have firmly made up my mind to follow four courses after the war," he penned in his diary. "I intend to get a college degree, a law degree, travel extensively, and have the best possible time in this best of all worlds!"[115]

Brewster said he started his diary, in part, to help him "clarify" who he was and what he wanted to achieve in life. As he reflected on his high school years, he realized something within him had fundamentally changed following a "worthless summer" before his senior year at St. Paul's. "I now wanted to get somewhere—be something—and do something worthwhile," he realized. This transformation, he said, paid immediate dividends, leading to his election as senior class president and winner of awards in academics, athletics, and public speaking. He received praise from his teachers and his high school peers alike, and he liked the feeling.[116]

"Today is the 19th of November 1943. I find myself at nineteen years of age a very ambitious, thoughtful, and determined person," he wrote the day he started the diary.[117]

Over the months he was to spend on transport ships or in barracks or tents, Brewster began reading every book he could get his hands on, especially biographies and books on politics and social issues. He began compiling a glossary of political and religious "isms" and their definitions—pragmatism, utilitarianism, communism, Zionism, capitalism, nationalism, fascism, humanism, and so on.

"I find myself often wondering as to what part I should play in this life of ours." He described himself as "conservative and quiet," but said he was "growing away from this," a shift reflected in his growing support for the New Deal policies of Franklin Roosevelt. He concluded he was not particularly amusing, but then dismissed that by saying "most amusing people are fools." What he really wanted, the young man said, was to be "a good conversationalist, for that is one of the greatest gifts any man can have."[118] Perhaps struck by his adulation for the erudite Ambassador Bullitt, he added, "I have an intense desire to improve my mind. I respect intelligence above all else. Stupid people are a bore; they accomplish nothing."[119]

"What it all narrows down to is, 'How can I influence the most people?'" Brewster wrote, although he never divulged to what end he wished to exert such influence.[120]

With the war over, Brewster returned in 1946 to Fernwood, his Green Spring Valley home, to discover he barely knew his own family. His father had died when he was ten, and he had spent most of the next eleven years away from home—first at the Gilman School and then away at boarding school at St. Paul's; at Camp Kieve in Maine in the summers with his brother, Andre; at his freshman semester at Princeton in New Jersey; and then three years in the Marines in South Carolina, Virginia, California, Hawaii, Guadalcanal, Guam, Okinawa, and Japan. His mother, Ottolie, now lived with her new husband, William F. Cochran Jr., whom she had married in 1939, although he died in October 1946, not many months after Danny returned from the war. Danny's grand-mother, Catherine Osborne Young Hobart Wickes, who had lived next door at Wickcliffe, also had passed away at home in 1942.

The biggest change was with his siblings, most of whom were just children when he left and were becoming young adults by the time he returned. Andre, the next youngest, had also joined the Marines and was sent to China during World War II. But the younger children, Catherine and the twins, Walter and Betty Baugh, hardly knew their elder brothers. By the time Danny and Andre returned home, Ottolie and her new husband had had another child who, of course, was even younger: Danny's half-sister, Frances Cochran.

"I never really knew Danny and Andre," recalled Walter, who was seven years younger than Danny and has few childhood memories of his older brothers. "I can remember sitting in the den with one of them on each side and they used to hit me in the arm—what do you call that, a 'noogy'? It hurts!"[121]

Walter said he was so young when Danny joined the Marines that "I didn't even know what war was." He said that when Danny returned, he "was a brother and an older man—he was the only man in the house at that time." Danny served as a surrogate father who would go to watch Walter's football games or wrestling matches at Gilman.[122]

"Danny never talked to me about the war," Walter said. "He talked mostly about fox hunting, football, and riding horses."[123] It was Danny who got the family back into owning, training, and racing horses, a part of his late father's life and legacy that Danny clearly missed while away. He converted an old coach house at Fernwood into a stable, had about six stalls built in the back, and filled the loft with straw and hay. Walter recalled that Danny would rouse him out of bed about five in the morning to help him exercise the horses.[124]

"Danny definitely was the one who got me started riding again," Walter recalled.[125]

Danny Brewster seemed in a hurry to make a name for himself as a horseman. In 1948, just two years after returning from the Pacific, he won two races in a single day—the John Rush Streett Memorial and the My Lady's Manor. That year he and Walter also began competing against each other in the annual Maryland Hunt Cup, the famous but dangerous four-mile race held each April at Worthington Farms and Snow Hill. Their mother, Ottolie, owned a jumper named Cliftons Dan, which eighteen-year-old Walter rode in '48, while twenty-five-year-old Danny rode Curwick Tim, owned by his aunt, Betty Wickes Sage. Walter finished third and Danny finished sixth. The following year, it was Danny's turn to ride Cliftons Dan and he finished fourth, while Walter fell from his horse, Dunlora. Walter was back aboard Cliftons Dan in 1950 and finished seventh, while Danny again rode Curwick Tim but pulled up the horse and never finished the race.

"Cliftons Dan was just a fabulous horse," Walter recalled decades later. In that 1950 race, Walter remembered being thrown off Cliftons Dan and quickly getting back in the saddle and finishing the race. Since then, the rules have changed. "You can't do that anymore. If you get thrown off, you're off," he said with a laugh.[126]

The whole steeplechase circuit—the My Lady's Manor, the Grand National, the Hunt Cup, and other races around Maryland and in neighboring Pennsylvania and Virginia—captivated young Danny Brewster. The race seasons generally ran from mid-March until the end of May and then picked up again in September through early November. When they weren't racing, they were fox hunting across the expansive pastures and woodlands that lined the valleys.

Between 1947 and 1950, Brewster rode in some fifty point-to-point races, won six and had a number of second- and third-place finishes. But it is a rough and tumble sport, with jockeys clinging to 1,200-pounds of horse muscle racing thirty miles per hour and hurdling shoulder-high timber fences. Brewster spilled at least ten times.[127] In 1951 and '52, Brewster again rode in the Maryland Hunt Cup, both times on a horse he then owned, Bachelor's Double. The 1951 race, however, turned tragic. Out of twelve starters, only four finished. One horse was killed and a second broke a leg and had to be destroyed. Two jockeys were hospitalized.

Brewster fell at the forbidding third of twenty-two fences—the so-called Union Memorial (Hospital) jump. Yet the following year, he was back aboard Bachelor's Double and raced to a fourth-place finish.

The horse country culture then—like it was for generations before and like it still is today—was one part horse flesh, one part rider courage, and at least two parts champagne, mint-flavored southside rum drinks, and tables groaning with prime rib, softshell crabs, deviled eggs, fried chicken, southern ham biscuits, marinated asparagus, pasta salads, brownies, cookies, cakes and pies, and almost anything else the palate might desire. In this setting, there is seemingly no end to the beer, wine, vodka, gin, or other beverages for the thirsty. There are luxurious lunches served in 150-year-old estate homes before the races; fabulous tailgate spreads on tables erected behind cars parked in the grassy fields a few steps from where spectators size up the horses in the paddock and await the start of the race; and posh receptions in other nearby homes after the last fence has been jumped. These days, the after-race parties often feature a looped videotape of the just completed race so those who just witnessed the real thing an hour or so before can cheer on their favorite steed anew, or groan again as rider and horse go unwillingly their separate ways. On the night of the Hunt Cup, there is a by-invitation-only, white-tie-and-tails ball, usually held at a country club or hotel in downtown Baltimore.

Year after year, members of the same families compete against each other in the various races, own or train many of the horses, and often live on the surrounding farms. In many cases they are leaders of business, industry, or the legal profession in the region, philanthropists, and not infrequently the beneficiaries of inherited money. Their names, intermingling like family trees, are etched each season on the silver trophies awarded to the lucky winners. Some family names first appear in the race records of the nineteenth century, reappear periodically throughout the twentieth century, and still resurface in the twenty-first.

"You didn't have to be terribly proficient to do it, just as today you don't have to be terribly proficient to participate," said Baltimore County horseman Charlie Fenwick, himself a member of one of the old valley families. "It was fun; it was exciting; it was social; and it was dangerous—lots of stuff that sort of fit into a lifestyle."[128]

State tourism signs planted throughout the region to highlight the area's scenic byways state simply enough: "Horses and Hounds," a nod to a multi-generational heritage for which locals clearly need no reminder.

"The idea of steeplechase racing in April was that the fox hunting season ends the end of March. That is when foxes begin to mate, and you have cubs and you're not going to be hunting cubs," Fenwick explained. "The season is over, the weather is wonderful and the horses are fit, so let's take it into April and see who has the best horses at the end of the hunting season... That was the natural progression of things. It was a part of the culture."[129]

Fenwick admits that the racing has become more professional in recent years. Jockeys are sometimes imported from Europe, and now there is a substantial purse for the winner, whereas in the early days the competitors raced just for the fun of it—for a trophy and the bragging rights. "It's gotten way beyond that now. Lot of times horses run in these races now and have never seen a fox or a hound," Fenwick said.[130]

Some individual races are named after members of these families whose personal histories are intertwined with steeplechase racing. There is, for example, the Daniel Baugh Brewster Memorial, a novice timber race at the Green Spring Point-to-Point that is named for Danny's father, who had been Master of the Green Spring Valley Hounds (1925-1930). Danny's grandfather, Benjamin Harris Brewster Jr., had also served as Master of Foxhounds (1914-1919), as did Danny's youngest brother, Walter (1994-1996). Four generations of Brewsters have competed in the Maryland Hunt Cup, including Danny's grandfather, Danny's father, various uncles, Danny himself, his two brothers, Danny's son, Gerry L. Brewster, and his daughter, Danielle Brewster Oster. To encourage a new generation of riders, Gerry Brewster now sponsors a pony race for young children in honor of *his* father, and – like the one named for his grandfather – is also called the Daniel Baugh Brewster Memorial. It is held each spring at the Pimlico Race Course in Baltimore.

That horses had moved back to the center of Danny's life was probably a big reason why he did not return to Princeton after the war. New Jersey was just too far away from his horses, the races, and the social gatherings he loved so much at home. Moreover, to return to Princeton as a freshman would have subjected him to restrictions on his driving and would have required him to wear a little freshman beanie known as a "dink." After commanding Marines in battle in World War II, Danny Brewster was not about to wear a dink.

During the war, he seemed already to have dismissed the idea of going back to Princeton, thinking instead that he might try Georgetown University because of its proximity to, and his growing interest in, political power in Washington. But even Georgetown seemed too far from home. He finally enrolled at the Johns Hopkins University, a short commute into nearby Baltimore, where he studied for two years and earned enough credits to enroll in the University of Maryland Law School, also in Baltimore. (In the aftermath of the war, veterans were often allowed to enter law school without first receiving an undergraduate degree, a milestone Danny Brewster skipped.)

Brewster passed the Maryland Bar in 1949 and began practicing law in Towson, the Baltimore County seat, with veteran lawyer and powerful state Senator John Grason Turnbull, who by then was also Majority Floor Leader in the Maryland Senate. Fourteen years older than Brewster and already in practice for some seventeen years, Turnbull would become Brewster's mentor and Brewster his protégé. From the start, it was a politically connected firm, which gradually expanded to become Turnbull, Brewster, Boone, Maguire, and Brennan. Boone was A. Gordon Boone, who would become Speaker of the Maryland House of Delegates; partner John Maguire also served in the House of Delegates; and all of the partners were active in Democratic politics, both in Maryland and nationally. In 1956, for example, Turnbull headed Adlai Stevenson's Maryland campaign for President of the United States.

John Howard, a young attorney in the firm, said the politically influential collection of lawyers became jokingly known around Towson as "Octopus, Inc."[131] They bought a three-story white clapboard house on Chesapeake Avenue and converted it into law offices and a small law library. The kitchen and bar were on the first floor.

"If you wanted to get something done, they were the firm to go to," Brewster's son, Gerry, said years later.[132]

After graduating from college, most of the educated young men of the valleys north of Baltimore generally stayed out of the public eye, moving into business or law, but Brewster was immediately smitten by politics. He barely had time to change out of his uniform before Governor Herbert R. O'Conor, a Democrat, appointed him to Maryland's Advisory Committee on Veterans Affairs. By 1950, Brewster ran for, and was elected to, the Maryland House of Delegates, adding to the political prestige of his new law firm.

Lawyering and legislating weren't Brewster's only avocations. He had also become partners with J. W. Y. "Bill" Martin and Donald B. "Squeaky" Culver in a farming business, which included breeding and training racehorses. They located their start-up at Worthington Farms, which is on Tufton Avenue and at the time was part of the one-thousand-acre Snow Hill Farm owned by the Martin family. Brewster brought with him from Fernwood his English horse trainer with a French name, Marcel "Marsh" LeMasson, and the partners called their new enterprise "Tufton's Folly." For years, Le Masson served as Brewster's farm manager and head of all equine operations.

Still in his late twenties, Brewster was practicing law and getting an insider's view of politics during the week, raising and training horses in the mornings and evenings, and racing, partying, and dating on the weekends. Every other year, Danny spent three months at the state capital in Annapolis when the Maryland General Assembly was in session and then attended one-month sessions in the intervening years. Young, strong, and virile, Brewster embraced life as if he were making up for lost time. "He didn't have trouble getting a date," his brother Walter said with a mischievous grin, adding that Danny's dates were often with girls a good bit younger than he.[133] As Danny had hoped, he was having "the best possible time in this best of all worlds!"

A year or two after he was back in Maryland, Brewster rode in the Whitemarsh races near Chestnut Hill, Pennsylvania, outside Philadelphia. At an after-race party for visiting riders, he met a beautiful woman named Carol Leiper de Havenon, a successful model, actress, and expert equestrian. Although she was six years older than Brewster, the two started dating.

As a model, Carol de Havenon's photos had appeared in *Life, Vogue, Harper's Bazaar,* and other magazines, including on a 1941 cover of *Mademoiselle.* She also was an actress who had played summer stock theaters and later became a stand-in for Ginger Rogers in the 1940 Academy Award-winning film *Kitty Foyle.* Also for the film, she was featured in a series of promotional photographs taken by Alfred Eisenstaedt, the famous *Life* magazine photographer probably best known for his V-J Day photo of a sailor's impromptu kiss of a nurse during the end-of-the-war celebration in Times Square. De Havenon, who used the stage name Carol Lorell, studied acting at the American Academy of Dramatic Arts in New York City and worked for the Conover Modeling Agency. Some said she reminded them of another beautiful Philadelphia actress: Grace Kelly.

In 1947, after about eight years of marriage and two children, Carol amicably divorced her first husband, Gaston de Havenon, a Tunisian-born perfume importer she had lived with in the Lower East Side of Manhattan. Gaston de Havenon became a renowned collector of African art and counted among his closest friends the artist Arshile Gorky, the sculptor Isamu Noguchi, and other artists who lived nearby or in Greenwich Village. But Carol had tired of big city life, missed her horses and riding, and yearned for Philadelphia society. "Simply put, her marriage to my father broke up [after] seven years because they came from two totally different worlds and she wanted to return to the world [she knew]," son Michael de Havenon said years later.[134] So, Carol Leiper de Havenon and her two sons, Michael and Andre, moved back to her father's house on Meadowbrook Lane in Chestnut Hill.[13] Soon after, she met Danny Brewster.

Just as Brewster's father had been Master of Foxhounds for the Green Spring Valley Hounds, so Carol Leiper's father, James Gerhard "Gerry" Leiper Jr., had been Master of Foxhounds and a co-founder of the White Marsh Valley Hunt in Pennsylvania. Gerry Leiper and his wife, Edith, were among the most prominent fox hunters of their era, regularly riding with members of the White Marsh Valley, Rose Tree, Radnor, and Andrew's Bridge hunt clubs in Pennsylvania. Like Brewster, Carol was born into the world of fox hunting and steeplechase racing. She began riding at the age of three, although she rode side-saddle in those early days, was fox hunting by age six, and became a prize-winning rider. She was one of the few successful female steeplechase jockeys of her day.

"It is effectively the same world Dan belonged to, just separated by 75 miles," explained Michael de Havenon, her son from her first marriage.[135]

Gerry Leiper is said to have always wanted a son, but instead he and his wife had three daughters, Polly, Edith, and Carol. Leiper nevertheless raised his girls much the way many families raised boys, imbuing them with a toughness that would prepare them for the challenges of their lives.

Carol, for example, always claimed she learned to swim when her father simply threw her into a pool. "It's the kind of story you're told, but in my case, it really happened," Carol said more than once, according to her son, Gerry L. Brewster.[136]

Gerry Brewster tells his own story about his stern grandfather and namesake, Gerry Leiper. While visiting the Leiper home in Pennsylvania as an eight- or nine-year-old child, Gerry recalled, he walked halfway down a flight of stairs one day only to be confronted by the Leiper family's pair of large huskies standing at the foot of the stairs, growling and baring their teeth. His mother, Carol, standing behind him, encouraged him to continue walking down, but Gerry said he was paralyzed with fear. At that, Gerry Leiper, watching from the floor below, grabbed a cane

---

13. Andre Victor de Havenon died in 2000.

66

from a stand, held it in the air above his head and warned the young boy, "Gerry, it is either me or the dogs." With that, Gerry Brewster descended the rest of the stairs, the dogs backed away, and that was that.

"It was clear to me that my mother wanted me to be raised the same way that my grandfather had raised her—tough—the way she would need to be later in life," Gerry Brewster said.[137]

The Leiper girls were not only riders but also horse trainers and owners. Polly Leiper Denckla's horse, Ned's Flying, won the Maryland Hunt Cup in both 1957 and 1958. The girls were also sailors. Gerry Leiper was active in the Corinthian Yacht Club[14] and took his girls along on races and offshore sailing excursions while they were still in grade school. "The girls like a hard blow and a heavy sea," Leiper was quoted as saying after he and his girls sailed their forty-five-foot sloop, "*Electra,*" through rough weather between Barnegat Bay and Atlantic City, New Jersey, in 1930. "They've sailed since they were seven years old and are particularly delighted when a strong breeze gives them an opportunity to test their skill at the tiller."[138]

During the early months of their courtship, Carol and Danny commuted between Baltimore County and Chestnut Hill, but Carol began spending more and more time with Danny in Maryland. Walter Brewster remembered Carol fox hunting aboard Cliftons Dan.

"[She] was a bea-u-ti-ful rider," Walter said, slowly stretching out the word "beautiful" for emphasis. "She was very capable, a very smart gal."[139]

With a chuckle, Walter also remembered a morning while still living at Fernwood when he was supposed to go riding with Danny around five a.m. Danny normally would come from the bedroom next door to shake him awake, but apparently had overslept. "I looked at the clock and it was five thirty so I jumped out of bed and ran into [Danny's] room and there was somebody under the covers and I shook it and this blonde head

---

14. Founded in San Francisco in 1886 by sailors who wanted a club for boats under forty-five-feet in length, Corinthian clubs can now be found in cities and towns up and down both the West and East Coasts as well as inland in ports such as Chicago. The Philadelphia club began operations in 1892.

popped up—it was Carol! I said, 'I, uh, I, uh, I'm sorry.' It was not the first time I met her, but the first time I met her in my brother's bed."[140]

In the summer of 1954, Bill Martin, one of Danny's partners in Tufton's Folly, died. His 1,017-acre Snow Hill and Worthington Farms property, as well as his partnership in Tufton's Folly, reverted to his widow, Nancy "Nannie" Martin. When the third partner, Squeaky Culver, sold his partnership interest to Danny and Nannie, it cleared the way for Danny to propose buying the property of his dreams: Worthington Farms.

By then, Danny and Carol had been dating for nearly seven years. Their plan was to buy Worthington Farms and run it together.

Even without a big land purchase, there was already pressure on Brewster to marry Carol, if for no other reason than the mores of the time. Brewster was a partner in a well-known, politically connected law firm as well as an elected member of the Maryland General Assembly. In 1950s America, public officials were expected to marry their lovers, not just live with them.

"Everybody in the family was saying, 'Danny, marry Carol, marry Carol, marry Carol,' until I think he got tired of hearing about it," Walter recalled.[141]

Finally, on September 25, 1954, Daniel Baugh Brewster Jr. married Carol Helme Leiper de Havenon at her father's home in Chestnut Hill, attended only by immediate members of the two families and other close friends. She was thirty-seven; he was thirty-one and in the middle of his race for re-election to the House of Delegates.

"Our courtship consisted chiefly of going to political meetings during the week and horse races on weekends," she later recalled.[142]

Two weeks after their marriage, Danny and Carol Brewster formally proposed to buy 395-acre Worthington Farms for $157,880, or about $400 an acre. Nannie Martin agreed on November 30 to sell it to them, albeit with some restrictive covenants that said the property had to be used for farming or the raising of livestock. The agreement also gave the Martin family the first right of refusal to repurchase the property, but only if Brewster's children did not purchase it from their parents first. The following February, the deed to Worthington Farms passed to the Brewsters.

From the start and throughout their marriage, Carol Brewster was a full, working partner in the farm. She had attended the Springside School in Chestnut Hill, then St. Timothy's School (then located in Catonsville, Maryland), and graduated in 1935 from the Shipley School in Bryn Mawr, Pennsylvania. She then went to "finishing school" at Brillantmont International School in Lausanne, Switzerland, where she became fluent in French and learned a smattering of other languages. After that, she attended Ambler College, now part of Temple University, where she majored in animal husbandry—training that helped prepare her to manage a large horse and cattle farm.

Spreading across the floor of the Worthington Valley, Worthington Farms not only was the verdant site of the annual Maryland Hunt Cup but also was close to the white-fenced horse farms of wealthy neighbors. Directly across the road, for example, stood Sagamore Farm, then owned by Alfred Gwynne Vanderbilt Jr., heir to the Vanderbilt fortune. He had been given the six hundred-acre thoroughbred horse farm by his mother as a twenty-first birthday present. Vanderbilt was a renowned horse breeder and, for a time, owned Pimlico Race Course in Baltimore where the Preakness Stakes are run each May as part of the Triple Crown of horseracing. Pimlico is also where Vanderbilt staged the famous 1938 match race between Seabiscuit and War Admiral. He died at age eighty-seven in 1999, and his farm is now owned by Kevin Plank, the founder of the sports apparel company Under Armour.

By the early '50s, the dashing, fast-moving Danny Brewster was already gaining regular notice in the local press. Maryland's biggest paper, the *Baltimore Sun*, ran a feature on the "gentleman jockey" that included nine photographs of Brewster riding, jumping, and feeding horses and talked about his budding political prospects.

Following his marriage to Carol, their purchase of Worthington Farms, and his re-election to the House of Delegates, a political newsletter called *The Maryland Report* singled Brewster out as a "Marylander of Promise."

"Of all the young men in Maryland politics today, Dan Brewster of Baltimore County is most apt to reach the top. There are many who firmly believe the youthful 32-year-old legislator will someday be governor."[143]

Chapter 6

THE GOLDEN BOY OF MARYLAND POLITICS

It all seemed so easy, so preordained. Young Danny Brewster emerged from the savage ferocity of World War II to become the golden boy of Maryland politics.

And why not? Hollywood handsome, gorgeous and talented wife, two young sons, inherited wealth, solid education, glamorous and fearless horseman, prominent friends and family, practicing attorney with a politically influential firm, working farmer, decorated war hero: his rise was that of a man effortlessly climbing a steep flight of stairs without breaking a sweat.

About eight years into this upward trajectory, a newspaper columnist remarked: "Daniel Baugh Brewster at age 35 appears to be a man who has everything. Someone who knows him commented, 'He's always tried to avoid choking on his silver spoon.'"[144]

The young man was in a hurry, perhaps because, as his first wife later revealed, what he really wanted to be was President. He briefly considered kick-starting his political career the very year he left active duty and returned home by running for the state legislature in 1946. But he did not have enough time to put together a campaign, plus he was convinced he first needed to finish his education.

Almost from the start, the speculation about Danny Brewster in political circles was how high would he go. Governor? Congress? The US Senate? The White House?

In September 1950, under the tutelage of his law partner, the powerful state senator John Grason Turnbull, the fresh-faced twenty-six-year-old Brewster easily won his first election by pulling down the second-largest vote total among eighteen candidates vying for six nominations in the Democratic primary for the House of Delegates from Baltimore County. Then, in the November general election, he was elected with the third-highest vote total among the twelve Democratic and Republican candidates running for the six county seats. In Annapolis, he was appointed to sit on the House Judiciary Committee, an all-star group of lawyer-legislators that included two future US Senators, four future judges, a future congressman, a future state Senate minority leader, and a future two-term governor, Harry R. Hughes, who became one of Danny's closest friends.

In those days, the Maryland legislature was a boys' club with a surfeit of high-energy hijinks and extracurricular activities, much of it fueled by hours of after-hours imbibing. It was no wonder: the General Assembly in the 1950s was full of World War II veterans, many of them happy just to be alive, and most of them supercharged and ready to blow off some steam and catch up on all they had missed while in combat. Hughes, in the final months of his life in 2018, still vividly recalled how—some sixty years earlier—the muscular Danny Brewster would bear-hug friends and lift them off the ground. "I recall that Danny was strong. He took pride in his strength," Hughes said.[145]

Other stories about Brewster in those days have been passed down through family lore, although they are harder to verify. Most of these stories were said to have taken place in Carvel Hall, a seedy hotel built over what are now the restored formal gardens of the historic, colonial era Paca House in downtown Annapolis. Legislators and reporters alike lived at Carvel Hall, which featured a heavily used taproom with a piano in the basement and an annex of rooms that for reasons unknown was grimly called "the Death House."

Perhaps the most enduring story involving Brewster tells of a night when his mentor, Senator Turnbull, was out carousing, so Brewster wrestled a parking meter out of the sidewalk and placed it in Turnbull's empty bed to let him know the meter was running. Another tale recounts the time Brewster allegedly threatened a fellow lawmaker into voting the right way by holding him by his ankles and suspending him from an upper story hotel window. And still another about how, in protest of the hotel's tardy room service, he dropped down the Carvel Hall stairwell a stack of dishes that had been piling up in the hallway outside his room. Or, finally, how after complaining to the hotel night clerk about the lack of heat in the rooms, he was told that if he didn't like it, to break up the furniture and throw it into the fireplace, so he did just that.

These drink-inspired episodes were not widely known outside the close-knit, boys-will-be-boys Annapolis fraternity. What the public saw instead were the breathless accolades for Brewster that routinely poured in, extolling—and often exceeding—the young delegate's record of service. "Where his rising star will lead him, whether to Washington or to a high place in the Government of his State, only a prophet could safely venture an opinion. But that he will go far few will doubt. For he combines to an extraordinary degree the ability to win friends with a sincerity of purpose so frequently lacking in the 'hail fellow well met' type of politicians," declared one flattering tribute to Brewster after only a single term in the state legislature.[146]

When he ran for re-election as a delegate in 1954, he finished first in the twenty-two-person Democratic primary and then finished first again in the twelve-person race for six seats in the general election. By this second round of elections, Brewster even eclipsed the vote totals of his more experienced law partner and future Speaker of the House, Delegate A. Gordon Boone, and he began to develop a reputation as a prodigious vote-getter who seemed unstoppable.

In his second term in the state legislature, Brewster was elevated to the position of Vice Chairman of the Judiciary Committee and from time to time ran the committee in the chairman's absence. He began to be named to various study commissions—one to look at the operations of the Port of Baltimore, another to study the state judiciary, and still another to evaluate the work of the State Roads Commission.

Meanwhile, his family began to expand. In September 1955, he and Carol Brewster welcomed the birth of their first son, named exactly as Danny had been: Daniel Baugh Brewster Jr. In September two years later, their second son, Gerry Leiper Brewster, was born. At the time, Gerry's father was thirty-three, his mother forty.

It soon became clear to Turnbull that Brewster's primary interest was politics, not law, although Brewster continued to practice. In the summer of 1957, for example, he appeared before the Baltimore County Council as the attorney for a group of dog owners opposed to a proposed county ordinance that would have required dogs to be confined in an enclosure, to be chained, or to be with their owners. Those supporting the bill said it would stop dogs from biting, barking, attacking shrubbery, or being hit by cars. But before a jam-packed audience of opponents of the bill, Brewster won the day, arguing that dogs in rural areas, such as where he lived, were used for hunting and protection and could not and should not be confined. He claimed the ordinance would allow a dog warden to chase a loose dog "right into one's bedroom."[147]

As a young member of the General Assembly, Brewster was out almost every night, speaking at "rubber chicken" dinners at fire halls, attending political bull roasts, visiting farmers or factories or businesses in his district, or simply having drinks with his constituents or his legislative colleagues. Absence from home, day or night, became Brewster's pattern for as long as he was in public office.

"In politics, a man seldom gets much time to spend with his family," Brewster commented in January 1959, as if he had no say in the matter. "During the last campaign, I missed 89 consecutive dinners at home in the days before the election."[148]

His son Gerry, commenting decades later on his father's political career, said succinctly, "He was never home."[149]

As Brewster looked to move up the ladder toward Congress, the political obstacle in his way was another war hero, James P. S. Devereux, known for his World War II heroics in the 1941 defense of Wake Island in the Pacific. Devereux, a Republican and retired Marine brigadier general, was first elected to the Second District seat in 1951, was re-elected three times, and was considered a formidable opponent. The question was whether Brewster, a hero of Okinawa, would prevail in a race against Devereux, the hero of Wake.

Speculation about a Brewster-Devereux race began as early as halfway through Brewster's freshman term in the state legislature, even though he was then still a back-bencher with no big accomplishments on his resume other than helping to form the Young Democrats club in Baltimore County in 1952. The *Jeffersonian*, a Democratic-leaning weekly paper based in Towson avidly read by the political set, began promoting a Brewster candidacy, saying residents of Maryland's Second Congressional District (which included Baltimore, Harford, and Carroll counties) were already looking for a candidate "who will not only inspire the trust of voters, but who will appeal to their imaginations and create a feeling of friendliness. Such a candidate is not easy to find." The newspaper then added, "The *Jeffersonian* has looked the field over carefully and has reached the conclusion that we have in our midst a man who possesses all of the qualities it will require to tumble Representative Devereux from his well-entrenched position. The man we refer to is Mr. Daniel B. Brewster... a likable man, a colorful man, and a man of recognized ability. As a candidate for Congress he would appeal successfully to every strata of the electorate. Representative Devereux was nominated and elected as the hero of Wake Island. In Mr. Brewster the Democratic Party could offer a man with a war record it would be difficult to surpass."[150]

When Brewster filed as a candidate for Congress on June 20, 1957, eleven months before the party primary, another local paper, the *Union News*, said of him, "One of the most respected leaders of the county Democratic organization here and a proven vote-getter, Mr. Brewster has most of the attributes which go to make up a successful candidate.... If anything, his war record is even more distinguished than that of Mr. Devereux, the 'Hero of Wake Island.'"[151] A couple months later, the Towson Junior Chamber of Commerce nominated Brewster as "one of the 10 outstanding young men in the US for the year 1957."[152]

But before the Brewster-Devereux contest could be joined, Brewster's law partner, Gordon Boone, unsuccessfully challenged Devereux in 1952. Two years later, both Boone and Brewster ran for re-election to the state legislature. For the 1956 congressional election, however, Turnbull said his two young law partners came to his office and cut a deal: they "flipped a coin" and agreed that Boone would challenge Devereux again in '56 and, if he lost, Brewster could have his shot in 1958. It was a good deal for Boone because even if he lost, he would not jeopardize his seat in the state legislature.[153]

Brewster supported Boone in '56 but clearly was eyeing the race for himself. At a Ladies Democratic Club luncheon in Dundalk, he toasted Boone by saying, "Here's to it and to it again, if you ever get to it and don't do it, may you never get to it again!"[154] Two years later, it was Brewster who "got to it" and was ready to challenge Devereux.

In most political circles, Brewster was considered a shoo-in to win his party's nomination. His lone challenger in the congressional primary was an Italian-born construction company owner named Peter Aiello. Brewster captured 81 percent of the vote and thumped Aiello by a five-to-one margin. Brewster was so popular that in the general election Aiello called him "a gentleman" and endorsed him. "Had I done my investigating before filing, I would never have run against him," he admitted.[155]

The long-awaited clash between two decorated World War II heroes, however, never happened. Instead of running for re-election as expected, Devereux opted instead to run for governor. Devereux may have been frightened by Brewster's growing popularity, although years later he explained that after eight years in Washington, he simply wanted to be home more often.[156] (Devereux got his wish as he went on to lose the gubernatorial election to J. Millard Tawes of Crisfield.)

Instead of getting two war heroes pitted against each other, Second District voters were offered a choice between two blue blood, Baltimore County horsemen: with Devereux out of the race, the Republicans quickly chose J. Fife Symington Jr. to be Brewster's opponent. Symington was born and raised not far from Brewster in Baltimore County and later married into money: his wife was Martha Howard Frick, granddaughter of the steel magnate, Henry Clay Frick. Both Brewster and Symington rode in local steeplechase races. Symington, slender with strawberry blond hair, was a 1933 Princeton graduate and a former Democrat who had become the head of Pan American Airlines' London office during World War II. By 1958, he was running a small hardware and lumber business.

Republicans tried to paint Brewster as the hand-picked stand-in for the Democratic political machine that essentially ran Baltimore County politics in those days, but the Symington-Brewster campaign was relatively lackluster and the outcome never really in doubt. Symington complained about Brewster's vote against a state movie censor board while he was in the General Assembly, worried aloud about communists in the State Department, and complained the federal government was too large. Brewster railed against federal farm subsidies—a topic he harped on throughout his political career—and voiced support for rural electrification, the United Nations, and a labor reform bill then pending in Congress. Powerful House Speaker Sam Rayburn of Texas became a visible Brewster supporter.

Perhaps the issue that got the most press was a stunt by the Brewster campaign that came after Symington opened a campaign headquarters in Towson immediately across the street from Brewster's. In response, the Brewster campaign affixed a huge Brewster sign on the roof of a two-tone station wagon with big white-wall tires—"Dan's the Man! Brewster for Congress"—and parked it directly in front of Symington headquarters, blocking the Symington signs in the window. Symington's people cried foul, and the candidate himself called it "unsportsmanlike." They complained the station wagon was parked at a meter longer than the two hours allowed, that the Brewster campaign was feeding the meter, and that no one was enforcing the two-hour limit. The Brewster campaign, asked to respond, stated, "That meter is not being fed by the Brewster campaign. That meter is being fed by loyal Democrats walking up and down the street."[157]

A couple weeks before the election, the Brewster campaign ran an ad in eighteen local community newspapers entitled, "Some Revealing Questions and Answers on… Why I should vote for Daniel B. Brewster." The ad said he not only supported vets but was a vet; that he not only supported farmers but was a farmer himself; that he not only supported working men and businessmen but, as a lawyer, knew labor and business law and was "an experienced legislator." The ad included a picture of Brewster in front of the fireplace at Worthington Farms, kneeling behind a chair where Carol was seated with baby Gerry in her lap and three-year-old Dan Jr. standing to one side.[158]

When he had entered the congressional race the previous year, Brewster issued a one-page statement explaining his reasons for announcing so early, saying he wanted ample time "to present myself and those things for which I stand to the people in a calm, deliberate, thoughtful and independent manner."[159] He said he was willing to "discuss any and all local and national issues and state my position on them." On almost the eve of the election in 1958, the rector of St. John's Episcopal Church, located on Butler Road not far from Brewster's Worthington Farms, wrote a letter to the editor of the *Baltimore Sun*, responding to a prior letter that had been critical of Brewster.

"I know him to be a gentleman," the Reverend Nelson Rightmyer said of Brewster, describing himself as a Republican but failing to disclose that Brewster was one of his parishioners. "Throughout this political campaign, which has not been noted for its cleanliness, I think Dan Brewster has earnestly tried to avoid the vilification, condemnation by innuendo, and general gutter-politics which has been so common. Both in public and in private, he has tried to deal in policies not personalities, and he has consistently tried to conduct his campaign in such a manner as to raise the general level of political morals." He went on to say that, by contrast, Symington was trying to "trade on his surname, which was made nationally known by a man who stands for everything the Republican Party opposes," a reference to US Senator Stuart Symington of Missouri, a popular Democrat.[160]

Several days later, the Democratic Symington endorsed Brewster over his cousin, the Republican Symington. "If I lived in your district, I'd vote for you," the Missouri Symington publicly told Brewster.[161]

Other endorsements poured in, almost predictably. The local *Union News* said Brewster "has all of the qualities which fit him for the job he is seeking," and talked about his "native intelligence and commanding personality."[162] The *Baltimore Sun*, the state's most influential newspaper, noted that Brewster was "of the gentry," yet "shows a keen awareness of the problems of an industrial civilization. In that sense, he has kept step with the growing industrialization of his district."[163]

Brewster breezed to victory, winning by more than 31,000 votes and capturing 61 percent of the total. In a rematch two years later, Brewster was so popular he ran unopposed in the Second Congressional District's Democratic primary and then soundly beat Symington a second time by a 37,190-vote margin, or 59 percent of a much bigger turnout in the year John F. Kennedy was elected President.

The *Baltimore Sun* exuberantly endorsed his re-election, saying Brewster "has the highest integrity and is a prodigious worker," adding that he "makes no bones about the fact that he is determined to continue a career in politics.... Everybody talks incessantly about getting 'better people' into politics. Mr. Brewster is one of those 'better people' and he is in politics."[164]

For a typical "new man in Washington" feature story following his election to Congress, Brewster followed advice given him by Speaker Rayburn and tried to avoid being categorized. "I vote on the merits of each issue and I prefer to be regarded as a Democrat from Maryland, not as a liberal or a conservative or a middle-of-the-road Democrat," he said.[165]

Campaign news stories frequently shared some of the credit for Brewster's popularity with his wife, Carol, and often cited her beauty as a campaign asset. When Brewster ran for a second term in Congress in 1960, Carol was favorably compared to Jacqueline Kennedy, the refined and glamorous wife of the then Democratic candidate for President.

"Carol Brewster is certainly another proof that pulchritude helps out at the polls. Mrs. Brewster is a well-poised natural beauty," one reporter wrote, adding that she not only ran the Brewster's horse and cattle farm in the Worthington Valley but also occasionally gave speeches on her husband's behalf.[166] Photos of Carol during the campaign sometimes showed her driving the family's huge Farmall tractor, riding horses, or doing other chores around the farm.

Once Brewster arrived in Washington, the Marine Corps veteran landed the plum committee assignment he wanted: a seat on the House Armed Services Committee. There, he was in his element. He fretted publicly about US defenses against the spread of communism. He spent days and weeks on fact-finding trips, visiting troops in West Germany, flying in a supersonic fighter plane, and diving underseas in a nuclear submarine in the North Sea off Scotland. He called for modernization of the US Army, full strength for the Marine Corps, and a build-up of the US Navy. He investigated the use of military manpower and concluded that combat trained soldiers were being misused as "orderlies, house boys, butlers, babysitters, cooks and chauffeurs."[167] He began developing a reputation as a hawk on military matters.

By 1960, he had captured the attention of Kennedy, who put Brewster on his presidential campaign's Natural Resources Advisory Committee, where Brewster worked on water pollution issues. That September, Brewster hosted a campaign rally at the Towson Plaza Shopping Center that was ostensibly for Kennedy but which featured himself as well. While Brewster sat on the stage just to Kennedy's left, the Senator from Massachusetts called him "my friend and colleague in the Congress" and urged Marylanders to return him to office, "not only for the benefit of this district, but for the country."[168]

Kennedy, of course, narrowly won that election against Richard Nixon, but Brewster's re-election to Congress was never in doubt, even though he lost in increasingly conservative Carroll County, one of three counties in his district. The ballots had barely been counted when news stories started to appear speculating that Brewster was now poised to run for the US Senate two years hence.

With a Democrat in the White House and his own stature growing, Brewster increased his focus on foreign affairs. He supported Kennedy when the President sent naval units off the coast of Laos in Southeast Asia, saying the United States would not stand by as communists threaten the Free World. He was only mildly critical of Kennedy's Bay of Pigs invasion fiasco in Cuba. He supported a resolution aimed at keeping China—in those days labeled "Red China"—out of the United Nations.

By summer of the final year of his second term in Congress, word began leaking out that he was already quietly touring the state in preparation for a run against the incumbent US Senator, Republican John Marshall Butler. When Butler decided not to seek re-election, the field of Senate candidates began to get crowded. Blair Lee III, a popular state senator from the Washington suburbs, joined the race, and several other prominent names were being mentioned, including the state Senate president, the mayor of Baltimore, and a controversial Baltimore County paving contractor named George P. Mahoney, who had become almost a perennial candidate for higher office in Maryland—as well as a perennial loser. By 1961, Mahoney had already run for governor twice and for the US Senate three times, with nothing to show for it except five defeats.

Governor Tawes, a crusty conservative Democrat from Maryland's Lower Eastern Shore, was about to launch his own re-election bid on a ticket with his Attorney General, Tom Finan, and the state Comptroller, Louis L. Goldstein. Brewster wanted to get his name added to the ticket as the Democratic organization's pick for the US Senate, but he was getting nowhere with Tawes or the governor's political adviser, a former beer lobbyist named George Hocker.

That July of 1961, Danny and Carol Brewster spent a weekend at nearby Rehoboth Beach, Delaware, with their friends Harry and Patricia Hughes, who rented a cottage there each summer. Also there were Harry's friends, a former Caroline County legislator named Jack Logan and his wife, Ann. The group spent most of the weekend sitting in the sun and talking politics, trying to figure out a way to pressure Tawes into placing Brewster on his ticket. The Tawes ticket represented the old guard, the powerful Democratic machine that was running Maryland politics, so it was the safe place to be if you wanted to move up.

They came up with a plan to leak a story to newspapers that suggested the fast-rising Brewster was considering running against Tawes for Governor on a ticket that would feature Blair Lee for the Senate, Hughes for Attorney General, and a well-known Baltimore businessman named Jim Lacey for Comptroller.

Charles G. Whiteford, then dean of the *Baltimore Sun* political reporters, took the bait. His subsequent story labeled the "group of young aggressive Maryland Democrats" as the "New Era Ticket" and suggested it would present "a major problem for Tawes."[169]

"Needless to say, Danny quickly got a phone call from the Tawes camp inviting him to go on their ticket as a candidate for the US Senate," Hughes later recalled. "Danny called me in Rehoboth, told me what was going on, and I agreed he should take their offer."[170]

It was the next predictable, almost inevitable, step in the ascent of Daniel Baugh Brewster in public life.

Chapter 7

SENATOR BREWSTER

Despite his aura of invincibility, Brewster's path to the United States Senate did not appear assured, at least not on paper. If he made it to the general election in November, it looked like he would face a two-term Republican in a state that had not elected a Democrat to the US Senate in sixteen years. His immediate and more serious concern, however, was whether he could win the May 1962 Democratic primary against a formidable competitor, state Delegate Blair Lee III of Montgomery County.

Like his twice-defeated congressional opponent, Fife Symington, Lee was another blue-blood opponent for Brewster, but one with much stronger legislative credentials and his own large voter base in a different part of the state, the populous Washington suburbs. Lee was the scion of a large and wealthy family with a heritage in American history and politics that dated to the founding of the country, a lineage that may well have eclipsed Brewster's notable family tree. Two of Lee's forebears were Francis Lightfoot Lee and Richard Henry Lee, the only brothers to sign the Declaration of Independence, which meant the two principal candidates for Maryland's US Senate seat in 1962 were each a direct descendant of signers of America's founding document. The Lee family lineage also included Montgomery Blair, postmaster general under Abraham Lincoln; newspaperman Francis Preston Blair, an ally of Andrew Jackson; and Confederate General Robert E. Lee, among other diplomats and military men. Lee's grandfather, Blair Lee I, was Maryland's first elected US Senator, and Lee's father, E. Brooke Lee, was a former Speaker of the Maryland House of Delegates and was still a player in Maryland politics.

Like Brewster, Lee had attended the St. Paul's School in Concord, New Hampshire, graduating eight years before Brewster, and then, like Brewster, attended Princeton University. He, too, was a World War II veteran, serving with the Navy aboard supply ships in the Atlantic and discharged in 1945 after four years of service with the rank of lieutenant commander. He was elected to the Maryland House of Delegates in 1954, the year Brewster won his second term there.

Five candidates filed to run in the 1962 Democratic Senate primary, but it was always just a two-man race (one of the other candidates campaigned in an Uncle Sam costume). Brewster and Lee were strikingly similar: polite, articulate, well-groomed, and educated. Lee had a quick wit and a wry sense of humor. Both said they were avid supporters of President Kennedy and, until the election's final weeks, both talked mostly about policies and issues.

Brewster drummed on some of his favorite issues: the need for a strong national defense to halt the spread of communism around the world, the economic foolishness of farm subsidies, and the high cost to taxpayers of carrying a large national debt. He introduced legislation designed to help East Coast shipbuilders, such as those in Baltimore, compete with Pacific shipbuilders. And he used his position as a member of the House Armed Services Committee to tour and advocate for federal facilities around the state, such as the Aberdeen Proving Grounds in Harford County.

For the most part, Lee's positions on issues were much like Brewster's. The important difference between the two was not policy but organization. Brewster was on the ticket backed by the Democratic Party machine, which could produce and circulate campaign materials and turn out voters, while Lee ran on a lower budget splinter ticket with George P. Mahoney, the paving contractor and perennial candidate, who had decided he would have a better chance challenging Tawes for Governor than competing against Brewster and Lee for the Senate.

Only toward the end of that primary campaign, when it became increasingly clear that Brewster was in the lead, did Lee attack him. For the previous two or three years, the General Assembly had been in turmoil over a burgeoning scandal involving corruptly run savings and loan associations and the absence of state regulation. To lure customers, S&Ls promised exorbitant and unsustainable interest rates on deposits. They made bad loans, enriched themselves through insider trading, and failed to adequately insure deposits. Suddenly, many S&Ls in Maryland were going belly up and taking with them the life savings of their depositors.

In 1961, the year before the Senate primary, the scandal hit close to home for Brewster when newspapers disclosed that a number of key state legislative leaders—almost all of them his political colleagues from Baltimore County—were officers or stockholders in a phony deposit insurance company called Security Financial Insurance Corporation. The company was soon shown to have woefully insufficient assets to insure deposits. More troubling, most of the Baltimore County politicians who were involved with the insurance company were also in a position to vote up or down legislation intended to clamp stiffer regulations and requirements on S&Ls. They included Brewster's law partner A. Gordon Boone, who was then Majority Leader of the House of Delegates (and who was eventually sent to prison over this issue), and Charles F. Culver, who was vice chair of the House Committee on Banking, Insurance and Social Security. Former Baltimore County Executive Michael J. "Iron Mike" Birmingham, by then a member of the Democratic National Committee; Delegate Roy N. Staten, then chair of the House's Baltimore County delegation; Baltimore County state Senator James A. Pine; and another of Brewster's former law partners, John Grason Turnbull, who was by then a judge, were all identified as shareholders in Security.

Lee implied Brewster must have been involved as well, although he produced no evidence.

"Well, there were rumors about it, but I never believed it," recalled Theodore G. "Ted" Venetoulis, who in the 1970s was elected as Baltimore County Executive and later ran unsuccessfully for the Democratic nomination for Governor. "I never thought it so," he said of Lee's allegations. "We all liked Danny, respected him."[171]

Lee, however, went after Brewster's alleged connections to Security. "This is the firm which thus far has not paid one cent to any depositor who has lost money in savings and loan associations that have gone under," he said. "Finally, this is the company for which charter application was made on the stationery of the Brewster-Boone law partnership."[172]

Brewster shot back. "On many occasions, I have publicly stated and now repeat that I have never been in any way connected with any company insuring savings and loan institutions." He added, "In 12 years in elective office, I have never indulged in personal attacks and do not propose to do so. If Mr. Lee chooses to follow the 'low road,' that is his privilege. I prefer the 'high one.'"[173]

His protestations notwithstanding, as the primary drew closer, Brewster also got personal. He called Lee's father, E. Brooke Lee, "a thoroughly discredited Montgomery County politician who is trying to make a comeback through the candidacy of his son," and criticized Jack Pollock, a Lee campaign ally Brewster described as "a selfish, ambitious Baltimore city boss who for years has sought to expand his sinister influence into state government." Together, he charged, Lee and Pollock wanted to install Mahoney as their "puppet governor."[174]

The back-and-forth didn't seem to matter to voters or to those who financed elections. Brewster won the support of both labor and management. The AFL-CIO was behind him, as were National Brewing Company President Jerold Hoffberger, a major political fund-raiser; Carl Murphy, board chairman of the *Afro-American Newspapers*; Clarence Miles, a Baltimore lawyer and general counsel for the Martin-Marietta Corp.; John Leutkemeyer, president of Equitable Trust Company of Baltimore; and William Marbury and Richard Emory, partners, respectively, in the silk-stocking Baltimore law firms of Piper and Marbury and Venable Baetjer and Howard.

"One of the few bright spots in an otherwise drab political picture is the candidacy of Congressman Daniel B. Brewster, who is running for the office of United States Senator," one Democratic-leaning local newspaper editorialized. "Mr. Brewster has devoted most of his adult life to serving the public.... Still relatively youthful, Mr. Brewster should be able to give the citizens of Maryland many more years of useful public service."[175]

On May 16, 1962, Brewster outdistanced Lee by more than 81,000 votes to win the Democratic nomination for the US Senate. He received more votes than his other four opponents combined and won Baltimore city and twenty-one of the state's twenty-three counties—all except Montgomery and Frederick, which constituted the core of Lee's base.

Mahoney, meanwhile, lost his bid against Tawes to become Governor, his sixth futile statewide race in a dozen years. A post-election editorial in the *Baltimore Sun*, entitled "Six are Enough," said, "The very phrase, 'Mahoney campaign,' now signifies to voters the breezy, slashing and often destructive brand of electioneering which comes naturally to Mr. Mahoney.... Mr. Mahoney must soon conclude that his heyday is past and that, for his own sake as well as the party's, other voices and different names would be more welcome."[176] To the later dismay of Brewster and other Maryland Democrats, Mahoney would reject this advice.

The Republican incumbent, two-term Senator John Marshall Butler, had decided not to seek re-election, likely fearing defeat by Brewster. To take his place, Republicans selected Edward T. Miller, an Eastern Shore lawyer who had represented Maryland's First Congressional District for six terms, from 1947 to 1959, before twice losing bids for re-election. The sixty-seven-year-old Miller was of a different generation. He had served with the Army in World War I and then served again during World War II in North Africa, India, and China. Between the wars and some three years before Brewster was born, he was admitted to the practice of law.

With a somewhat competitive primary behind him, Brewster's general election campaign against Miller proved to be as easy as the rest of his rise through the political ranks. Under the headline "Golden Boy of Maryland Politics," a local suburban Washington newspaper said Brewster "has made quite a name for himself since he first entered politics. The question has often been asked: is he gifted or lucky or talented—or a fortuitous combination of all three?"[177]

A lot of attention was focused on Brewster's wife, Carol, which in the early 1960s meant talking about her beauty before mentioning her accomplishments. One feature story referred to Brewster's "pretty, blonde wife, Carol," and described her as "a trim, 123-pound, 5-foot-6-inch blonde with a golden tan and brown eyes."[178] Another carried a headline that said, "Brewster's Vivacious Wife Should be Political Asset."[179]

A *Washington Post* writer called her "a talented campaigner with a firm handshake and a knack for getting acquainted with voters."[180] Both Brewster and his wife tended to speak extemporaneously, he without need of a speechwriter and she employing talents acquired during her stage career.

"While her husband travels around the state, campaigning day and night, she divides her time between the farm, where they breed and train horses for the track, and the campaign trail, where she makes speeches and meets voters."[181]

Carol Brewster noted that between her husband's official Washington duties and the long hours he spent campaigning, he was "away from early morning until past midnight most days," leaving her to run their farm, exercise some of the horses, occasionally drive the big Farmall tractor to the hay or corn fields, and keep tabs on their two young boys, Dan Jr. and Gerry, who were taking lessons in riding, swimming, and skiing.[182] She hired a mother's helper because, increasingly, her husband had become a stranger to his own family.

Brewster's young campaign driver in the summer of 1962, DeCourcy "Dick" McIntosh, saw a different side of Brewster's routine. "The way he campaigned... was to go to bar to bar to bar to bar. He said to me early in the game that this was what he did. He'd stop in these roadhouses and other places where he knew people were congregating and have a drink, chat it up with them, shake hands, then go on to the next. I remember he said to me early on, 'Now I don't want you getting drunk on me!' Well, I was thinking, 'Well, I don't want *you* to get drunk on me!'"[183]

McIntosh said he frequently went inside the taverns with Brewster who "tended to know everybody, everywhere." The young aide came to believe that, on balance, the bar-hopping was an effective means of campaigning because it was a way for the refined and "elegant" Brewster to mix with voters he otherwise would likely never meet. It was a way for him to appear to be more like one of the guys. "He got to the common man," McIntosh said.[184]

When Brewster and Miller met in a public debate in September, the only fireworks involved an accusation from the Republican that Brewster stood to enrich himself because he and his law firm were representing a defunct amusement company that was trying to sell its land on Assateague Island at a big profit to the state of Maryland. Brewster said he had already given up his law practice and within days after the debate he had his name formally removed from the Assateague legal case.

Such small-bore charges, however, were quickly overshadowed by a huge Democratic rally in early October at the Fifth Regiment Armory in Baltimore headlined by President John F. Kennedy, who flew by helicopter from Washington to Baltimore with Brewster and two other Maryland congressmen. They were greeted by an estimated 30,000 in Patterson Park, while 200,000 were said to line the motorcade route, 8,000 waited inside the armory, and another 12,000 crowded outside. Baltimore police estimated that at least one out of every five Baltimore residents turned out during the one hour and twenty-two minutes the glamorous President was in the city.[185]

Kennedy urged the Democrats to support Brewster for the Senate, saying his election "is vitally important for the interest of this state, so the state will have someone to speak for it and for the country."

"We're talking about members of the House and Senate who support those programs of minimum wage, and medical care for the aged, and urban renewal, and cleaning our rivers, and giving security to our older people, and educating our children, and giving jobs for our workers," Kennedy said, and then quoted Woodrow Wilson: "What use is the success of any political party... unless it serves a great national purpose."[186]

The only hint of the deep racial strife that was to overwhelm America in the years to come was a small group of eighteen picketers outside the armory representing a group called Fighting American Nationalists. They carried a sign that read, "Impeach President Kennedy. Beware Traitors. Whites Will Win."[187]

Just over a year later, on November 14, 1963, Kennedy would make his final visit to Maryland to dedicate the I-95 expressway across northeastern Maryland. Brewster would have attended, but as Kennedy explained in his remarks, he had to be in Washington for a Senate floor vote, so Carol Brewster joined the President in Brewster's place. Eight days later, Kennedy was assassinated in Dallas.

A brighter story, however, involves the day Kennedy was invited to speak at that dedication. Maryland Governor J. Millard Tawes, Delaware Governor Elbert N. Carvell, and Brewster, by then the state's junior Senator, delivered the invitation in person to the Oval Office where two-year-old John-John Kennedy stole the show. After shaking hands with each of the visitors, John-John hid under his father's desk, came out to shake hands again, and went back under the desk. When he emerged to repeat the greeting a third time, the President told his son, "That will be enough, John-John. It's not time to start campaigning yet."[188] Following JFK's death, the freeway he'd dedicated days earlier was quickly named in his honor.

Within two weeks of Kennedy's 1962 speech at the armory in Baltimore, endorsements for Brewster started to pour in. The *Baltimore Evening Sun* said Brewster "has developed into an intelligent moderate with a healthy streak of independence."[189] The sister morning *Sun* said it liked Brewster because he represented the younger generation and because he was "a middle of the road Democrat."[190] The city's third daily newspaper, the *Baltimore News-Post*, also endorsed him.

Brewster's victory was a blow-out. He defeated Miller in Baltimore and in eighteen of the state's twenty-three counties and won by a 170,592-vote margin, 62 percent to 38 percent—the first Democrat to be elected to the US Senate from Maryland since 1946. He was thirty-nine years old.

Vice President Lyndon Johnson sent his congratulations and urged

Brewster to "immediately" communicate his committee assignment requests to Majority Leader Mike Mansfield and suggested the Senator-elect also reach out for help to Johnson's former Senate aide and political fixer, Bobby Baker.[191]

Brewster's initial committee assignments were to the Government Operations Committee, a watchdog panel that could review any government expenditure; the Public Works Committee, which oversaw federal construction of roads and buildings, water pollution programs, flood control projects, and river and harbor improvements; and the Post Office and Civil Service Committee, which monitored the performance and organization of the US Postal Service and oversaw salary, pension, and other bread-and-butter issues related to federal workers. But he could not land a seat—at least not yet—on the panel for which he had the greatest interest, the Senate Armed Services Committee. Republican J. Glenn Beall Sr., Maryland's senior Senator, already served on that committee and Senate rules prohibited two Senators from the same state from serving on the same major committee at the same time. In 1964, voters would provide Brewster with the opening he desired.

During the Christmas holidays that year, Paul B. "Red" Fay Jr., a close friend of Kennedy's who was then Undersecretary of the Navy, sent Brewster a holiday card that said, "Dan—the poll is completed and you and Carol are now voted the nation's finest looking Senatorial couple."[192]

By the time he was sworn into office as "Senator Brewster" on January 10, 1963, he had begun to put together a staff. It was to be led by an old Towson friend and occasional drinking buddy, William S. Townsend, who had also been his top Administrative Assistant when Brewster was a congressman. Ellen T. Lynch, sister of Brewster's early mentor, John Grason Turnbull, became his personal secretary in his district office in Towson, and Diane Dilweg, daughter of a former Green Bay Packer football player, LaVern Dilweg, who was later elected to Congress, became Brewster's personal secretary in Washington.

The new Senator also named Ellery B. "Woody" Woodworth, a Harvard grad from Glyndon who had taught music and political science at the Gilman School in Baltimore, as his legislative assistant. And he hired Robert "Bobby" Knatz, an old friend with Baltimore County political connections, to head his Baltimore constituent office.

Two of the most interesting hires to Brewster's staff were his first receptionist, a young Trinity College graduate named Nancy D'Alesandro, and Steny Hoyer, a University of Maryland senior and student body president who had interned in Brewster's congressional office in 1962, running the mimeograph machine and doing other menial tasks in the office mail room. Hoyer put in so many volunteer hours that Townsend, the Administrative Assistant, put him on the payroll. When Brewster was elected that fall, Hoyer just moved with him from the House to the Senate.

D'Alesandro was the daughter of one Baltimore mayor and sister of another future Baltimore mayor. She spent most of 1963 seated behind a large sign on which the Senator proudly displayed her well-regarded Maryland name. "Well, I don't know how large the sign was, but I do know I was the first desk when you came into the office," she recalled of her first salaried job in politics.[193] In the fall of 1963, D'Alesandro married Paul Pelosi (Danny and Carol Brewster danced at their wedding), and the young couple moved to California. There, Nancy Pelosi was eventually elected to Congress, where she ultimately rose twice to become Speaker of the US House of Representatives, the only woman ever to hold that high post.

"I know how respected [Brewster] was in our family. I was so honored to have that opportunity," Pelosi recalled of that first job, sitting in her second floor Speaker's office in the US Capitol with its commanding view down the length of the National Mall. "And, for my family, it was a big thing."[194]

Hoyer, after graduating from Maryland, began classes at Georgetown University Law School and worked in various capacities for Brewster— driver, mail opener, letter writer, screener of service academy applicants, policy researcher, and campaign aide. In May 1966, at the age of twenty-six, he wanted to run for the Maryland House of Delegates but got shut out by more senior Democrats.

"One day we were all sitting there talking about it and Steny had this ashen look on this face and said, 'The Senator says I'm going to run for [state] Senate,'" recalled Robert A. Manekin, who was a seventeen-year-old office intern in 1966. "He [the Senator] said, 'If we can't get you on the ticket for House of Delegates, we're going to run you for state Senate.' I think Steny was a little bit overwhelmed by it, but the Senator was not to be denied. He just thought if the Democratic machinery couldn't put Steny on the ticket for the House of Delegates, then goddamn it we're going to just run him for the Senate."[195] Hoyer not only won the Senate seat but rose to be the state Senate President, then won a seat in Congress, and eventually became House Majority Leader—the second highest position in the House—each time that Pelosi served as Speaker.

"You know, I'm surprised that doesn't get more attention," Hoyer said of the fact that two low-level aides working for the same United States Senator in 1963 would rise to become the two most powerful members of the US House of Representatives a half century later. "It is serendipitous," he said with an amused shake of his head. "Out of that little office—she is at the receptionist desk and I'm in the back office—there is nobody on God's green Earth who would have walked through that door and said, 'She's going to be the Speaker and he's going to be the Majority Leader.' It really is amazing."[196]

Brewster made one other hire that first year that would have an outsized effect on his life. The young man was John F. "Jack" Sullivan, a record-setting basketball star at Mount St. Mary's College in rural Emmitsburg, Maryland. Brewster may have come to know Sullivan through the young man's father, who had been chief of the Capitol Police. Jack Sullivan's initial title was that of executive assistant, but his real job that first year was to be Brewster's driver.

Hiring Sullivan surely seemed unexceptional at the time, but as his importance in the office and his influence with the Senator grew, his hiring would eventually prove to be one of the most politically fateful decisions made by the new United States Senator from Maryland.

Chapter 8

TRAITOR TO HIS CLASS

Danny Brewster grew up in a country dominated by white men. It wasn't Danny's doing; it was just the way it was.

Brewster's neighbors, his friends, his classmates at Gilman and St. Paul's, his teachers, his law partners and business associates, his fellow state legislators and congressional colleagues, were—almost without exception—white and male. At the time Brewster was elected to the US Senate in 1962, there had never been in the nation's history a President or a US Supreme Court Justice who was not a white male.

Since at least the beginning of the twentieth century, Maryland's state government pursued the same white supremacy principle that had been espoused in other southern states since the collapse of Reconstruction in the 1870s. It enacted Jim Crow laws that separated black and white Marylanders in schools, restaurants, theaters, bowling alleys, trains, steamboats, parks, and waiting rooms. White teachers were paid more than black teachers, who were further humiliated by being required to scrub schoolroom floors. Intermarriage between the races was forbidden, as it had been since Colonial times, and the Democrats who controlled the General Assembly did everything they could to bar African Americans from voting, despite passage in 1870 of the Fifteenth Amendment to the US Constitution, which provided that the right to vote may not be denied due to race.

In his inaugural address in 1908, newly elected Maryland Governor Austin L. Crothers said he supported "the elimination of the illiterate and irresponsible Negro voter from the electorate of the State…. Let us execute unflinchingly the purpose of the Democratic pledge by all lawful and constitutional means to maintain the political supremacy of the white race in Maryland."[197]

Starting as early as 1912, there were repeated efforts to repeal Maryland's Jim Crow laws requiring segregation of the races, but it was not until March 1951, Brewster's first year in the House of Delegates, that the repeal was finally enacted.[198] That legislation passed through the Judiciary Committee, where Brewster's voice and vote were needed.

When Brewster joined the US Senate a dozen years later, only five of the 535 members of the Eighty-eighth Congress were African American, all of them in the House. Two years later, there were six. And then, as the Ninetieth Congress opened in 1967, the six African Americans in the House were joined by Republican Edward Brooke of Massachusetts, the first African American to be elected to the US Senate since 1879—a span of eighty-eight years. Brooke's election may have been a delayed result of the passage, back in 1913, of the Seventeenth Amendment to the Constitution, which provided for direct election of Senators by voters.[199] Prior to that, the Constitution had given state legislatures the authority to elect Senators, and most state legislatures were controlled by rural white voters.

The wider world Danny Brewster was born into was a world of legal and cultural racial segregation, especially throughout the southern states from Florida to Louisiana but also as far north as Maryland and beyond. State Department officials, for example, complained that African diplomats traveling between Washington and New York were refused service at a restaurant on US Route 40 just north of Baltimore—an insult faced every day by average black Americans almost wherever they traveled.

A century after the Civil War and abolition of slavery, African Americans were still discriminated against in almost every way that mattered: in employment, education, public transportation, and equal access to hotels, lunch counters, stores, and other accommodations. Federal policies "redlined" black areas of cities and then intentionally steered business loans to the white parts of cities instead. Real estate agents refused to show African Americans houses in white neighborhoods. Bus stations had separate "white" and "colored" waiting rooms, bathrooms, and drinking fountains. Most public schools throughout the south were not integrated despite a 1954 ruling by the US Supreme Court that outlawed school segregation. Segregated schools were so much a part of the fabric of the nation that for years after the ruling many states either slow-walked implementation, challenged the decision in court, or simply ignored it.

Using poll taxes, literacy tests, and blatant physical intimidation, black Americans were routinely prevented from exercising their basic right of citizenship, voting. Lynching or other incidents of racial violence were frequent, even as insidious, less violent, small indecencies were acted out against African Americans every day. A large segment of white America paid little attention to how unfair, hurtful, or demeaning the treatment of black Americans was.

Joseph D. Tydings, who became Maryland's top federal prosecutor, the US Attorney, in 1961, told a poignant example. Tydings selected as his top assistant a veteran prosecutor named John R. Hargrove. Hargrove was a highly regarded lawyer and well liked by his staff, but because he was African American—simply because of the color of his skin—he was not allowed to dine in most Baltimore restaurants frequented by his white colleagues. Tydings and some of his Assistant US Attorneys related how ashamed they were that Hargrove could not go out to eat with them and how they would often bring their lunches to the office so they could eat with him and avoid their mutual embarrassment.[200]

In well-to-do homes, such as the home where Brewster was raised just north of Baltimore, the hired help—the cooks, maids, chauffeurs, and gardeners—were often, although not always, African American. (At Wickcliffe, the castle where Brewster's grandmother lived, for example, almost all the live-in servants were European immigrants, although their work was supplemented by additional daytime servants, both white and black.)[201] At Fernwood, Brewster's parents' home, Pearl was the maid, Hawkins the butler, Vera the cook—all of them African American and all known to the family by their first names.[202] No one in the Brewster family would have thought twice about it.

It was not until 1963 that Maryland's General Assembly finally passed a public accommodations law ending discrimination in hotels, restaurants, and other establishments that provided sleeping accommodations or food for the public. But the only way legislative leaders could get the measure approved was to exempt the nine counties on Maryland's Eastern Shore and allow Carroll County to hold a county referendum before the law could go into effect there. After blacks were denied service in a restaurant in the Eastern Shore town of Cambridge that summer, race riots broke out. Within a year, the General Assembly repealed the Eastern Shore and Carroll County exemptions.

Racial discrimination was also the rule in the American military, even as the nation was desperate to recruit more troops at the outbreak of World War II. First there was resistance to letting African Americans serve in the military, and when they were finally admitted, they were restricted to segregated units and used primarily for field support services rather than front line fighting. The races were separated at military parades, at church services, and in buses and canteens. There was virtually no chance an African American would be made an officer because most white soldiers—especially those from the South—would not abide having to answer to or salute a black officer, much less call him sir.

In the US Marine Corps, in which Brewster served, it was worse. African Americans had never been allowed in the Marine Corps since its founding in 1798 and Major General Thomas Holcomb, the Marine Corps Commandant, had no intention of changing that. In April 1941, after World War II began in Europe, Holcomb told a high-ranking Navy board, "If it were a question of having a Marine Corps of 5,000 whites or 250,000 Negroes, I would rather have the whites."[203] In 1942, under pressure from President Roosevelt, the US Navy and Marine Corps began to integrate, but black Marines were kept in segregated units, trained by white officers. Holcomb complained that black recruits were "trying to break into a club that doesn't want them."[204]

Once black Marines left training, they were often assigned as truck drivers, cooks, mess hall stewards, or typists. Many were given jobs as stevedores, moving supplies from factories or warehouses to ships and from ships to support bases or to the beaches where the white Marines were fighting.

Black Marines were commonly given the most dangerous jobs, often sent out as stretcher bearers to retrieve wounded soldiers under intense Japanese fire. They also were regularly assigned the perilous task of moving heavy crates of ammunition to the battle, then forward through the mud and chaos to the front lines, often with whizzing bullets and enemy shells exploding all around. This vital resupply work was performed with the same sense of patriotism that propelled their white counterparts. "It was a heroic, thankless job that few of us wanted," one soldier admitted.[205]

Even though these black Marines carried rifles, carbines, or submachine guns, they were not supposed to be involved in the actual fighting. Yet some voluntarily filled in when Marines on the line were killed or wounded.

"[Historian] Stephen Ambrose identified the lamentable American irony of WWII, writing [in his book, *Citizen Soldier*], 'The world's greatest democracy fought the world's greatest racist with a segregated army.'"[206]

There were about four thousand African Americans in the military at the outset of the war. By 1945, there were more than 1.2 million. Just under twenty thousand served in the Marines, and nearly thirteen thousand of them served overseas. About two thousand African American Marines participated in the battle for Okinawa, a larger concentration than for any previous operation.[207]

When the war abruptly halted with the Japanese surrender two months after the battle for Okinawa ended, veterans returning home from the Pacific—black and white alike—received little in the way of a celebratory homecoming. Americans were eager to get on with their interrupted lives, acting in many ways as if the intervening war had changed nothing. But it had.

African American newspapers and churches and many black soldiers themselves embraced what they called a "Double-V Campaign"—victory against the enemy overseas and victory against racism at home. Yet when black soldiers came home smartly dressed in their uniforms and proud of the service they had rendered, they were treated in many parts of the country just as they had been before the war: as inferiors undeserving of the same rights bestowed unquestionably on their white counterparts.

Such treatment infuriated Danny Brewster.

"I would have to guess," his brother Walter surmised years later, "that when he was thrown into the military with people from a poorer state of life than he had, I think he was definitely influenced by the boys from the right and the left—and the blacks—who were getting killed."[208] The year after the war ended, Governor Herbert R. O'Conor appointed Brewster, the young war veteran, to serve on the state's Advisory Commission on Veterans Affairs, his first entry into civilian public service.

Soon, Brewster and his childhood friend Francis N. "Ike" Iglehart became involved with the American Veterans Committee, a Maryland group started by a man named Charles Bolte, who had lost a leg at the battle of El Alamein in Egypt. The group purposely enlisted African Americans as members and had as its slogan "Citizens First, Veterans Second." They favored a GI Bill but not bonuses for those who had served in the war because, they believed, participating in the war was everyone's obligation.[209]

The group began planning a banquet at the local Green Spring Inn in Brooklandville, but the proprietor said he would not serve blacks, veteran or not. Brewster was so outraged he invited the African American vets to his home for dinner—a breach of social protocol that simply was not done in the Green Spring Valley in those days. As gossip about such visits spread around the cocktail parties, race meets, and church services in the area, word began to filter back to the Brewster family that neighbors thought Danny was behaving like a "traitor to his class."[210]

Unable to use the Green Spring Inn, the veterans group managed to integrate the previously segregated Park Plaza Hotel near Mt. Vernon

Square in Baltimore by holding dinner meetings there, recounted Iglehart, who at the time was a freshly returned-from-the-war student at Princeton. He told of talking with a young black GI in uniform at Baltimore's Penn Station as the two waited for a train to New York. The soldier told him he had re-enlisted because he could not stand the segregation of civilian life that he encountered after coming home.[211]

"Danny was really concerned about working people and black people. He was the first one to bring black people to the dining table at Fernwood. And Mortison would wait on them!" his brother, Walter, recalled, referring to Theodore Mortison, the Swedish butler who had previously worked for their grandmother next door at Wickcliffe. "Danny really, really cared about working people (and) was very generous too."[212]

Brewster's son, Gerry L. Brewster, explained, "To Dad, these men had fought for their country and, dammit, he was going to do something about it."[213]

Michael de Havenon, a son of Brewster's wife, Carol, from her first marriage, observed, "An important quality that Dan had is he was totally without social pretension." Despite being raised in what de Havenon described as a "claustrophobic social world" of money, horse riding, and connections, "He was in no way a snob."[214]

Charles McC. Mathias Jr. was a close friend of Danny's who lived with him for a while at Fernwood while they attended law school together. Years later, after Mathias had been elected to the US Senate, he remembered how "highly motivated" Brewster was and recalled how he was "one of the first people to break down the racial barriers. We had a certain number of blacks we would invite out [to Fernwood]."[215]

During the war, millions of African Americans migrated to northern cities to work side by side with white workers in war-related factories. Out of that shared war-time experience, a broader, more national push for civil rights began. At the 1948 Democratic National Convention in Philadelphia, the young mayor of Minneapolis, Hubert H. Humphrey, planted a stake for racial equality by proposing adoption of a first-ever civil rights plank in the Democratic Party platform.

"There are those who say to you—we are rushing this issue of civil rights. I say we are 172 years late," Humphrey said. "There are those who say—this issue of civil rights is an infringement on states' rights. The time has arrived for the Democratic party to get out of the shadow of states' rights and walk forthrightly into the bright sunshine of human rights."[216]

The civil rights plank was adopted, but it immediately revealed the national split on race when the entire Mississippi delegation and most of the Alabama delegation walked out of the convention and formed their own party, the Dixiecrats, and ran their own nominee for President.

Just twelve days later, President Harry S. Truman moved to correct the longstanding racial prejudice within the military, issuing an Executive Order that prohibited discrimination in the military based on race, color, religion, or national origin.[217] When his Secretary of the Army dragged his feet in implementing the order for nearly a full year, Truman fired him.

The fight over civil rights would play out slowly, painfully, and often violently over the next several decades and, in many ways, is still playing out today. Most of the early post-war civil rights victories were achieved through the courts, such as the 1954 school desegregation ruling, not in Congress and certainly not in state legislatures. Not until 1954, Brewster's second term in the House of Delegates, for example, were black lawmakers first elected to the Maryland General Assembly.

By the end of the 1950s, around the time Brewster was elected to Congress, the national civil rights movement was gaining strength, largely out of frustration with the pace of change. It had become increasingly clear that if civil rights were to be expanded to all Americans, it would not happen piecemeal at the state level but would have to be dictated by the federal government. A stark early example came in 1957 when President Dwight D. Eisenhower ordered National Guard troops to enforce desegregation of Little Rock Central High School in Arkansas. By the end of the decade, African Americans were regularly staging sit-in demonstrations at white-only lunch counters and protesting in countless other ways to demand equal treatment under the law.

In 1960, the young, vibrant voice calling for such change was Massachusetts Senator John F. Kennedy, the Democratic candidate for President. Fully 70 percent of African Americans who voted in that election voted for Kennedy, in part because late in the campaign JFK and his brother Robert were instrumental in getting the Reverend Martin Luther King Jr. released from a Georgia jail amid fears that the civil rights leader might be seized by a white mob and lynched.

While Kennedy, like Brewster, knew the time had come for broad changes in civil rights for African Americans, the new President had won the election by the slimmest of margins and now faced the practical political constraint of a filibuster-prone US Senate almost totally controlled by Southern segregationists. Still, his administration could not help but be drawn into the simmering domestic war over civil rights: the sit-in demonstrations; the Freedom Riders attempting to integrate interstate buses; the angry opposition that African American students faced while trying to enroll at all-white Ole Miss or the University of Alabama; or the brave souls, black and white alike, trying to register blacks to vote in Southern states under threat of job loss, beatings, and even murder.

"I tell people to this day how difficult it was [but] people don't understand how difficult it was just to support civil rights," said Clarence Mitchell IV, grandson of Clarence Mitchell Jr., the NAACP lobbyist from Baltimore who was so instrumental in passing civil rights legislation that he became known as the "101st Senator." "Back in those days, it was political suicide and those people knew that because of their votes—and Lyndon Baines Johnson knew—that we had lost the South forever."[218]

In 1963, the year Brewster joined the Senate, Kennedy introduced a comprehensive civil rights bill, but while it received the endorsement of House and Senate leaders, there was no way it could overcome the blockade by Southern Democrats. Then, in November, Kennedy was assassinated, and it became unclear what, if anything, would happen to the push for civil rights, especially with a Southerner, Lyndon B. Johnson of Texas, taking Kennedy's place.

By personal temperament and perhaps because of what he had seen both during and after the war, Brewster easily supported the civil rights movement. To him, it was simply a matter of fairness. He believed, without fanfare or chest-thumping, in Thomas Jefferson's words—that "all men are created equal." Like his political idol Franklin Roosevelt, he also had faith that the federal government could be engaged to achieve great and beneficial change for the nation.

From his earliest years, Brewster believed that because of his upbringing, his education, and his opportunities, he had a duty to help improve the world. As senior class president at the St. Paul's School in 1941, in the annual "President's Speech" to fellow students, Brewster gave an insight into what was then in his heart—and what those who knew him best would say remained in his heart throughout his life.

"The word duty has been used so much that it almost seems commonplace—but duty is the most important factor in every man's life," Brewster told fellow students.[219]

"To state it simply would be to say that it is our duty to grow up into loyal citizens of our country." By that, he said, he did not mean simply staying out of trouble and minding your own business. "That course would be easy for most of us. We could either join the family business or take advantage of our connections to obtain for ourselves a job. Then life would be easy, but futile—an idle and selfish life of leisure would be our lot."[220]

Showing a maturity beyond his seventeen years, Brewster then encouraged his fellow students to choose "another way of life. This latter way will be for the men who realize that their education and environment have put them in a position to accept a responsible place in society. Some of these men will enter government posts, while others will be leaders in their home communities. Gentlemen, that is the kind of men St. Paul's ought to turn out."[221]

This was Brewster's personal preparation, his outlook, and the character he brought to the United States Senate in 1963. He would need all those qualities to confront the challenges and setbacks he was to face in the years to come—problems he could not possibly have foreseen as he moved into the highest political position of his life.

Chapter 9

THE TURNING POINT

Marines sometimes offer a bit of combat advice to their fellow Marines: "Stay off the skyline." Translated, that simply means don't expose yourself needlessly. Don't take unnecessary risks.[222]

But the explosive decade of the 1960s was full of risks, and Danny Brewster—silhouetted against the bright light of public controversy—had trouble staying off the skyline.

For the country, it was a decade of enormous change, both good and bad, alternately exhilarating and crushing. For Brewster, it also was a decade of life-altering change, although with each passing year, the bad increasingly eclipsed the good.

In the first half of the decade, the overarching political issue was civil rights. In the second half, it was the expanding and increasingly unpopular American war in Vietnam.

From his earliest days in Maryland's House of Delegates, Brewster's support for civil rights was never in question. As a candidate for the US Senate in 1962, he lambasted the use of poll taxes that kept African Americans from voting, calling them archaic and undemocratic vestiges of a bygone era. Days before his election that year, he cemented his already strong support among black Marylanders by telling the *Baltimore Afro-American* newspaper that he favored a fair housing law for Maryland, establishment of a federal Department of Urban Affairs, and abolition of literacy tests for voters that were then employed as a way to suppress African American voting in a number of Southern states.[223]

But the clash over civil rights would test the young US Senator almost before he had had time to settle in. Five months after he took office, race riots erupted in the small Dorchester County seat of Cambridge on Maryland's Eastern Shore after African Americans who were already relegated to the balcony of the local movie theater were informed they now had to sit in the balcony's back rows. The previous spring the General Assembly had passed a public accommodations law that opened restaurants, hotels, theaters, and other public establishments to all Marylanders regardless of race but which explicitly exempted the law from applying to the nine counties on the Eastern Shore, including Dorchester. The riots worsened following the June 12 assassination in Jackson, Mississippi, of civil rights activist Medgar Evers, gunned down in his front yard after his bodyguards mysteriously disappeared. Evers was returning from an NAACP meeting at which T-shirts were distributed with the slogan "Jim Crow Must Go."[224]

Maryland Governor J. Millard Tawes, himself an Eastern Shoreman, responded to the Cambridge riots by sending in the National Guard to restore order. The National Guard would remain deployed as a peace-keeping force in Cambridge for the next two years.

Throughout the summer and fall of 1963, the nation became convulsed by the struggle over civil rights, a condition that would persist and evolve for the remainder of the decade. President Kennedy's civil rights legislation got the tepid support of Senate Majority Leader Mike Mansfield of Montana and Senate Minority Leader Everett Dirksen of Illinois—tepid because both knew it would never survive against the "Old Bulls" from the South who chaired virtually every major committee in the Senate. In August, the Reverend Martin Luther King Jr. upped the pressure with his "I Have a Dream" speech from the steps of the Lincoln Memorial before a crowd of more than 250,000, just blocks from the US Capitol where the civil rights legislation was awaiting action. He urged America to "make real the promises of democracy."

"It would be fatal for the nation to overlook the urgency of the moment," he said. "This sweltering summer of the Negro's legitimate discontent will not pass until there is an invigorating autumn of freedom and equality.... There will be no rest nor tranquility in America until the Negro is granted his citizenship rights."[225]

Yet less than a month later, four little black girls, ages eleven to fourteen, were killed and twenty others injured when Ku Klux Klan members used dynamite to bomb the Sixteenth Street Baptist Church in Birmingham, Alabama, a predominantly black church often used as a meeting place for civil rights groups. The crime stirred the nation but still was insufficient to push the civil rights bill to passage. In October, the legislation passed the House Judiciary Committee but was then referred to the House Rules Committee where it was bottled up by the committee's proudly segregationist chairman, Democrat Howard W. Smith of Virginia.

That same month riots erupted for a second time in Cambridge following the narrow defeat of a public accommodations' amendment to the city charter. Opposition was led by the Dorchester [County] Businessman's and Citizens Association. Cambridge's mayor asked Senator Brewster to mediate the resulting dispute and Brewster dispatched Billy Townsend, his Administrative Assistant, and Woody Woodworth, his Legislative Assistant, to see if they could help.

"I believe the present situation in Cambridge represents an acute embarrassment to the state and to our country. I have found it personally embarrassing to me as the junior senator from Maryland. I believe that some reasonable and just solution must be found," Brewster said, but the stalemate in Cambridge persisted, punctuated with protest marches that, in turn, incited more violence.[226]

Then, in late November 1963, President Kennedy was assassinated, and, with the unexpected suddenness of a bullet, Lyndon B. Johnson was President.

For those pushing for true equality for those Americans then commonly referred to as "Negroes," "colored," or—in many instances—much worse names, the ascension of Lyndon Johnson to the presidency provided little cause for optimism. Throughout his long career in Congress, Johnson had almost always voted along with his fellow Southerners against efforts to end racial discrimination. Congress in those days would not even outlaw the heinous practice of lynching.

But there was another side of Johnson that the public rarely saw, a side in which he demonstrated genuine personal concern for the plight of impoverished Hispanics, African Americans, and others, concluded his biographer, Robert Caro. His votes against civil rights over the years may well have been more about advancing his own political fortunes within a Congress ruled by segregationists than it was a reflection of how he really felt. "Throughout his life, there had been hints that he possessed a true, deep compassion for the down-trodden, and particularly for poor people of color, along with a true, deep desire to raise them up," Caro wrote as part of his multi-volume biography of Johnson.[227]

Five days after President Kennedy was killed, Johnson appeared before a joint session of Congress and surprised many by urging the nation to adopt a sweeping civil rights law in the late President's memory. "We have talked long enough in this country about equal rights," he said. "We have talked for one hundred years or more. It is time now to write the next chapter, and to write it in the books of law."[228]

Danny Brewster had the rare distinction among his Senate colleagues of being the only Democrat from a state south of the Mason-Dixon line to co-sponsor both the Civil Rights Act of 1964 and, the next year, the equally controversial Voting Rights Act of 1965.

Before year's end, supporters, led by Democratic Representative Emanuel Celler of New York, began collecting votes on a petition to pry the civil rights bill out of Smith's Rules Committee and send it to the full House of Representatives for a vote. Once free from Smith's clutches, the legislation passed and was forwarded to the Senate. President Johnson, who had built an unmatched reputation as the "Master of the Senate" in his years there, began to work his parliamentary magic. The House bill landed in the Senate Judiciary Committee that was headed by Senator James O. Eastland of Mississippi, who, like other Southerners, was no friend of civil rights and whose intention was to kill the legislation or simply never bring it to a vote. In late February 1964, however, Majority

Leader Mansfield, surely working in concert with the President, used a parliamentary maneuver to extricate the bill from Eastland's control and put it on the Senate floor.

Already, Brewster's office was receiving an avalanche of mail about every aspect of the civil rights struggle then permeating the nation. Even though Brewster publicly stated that letters supporting civil rights were running ahead of those opposed, the thousands of letters on civil rights among Brewster's official papers at the University of Maryland seem to tilt more heavily against the landmark changes in racial practice then under consideration. That is not altogether surprising as letter writers are generally more prone to protest something they do not like than praise something they do. What is shocking in those letters, however, is the fear and deep racial hatred many writers admitted to and the bald threats of political retribution directed at Brewster or anyone else who dared side with Negroes.

The complaints took many forms: opposition to the federal government forcing businesses to accept patrons they did not want, fear that uneducated African Americans would be allowed to vote, and scurrilous allegations that Martin Luther King Jr. and others in the civil rights movement were actually trained communists intent on undermining American democracy. "I don't know of anyone," one Baltimore woman wrote, "that wants to live with the black(s) and I hope you feel the same."[229] Some writers ominously predicted a nationwide race war was about to erupt. Among the most prejudiced letters were those from a frequent writer to Brewster and to other members of Congress named William M. Werber, who ran a Washington, DC, insurance agency.

"Black people the world over, and this includes the United States, are basically uneducated, unambitious, and unproductive, except in the area of self-propagation," Werber wrote Brewster on January 24, 1964. "In all of our major cities the blacks are the principal recipients of relief and the chief perpetrators of our crimes. Their contributions in taxes and services are minimal. They are dissidents and are constantly shoving for preferential treatment that their abilities cannot earn for them."[230]

In March, Werber was at it again, pressing Brewster to agree that hiring more blacks into the federal government would decrease the number of whites and that would not be in the "long range interest of the country." [231] Brewster replied, "I am firmly convinced that the best interest of this nation—one nation under God, indivisible, with liberty and justice for all—will be best served when we talk of each other as citizens and Americans, not blacks and whites."[232]

Philip James Bunch of Hyattsville, Maryland, wrote, "Maybe you are prepared to tread the utopian path in 1964, but we white Marylanders are not. Are you forgetting that Maryland was a slave state 100 years ago?" Bunch then delivered the political threat, "The negro vote didn't put you in office; the white man did. And the white man can just as easily take that vote away come your next election. Keep that in mind, Senator."[233] Brewster replied, "I failed to see how the argument that Maryland was once a slave state is either cause for pride or justification for opposing Civil Rights legislation 100 years later."[234]

The letters poured in with worries about federal overreach: forced housing pushing blacks into white neighborhoods, forced hiring of blacks in white businesses, forced busing of white students to bad—that is to say, black—neighborhoods, and general fears of increased racial violence.

"Unless you radically change your stand on 'Civil Rights,' my vote will never be on your side hereafter," wrote Adolph F. Sckow of Bethesda.[235]

There were also plenty of letters supporting civil rights and Brewster's efforts.

"Please do not waste government time and money answering this letter. Just get busy and get a good and complete civil rights bill passed," wrote Mr. and Mrs. Harald Rausch of Kensington. "It is time after 100 years for negroes to be first class citizens!"[236]

Brewster received other letters on related issues, including a number of letters urging him to vote for "cloture," the parliamentary maneuver necessary to cut off debate and end the Southern filibuster. Atheists sent letters complaining that discrimination against them was still exempted in the draft bill. Mothers whose sons were involved in the dangerous work of trying to register black voters in places like Mississippi and Alabama implored the Senator to do something to guard their children's safety.

Brewster took to the Senate floor in the bill's defense, saying he need not look any farther than the racial strife playing out in the Maryland town of Cambridge to appreciate the necessity of enacting federal civil rights legislation. In a letter at the time to Juanita Jackson Mitchell, then head of the Maryland State Conference NAACP Branch, Brewster said, "All Americans must be conscious of their responsibility to live together in harmony and in peace," adding that he hoped "every effort will be made to negotiate differences in a constructive manner and in an atmosphere of calm."[237]

Then a new, more serious and immediate threat to both the fate of the civil rights bill and Maryland's broad support for the country's new President arrived in the person of George C. Wallace, segregationist Governor of Alabama. On March 9, 1964, Wallace filed to run for President in Maryland's May 19 Democratic presidential primary. The winner would control all forty-eight of Maryland's delegates to the Democratic National Convention in August in Atlantic City, New Jersey, meaning if Wallace won, the delegates, by law, would be required to support him for President.

"People go to the polls and they vote their angst, they vote their anger, and these people that prey upon their fears—like Donald Trump is doing now—that's what George Wallace did," said Maryland Senate President Thomas V. Mike Miller Jr., a lifelong student of Maryland politics.[238]

Out of deference to the memory of his slain predecessor, Johnson had opted not to enter his name in the handful of state presidential primaries that were held that year, although he fully intended to seek a full term in the presidency come November. Instead, he enlisted "favorite son" candidates to stand in for him. Wallace had already entered the April 7 presidential primary in Wisconsin and the May 5 primary in Indiana and would face as surrogates the incumbent Democratic governors of each of those upper Midwestern states.

Until Wallace filed his candidacy in Maryland, however, there seemed to be no urgency to select someone to stand in for Johnson, but once Wallace filed, the immediate question for Maryland Democrats was: Who can stop him?

One possibility was Governor Tawes, then midway through his second term. But Tawes came from the conservative Lower Eastern Shore of Maryland where racial discrimination was still a way of life and he made clear he did not want the task. On the Sunday following Wallace's filing, state Attorney General Thomas B. Finan, speaking for both himself and Governor Tawes, telephoned Brewster at his Worthington Farms home and convinced the forty-year-old first-term Senator to take on Wallace. LBJ had personally asked Brewster to do it, and Brewster's selection had been cleared by Cliff Carter, Johnson's political aide. Brewster, after all, was not up for re-election himself for another four years and had a well-deserved reputation as the most prolific vote-getter in Maryland.[239]

"To allow Governor George Wallace to run unchallenged in Maryland's presidential primary would be unconscionable," Brewster explained the day he filed to run. "It is unthinkable that our state's delegation to the Democratic National Convention might be forced to bear the shame and embarrassment of casting Maryland's votes for such a man."[240] Just the year before he entered the Maryland primary, Wallace had gained national notoriety by standing in the entrance of the all-white University of Alabama in an attempt to block entry by the school's first African American student—his effort failing only because of federal intervention.

A decade after Brewster's fateful decision to oppose Wallace, Townsend, Brewster's then top aide, recalled, "The Senator had nothing to gain and everything to lose. As his political adviser, I begged him not to run," but he said Brewster told him, "The President called me to the White House and asked me to undertake this campaign on his behalf and I simply could not refuse."[241]

Unfortunately for Brewster, Townsend soon suffered a heart attack and was forced to leave the campaign against Wallace in the hands of another Brewster aide with only limited political experience, John F.

"Jack" Sullivan.

"At the time that the Senator filed to run against Governor Wallace, it was pretty well decided that it would be a pretty easy election. It wouldn't be much of a problem running against a man from Alabama in Maryland," Sullivan later recalled.[242]

Sullivan's assessment was dead wrong. Within two days, Brewster's personal secretary, Ellen Lynch, received an anonymous telephone threat that said if Brewster did not immediately withdraw from the race, his "wife would be taken care of." Baltimore County police detectives had to be brought in to guard the safety of Brewster and his family.[243]

Then, on March 29, Brewster and Wallace faced off in a nationally televised debate on ABC's *Issues and Answers*, moderated by the journalist Howard K. Smith. Brewster asked Wallace to withdraw; Wallace respectfully declined. Then Wallace read a forceful statement that supported states' rights, attacked the federal judiciary, and advocated a generally racist approach. He asked Brewster what he thought about it and Brewster, predictably, said he disagreed with and disapproved of the statement. Then Wallace sprung the trap, revealing that the statement he had just read aloud to TV viewers had not been written by him but, rather, had been the words of Lyndon Johnson, the man Brewster was standing in for, delivered years earlier on the floor of the Senate.

Stunned, Brewster was momentarily at a loss for words. When he recovered, he attributed the statement to a time years earlier when Johnson was a junior Senator from Texas and was representing his constituency at the time. The President's current position, he said, is boldly in support of civil rights.

"You show me a man who has never changed his views, and I'll show you a fool," Brewster countered.[244]

From that point on, the campaign turned bitter and mean, with name-calling from both sides. The steady, methodical, patrician Brewster came off almost as an innocent against the glib, wily, and street-savvy Wallace.

"In his less than two years in the Senate, he has left the impression of a man who thinks before he speaks. Sometimes, after thinking, he does not speak at all. The net of it is a political personality not yet filled out to the edges, its very central parts blurred here and there by prudence," stated one unsigned political opinion piece in the *Baltimore Evening Sun*. "For Mr. Brewster, this non-controversial era is about to end. The first three weeks of May, consequently, are likely to tell more about what the Senator is made of than all the fourteen years he has held public office."[245]

Brewster appeared knocked off balance by the vitriolic reception he received on the campaign trail. For him, it was a turning point in his career. Here was a politician accustomed to accolades and high vote totals suddenly being shunned, booed, cursed, and even spat upon. Such a reaction shook him to his core. He—and many other progressive Democrats—had completely and naïvely underestimated how pervasive was the opposition to civil rights in Maryland and how angry voters had become.

"Social revolution involving blacks was at its zenith," Townsend said as he reflected on the Wallace campaign years later. "People that were Dan's normal political allies wanted to register a protest against social change and economic pressure. They thought they were not going to hurt Dan by voting for Wallace. But in reality, it hurt him deeply."[246]

Undoubtedly, much of the anger directed at Brewster felt was really aimed at the civil rights bill, and at the racial unrest, demonstrations, and riots that erupted across the country. Brewster wasn't even the real candidate—he was merely a stand-in for Johnson. Much of the animus may have been directed at Johnson, but it was Brewster who was visible on the skyline and the one being targeted.

Brewster's campaign had trouble raising money and Brewster later complained that this difficulty was because his race against Wallace was somehow a "side-show" to the main event, by which he meant the Democratic primary for Maryland's other US Senate seat. That contest pitted the popular state Comptroller, Louis L. Goldstein, against a young reform candidate and former US Attorney, Joseph D. Tydings. But most voters and certainly most newspapers clearly understood that Brewster's contest with Wallace carried implications far more significant than who would win the other Senate seat or the disposition of Maryland's forty-eight delegate votes at the national convention. On more than one occasion, Wallace declared that his candidacy for President should be viewed as a public referendum on the civil rights legislation, believing the outcome of the primary could either propel it to passage or stop it in its tracks. Johnson knew that, civil rights proponents knew that, and Brewster knew that.

"It is very difficult to be a stand-in. They are not voting for you—it is Wallace or Johnson. You are not pretending to run for President. And Johnson, very frankly, asked him to do it, and it was a terrible thing to ask somebody to do," recalled Steny Hoyer.[247]

Brewster repeatedly tried to make the point that Wallace either didn't understand the civil rights bill or was intentionally misconstruing its purpose. But Wallace undoubtedly understood it clearly enough to know what it would mean to the everyday Marylanders, many of whom, from instinct, upbringing, and history, burned with opposition to it.

Half a century before Donald J. Trump burst onto the national political scene, George Wallace cobbled together a similar coalition of political extremists, white supremacists, and disaffected, lower income Americans with a distrust for government and a sense of abandonment. "The issue was so simple," Townsend later reflected. "Wallace offered an undisguised appeal to basic instincts—racism, competition for jobs, opposition to integrated housing, busing of school children. The little man against the establishment. States' rights. Against interference and oppression of the federal bureaucracy."

"It was a blow to [Brewster's] ego that people he thought were his friends voted against him," Townsend said.[248]

On March 30, Senator Richard Russell of Georgia and seventeen other Southern Democrats plus one Republican began a filibuster designed to block passage of the civil rights legislation. "We will resist to the bitter end any measure or any movement which would have a tendency to bring about social equality and intermingling and amalgamation of the races in our [Southern] states," Russell said.[249]

In early April, the head of the Democratic party in Wisconsin said it would be catastrophic if Wallace were to win 100,000 votes in the primary there, but the Alabaman won 266,000, or about a third of the votes cast. Wallace opponents attributed his better-than-expected performance to crossover votes from Republicans intent on embarrassing LBJ.

In the Indiana primary on May 5, Wallace won 30 percent of the vote, but that turned out to be his worst showing in the three presidential primaries he entered that year, even in a state with a strong history of Ku Klux Klan activities. Now he was turning his attention to Maryland, essentially a Southern state where his racist appeal would likely be more acceptable.

"George Wallace had a touch of the fear-monger that we see now in [President Trump]," said House Speaker Nancy Pelosi, who had worked in Brewster's office the year before the Wallace campaign.[250]

Much like Trump's critics, Brewster just could not believe that the Maryland public didn't see through Wallace. "His only strength is rooted in the ignorance of those who may be duped by his lies. He is a man who proclaims himself 'champion of Constitutional government,' but who has blatantly defied the decisions and orders of the nation's highest court. He is a man who says he is not a racist, but who campaigned for the public office he now holds on the same platform with the Imperial Wizard of the Ku Klux Klan... A vote for this man," Brewster continued, "would desecrate the memory of our fallen President. It would be a shocking insult to our current President. It would, most of all, make a mockery of the democratic process in the state of Maryland. In all sincerity, I believe it would shame us for years to come."[251]

"Danny had total contempt for Wallace," recalled Brewster aide Bill Miller, who helped in the campaign against Wallace.[252]

In response, letter writers turned up the heat. One Glen Burnie man addressed his letter to "Fork-Tongued Brewster," began with the salutation, "Dear Two-Faced," and called him a "phony double talker" but said he was pleased that "a man of your low caliber was selected to oppose that great statesman, Governor Wallace." Another writer from Takoma Park said, "Marylanders are sick to death of their weak-kneed 'leaders' who are attempting to cram the Congo down our throats."[253]

The country seemed to be coming unglued. In early May, police in Birmingham, Alabama, quelled a demonstration by African Americans by unleashing police dogs and spraying protesters with high-powered water hoses. Then, back in Maryland, Wallace decided the best way to rub salt in the state's racial wounds was to deliver a speech in Cambridge, epicenter of the state's racial unrest. In addition to his own bodyguards, at least fifty state police and another four hundred Maryland National Guardsmen were stationed nearby. A crowd of twelve hundred showed up at a fire hall to hear Wallace, and another three hundred or so protesters held a counter-rally nearby. Before it was all over, rocks and bottles were thrown, tear gas used, and thirteen African Americans arrested. Similar violence continued for the next three nights.[254]

Brewster recoiled at even being in the same room with Wallace. Other than their nationally televised debate early in the campaign, the only time the two crossed paths was at the Baltimore television station WBAL where both were recording addresses for the close of their campaigns. Here is how Wallace later described that chance encounter:

"Although I was a guest in his state and he should have made the initial gesture of greeting, I strode across the stage and held out my hand. 'Senator Brewster, I am glad to see you again.' Although portrayed as a genteel country gentleman, Brewster replied coldly, 'I shake hands with you out of respect for the system that allows you to be in the state, but I don't respect you or your principles.' I bit my lip and turned around and went back to my seat without replying. Perhaps there is truth to the saying that politics is no game for a gentleman."[255]

Johnson and the Democrats knew what was at stake in Maryland. If Wallace were to win, not only would Brewster be humiliated but Johnson, too, and such a defeat could spell the end of the civil rights legislation. In the campaign's final two weeks, the best-known Democrats in the nation paraded into Maryland to campaign for Brewster (and the

President) and against Wallace. Johnson himself visited Cumberland in Western Maryland, ostensibly to look at federal projects in Appalachia, but Brewster stuck by him like a shadow. Then to Maryland came, among others, Senator Frank Church of Idaho; Senator Claiborne Pell of Rhode Island; Senator Abraham Ribicoff of Connecticut; Senator Birch Bayh of Indiana; Senator Daniel Inouye of Hawaii; and finally, Senator Edward Kennedy of Massachusetts—one of his first public appearances since the assassination of his brother six months earlier.

Kennedy, standing beside Brewster in ethnic areas of south Baltimore, said, "The Irish and the Poles came to this country looking for a better life. The Democratic party gave it to them." He recalled his older brother's visits to Maryland. "You in South Baltimore gave him your help and your support. The man who is running against Danny Brewster is against everything the President lived for and worked for. I am here because I felt he would have wanted me to be here."[256]

Sometimes, when Brewster had to be on the Senate floor for the civil rights debate, his wife, Carol, campaigned against Wallace on his behalf despite the earlier threats on her life. Two days before the primary, the *Baltimore Sun* ran the entire text of the civil rights bill so readers could read the legislation for themselves to determine which of the candidates was telling the truth about what it would do.

Then, mercifully, the election was over. Brewster won with 54 percent of the vote to Wallace's 43.5 percent, yet Brewster was clearly embarrassed that Wallace had done so well. The Alabama Governor won sixteen of Maryland's twenty-three counties, including the nine counties of the Eastern Shore, the three in Southern Maryland, and Howard, Anne Arundel, and Harford counties in Central Maryland. Brewster, who had long been popular with black and working-class voters, handily won Baltimore city, but in Baltimore County, his home turf, he barely won by a scant 324 votes out of the 94,878 cast.

On election night, Brewster aide Woody Woodworth emerged from the Brewster campaign's hotel suite after the race had been called and admitted, "How can we be elated? We'd be elated if we had held him to less than Indiana."[257]

But Senator William Proxmire, a Wisconsin Democrat and outspoken civil rights supporter, understood the Maryland vote's impact. On the Senate floor, Proxmire mentioned how candidates who supported civil rights—Democrats and Republicans alike—had won the primary in every congressional district in Maryland "and those who opposed it lost."

He singled out Brewster as "a wonderful human being, a fine Senator, competent, intelligent, charming. He took on a very tough task in running as a stand-in candidate for President Johnson. This is always a hard role. Brewster won and deserves the thanks and acclaim of all civil rights adherents."[258]

The same day Wallace lost, Senate Minority Leader Everett Dirksen convened the Republican caucus in Washington and emerged to say that amendments that he and Democratic floor leader Hubert H. Humphrey had worked out with Attorney General Robert F. Kennedy had convinced enough Republicans to join Democrats in a vote for cloture to end the Southern filibuster, thus clearing the way for passage of the Civil Rights Act of 1964. Brewster's victory over Wallace had extinguished the last best hope the Southern Senators had to defeat the bill, which was to keep the Republicans from joining the cloture vote.[259]

The Brewster victory over Wallace had a more personal impact on African Americans in Maryland. "I remember when George Wallace ran in Maryland," said former Baltimore County Public Schools principal Barry Williams, the brother of Maryland House Speaker Adrienne Jones, the first African American and first woman to hold that position. "There were several children in my elementary school who parroted the language of their parents without understanding the real meaning. I remember thinking if George Wallace won, I would not be allowed to attend the same school as I had been.

"Fortunately," Williams continued, "Maryland landed on the right side of history."[260]

The same night that Brewster won, reform candidate and civil rights advocate Joseph D. Tydings also won a lopsided upset victory over the favored Louis L. Goldstein for the Democratic nomination for Maryland's other Senate seat. Goldstein, whose civil rights support had come into question, had been backed not only by the dominant Democratic organization but also by Brewster.

Reflecting back on the Brewster-Wallace race a decade later, Tydings said, "Danny didn't really evaluate the race before he got in. He didn't feel it out. He underestimated Wallace. It was the first time [Brewster] had been booed in his life. He was very upset when [Wallace] got the amount of vote(s) that he did." Having said that, Tydings also said Wallace would have won in Maryland had it not been for Brewster, whom he called "the most effective political figure at the time."[261]

In 1972, Wallace returned to Maryland as a presidential candidate and easily won the state's presidential primary. But while campaigning in Laurel, Maryland, the day before that election, Wallace was shot and paralyzed in an assassination attempt, essentially ending his national aspirations.

"Wallace," concluded the historian Theodore H. White, "astounded political observers, not so much by the percentage of votes he could draw for simple bigotry… as by the groups from whom he drew his votes. For he demonstrated pragmatically and for the first time the fear that white working-class Americans have of Negroes… and in Maryland he did better, running almost as strong among the steelworkers of Baltimore as among the hereditary racists of the Eastern Shore."[262]

An odd result of Brewster's success against Wallace is that the victory seemed so disappointing even though an electoral margin of ten percentage points or more is often viewed as overwhelming. But the expectations about how a home-grown candidate of Brewster's character, qualifications, and prior electoral performance would do against the racist Governor of a Southern state were such that even in victory, it felt to many like a defeat, or at least an unsatisfying victory. Yet, by comparison, Brewster received more votes in the 1964 Democratic presidential primary in Maryland than all but one other Democratic candidate in a Maryland presidential primary in the twentieth century, including

Kennedy, Jimmy Carter, Walter Mondale, Michael Dukakis, and Bill Clinton. The exception was Edmund G. "Jerry" Brown in 1976.

Brewster's victory was important enough to garner front page banner headlines in newspapers from Los Angeles to Chicago to Philadelphia and from Spokane to Des Moines to Tampa. Almost all the headlines noted how "close" the race was, one even proclaiming that Brewster had "edged" Wallace even though the Marylander had won by more than ten percentage points.[263] In the South, Wallace's loss was portrayed almost like a victory. "Strong Anti-Rights Vote Given Wallace," blared the *Pensacola Journal* in Florida. The smaller sub-head said, "44 Per Cent in Maryland Say No to Brewster."[264]

Even today, when some of Brewster's contemporaries are asked to think back on that long-ago 1964 Wallace campaign, what lingers in their memory is that Brewster got clobbered, even though he didn't.

"Now that Maryland has spoken very loudly through a majority of the white people voting for Wallace… don't you feel that common sense should dictate that you start to represent the majority of the white people of the state of Maryland and change your stand on the so called Civil Rights Bill?" inquired V. J. Hughes Sr., a Baltimore resident. "If you do not, you can kiss your political future goodby [*sic*]. Yours respectfully."[265]

Neither swayed nor intimidated, Brewster followed the lead of Senator Humphrey and joined the mostly northern majority in the Senate on June 10, 1964, and voted for cloture to end the Southern filibuster. The 71-29 vote marked the first time cloture had ever been invoked in support of a civil rights bill and only the second time cloture had been invoked in the Senate for any purpose since 1927.

The very next day Brewster received a letter from another Baltimore resident who said in no uncertain terms, "In light of your recent actions, I would never vote for you for Senator or any other public office."[266] Still another was even more threatening, saying, "Your time is coming and I'll assure you I'll do everything in my power to defeat you. I made one mistake voting for a 'yes' man to the president. I'll not do it again."[267]

Fifteen years after that primary election, Brewster admitted, "I totally misunderstood the depth of racial hatred and bigotry in the state. I was amazed, staggered, disheartened and bitterly disappointed, and I seriously considered dropping out of politics."[268]

Hoyer, who was then on Brewster's staff, reflected, "I think [the Wallace campaign] really undermined his confidence in himself and probably his view of himself. I think he felt, 'I've screwed this up.' You know, 'I'm a United States Senator and I have been at this for two years, never lost an election,' sort of the bright shining star of Maryland, and I think he was just feeling probably self-guilt."[269]

But he also began receiving letters praising his courage and assuring him that he was in the right, that his was the moral position. Most came from constituents, but at least one came from the Reverend Martin Luther King Jr., who wrote to Brewster, "The devotees of civil rights in this country and freedom loving people the world over are greatly indebted to you for your support in passing the Civil Rights Act of 1964."[270] After the filibuster ended, the Civil Rights Act of 1964 passed the Senate, 73-27, and the House of Representatives accepted all of the Senate's changes. It then went to President Johnson, who signed the landmark legislation into law on July 2, 1964.

Brewster could have stayed off the skyline by avoiding the Wallace race or by taking a lower profile on the civil rights legislation. But he took those positions out of loyalty to Johnson and loyalty to his political party, and, most importantly, out of the certainty that his support for civil rights was the only defensible position a fair and decent person could take.

The primary campaign against George Wallace became a turning point for Brewster, both professionally and personally. He was taken aback by the public's reaction. The man who, as a teenager, spoke so eloquently of the duty one has to one's country, who, as a Marine, was wounded multiple times while fighting for his country and decorated for his actions, and who had served the people of Maryland in the General Assembly, the House of Representatives, and now the US Senate, was not only booed, cursed, and spat upon, he now began to receive threatening letters calling him a traitor to his nation for supporting the civil rights bill.

"That was the first political blow he experienced," said his good friend Harry Hughes. "I don't know whether that triggered it, but [after that campaign] he started drinking."[271]

"Danny underestimated Wallace and the redneck backlash," said Senator Tydings.[272] That campaign changed Danny Brewster, changed the trajectory of his political career, and ultimately changed his life. "It did, very much, hurt Danny's political future. Emotionally, it upset him and shattered his confidence. It damaged his effectiveness as a future candidate. Brewster took it way too seriously."[273]

Chapter 10

SAVING ASSATEAGUE

Two big storms shaped Danny Brewster's most lasting personal legislative achievement, the permanent protection of Assateague Island.

The first, in August 1933, was a hurricane that hit Maryland's Atlantic coast with such force that it carved a twelve-foot-deep, two-hundred-foot-wide inlet through the barrier island at the south end of the Maryland beach resort of Ocean City. South of that new inlet and suddenly disconnected from Ocean City lay Assateague Island, a thirty-seven-mile-long, wind-blown strip of sand dunes, scrub brush, and loblolly pines that was mostly undeveloped and unoccupied save for some scattered waterfowl hunting lodges, a few small private beach cottages, and an ancient herd of wild ponies. The northern two-thirds of Assateague were in Maryland and the bottom third, which included Chincoteague and the somewhat developed Chincoteague Island, was in Virginia. Once Assateague was cut off by that 1933 storm, the only way to get there was by boat or on a small vehicle ferry until two small bridges were built from the Virginia mainland in 1939 and 1940: the first across Chincoteague Channel to Chincoteague Island, and the second from Chincoteague Island across Assateague Channel to the preserved portion of Chincoteague on the southernmost end of Assateague Island.

Largely as a result of World War II, not much changed on Assateague Island until the early 1950s when the first bridge spanning the Chesapeake Bay opened near Annapolis. That bridge opened the entire Eastern Shore—including the beach-lined barrier islands fronting the Atlantic—to easier access and made all of it ripe for development. As building exploded in Ocean City north into Delaware, developers also envisioned huge development potential—and profits—on Assateague.

Almost immediately after the Bay Bridge was built, a lawyer from Silver Spring, Maryland, a suburb of Washington, DC, assembled a group of investors who then purchased most of the Maryland portion of Assateague, subdivided almost every square inch, and began marketing the eight thousand-lot proposed development as Ocean Beach, Maryland, a "new Atlantic coast playground." Sales brochures with a photo of a herd of wild ponies on the cover contained page after page of plats depicting row after row of half-acre building lots, most rows eight or nine lots deep, stretching from the ocean front on the east to the island's western shoreline on Chincoteague Bay.[274] A number of lots were sold sight unseen to residents of Florida, the Midwest, and elsewhere through out-of-state advertising, but because there was no bridge to the Maryland portion of the island, actual development was sparse. By 1958, there was only one road and about twenty-two buildings, even though optimistic developers had planted scores of white, numbered street markers where one day they hoped to build actual streets.

Frustrated by the inaccessibility of their investment properties, lot owners formed a private corporation to raise money to construct a bridge to the mainland. Worcester County officials were cool to the idea, but the Ocean Beach developers offered the state of Maryland about three miles of shoreline to develop a state park if the state would build the bridge. By 1961, Governor Tawes signed legislation authorizing the state to spend $1.5 million to build a bridge to Assateague.

Then, beginning on Ash Wednesday 1962, the second big storm hit, a three-day nor-easter that devastated Assateague and the mid-Atlantic coast. Water crossed the low-lying island in at least five places, flattening dunes and filling marshlands with sand. All but about a dozen of the forty-some buildings that had been erected by that time were knocked down, and the only paved road was obliterated. Perhaps most disturbing, part of the shoreline of the island shifted some 420 feet to the west.[275]

One of the most famous pictures from the period depicted William

Green, a Worcester County activist who lived across Sinepuxent Bay from Assateague and who thought the Ocean Beach plan would be a disaster. Green had his photograph taken while he leaned against one of the street signs—"So. 54 St."—with water up to his shins. The water stretched as far as the eye could see beyond him past rows of additional perfectly aligned signs marking the locations of streets that had never been built.[276]

To many, the Ash Wednesday storm illustrated the folly of trying to develop Assateague. The *Washington Post* called would-be residents "gamblers in hip boots."[277] The Audubon Naturalist Society and other environmental groups questioned how development could be supported on such a vulnerable strip of sand. Joining the chorus of skeptics was Stewart Udall, President Kennedy's preservation-minded Interior Secretary and a man with big ideas who thought Assateague should be protected in its pristine state. Kennedy was sympathetic to this plan after co-sponsoring legislation as a US Senator that created the Cape Cod National Seashore, a portion of which was developed for recreation and the rest set aside as "primitive wilderness."

Danny Brewster, a supporter of President Kennedy, embraced the idea of federal acquisition of Assateague. In July 1963, just seven months into his first year in the Senate, Brewster accompanied Udall, state Comptroller Louis L. Goldstein, and Maryland Congressman Samuel Friedel on a walking tour of the Assateague beach.

Udall was concerned that almost all property along the coasts of the United States was in private hands and argued that the public deserved access to areas still unspoiled by development. He said Fire Island in New York and Assateague Island in Maryland were two prime candidates to become National Seashores, a new type of park that he said would compare favorably to Cape Cod, Cape Hatteras, or Point Reyes, California.

By the time Brewster took him to tour Assateague, Udall's office had already proposed a plan that called for the state park on the northern portion of the island, more roads, improvements for the Chincoteague National Wildlife Refuge in Virginia at the southern end, and federal acquisition of the bulk of the island that remained in Maryland.

Goldstein was the first Maryland official to endorse Udall's plan, and two months later Brewster introduced legislation that would establish the Assateague Island National Seashore, much as Udall had planned it. A nearly identical bill to Brewster's was introduced on the House side by Representative Rogers C. B. Morton, a progressive Republican from the Eastern Shore, who worked cooperatively with Brewster.[278]

Not everyone liked the idea of the federal government taking over Assateague, especially the purchasers of some of the eight thousand lots at Ocean Beach, the Worcester County commissioners who envisioned a tax revenue windfall from such a huge development, and some within the state government who had already paid for a bridge to connect the island to the mainland and had plans for the new state park on the island. Depending on location, half-acre residential lots at Ocean Beach sold from as low as $1,500 to as high as $7,250 for oceanfront lots on the corners of proposed blocks of houses.[279]

Before in-depth hearings on Brewster's bill could be held, he and the rest of Congress became distracted by much weightier and time-consuming issues, including passage of the Civil Rights Act of 1964 and Brewster's fearsome confrontation with George Wallace in that spring's Maryland presidential primary. Brewster interrupted his campaign against Wallace just long enough to speak to an Atlantic coast parks and recreation group meeting in Baltimore in early May and repeated phrases Udall sometimes used to describe Assateague as the last undeveloped strip of shoreline between Cape Cod and Cape Hatteras. Moreover, he noted that Assateague beaches were within 150 miles of 34 million people living in and around Washington, DC, Baltimore, Wilmington, and Philadelphia.

Perhaps the most hotly debated question was: If Assateague is to become a National Seashore and state park, how much development should be allowed? Opinions ranged from encouraging intense commercial development in or near the state park and constructing a paved road from the Maryland bridge all the way to Chincoteague to leaving the island in as natural and primitive a state as possible, virtually untouched by man. Udall, and ultimately Brewster, were in the latter camp.

The proposal, however, was beset by controversies. Ocean Beach lot owners hated it, even though Udall promised them fair market value for their property, a costly promise that concerned some members of Congress. Hunters who frequented the rustic lodges that dotted the remote island worried about losing their beloved sanctuaries for shooting ducks, geese, other waterfowl, and deer. Moreover, if the federal government was going to take over, Maryland wanted to be reimbursed for the cost of building the bridge to Assateague, which finally opened to traffic in fall 1964. As the debate dragged on, a large and diverse collection of environmental groups became engaged, and often they, too, were at war with each other over what kind of park Assateague should become.

In the end, there was not enough time to resolve these disputes in 1964, so on the first day the new Eighty-ninth Congress convened in January 1965, Brewster re-filed his Assateague legislation, which became known as Senate Bill 20. Days later, President Johnson gave the proposal a boost by mentioning it in his annual State of the Union address to Congress, linking it to his broader efforts to protect wilderness areas and the nation's natural beauty. Johnson and the Democrats had won an overwhelming landslide in the November 1964 election and the Democratic majority seemingly had the power to do almost anything it wished.[15]

Even with that, remembered Bill Miller, who was then a special assistant to Brewster, "It was a very difficult bill to pass." One unexpected problem, Miller recalled, was that Brewster received push-back from Senators from Ohio, Indiana, Illinois, and elsewhere in the Midwest because many of their constituents had bought lots on Assateague as investments, sight unseen, and did not want the federal government to push them off their bit of sand. "They bought lots with the idea that that would be their retirement," said Miller. By 1965, however, many of those who had originally purchased waterfront lots now found that they owned lots that were already under water, and that made it a hard sell

---

15. At the beginning of the Eighty-ninth Congress, Democrats held a 68-32 margin in the Senate and a 295-140 margin in the House, the biggest Democratic margin in Congress since Franklin Roosevelt's election in 1936.

to convince members of Congress that such land speculators should be rewarded by being reimbursed in full.[280]

Nevada Senator Alan Bible, chairman of the Subcommittee on Parks and Recreation, balked at the growing cost of the Assateague proposal. Then Representative Morton threatened to unravel the various negotiated compromises incorporated in the Assateague legislation by announcing his support for a road the length of the island. Brewster disagreed but accepted Morton's amendment, saying, "A National Seashore with a road is better than no National Seashore."[281]

As for Bible, Brewster, supported by the newly elected junior Senator from Maryland, Joseph D. Tydings, put on a full-court press. Brewster enlisted fourteen of his colleagues, including Senators from as far away as Alaska, to be co-sponsors. He and Morton opened an exhibition of sketches and photographs of Assateague done by students at the Maryland Institute of Art in Baltimore and displayed them in the rotunda of the Old Senate Office Building. He took Bible and three other subcommittee members to walk the sands of Assateague and then to take a ride several miles down the beach between the seashore and the dunes. The delegation was also taken on a low-altitude helicopter tour of the entire length of the island. Brewster quietly arranged for a range of environmental and preservation groups—the Federated Garden Clubs, the Izaak Walton League, the Citizens Committee for the Preservation of Assateague Island, and others—to lobby Bible to support Senate Bill 20.

On March 17, 1965, Bible's subcommittee opened the first of what would become four full days of hearings on Assateague. Brewster, as the bill's primary sponsor, was first to testify, and he urged quick action, saying Worcester County officials were ready to drive bulldozers onto the island, developers were seeking building permits even though there were no plans for sewage disposal, and opponents were already suing in state court to stop the federal takeover. "I have continued to stress the need for prompt action because I know that without prompt action the opportunity to bring Assateague into the public domain for the enjoyment of all will be lost," Brewster said. With the bridge now built and open to traffic,

1965 had become "the decision year," Brewster declared.[282]

C. A. Porter Hopkins, a farmer, hunter, conservationist, and friend of Brewster's from Baltimore County who later would serve as a Republican member of the Maryland General Assembly, headed the Citizens Committee for the Preservation of Assateague Island. "My adult life has been spent so far seeking to conserve and to preserve those features of our natural and cultural heritage without which future generations of Marylanders and Americans would, in my opinion, be spiritually handicapped," he testified, adding that he had hunted and fished on Assateague for a decade and had "watched the ponies, turtles and birds, and I have taken my family there before the bridge was built so they could know what the Lord created before man messed it up."[283]

Half a century later, Hopkins summed up what he was trying to accomplish: "The idea was, you don't develop the whole East Coast."[284]

Udall, Tydings, Morton, Tawes, Goldstein, Baltimore Mayor Theodore R. McKeldin, and other Maryland, Virginia, and federal dignitaries, environmentalists, park organizations, and garden club officers paraded to the witness table one by one to express their support. But opponents, led principally by lot owners, also made a strong and determined showing, disputing the notion that Assateague was unbuildable when just a mile or so to the north, the resort of Ocean City was booming with motels, restaurants, stores, and major highways.

"I was born in Virginia. I live in Virginia. But I hope to die on Assateague Island," said Fred C. Lewis of Fairfax, Virginia, a lot owner on Assateague for fifteen years.[285] He said lot owners had paid for their land, paid property taxes, paid for maintenance, and were willing to assure that the island's protective dunes would be safeguarded, especially now that the bridge that property owners have long dreamed about was now a reality.

Another six-year owner of a half-acre lot, a US Civil Service employee named William R. Perl, PhD., of College Park, Maryland, protested that his land was now about to be "nationalize[d] in the Communist fashion."[286]

Wallace M. Smith, a lawyer representing Ocean Beach, read into the record old letters from Brewster and Morton that predated their support for the Udall plan in which both lawmakers expressed explicit support for the private landowners on Assateague. The Brewster letter, written on October 12, 1962, when he was in his final month of candidacy for the Senate and about two years before the bridge to the island was opened, stated his belief that the private Ocean Beach development would be economically beneficial to Worcester County and could function side by side with the proposed state park. The Morton letter stated that the Congressman "would not in any way support a 'Federal Government takeover.'"[287] By 1965, however, both men had bought into the idea of turning Assateague Island into a federally controlled National Seashore and nothing more was said about their change of position.

As the long hearing drew to a close, Senator Bible remarked that he owned a "little home" on Lake Tahoe back in Nevada and would be "mighty unhappy and upset" if the government took it "for some higher use." But he said Congress had both the Constitutional authority and the responsibility to decide if and when property should be taken for such a purpose. It seemed clear by then which way the chairman was leaning.[288] Presidential aide Bill Moyers then added the final touch, placing a call to Bible to say the President urged him to back Brewster's bill. The combination of pressure and stroking worked, and by September, with Bible's support, President Johnson signed into law Danny Brewster's legislation creating the Assateague Island National Seashore.

Some of the Assateague photos that had been on display in the Old Senate Office Building were set up on easels at the bill signing. One in particular, taken by an art student named Santo Mirabile, was an elevated photo looking down on waves lapping the ocean front shoreline with the two large words—"Save Assateague"—dug into the sand. At least eighty-five of the bill's supporters signed the mat surrounding the photo, starting at the top center with the signature of Lyndon B. Johnson. Signers included Governor Tawes; Secretary Udall; Senators Bible, Tydings, Henry M. "Scoop" Jackson of Washington, and Ralph

Rivers of Alaska; Baltimore Mayor McKeldin; Comptroller Goldstein; Chincoteague Mayor Elwood Turlington; Representative Morton and the other seven members of Maryland's congressional delegation; future Baltimore County executive Ted Venetoulis; Porter Hopkins from the Citizens Committee for the Preservation of Assateague, plus representatives of the Izaak Walton League, Federated Garden Club, National Wildlife Federation, and other environmental groups; and several news people who had covered the long-running issue, including well-known Maryland outdoor writer Bill Burton. Once signed and framed, the photograph was presented to Senator Brewster, who proudly displayed it in his office for years.

"His crowning achievement was Assateague," Brewster's special assistant, Bill Miller, said years later.[289]

The following year, the Interior Department dispatched an employee named Joseph W. Fehrer Sr. to begin buying up the eight thousand or so privately owned pieces of property on Assateague Island—a process that "remains to this day the largest acquisition ever done by the National Park Service per parcel," according to his son, Joseph W. Fehrer Jr.[290]

Opponents of the federal government's plan to acquire Assateague had criticized Secretary Udall's prediction of a million visitors a year and of that number rising to as many as three million by 1975, saying such numbers would never be realized. Liz Davis, a National Park Service ranger at Assateague in 2019, said the number of yearly visitors appears to have leveled off at about 2.3 million, but she said that number is intentionally constrained by the decision to limit parking on the Maryland portion of the island to a maximum of about five hundred vehicles. The island in general and the Chincoteague Wildlife Refuge on the island's southern end in particular have become world-class destinations for visitors interested in watching waterfowl and other birds. The primary use of the Maryland portion of the island is for beach-goers, campers, and surf fishermen. In late July each year, thousands of people crowd into Chincoteague for the annual wild pony swim and pony auction that benefits the Chincoteague Volunteer Fire Company.[291]

A four-mile section of the Maryland part of the island that includes the state park is now developed for campers, beach users, and other visitors and their vehicles. Bill Huslander, another National Park Service Ranger, said, "I would say all the rest is undeveloped and is still in its natural state and we have been trying to manage more for those natural processes more than ever—let natural processes dominate."[292] Some driving on the beach is permitted, but it is limited and closely regulated.

Just as Brewster had hoped, there are no motels on the island, and the controversial road from the Maryland bridge to Chincoteague was never built and likely never will be. When Hurricane Sandy swept over the island in 2012, that storm uncovered chunks of old asphalt left from the original island road destroyed by the Ash Wednesday storm of 1962. That debris is now being removed.

Storms created the opportunity at Assateague Island and storms continue to define what happens there. The National Park Service, which works with the US Fish and Wildlife Service to administer the National Seashore and the Chincoteague Wildlife Refuge, is gradually converting many of the island's fixed structures – such as campground showers or bathrooms -- to mobile structures rather than see them destroyed by storms and then have to be rebuilt at taxpayer expense. That way, said Huslander, "we can get them out of the way, if necessary."[293]

Brewster, Udall, and their allies had the vision to prevent development on one of the last remaining, largely unspoiled pieces of oceanfront property on the Eastern Seaboard. Brewster had the support of President Johnson, who was indebted to him for waging the campaign against Wallace the year before, and the President's support undoubtedly helped push the bill to passage.

When Stewart Udall signed his name to the edge of the "Save Assateague" photo, the forward-thinking Interior Secretary left a simple message for the bill's sponsor: "Great Work Dan."

Chapter 11

THE BIGGEST MISTAKE

Throughout his long life, even in later years when he was threatened and harassed by the government he had served so loyally, Danny Brewster tried to embody the US Marine Corps motto *Semper fidelis*, "Always Faithful," both to the Marines and to his country.

Another Marine Corps slogan that surely carried Brewster and his fellow Marines through the horrors of Okinawa—as it must have done for Marines elsewhere in the war—was "Over fear and doubt, through fatigue and scrutiny—Marines win."[294] It was a simple, declarative statement of attitude and intention. "Marines win." They did what needed to be done to win. That was clearly the attitude that shaped US Senator Daniel Brewster's view of the war in Vietnam: that America must do whatever it takes to win.

That hardened view, he painfully admitted decades later, constituted the biggest policy mistake of his life.

There is little question that Brewster's relentless support for the war in Vietnam was driven by his military background and personal experiences in war. He had been in the thick of it and in the worst of it, and he knew what it took to prevail when you were on the ground, what kind of support troops required.

But Brewster also was a product of the post-World War II era's almost irrational fear of communism, and he embraced the argument that Vietnam was a place where the United States must draw the line to block communism's spread. Brewster's entry into public life in 1950 coincided with the rise of another Marine with World War II experience,

US Senator Joseph McCarthy of Wisconsin. McCarthy, as is now well known, exploited the post-war fear of communism with a series of unsubstantiated claims about communists in the US State Department, in the US Army, and elsewhere in the American government. Even though McCarthy's damaging demagoguery eventually resulted in his formal censure by the US Senate, the fear he fostered of communism seeping into American institutions and into governments around the globe became a ghostly presence in the political affairs of the United States for the next generation and beyond.

Like others of his era, Brewster believed in the so-called "domino theory," which held that once communists toppled a government in one nation, neighboring countries would be next to fall until, step by step, communists dominated the world. In the Cold War era of the 1950s and 1960s, the "Red Scare" was considered a serious threat to the future of Western democracies. America's principal adversaries were the Soviet Union and China. Behind what was known as the Iron Curtain, the Soviet communists controlled virtually all of Eastern Europe. As for "Red China," American military leaders remembered all too well how that nation poured nearly three million of its own troops into North Korea against the United States and its allies during the Korean War of the early 1950s. China now was seen as the invisible hand behind North Vietnam's communist incursion into the Republic of South Vietnam, which was nominally a democracy and, by treaty, an ally of the United States.

"The Communists will continue to probe here and there in search of a soft spot in free-world defenses. The present situation in South Vietnam is an example of this continued pressure," Brewster said in 1962.[295] By then a member of the House Armed Services Committee, he had been briefed on the initial military foray into Vietnam begun by Presidents Eisenhower and Kennedy. At that early stage, however, the number of troops was low, casualties were limited, and later expansion could not be foreseen.

"This was a different time and people felt a different obligation to the country, to get out there and do what had to be done for the country, that was the sense of it," recalled Tom Kelleher, who in 1964 was a seventeen-year-old office boy in what was by then Senator Brewster's Towson office. "Let's face it, we didn't understand anything about being able to say no—it was, 'What do we have to do?' That was [the message] we were getting from our families."[296]

There are those who believe that had Kennedy not been assassinated in late 1963 and, instead, lived to be re-elected in November 1964, he would have withdrawn American troops from Vietnam. What did happen, however, was that Lyndon Johnson replaced Kennedy and as the election of 1964 approached, he and the Democrats who controlled Congress wanted to project for the new American President an image of military strength and the resolve to staunch the spread of communism. Conservative Arizona Senator Barry Goldwater, nominated in July to be Johnson's Republican opponent, was already criticizing the President as being "soft on communism."

The Democrats' opportunity came on August 2, 1964, when the *USS Maddox*, an American destroyer, reported being attacked by three North Vietnamese Navy torpedo boats in the Gulf of Tonkin. It took Congress only five days to enact what became known as the Gulf of Tonkin Resolution, which said in effect that President Johnson could do whatever was necessary to support a member of the Southeast Asia Collective Defense Treaty, the treaty the US had with South Vietnam.

When the resolution first came up for debate on the Senate floor on August 6, Brewster was among the first of several Senators who expressed reservations to Foreign Relations Committee Chairman J. William Fulbright of Arkansas.

"I had the opportunity to see warfare not so very far from this area, and it was very mean," Brewster said. "I would look with great dismay on a situation involving the landing of large armies on the continent of Asia. So, my question is whether there is anything in the resolution which would authorize or recommend or approve the landing of large American armies in Vietnam or China?"[297]

The long-serving and widely respected Fulbright replied as candidly as could be expected. "There is nothing in the resolution, as I read it, that contemplates it. I agree with the Senator [Brewster] that that is the last thing we would want to do," he said, but added, "However, the language of the resolution would not prevent it. It would authorize whatever the Commander in Chief feels is necessary. It does not restrain the Executive from doing it."[298]

Fulbright said the question might be better posed to Senate Armed Services Committee Chairman Richard Russell of Georgia, but said, "Everyone I have heard has said that the last thing we want to do is to become involved in a land war in Asia; that our power is sea and air, and that this is what we hope will deter the Chinese Communists and the North Vietnamese from spreading the war. That is what is contemplated. The resolution does not prohibit that, or any other kind of activity."[299]

In answer to another Senator's question, Fulbright stated, "This action is limited, but very sharp. It is the best action that I can think of to deter an escalation or enlargement of the war. If we did not take such action, it might spread further. If we went further and ruthlessly bombed Hanoi and other places, we would be guilty of bad judgment, both on humanitarian grounds and on policy grounds, because then we would certainly inspire further retaliation."[300]

The debate stretched over two days and lasted for hours. Among the others expressing deep concern were two Democrats, Wayne Morse of Oregon and Ernest Gruening of Alaska, and Republican Thurston Morton of Kentucky. Nevertheless, on August 7, the Gulf of Tonkin Resolution passed the Senate 88-2, with only Morse and Gruening voting no. Brewster, as fate would have it, was temporarily serving as the Senate's presiding officer the day the resolution passed. The House of Representatives had already approved an identical resolution, 414-0.

Despite his concerns, Brewster joined the majority that gave Johnson carte blanche authority "to take all necessary measure to repel any armed attack against the forces of the United States to prevent further aggression."[301] As a Marine, Brewster believed that the military should always be supported in any way that would make winning not just possible but all but inevitable. This Senate vote was the action that opened the door to the huge commitment of troops and resources and the wide escalation of the Vietnam War that was to follow.

Presciently, Morse warned, "I believe this resolution to be a historic mistake."[302] Years later, with the benefit of hindsight, Brewster agreed. "I really regret I did not pursue the line I initiated. I was right. But I was too committed to the Johnson Administration to openly buck them."[303]

The lopsided approval of the Tonkin Resolution was not all that surprising. On foreign military matters, Congress had historically manifested a level of trust in the President and the generals who advised him, a faith that today seems almost quaint and naïve. "Well, yeah, [Brewster] trusted," explained House Speaker Nancy Pelosi. "What can you do? He trusted them."[304]

This, of course, was years before publication of *The Pentagon Papers*, the secret, government-commissioned history of the Vietnam War that exposed the lies told to the American people by the President, the generals, and other administration officials about their claims of success in the conduct of the war. In the early days of fighting in 1964, however, neither Brewster nor most others in Congress seriously questioned what Johnson or others in the administration were telling them about Vietnam, although members of the general public were beginning to do so.

Fully eight months before the Tonkin Resolution was enacted, when the struggle in far-off Vietnam was still relatively new, a concerned constituent from Greenbelt wrote Senator Brewster: "I fervently hope that you and the new Senate will be able to do something to help stop the stupid war in South Viet Nam. It is extremely costly in men and money and is doing nobody any good. The money would be much better spent on [President Johnson's] War on Poverty."[305]

By year's end, the pace of letters against the Vietnam War began to pick up and really accelerated in 1965. Just before Christmas 1964, a Silver Spring doctor named George J. Cohen urged Brewster to get the United Nations involved in negotiating a peace agreement in Vietnam. If not, he predicted, the US "will continue to spend many American lives and dollars in what has so far been a totally fruitless endeavor. If we try to 'finish it off in a hurry,' we will be taking over a war in which we have no direct interest, which will cost ever more dearly in both life and money, and which could easily be escalated to a prolonged major conflict with Communist China."[306]

A Quaker group also urged a United Nations intervention, writing, "Now innocent civilians [are] bombed, precious crops destroyed, hated dictatorships subsidized and a steady growth of support for rebel Vietcong. Allegiance of the emerging populations to the United States can hardly be won by this kind of activity."[307] Writers frequently lamented the "immorality" of the war.

Brewster was largely unmoved, remaining instead in lockstep with President Johnson. After Johnson addressed the nation about the Vietnam War in April 1965, Brewster wrote a personal note to the President praising his remarks, which prompted a reply from Larry O'Brien, the President's congressional adviser. "The President has asked me to acknowledge and thank you for your letter.... He is grateful for the warmth of your comments on his address to the nation on Vietnam and wants you to know that he is greatly encouraged by your reactions to his proposals."[308]

A month later, Brewster issued a strong statement in support of Johnson's Vietnam policies to which Jack Valenti, a special assistant to the President, wrote, "It's mighty comforting to have you in our corner."[309]

"He was a down-the-line Johnson loyalist [starting] from the Bay of Tonkin, as long as I was with him," said W. Shepherdson Abell, an intern and part-time legislative assistant in Brewster's office from 1965 until 1967. "If the issue came up [with staff], he wouldn't take any direction—he'd just go and vote for it."[310]

Brewster gradually became President Johnson's go-to man on Vietnam in the Senate. If Brewster had second thoughts, it was not that the US was doing too much in Vietnam, but rather not enough to assure victory. When members of the Joint Chiefs of Staff asked for something,

Brewster remembered years later, "As an old military man, I took them at their word. When a general or an admiral told me that was the way it was, I believed them. I should've questioned it further, but we were in a fight. My point of view as an old Marine was that there was no backing down—when you're in a fight, you win it."[311]

"He had a sense of loyalty toward the troops. If you were going to have troops there, you've got to give them support. That was his framework," recalled Bill Miller, who was on Brewster's staff his entire time in the Senate.[312]

Beginning in 1965 and continuing well into the 1970s, the anti-war protest movement grew larger and more vocal. Miller said the Senator knew that he personally opposed the war so he was intentionally sent out to talk to the "peaceniks" when they showed up at the office or events. To Brewster and to his top staff aide, Jack Sullivan, another former Marine, these protests were un-American and gave succor to the enemy. American troops in the field in Vietnam said they couldn't understand what was going on back home while they were fighting for their lives in the jungles of southeast Asia.

That October, John Bambacus, a young Marine private first class from Western Maryland stationed as a courier in the port city of Da Nang, sent Brewster a three-page handwritten letter asking, "What do these protesters back home plan to achieve from these attacks against US policy? If some of these protesters could only see how much these people hunger for a free society then maybe a different attitude would prevail. I respect these opinions because we live in a democracy where everyone can speak as he wishes, but sir, it makes me mad when myself and others over here have to read this in the newspaper."[313] Brewster replied that he had spoken to other soldiers in Vietnam who felt the same way. "I can tell you, however, that the vast majority of Americans support our foreign policy in the Far East. The vocal protest we now hear comes from a small minority in our nation."[314]

Neither Brewster nor Bambacus could have known that after spending three years in Vietnam, Bambacus would return home, earn his degree, become a college professor, later become an assistant to Brewster's friend and 1968 political opponent, US Senator Charles McC. Mathias Jr., and then later go on to represent Western Maryland in the Maryland Senate.

By his third year in the Senate, Brewster finally secured the committee assignment he wanted most, a coveted seat on the Senate Armed Services Committee. His path to the assignment was cleared when J. Glenn Beall Sr., the Maryland Republican who had served on Armed Services, was defeated for re-election by Tydings in 1964. But even then, Brewster's appointment was delayed several months by the committee's powerful chairman, Richard Russell of Georgia, who wanted to impress on the young Senator from Maryland that the chairman was none too happy about Brewster's vote to end the Southern filibuster during the civil rights debate in 1964.

The worried letters about Vietnam poured in regardless of Brewster's committee assignment. He began hearing from constituents who accused protesters of committing treason, charging the protesters were probably communist-inspired and saying that those who publicly burned their draft cards (then a highly visible form of dissent) should be arrested and prosecuted. One writer said colleges where anti-war protests are held should be denied federal aid. Another suggested a big military parade might stir up support for the war.

"It is men like you that will make this country better...," one Baltimore man wrote Brewster. "You know... I am a veteran of World War II and when I read about all this clap trap like burning of draft cards, pickets and the like carrying placards urging this great country to get out of Vietnam, it... is terrible."[315]

Brewster also received his share of emotionally painful letters. One woman who described herself as a war widow wrote plaintively that she hoped Brewster could help her to continue to receive her late husband's government benefits. Another wrote that her nineteen-year-old nephew had been killed in Vietnam just twenty-seven days after arriving, saying she and her family were waiting for his body to be returned home. "Our country failed him," the woman wrote. "My God, help us! I certainly don't say withdraw. Never. But fight to win it completely, not another Korea, and let the remainder of our boys live."[316]

Some letter writers began to voice Brewster's privately held doubts about the exit strategy for the ever-expanding war. In one five-page, handwritten letter, a Greenbelt man, Milton Hoffman, asked Brewster the question no one so far had been able to answer: What does it mean to "win" in Vietnam? Hoffman said he understood winning in poker or craps but said the American tactic of burning Vietnamese villages was "like burning down the house to get rid of roaches. What kind of winning is that?" He predicted that the President would need to commit a million troops to Vietnam if he cannot come up with a political solution.[317]

"The many questions which you raise deserve to be raised," Brewster replied but added, "Many of them cannot be positively answered today or tomorrow." He then tried to put the best light on the situation, saying he was convinced the Vietnam War would lead to "a safer world."[318]

The war was fast generating strong political divisions in the country. One man reported that for years he would go door to door collecting Dollars for Democrats, but suddenly many households refused to give because of Vietnam. Another sign came when Mathias, Brewster's former law school roommate who was then serving in the House of Representatives, called on the Johnson administration to begin de-escalating the war. That position, the Republican from Western Maryland said he later realized, was what provided "a point of entree for me with Democratic voters."[319]

Probably the most stubborn opponent was Oregon Senator Wayne Morse, who frequently gave long, late afternoon floor speeches against the war—so frequent, in fact, that he was known to other Senators as "the five o'clock shadow." Morse was at it again on the evening of July 15, 1965. The presiding officer—a ceremonial post that often rotated among junior members of the Senate—that night was Daniel Brewster of Maryland, dressed handsomely in a black tuxedo. He had warned Senate aides that he had to depart at seven p.m. sharp to make an important dinner engagement. As Morse droned on, the hour arrived with no relief in sight. So, against Senate rules and protocol, Brewster simply gaveled the Senate into adjournment and left.

The reaction in the staid Senate chamber became the stuff of history. Morse, incensed, never finished his speech but instead entered remarks into the *Congressional Record* condemning Brewster. While some Senators privately snickered at the snub, both Majority Leader Mike Mansfield and Minority Leader Everett Dirksen "came around with properly long faces and agreed how terrible it was."[320] Mansfield pushed Brewster to publicly apologize the next day and afterward praised both Morse and Brewster as "big men with a capital B" for their amity.[321]

Decades later, Senator William Proxmire, who had been a friend of Brewster's, was introduced to Brewster's son Gerry during a speaking engagement at Maryland's Goucher College. "Gerry," the Wisconsin Senator intoned, "in the history of the United States Senate, the only two people who could stop a Senator from speaking on the floor of the Senate were God and Danny Brewster."[322]

But the war was no laughing matter. In a speech to disabled veterans in New Orleans that August, Brewster said, "The United States is stuck with a dirty, ugly situation there. The alternative is clear to press for a settlement which would leave South Vietnam independent, or to abandon a free people to the communists. Such an abandonment would ratify the action of the aggressors. It would strengthen the militant position of the Chinese Communists, and perhaps encourage similar communist-dominated insurrections around the world."[323]

By then, however, Brewster was already wondering aloud how to extricate the US from such a stalemate without further escalation. "We cannot withdraw, we must not lose, and we should not broaden the conflict," he said.[324]

For Brewster, the late 1960s were a baffling time, made more confusing by his steady increase in drinking. As a believer in each person's obligation to do one's duty, he could not understand anti-war protests. As a Marine, he could not comprehend how his fellow politicians balked at giving the military in Vietnam anything it requested. As a proper and well-groomed member of the upper echelons of polite society, he could not fathom what was driving the emerging long-haired, Hippie culture and its embrace of drugs and psychedelic music and its disdain for authority. As a believer in the rule of law, he bridled at the riots and other acts of lawlessness in American cities perpetrated by "black power" leaders in the name of civil rights. He desperately wanted to support Johnson but watched helplessly as the President's grand social programs, such as his War on Poverty, were steadily subsumed by the conflagration in Vietnam.

"Johnson was thought of as being a big Texas blow-hard, but he wasn't anything vaguely close to that," said Tyler Abell, a former Assistant Postmaster General and family friend of both Johnson's and Brewster's. "[Johnson] was absolutely one of the most brilliant people I've ever been associated with, and I've been with some good ones.... One of his best friends in the Senate, [Georgia Senator] Dick Russell, told him there is no way we can win this war, but they both agreed with each other that there is no way we can get out. This was back at the beginning."[325]

"Johnson somehow or other got himself talked into the idea that more Marines were going to win it. I still don't see how he could have looked at it himself and not say, 'You can't win, so let's get out!'" said Abell, whose wife, Bess, served as Social Secretary in the Johnson White House. "But when you're the most powerful country in the world, to let this little snippet of a place defeat you, and five hundred thousand Marines?"[326]

In October 1965, Brewster decided to see the war for himself. He embarked on a three-week tour of Asia that took him to South Korea, Japan, back for the first time in twenty years to the island of Okinawa, to Taipei and Hong Kong, and finally to Saigon and a full week traveling from south to north and back in Vietnam. As a colonel in the Marine Corps Reserves, he donned green fatigues and jungle boots, toured US camps, boarded an armed river patrol craft, fired a howitzer, rode in tanks, and visited local hamlets and markets. His tour took him from the swampy delta in the south to within a few miles of the North Vietnam border. He even hooked up with his old World War II unit, L Company, Third Battalion, Fourth Marines. He was drenched by rain and splattered by mud and ate both in the enlisted men's mess and with generals in the field. When he could, he sought out Marines or other soldiers from Maryland.

"The people back home know about the good job you are doing," Brewster told the troops, minimizing the growing anti-war chorus he was hearing at home. "The overwhelming majority of Americans support you. They're mighty proud of you."[327]

Of his side trip to revisit Okinawa, he said that he found Sugar Loaf Hill after some difficulty, "and it was a bloody housing development with a water tank on it. No more sign of war than downtown Baltimore."[328]

He returned from Vietnam more of a hawk than when he had left, declaring, "There's no danger we will pull out," and calling for the immediate mining of Haiphong Harbor to stop the flow of petroleum and missiles into North Vietnam.[329] "I was very gung-ho and very much wanted to bring back an authentic report on Vietnam," he later recalled.[330]

Johnson summoned him to the White House for a report and his advice to the President was to continue to send in more troops and bombs. Publicly he said, "I have just returned from Vietnam and it was clear there to me that we stepped in just in the nick of time with real military force. In a military sense we have stabilized the situation. There is no chance in the world that we will be pushed into the sea."

He even talked openly and aggressively about the prospect of an expanded war with China. "If Red China enters the situation openly in South Vietnam with land armies, there will be no safe haven for them or for any of their forces anywhere on the Asian mainland," he said, adding that the US cannot compete with the Chinese army man to man but that the US can "shatter them with our air and sea power." He said America would have to hold its place in Vietnam while "we took a terrible toll on every industrial complex in every major city in Red China."[331]

Then, as if to moderate such bellicose language, Brewster said the

US should not go after women and children. "You must remember, our purpose is not to destroy here, our purpose is to maintain peace."[332]

As both the war and the politicians waging it grew ever more desperate, Brewster began calling for ever heavier bombing raids on military targets in North Vietnam, although he was careful to say, "The unrestricted destruction of residential areas would be both inhuman and unwise, and the use of nuclear weapons unthinkable."[333]

"If we are going to send men overseas and into battle, and accept the casualties that they are now sustaining, then we must be prepared to back them up," he said during a half-hour Senate floor speech in early 1966. "In light of espoused objectives of both sides in this struggle, I see no reasonable ground on which to question the validity or, indeed, the essentiality of the American commitment."[334]

Then, starting in 1967, a cascade of events—most beyond his control but some self-inflicted—began to alter Danny Brewster's life and his future in politics. Most disturbing, those around him could see that his alcoholism was worsening and, with that, his judgment. Suddenly, he became undependable and staff were never certain if he would show up. The one-time Golden Boy of Maryland Politics was also in trouble politically even though he was the incumbent senior Senator, part of an overwhelming Democratic majority in Congress, and had close ties to the White House. But he had backed the wrong candidate in the 1966 Maryland Democratic gubernatorial primary and then angered many in his party by refusing to support the victorious Democratic nominee, a decision that helped a Republican be elected as Maryland's Governor. Sensing Brewster's vulnerability, opponents to his re-election in 1968 began popping up in both political parties. The Democratic field was led by George P. Mahoney, followed by Congressman Clarence Long of Baltimore County. Two strong candidates surfaced on the Republican side, Congressmen Rogers Morton of the Eastern Shore, who had helped Brewster turn Assateague Island into a National Seashore, and Brewster's old friend, Charles McC. Mathias Jr. of Western Maryland.

Letters both for and against the war poured into his office at such a high rate that staff divided them into monthly files titled "Vietnam Hawks" and "Vietnam Doves." There are so many letters from the Vietnam period that they are difficult to count, but by 1967 the letters from Doves seemed to greatly outnumber those from Hawks. Americans were tiring of Vietnam.

Brewster realized he was beginning to lose young people and some of the liberals in his political base who opposed the war. More than ever, he hitched his star to Johnson's, hoping the President's coattails would help pull him through. He became an Assistant Majority Whip in the Senate, a leadership post that helped round up votes for the Democratic caucus and the administration's priorities. But in 1968, even Johnson would let him down by not seeking re-election.

Against this backdrop, and seemingly against all odds, while attending a conference in Europe in January 1967, Brewster reunited with Anne Bullitt, the woman who had jilted him in 1943. Smitten anew, he came home and almost immediately divorced his wife, Carol, so he could marry Anne. Brewster's split with Carol was so unexpected it became front page news in both Washington and Baltimore, and his courtship of the exotic and wealthy Anne Bullitt, who then ran a horse farm in Ireland, made news overseas. The sudden marital switch sent political reverberations throughout heavily Catholic Maryland. It became hard for the Senator to focus on the war, on his job in general, or on his re-election campaign. Huge anti-war protests were held in Central Park in New York in the spring and on the National Mall in Washington, DC, that fall. Bobby Kennedy broke with the President over the war and then so did Joe Tydings, Brewster's fellow Senator from Maryland. Other Senators from both parties soon followed.

By early October 1967, Brewster, under pressure, also appeared to be getting cold feet about the war, announcing that he was "re-evaluating" his Vietnam stand by noting that Marylanders appeared to favor de-escalation. "There is little or no support in Maryland for the present course," he said. "The war is becoming more and more unpopular among the citizens of Maryland."[335]

But just two weeks later, he flopped back to full-throated support of the Johnson administration policy as "the best course among the choices available to us." Whether Johnson leaned on him or Brewster simply reverted back to his hawkish views, he once again said withdrawing US troops would be "unthinkable and impossible" and that a pause in the bombing of North Vietnam would be "inconsistent with our goals."[336] He called for the bombing to be intensified and repeated the administration mantra that "the freedom and security of South Vietnam are vital to the interests of the United States."[337]

In response to this, one constituent wrote, "The new image you are presenting of yourself—bigger war, more bombs, more American boys killed—places you right with the so-called 'hawks.' I must say, I liked you better the other way. A disappointed voter."[338]

Then, in January 1968, Brewster and the country were shaken by the news of the massive Tet offensive launched by North Vietnam and the Viet Cong throughout South Vietnam. The size and breadth of the attack caught the American and South Vietnamese forces by surprise and stood as a sobering rebuke to Johnson administration claims that the US was winning the war. Brewster first heard of the Tet offensive in a telephone call from his new wife, Anne, who happened to be in Paris where the attack was featured on the front pages of French newspapers. When the Senator, a member of the Armed Services Committee, called the Pentagon for confirmation, he was told that whatever was happening in Vietnam was confidential information and not yet ready for public release.[339]

"That," said Bill Miller, who witnessed the exchange, "really pushed him to start shifting his own thinking.… It was the beginning of his feelings that we weren't being given the truth or factual information. He got to the 'misgivings stage.'"[340]

It was as if the war was both unstoppable and unwinnable. It dragged on until 1975, from Eisenhower to Kennedy to Johnson to Nixon to Ford. More than 58,000 Americans were killed, as were hundreds of thousands of North and South Vietnamese, Cambodian, and Laotian soldiers and civilians, not to mention the thousands upon thousands more who received life-altering wounds. Cities were bombed into rubble; hamlets, burned. More than twice as many bombs were dropped on Vietnam, Laos, and Cambodia than were dropped on Europe and Asia during World War II.[341] At home, the war destroyed the American economy, Lyndon Johnson's hopes for a "Great Society," and Johnson's personal political legacy.

"Now I consider it the worst mistake I ever made in my whole public career, supporting the war policy in Vietnam," Brewster admitted in an extraordinarily candid interview with Towson historian Blaine Taylor in 1999, three decades after leaving the Senate. "I pressed the Administration to win the war, but if I had done my job properly as a Senator, I would have asked the Administration: 'Is our presence in Vietnam vital to the security of the United States?' Of course, it was not."[342]

"You must remember that President Kennedy and President Johnson and, of course, myself, and the majority of the members of... Congress, for that matter, were all products of World War II. Most of us felt that had we stopped Hitler through international force at the time of Munich, or at the time of the invasion of Poland, we might've avoided the Holocaust and World War II in its enormity, but the United States and the Free World did nothing about the rise of Hitler, and oppression and tyranny, and we paid a bitter price.

"Afterward, we felt that the threat of international communism was similar to the threats that we had seen in the days of Hitler—that the stated intent of international communism of world domination was not very different than that of the Nazis."[343]

Mike Merson, a Baltimore hospital administrator who became close friends with Brewster and his family late in Brewster's life, said, "If I could find one thing that Dan had remorse about—and many, many times he revisited it with me—it was Vietnam. He said he's thought about it over and over and over, and just thought it was a mistake," both the war and his support for it. "He also talked about how easy it is to be brought in and—not duped, because he always felt like he was using his own judgment—but not to ask the right questions when you were deeply engaged in a big policy decision."[344]

Brewster said he belatedly came to realize, "Our supply line was 10,000 miles long. We were fighting a war on somebody else's terms in a jungle where we couldn't use our sophisticated military weapons."[345] He said he gradually "became disenchanted" and said others around him, such as Vice President Hubert H. Humphrey, felt the same way, but because they supported the Johnson administration, they could not publicly object.

Or, at least they *chose* not to publicly object. Marines win, and for Brewster, giving up was unthinkable.

As he looked back over his career in public office, Brewster said, "Of the thousands of votes I've cast in some 20 years in elective office—in the state and federal governments—I believe my proudest moments were the passage of the Civil Rights Act of '64 and the Voting Rights Act of '65.

"My dreariest performance was on the Gulf of Tonkin Resolution."[346]

Photographs

Brewster's father, Daniel Baugh Brewster, and his mother, Catherine Ottolie Young Hobart, going out for a ride at the Green Spring Valley Hounds in 1931. *Brewster Family Photo.*

Brewster and his siblings, from top-to-bottom: Danny, Andre, Catherine, Walter, and Betty Baugh. *Brewster Family Photo.*

Wickcliffe, the 65-room castle built between 1914 and 1916 by Brewster's grandparents, Dr. Walter Wickes and his wife, Catherine Osbourne Young, as their home in the Green Spring Valley of Baltimore County. *Brewster Family Photo.*

A 1940 photo of young Anne Bullitt, daughter of American journalist Louise Bryant and the first U.S. Ambassador to the Soviet Union, William C. Bullitt. She was Brewster's first love, but when she broke off their brief engagement he immediately volunteered for combat in the South Pacific. *Brewster Family Photo.*

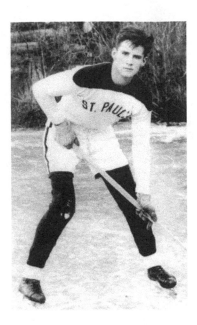

Danny Brewster on the outside hockey rink at the St. Paul's School in New Hampshire in 1940. Danny spent four years at the prestigious college preparatory school before attending Princeton University. *Brewster Family Photo.*

Lieutenant Brewster, who at age 20 may have been the youngest commissioned officer in the Marine Corps at the time, is pictured with an unidentified fellow Marine in the South Pacific in 1944. *Brewster Family Photo.*

This is the helmet Brewster was wearing when he was wounded as his platoon was ambushed on the second day of the US invasion of Okinawa in April 1945. Danny was wounded seven times during his time on Okinawa. *Brewster Family Photo.*

Carol Leiper de Havenon and Danny Brewster in 1949 during the early years of their courtship. *Brewster Family Photo.*

Danny jumps Clifton's Dan in 1950 while training for the Maryland Hunt Cup. *Photo by A. Aubrey Bodine – Copyright Jennifer B. Bodine – Courtesy of AAubreyBodine.com*

At their 1954 wedding, Carol and Danny Brewster (center) share a drink with close friends Charles McC. Mathias Jr. (left) and St. Paul's classmate Crocker Nevin (right). *Brewster Family Photo*

Danny at his wedding with his brothers, Walter (left) and Andre (right). *Brewster Family Photo*

Congressional campaign poster from Brewster's 1958 election to Congress. *Brewster Family Photo*

Presidential candidate John F. Kennedy boosts Brewster's re-election campaign during 1960 political rally hosted by Brewster in Towson, Md. *Brewster Family Photo*

Brewster, who was also president of the Maryland State Fair, hosts the Ghanaian Delegation on a tour of the Maryland State Fairgrounds in 1961, an era of segregation when people of different races rarely sat together. *Courtesy of the Maryland State Fair*

President Kennedy comes to Maryland to endorse Brewster for U.S. Senate, joined by Governor J. Millard Tawes. Barely a year later, President Kennedy will be assassinated in Texas while riding in this same limousine. *Photo by Thomas Scilipoti*

In a photo intended for political use, Danny and Carol walk across a field at Worthington Farms in 1962 with their two boys, Dan Jr. (left) and Gerry (right). *Brewster Family Photo*

Brewster joins President Kennedy behind the Resolute Desk in the Oval Office in 1962. *Courtesy of the White House*

President Kennedy stumps for Senatorial candidate Daniel Brewster at a rally held at the Fifth Regiment Armory in Baltimore on October 10, 1962, along with Maryland Governor J. Millard Tawes (left) and state Comptroller Louis L. Goldstein (right). *Photo by Thomas Scilipoti*

President Kennedy and Vice President Lyndon B. Johnson congratulate newly elected Senator Brewster in 1963. *Brewster Family Photo*

Among the young staffers in Brewster's Senate office was Steny Hoyer (standing, center), now the Majority Leader of the U.S. House of Representatives. *Brewster Family Photo*

Vice President Lyndon B. Johnson swears in Brewster to the United States Senate. *Brewster Family Photo*

Brewster, Maryland Governor Tawes and Delaware Governor Elbert N. Carvel join President Kennedy in the White House in 1963 to discuss I-95, a new federal highway linking the two states. *Courtesy of the White House*

The 1963 Valachi-McClellan Hearings exposed the country to the American Mafia for the first time. Senator Brewster questioned both lead-off witness Attorney General Robert F. Kennedy and mobster Joe Valachi – See one exchange below. *Courtesy of U.S. Senate Historical Office*

The Valachi-McClellan hearings of 1963 were historic for exposing the American Mafia to the American people. Attorney General Robert F. Kennedy was the leadoff witness, and mobster Joe Valachi's testimony riveted the nation. Senator Brewster was a member of this Committee that held these nationally televised hearings in the Senate Caucus Room, where the Watergate hearings and other infamous hearings have been held. Senator Brewster's exchanges with Attorney General Kennedy and with mobster Joe Valachi added some highlights to the hearings:

Senator Brewster: One last question. You mentioned oath. Do the members of the syndicate literally take an oath of allegiance to the syndicate?
Attorney General Kennedy: Yes, they do, Senator. They literally take an oath and they have the bloodletting … I might say in that connection that part of the requirement formerly was that you had to kill somebody in order to come into the organization. That seems to have been waived lately. But you could not go into the organization unless you had murdered somebody.
Senator Brewster: That is unbelievable.

Senator Brewster: Do you know if Vito tried to kill anybody, any other people in jail, by poison or by hanging? …
Mr. Valachi: There was a Peter Latempo poisoning.
Senator Brewster: What happened to him?
Mr. Valachi: They found him poisoned in Raymond Street jail while he was there waiting to testify against Vito. There was another one, Abe Reles. He was also supposed to testify. He fell out of the window.
Senator Brewster: How did he fall out of the window, do you know?
Mr. Valachi: They threw him out.
Senator Brewster: These men were waiting to testify?
Mr. Valachi: Against Vito and Albert Anastasia.
Senator Brewster: One was poisoned and one was thrown out of the window?
Mr. Valachi: Yes.

Brewster faces off against the segregationist Governor of Alabama, George C. Wallace (right), in a nationally televised 1964 presidential debate on ABC's Issues and Answers moderated by journalist Howard K. Smith (center). *Photographer/©ABC/Getty Images*

President Johnson boosts Brewster's campaign against Wallace in 1964 by flying with him aboard Marine One to an Appalachian Regional event in Western Maryland. The President's daughter, Linda, is on the steps in front of Brewster. *Brewster Family Photo*

Brewster's victory over Wallace depicted in 1964 *Baltimore Sun* cartoon by editorial cartoonist Richard Yardley. *Courtesy of the Baltimore Sun*

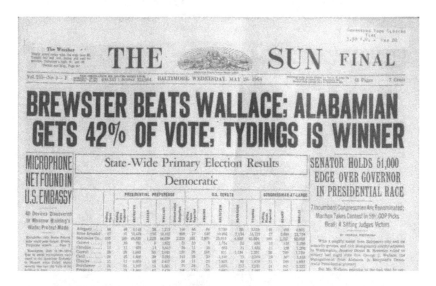

Baltimore Sun frontpage on May 20, 1964, announcing Brewster's victory over Wallace in the Democratic presidential primary and Joe Tydings's upset victory over Louis Goldstein in the Senatorial primary. *Courtesy of the Baltimore Sun*

In a 1964 Oval Office meeting, President Johnson thanks Brewster for standing in for him in the bitter Maryland presidential primary contest with Wallace. *Courtesy of the White House*

Brewster joined the vote for cloture, which stopped the Southern-led filibuster and cleared the way for passage of the Civil Rights Act of 1964. *Courtesy of the U.S. Senate Historical Office*

Interior Secretary Stewart Udall (center) joins Brewster (second from right) and other Maryland officials on a 1965 tour of Assateague Island, which under Brewster's legislation was later designated as a National Seashore. *Brewster Family Photo*

Brewster joins President Johnson at a 1965 bill signing on the White House grounds. Brewster was a strong Senate supporter of the Administration's legislation. *Courtesy of the White House*

Senator Brewster, a colonel in the Marine Corps Reserves and a member of the Senate Armed Services Committee, makes a fact-finding tour of the war in South Vietnam in 1965. *Courtesy of the United States Marine Corps*

Brewster on his tractor at Worthington Farms in Baltimore County, Md. *Brewster Family Photo*

Brewster with Sargent Shriver, founder of the Peace Corps, in 1965. *Brewster Family Photo*

Brewster (right) with his top aide, John F. "Jack" Sullivan (left), and Sullivan's Mount St. Mary's College basketball coach, James Phelan, in 1966. *Brewster Family Photo*

Danny and Carol Brewster (left and right), with Lady Bird and Lyndon Johnson at a White House event in 1966. *Courtesy of the White House*

Brewster (right), with fellow Maryland Senator Joseph D. Tydings and New York Senator Robert F. Kennedy, greet Roman Catholic Cardinal Lawrence Sheehan, Archbishop of Baltimore, during a tour of Maryland. *Brewster Family Photo*

Colonel Daniel B. Brewster, US Marine Corps Reserves, 1967. *Courtesy of the United States Marine Corps*

Senator Brewster sits next to Senator Robert F. Kennedy and in front of Senator Edward M. Kennedy for the President's 1967 State of the Union Address. *Courtesy of the Democratic National Committee*

Brewster (center) and his new wife, Anne Bullitt, greet Postmaster General Marvin Watson during 1967 campaign event. In the Senate, Brewster was a strong supporter of the Post Office. *Brewster Family Photo*

Hubert H. Humphrey with Dan Brewster and Anne Bullitt at an event in 1968, during which the Vice President endorsed Brewster's re-election to the Senate. *Brewster Family Photo*

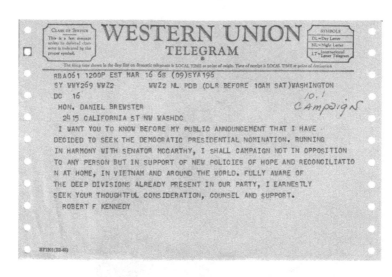

Telegram from Senator Robert F. Kennedy seeking Brewster's support for Kennedy's bid for the presidency. Sent on March 16, 1968, RFK was assassinated in Los Angeles less than three months later. *Brewster family photo*

Serving as a floor leader, Brewster addresses delegates to the infamous 1968 Democratic National Convention in Chicago. Among those in this picture are North Carolina Senator Sam Ervin (center, about three in from the right), Maryland Comptroller Louis L. Goldstein (center, far left), Congressman Carlton Sickles (immediately below Goldstein), Baltimore Mayor Tommy D'Alesandro III (to the right of Sickles) and Baltimore City Council President William Donald Schaefer (in front of D'Alesandro). *Uncredited/AP/Shutterstock*

Vice President Hubert H. Humphrey, the Democratic candidate for President in 1968, with Brewster. *Brewster family photo*

Palmerstown House, the historic Irish estate west of Dublin where Anne Bullitt ran a successful stud farm for race horses and became Ireland's first woman licensed horse trainer. *Photo by John W. Frece*

Brewster and his family in 1975. (front row, left to right) Catherine Jackson, Betty Baugh Towers, Walter Brewster, (back row, left to right) Frances Cochran Smith, Danny, mother Ottolie, and Andre Brewster. *Brewster Family Photo*

At the age of 54, Brewster still loved to ride and jump horses over tall timber fences, as he did aboard Jay's Trouble in the April 1978 running of My Lady's Manor steeplechase races. Look at the joy on his face! *Courtesy of Mid-Atlantic Thoroughbred Magazine*

Brewster with his family at Windy Meadows Farm in 1980. Pictured (left to right) are Kurt Aarsand, Jennilie Brewster, Judy Brewster, Gerry Brewster, Dana Brewster, Danny Brewster, Danielle Brewster, and Krista Aarsand. *Courtesy of the Baltimore Sun*

Brewster, former Senator Joe Tydings, Brewster's son, Gerry, former Governor Harry Hughes, and former Baltimore Mayor Tommy D'Alesandro III join in support of Gerry's 1994 run for Congress at a Harford County rally. *Brewster Family Photo*

The Brewster family at Windy Meadow Farm in 2005. (back row, left to right) Gerry Brewster, Laurence Oster, Kurt Aarsand, Jeanne Aarsand, Jeff Bedford, (middle, left to right) Judy Brewster, Danny Brewster, Danielle Brewster Oster, Kasey Bedford, (front, left to right) Dana Brewster, Jennilie Brewster, Hailey Bedford, Krista Bedford. *Brewster Family Photo*

Part II

The Fall:
Booze, Bullitt, Betrayal, and Bribery

Chapter 12

A DESTRUCTIVE FAMILY TRAIT

Danny Brewster was just ten years old when his father died of acute alcoholism. His widowed mother, Ottolie, hoping to protect her eldest son from a similar fate, offered him $5,000 if he would refrain from drinking until he was at least eighteen.

Even though it could be against his own self-interest, Danny Brewster – even as a teenager – was dependably honest. At the age of sixteen, while still a student at St. Paul's in New Hampshire, Danny confessed to his mother that her deal with him was off. "I have to tell you that I did drink," he confessed.[347]

Brewster developed a taste for drink early. Chris Kahl managed the exclusive Green Spring Valley Hunt Club, located a few miles from the Brewster home and where the Brewster family were longtime members. Kahl recalled how young Danny and other local teenagers would try to sneak into the club and get others to buy them drinks. "I'd be constantly chasing them out," he remembered.[348]

Thus began an embrace of drinking that at first punctuated, later dominated, and ultimately destroyed Danny Brewster's life. Like his father, and like more than a half dozen others within his immediate family, Danny Brewster became addicted to alcohol. It was a destructive family trait that transcended generations, affected members of both sexes, young and old, and was oblivious to rank, fortune, or public stature. Because of Danny Brewster's prominent, highly visible place in public life, what alcoholism did to him may have made him the most tragic victim of them all.

While he was growing up, his drinking was normalized within the posh hunt club society in which he was raised. It was enabled by the social drinking among those in public office, both in Annapolis and Washington. Even his grandparents, who lived next door in the Tudor-style castle, Wickcliffe, were said to have had an alcohol still on the premises during Prohibition and hid their illicit spirits behind secret panels in the walls and ceiling.

John Howard, as a young lawyer in Brewster's law firm, was in their Towson office working one Saturday morning when Brewster showed up. "We had this cute little blonde who was a receptionist and she had come in to help on that Saturday. And I'm up on the second floor, and I hear this [noise] on the stairs, and he chases this little girl right up the stairs like a bull—he was like a bull. A couple of us got a hold of Danny and had him settle down, but he was in a rage. That is the only time I remember seeing him [drinking] and that was a Saturday morning! He was drunk as hell."[349]

"We saw Danny drinking all the time," said his lifelong friend and neighbor C. A. Porter Hopkins. "But you would start hearing rumors that maybe Danny had too much to drink here, or maybe the girls thought that the wife [Carol] was unhappy. I can remember him coming down [to the Eastern Shore] to go gunning on Wroten Island, and Danny had stopped to get a bottle of sherry on Kent Island because he wanted the sherry to drink before he got to the boat to go over to the island, where he knew he could get some more to drink. That's the sign of somebody who was thinking, 'I've got to have a drink right now.'"[350]

By the late 1960s, drinking had begun to overwhelm Brewster's life, perhaps as he tried to forget the hostility and personal indignities he experienced during the awful Wallace campaign of 1964. Perhaps he used alcohol to smooth the rough edges of his political ambition. As the years slipped by, perhaps he turned to heavy drinking to help him bury once and for all his memories of the bloody horror he had witnessed and been part of in the war. Or, maybe it was to hide from the pain he surely realized he was inflicting on his wife and two young sons through his drinking, carousing, and chronic absenteeism.

Brewster claimed to be devoting up to six nights a week to politics, but some portion of that time away from home was surely spent with a drink in hand. "He was never there," Gerry Brewster, the younger of his two sons, painfully remembered.[351]

Dan and Carol Brewster were financial partners in Worthington Farms, and Dan treated his wife as an equal, which men rarely did with their wives in those days. She ran the farm while he was in Washington and made political speeches on his behalf when he was unavailable or incapacitated. Neither spent much time with their boys, who were raised primarily by nannies, often brought from Europe.

"Some kids are brought up by nannies but have parents who are quite engaged," observed Michael de Havenon, Carol's son from her first marriage. "Here, neither Dan nor my mother were engaged with the kids, really, so it went a little beyond just having nannies take care of them. Dan was so passionately involved in politics it left little room for other things in his life…. No, he didn't have much interest in his kids. And their mother was not a particularly good mother, or a good parent, at least by our standards today."[352]

Whatever the root causes, drink eventually ruined Danny Brewster's health, two of his three marriages, and his political and personal reputation. His associates reported that Brewster showed up drunk in his Towson law office, drunk in his Washington Senate office, drunk on the Senate floor, drunk while campaigning, and drunk behind the wheel. It cost him his beautiful farm and most of his fortune and lost him the respect of his family, friends, and colleagues, including some of the nation's highest-ranking leaders. It eventually contributed directly to his being accused of the serious felony of bribery. At its nadir, alcoholism nearly killed him.

"He was a very bad alcoholic. He didn't have control. He was an addict," sadly recalled Steny Hoyer, who was on Brewster's Senate staff for four years. "He started missing a lot of events and sending people on his behalf."[353]

Another Brewster staffer, Dick McIntosh, was Brewster's nineteen-year-old driver during his 1962 Senate campaign. Their practiced strategy was to drive to one bar where the candidate would go in, have a drink, and shake hands with voters and then drive to the next tavern to do it all again. Brewster's drinking, McIntosh later recalled "was all under control in '62. I used to say [to him], 'My God, look at all these bars we'd go to and all those beers, and you never show anything!' And he was fine. He had… a hollow leg."[354]

After that summer, McIntosh left the staff and went to college. When he rejoined the staff in 1966, he said "Danny was a different person, a changed man when I came back in '66. The change had been the devastating [Wallace] campaign of '64. I wasn't a part of it; I wasn't aware of it; I didn't know what the hell was going on. I've never really quite understood why that whole Wallace campaign was so devastating to Danny, but it seemed to have forced him back to heavy drinking."[355]

When he was seriously in his cups, Brewster would drink almost anything—vodka, bourbon, even mouthwash if it contained alcohol—but he was partial to beer. He could guzzle a full can of beer in the time others might take a couple sips.

Maurice Wyatt, a longtime player in Maryland politics who ran Brewster's Baltimore constituent office in 1967 and 1968 and eventually ran his '68 re-election campaign, is not the type to be easily surprised, but he said he was taken aback to discover that Brewster's top Senate assistant, Jack Sullivan, had installed a full-sized refrigerator in Brewster's Capitol Hill office and kept it stocked with Budweiser.

When Wyatt expressed his astonishment, he said Sullivan nonchalantly replied, "That's how I keep the boss happy." "Imagine that," Wyatt mused, 'That's how I keep the boss happy.'"[356]

W. Shepherdson Abell, a descendant of the family that long owned the *Baltimore Sun* and who became a prominent Maryland attorney, was an intern and part-time legislative assistant in Brewster's Capitol office from summer 1965 until summer 1967. His first impressions of Brewster were how good looking he was and how articulate and personable he was with the staff. "I was very impressed by him."[357]

But then he noticed the extent of Brewster's drinking. "He was in the office a lot, but he was drinking a lot too. You would actually hear the beer can pop in the morning. And I said to myself, 'This guy has the greatest job in the world, he has all the gear, but'… you knew that he was drinking."[358]

Like some other addicted drinkers, including some in his immediate family, Brewster for years was a functioning alcoholic. He drank too much, but he somehow managed to do his job and meet his responsibilities. During the second half of his six-year Senate term, however, that began to change. He began showing up at events too drunk to speak or just drunk enough to slur his words and embarrass himself. With increasing frequency, he was too drunk to show up at all.

Michael Olesker of Baltimore was a freshman at the University of Maryland in the spring of 1964 when Brewster and Wallace both showed up to speak on campus the same evening. Brewster, appearing along with Wisconsin Senator William Proxmire before an estimated one thousand to three thousand students in a steady drizzle outside of McKeldin Library in the center of campus, called for support for President Johnson and support for "decency." An hour later, Wallace attracted nearly ten thousand students inside Cole Field House, but most of them were there to boo and jeer the Alabama governor and hold up protest signs promoting equity among the races by displaying the mathematical symbol for equal.[359]

Olesker, who would go on to work for about twenty-five years as a reporter for the *Baltimore Sun* and a commentator on Baltimore TV station WJZ, recalled that he had been eager to hear Brewster speak. Still shocked by the Kennedy assassination and yet encouraged that Johnson was pushing for passage of civil rights legislation, Olesker said that the students viewed Brewster, as a surrogate for Johnson, as a representative of their ideals of racial inclusiveness. But his speech, Olesker said, just left them flat.

"I can still feel the frustration. Our hearts were really in it. And there was just nothing there. He rambled through the speech lifelessly, stumbled through it. It wasn't a sense of anger; it was a sense of 'Gee whiz, is this the best that he had to offer? Did he not get why we were there?'" Olesker said he did not recall Brewster slurring his words, but that after later learning of Brewster's problems with alcohol, he came to believe that Brewster must have been inebriated that night.[360]

Such recurring problems brought a new level of stress on members of Brewster's staff, who felt they had to conceal their boss's illness, had to make alibis when he unexpectedly missed meetings or events, or had to substitute for him when he was too incapacitated to do his job.

"Certainly by 1965, Danny's drinking was pretty serious," said staffer Bill Miller. "I was press secretary and I was never sure he would show up. He was missing some things. We were taking turns staying with him to make sure he would make it to the next event. Sometimes he wouldn't show up in the mornings and we didn't know where he was. Jack's [Sullivan] father had been the chief of the Capitol Hill police, and so Jack had a way of finding him when he was missing in action."[361]

W. Shepherdson Abell, who assisted with legislative matters, remembered, "He just wouldn't be there when the time came to go to the [Senate] floor."[362]

Miller said Brewster would not come into the office drunk but it was often clear he had already been drinking. "Like most advanced alcoholics, he could function with a good deal of intoxication. And that wasn't helped by the nature of the Senate, where they had drinking rooms right off the floor of the Senate and in many Senators' offices." Miller said Brewster was painfully conscious of what his drinking was doing to his staff and to the work of his office, and in the short intervals when he would get sober, he would tell his staff "that we should all quit."[363]

Wyatt and Miller had opposite opinions about whether Sullivan, who died in 2010, was an enabler of Brewster's drinking. Wyatt believes that by intentionally feeding Brewster's drinking habit, Sullivan believed he could exert his own power in the office and over the Senator's affairs.[364] Miller, however, thought Sullivan was trying to keep Brewster sober. "[Sullivan] needed [Brewster] to function. We took turns babysitting. We had a staff person that Jack hired, an African American young man, that became [Brewster's] more constant companion, and that was his job. I think for the most part, we helped Danny. He could empty a can of beer without swallowing. And sometimes when we'd go over to the Senate for a vote or something, I had to make sure he was stable. He'd get glassy."[365]

Brewster's drinking also began to affect his relationship with his important patron in the White House. In the summer of 1964, just a couple months after Brewster had stood in for President Johnson to successfully hold off Wallace in the Maryland presidential primary, Dan and Carol Brewster invited a small gathering to their Georgetown home to discuss ways to help one of Brewster's Senate friends, Vance Hartke of Indiana, get re-elected. Suddenly, the President of the United States walked in, saying he had "sneaked out the back door of the White House" to come over to pay his respects. According to a brief in the next morning's Washington Post, Johnson shook hands with a few guests and, within five minutes, was gone.[366] What the Post did not say, according to Carol Brewster, was that the President was to have stayed longer, but when he arrived he found that Brewster was drunk and most of the guests had already departed. The embarrassed President turned on his heels and left.[367]

It happened again in late October 1964 when Johnson appeared at the Fifth Regiment Armory in Baltimore for a big Democratic Party rally promoting Joe Tydings for the Senate, Carlton Sickles for the US House of Representatives, and other Democratic candidates in Maryland. Brewster, who was about to become the state's senior US Senator, was tapped to introduce the President, but when he stepped to the microphone, he paused for an embarrassing moment as if trying to collect his thoughts before finally giving the President of the United States possibly the shortest introduction of his career. "My fellow Marylanders, it is a distinct privilege and high honor for me to present to all Marylanders a truly great American, the President of the United States. Mr. President," he said and returned to his seat.[368] Almost certainly under the influence, Brewster appeared to be afraid that if he tried to say more, he would somehow mess it up.

White House staff also realized the extent of Brewster's illness. An internal congressional memorandum in February 1966 to the President from Harry C. McPherson Jr., a special assistant to Johnson, discussed Majority Leader Mike Mansfield's difficulties dealing with Louisiana Senator Russell B. Long, who was having his own problems with excessive drinking. McPherson told the President that Mansfield had to rely instead on Maine Senator Edmund Muskie or Hawaii Senator Daniel Inouye because Michigan's Philip A. Hart was often out of town and because "Brewster has his problem," an almost certain reference to his alcoholism.[369]

Although stories began to appear about Brewster's increasingly frequent habit of last-minute cancellations of meetings or events, he had kept his growing problem with alcohol somewhat hidden from the general public. But in the summer of 1967, his drinking suddenly became a statewide political scandal. The State of Israel was coming under increasing pressure from its Arab neighbors—Egypt, Jordan, and Syria—and war there seemed imminent. Jews in America began to raise money and political support for the Israeli cause. In Baltimore, a big pro-Israel rally was scheduled the evening of June 4 at the Pikesville Armory. The event came literally on the eve of what later became known as the Six-Day War, and Senator Brewster was to be the primary speaker. After he arrived, however, it became clear to his staff he was too intoxicated to speak and they steered him away from the microphone, explaining that the Senator was ill. Tydings, by then the Democratic nominee for the state's other US Senate seat, took his place.

Brewster might have gotten away with the subterfuge had it not been for some odd reporting about the event in the next day's *Baltimore Sun*. The *Sun's* reporter arrived at the rally late and Tydings was already speaking. He was handed a copy of Brewster's remarks, which had been prepared in advance, and assumed Brewster had already given his speech. When he reported in the *Sun* the next morning that Brewster had told the audience that, "We have a moral and political commitment to see this nation [Israel] thrive in peace," he did not realize Brewster never spoke those or any other words.[370] The day after the *Sun's* story, the rival *Baltimore News American's* political reporter, Frank DeFillipo, set the record straight, revealing that the reason Brewster did not speak was that he may have been drunk and that the incident probably damaged his support within the city's large and politically active Jewish community. DeFillipo quoted Brewster's press spokesman, Alan Dessoff, as saying the Senator "fully intended to address the rally... but suddenly decided against speaking because he wasn't feeling well." DeFillipo also quoted an unnamed source as saying, "The Senator looked as though he were ill, the sort of illness we've seen many times."[371]

A day later, the *Sun* ran what it called "A Correction and Apology." "The *Sun* committed a grievous error of fact when it reported on Monday morning that Senator Brewster (D., Md.) had spoken the night before at a pro-Israel rally at the Pikesville Armory. Senator Brewster had been scheduled to speak at the rally, but he did not, in fact, speak there."[372]

The effect was that just a little more than a year before he was to stand for re-election, Brewster's problem with drinking had suddenly become common knowledge. And the strong support he had heretofore enjoyed from the Jewish community appeared to be unalterably damaged. He didn't blame the press; he blamed himself.

While it was some time yet before Brewster conceded he needed medical help, he was aware that his drinking was out of hand and that he had to do something about it. A decade later, after he had finally quit drinking, Brewster recalled in a remarkably candid interview with the *Maryland State Medical Journal* that between 1964 and 1968, "I tried every halfway measure there was—only beer; only wine; only champagne; not after 5 p.m.; not before 5 p.m.; not in the state of Maryland; not in Washington; only at meals, etc. But I'd now become an alcoholic. No halfway measures worked."[373]

"I didn't admit it to myself in all my years in public life—that I was an alcoholic…. I knew I drank too much and that it impaired my intellectual agility—and I desperately tried to cut it back. I really wanted to stop—but I thought I could control it, not knowing that control was impossible for the alcoholic."[374]

So many of Brewster's close relatives have suffered from alcoholism that family members and friends alike are certain it must be hereditary. While medical research does show that those who have a family history of alcoholism have a greater tendency to develop a drinking problem than those who do not, genetics are believed to be the cause of alcoholism only about half the time. Otherwise, it is attributable to "social or environmental factors."[375]

"Some who have inherited genes making them susceptible to alcoholism are responsible drinkers or never take a drink in their life," according to studies on alcoholism presented on a treatment center website called the Addiction Center.[376]

One possible factor that could have prompted Brewster's excessive drinking—although he always denied it—was post-traumatic stress disorder, or PTSD, the prolonged and recurring anxiety that many combat veterans experience after returning from witnessing the horrors of war.[377] In World War I it was called shell shock and in World War II it was called combat fatigue. The nearly three-month-long campaign to conquer the Japanese on Okinawa produced 26,211 incidents of what were then listed as "non-combat casualties," the most incidents of combat fatigue ever recorded in a single campaign. Of those, 4,489 were from within Brewster's Sixth Marine Division. And, of those, 1,289 occurred during the seven-day battle for Sugar Loaf Hill, in which Brewster fought and in which 2,662 of their comrades were killed.[378]

Slogging those muddy, stinking, fly-infested killing fields, soaked with rain, working with little sleep or food, and constantly tormented by being under attack and bombardment for days on end, the only way soldiers could function was to suppress their fears. No one wanted to be accused of being a coward, yet the human psyche often couldn't cope.

Veteran fighters simply broke down, or became catatonic, developing what was called "a thousand-mile stare." Some sobbed; some screamed; some developed a dull detachment. Some, said author and Marine veteran of Okinawa, E. B. Sledge, "wore expressions of idiots or simpletons knocked too witless to be afraid anymore.... Some of those... probably never recovered but were doomed to remain in mental limbo and spend their futures in a veteran's hospital as 'living dead.'"[379]

After surviving the battle, Brewster was strongly dismissive of those who claimed combat fatigue. "I firmly believe that nearly 80 percent of the men who turn in with combat fatigue are fakes and cowards," he wrote in his handwritten war diary two months after the battle had ended. He said he understood the nerve-shattering effects of bombs and artillery shells bursting at close range and said those who suffered concussions from such blasts were "legitimate" casualties. But some of the men who left the fighting on Sugar Loaf, he angrily charged, "merely didn't have the guts to stick it out. They took the easy way. They left their friends when the going was tough. All of us certainly thought of this [way] out, but most men would rather die than leave."[380]

Brewster's closest relatives say he insisted he did not suffer from PTSD and, in fact, didn't really recognize it as a medical or mental condition, yet they also believed he had to have been affected by what he saw and experienced in the war. Stories abound among Brewster's family about the times he was seen after the war waving his Colt .45 in the air, holding it to his mouth or temple, being drunk and sitting in his boxers and T-shirt with the loaded pistol cradled in his lap, or jolted from sleep in the torment of a war-related nightmare.

Kurt Aarsand, who as a teenager moved into the Brewster household in 1976 after his mother, Judy, married Brewster, said his stepfather "really didn't like to talk about [the war], but I know he had nightmares pretty much all of his life."[381]

Daniel Perskie, whose father, Lieutenant Marvin Perskie, helped save Brewster's life and his platoon on Okinawa, said his father suffered from nightmares for years. On nights when there was lightning and thunder outside, his mother would leave the bedroom to sleep on the couch because his father "would have his .45 up on his chest and he'd be asleep on his back with his eyes open. It was creepy," he said. "Those nights we are talking about, if you woke him with the top half of his body… I mean, I'm a pretty big guy, but I always shook him by the toes so he didn't shoot you or twist around so quick, so violently. I guess he just got conditioned."[382]

While Danny was off in the South Pacific, his childhood neighbor and friend, Ike Iglehart, was fighting Germans at the Battle of the Bulge in Belgium. When Ike got back to the Green Spring Valley, he admitted to being disoriented by the war.

"As I drove or walked around the friendly hills of home, I found myself constantly looking for a place to put machine guns or mortars, and I kept a loaded .45 near at hand in my bedroom for a long time," he wrote in a personal memoir.[383] If Brewster felt that way, he kept it to himself.

Jennilie Brewster, Brewster's younger daughter from his third marriage, recalled how in later years her father would spend hours on his tractor mowing the fields of their farm, often dressed in the khaki clothes he wore as a Marine. "I would say, 'What are you thinking about [while] you're out there mowing in the field for hours on end?' It is not like he was listening to a Walkman. And he would replay things that happened in the war and decisions he had made, and if he had made different decisions would some of those guys have died? So, I definitely think it was something that he really dwelled on."[384]

"I think he was haunted by his experiences in the war. I think drinking was a way to deal with that," Jennilie said.[385]

"He suffered with depression," said Danielle Brewster Oster, Jennilie's older sister. "He used to sit like this, with his head in his hands.… He openly talked about alcoholism and his mistakes and how he could have been great. He had a lot of remorse about that. What his life [might have been]. He said, 'I had everything. I could have been President.'"[386]

Shep Abell, who had worked as a young man in Brewster's Senate office, remarked decades later that "there were some terrible people in the Senate, but there were also some giants in the Senate in those days. You just couldn't help measuring Dan against [the giants]. He was with them for most things, but he wasn't a giant because he couldn't be relied upon to stand up and give a speech. Because of the alcoholism, but maybe because of [his hawkish stand on] Vietnam too."[387]

Abell said he thought Brewster, absent the alcohol, would have been re-elected and that he could have become a very good Senator. "I think he would have been more like one of the giants. I think he had a curiosity that could have made him potentially a good legislator."[388]

Chapter 13

A DISASTROUS REMATCH

At the end of January 1967, Danny Brewster found himself among select members of Congress at a palatial estate in the English countryside where they were invited to spend a long weekend with their British counterparts candidly discussing "The Future of Europe and the Atlantic Community."

Seven US Senators, including Democrats Joseph D. Tydings and Robert F. Kennedy of New York and nine members of the US House of Representatives (including Donald Rumsfeld, a young Republican from Illinois) attended the prestigious conference. It was hosted by a British delegation that featured more than two dozen dukes, viscounts, field marshals, and other nobility, as well as foreign ministers and generals. A young Margaret Thatcher was among the English participants. A primary discussion topic was whether Great Britain should join the then developing European economic union.[16]

But Danny Brewster's mind and heart were elsewhere.

The senior Senator from Maryland, married for more than a dozen years and father of two young boys, was transfixed by the prospect of reuniting with Anne Bullitt, the Ambassador's daughter to whom he

---

16. Other Senators who attended included Republicans Charles Percy of Illinois, Gordon Allott of Colorado, Jack Miller of Iowa, and Hiram Fong of Hawaii. Representatives included Republicans Herman T. Schneebeli of Pennsylvania, Albert Quie of Minnesota, and Frank Horton of New York and Democrats Cornelius Gallagher of New Jersey, Morris K. Udall of Arizona, Otis Pike of New York, Richard Ottinger of New York, and John Dingell of Michigan. Source: Ditchley Conference program, Jan. 27-30, 1967, in Daniel B. Brewster papers, Hornbake Library, University of Maryland, College Park, MD, series IV, box 3.

had been briefly engaged in 1943, more than twenty-three years before. She had walked out of his life to marry instead a childhood friend from Philadelphia, Cappy Townsend. After three years, Anne divorced Townsend in order to marry another Philadelphian, Nicholas Duke Biddle, the son of a well-known Ambassador, to whom she was married for about seven years while living in Spain and England. She divorced Biddle to marry an Irish horse breeder, Roderic More O'Ferrall, who introduced her into Irish horse racing circles. But that marriage lasted barely a year. Separated in 1955, with More O'Ferrall accused in court to have hit her, Anne arranged to have the Pope annul their marriage. She reverted to her previous married name, Anne Bullitt Biddle.

After she and More O'Ferrall split up, Bullitt's doting father, William Christian Bullitt, helped Anne buy at auction the seven hundred-acre Palmerstown House in County Kildare just west of Dublin, the historic home of Ireland's Earls of Mayo. There, beginning in the mid-1950s, Anne Bullitt owned and ran one of the largest and most successful horse stud farms in the country. Her colt, Sindon, won the Irish Derby in 1958, beginning a string of race victories that pushed her to the top of the owners' list in Ireland. The thoroughbreds she bred at Palmerstown, notably the offspring of the resident stallion, Milesian, produced 110 winners in competitive races between 1958 and 1964.[389] Before her racing days were over, Anne's horses won races in Ireland as Mrs. Anne Bullitt Biddle, as Mrs. Anne Bullitt More O'Ferrall, and as Mrs. Anne Bullitt Brewster. In 1966, she became the first woman ever licensed as a horse trainer in Ireland.

A love of horses and racing was a central attraction between Danny Brewster and his wife, Carol, and it was the same between Brewster and Anne Bullitt. Yet there was something more, something different, something that felt almost preordained in his relationship with Anne. He had, after all, written in his wartime diary in 1943 that "Anne was the finest girl I have ever met," and also predicted, "If I had to bet my life on it, one way or the other, I would say that someday I will marry that girl."[390]

It is unclear how or precisely when or where she and Brewster rekindled their long lost affair, but by the time he arrived at the by-invitation-only conference at historic Ditchley Park near Oxford, she was all he could think about.

Almost immediately after arriving at the English conference, Brewster disclosed to Tydings that he intended to fly over to Ireland as soon as possible to visit Anne. "The first day [Danny] came to me and talked to me about Anne Bullitt, and he said he had bumped into her, that she had done really well, she had married some rich guy... and she got a lot of money and a big estate in Ireland. They had met and Brewster had fallen back in love with her. And so, he said, 'Would you cover for me?' And I said, 'Yeah, I'll cover for you.' I didn't have to. Nobody was calling for him, but I would have covered for him. I would have protected him."[391]

Although Tydings remembered Brewster as leaving the conference early to visit Anne, official records indicate he probably stayed until the conference was over, then moved into Claridge's Hotel in London where he was interviewed by the *Baltimore Sun's* London reporter, Charles Flowers, and then attended a dinner for the American delegation held at the House of Commons, arriving at a special door known as the "Strangers' Entrance." The following morning, January 31, he boarded a flight for Dublin.

By then, Anne Bullitt must have been distraught over the medical condition of her beloved father, who was living in Paris but was so sick with leukemia that he was trying to arrange a flight to the States so he could die peacefully at home in Philadelphia. Twice, however, his flights were canceled due to snowstorms blanketing the East Coast, and by February 14, when Anne joined him, he had fallen into a coma. The seventy-six-year-old former Ambassador to the Soviet Union and France died the next day. Anne arranged to have his body returned to the US, and he was buried following a funeral in Philadelphia on February 20 attended by, among other dignitaries, former Vice President and future President Richard Nixon and his wife, Pat.

Tydings recalled that at Ditchley, Brewster was drinking heavily, although he said Brewster's alcoholism actually seemed to worsen the following year when he stood for re-election. Whatever his level of sobriety, there is no question he was all but overwhelmed with his renewed love of Anne Bullitt. "He was a little bit gaga over Anne Bullitt," Tydings observed.[392]

For the last several years, Brewster's drinking and his prolonged absences from his Baltimore County farm had increased the stress on his marriage to Carol. He had bought a house in the Georgetown neighborhood of Washington, DC, but she refused to move there from their farm. On March 23, 1967, not even two months after reconnecting with Anne in Ireland, Brewster's office announced that the state's senior United States Senator—"the gentleman jockey," as he was described in one front-page news story—and his wife had separated and were discussing conditions of divorce.[393] Both their separation and later divorce were reported in newspapers around the country.

"I think Carol was pretty fed up," recalled Brewster's former staffer, House Majority Leader Steny Hoyer, who knew Brewster well and was empathetic about his drinking. "It is tough to be married to an alcoholic. It is tough to be the son of an alcoholic. And you get very angry. And you may love somebody, but you get very angry and you just say, 'I can't handle this.'"[394]

Dick McIntosh, another member of Brewster's staff, said, "There was this period of time that Danny disappeared to Ireland, and [staff wondered] 'Where is he?' And sometime when he came back, he was in just disastrous shape—this was before he married Anne. There was a period of time when he was getting divorced from Carol, and maybe Anne was giving him trouble about something, and I remember he was absolutely miserable from morning to night. He was really drinking heavily."[395]

Bill Miller, yet another Brewster staff member, said Carol was well-liked in the office, "unlike Anne." He said he never knew whether Carol refused to move to DC because her boys were in school, because of her social network in Baltimore County, or because of some other reason, but that it "left [Brewster] at some loose ends." He described Anne as "attractive, energetic, well-spoken, and Danny was crazy about her. When they were courting, he was on the phone with her every day for an hour or two, with an overseas operator, talking with her."[396]

"My impression of Anne is that she thought Danny was her ticket back into Washington, DC, society," Miller observed. "She was very clearly mistaken."[397]

John Grason Turnbull, Brewster's first law partner and unofficial political adviser, later said, "His divorce from [Carol] didn't do any good. That was a big mistake. It didn't help him any. A lot of people knew [Carol] and liked her. That [breakup], too, was the result of his drinking." Turnbull said he tried to convince Brewster to wait to marry Anne at least until after his re-election. "[I said] Dan, for Chrissakes, wait for two years. [But] he found out [why it would have been politically prudent to wait]."[398]

By the time she had reunited with Brewster in 1967, he had moved into the Madison Hotel in Washington and began writing a stream of gushing love letters to Anne, virtually all of them undated. "Your presence at my side is all that matters," he wrote to her, probably shortly after his return from Ireland. "There is nothing that means anything other than you. The only future is you; all centers about you. This is one hell of a way to live. I am only going through the motions of being a Senator."[399]

Writing to Anne on Madison Hotel stationery, Brewster recounted his initial conversation with his wife and said, "Carol will be OK. She was really decent today. I will see [personal attorney] Dick Emory at noon tomorrow. With luck he should be able to get all decisions tied down on paper. This will sound very final and definite and should stick."[400]

Then, almost as if he could not believe it himself, he added, "We somehow have a second chance. We will be happy. There may be trouble, but it will pass. Just stay with me.... I will need help from you during the next months. Just keep telling me this is a real partnership, that it is for keeps, that you love as deeply as I do."[401]

In a follow-up letter, Brewster said Emory had prepared a property settlement and child custody agreement and would take it to Carol the following day. Brewster also discussed a separate meeting he had held with Jerold Hoffberger, a close friend who owned the National Brewing Company in Baltimore and was a major financier of Maryland Democratic political candidates. "All are convinced I win [re-election in 1968] with ease," Brewster wrote. "Told men there (this is just the home team) that Carol and I would split up before the election. No mention of us, of course. No apparent problem here."[402]

Brewster was so infatuated with Anne that he could not keep her off his mind even when assigned the temporary task of running the United States Senate. "Dearest Anne—I am now presiding over the Senate," he scribbled on a note pad, the top of which was printed, "United States Senate—MEMORANDUM." "Joe Clark of Pennsylvania is speaking— God only knows about what. My thoughts are only about you." Anne was apparently due to arrive in the States the following day. "I can't wait to see you.... We must bring these separations to an end, too much time has already passed us by. Clark is about to stop—I must get to work. Love, Danny."[403]

Brewster's string of love letters is on file as part of the William Christian Bullitt papers, which are housed at Yale University's Sterling Memorial Library. One, written in dark blue ink on a plain piece of yellow legal pad, simply said, "Dearest Anne. I love you. DB." If Anne replied to any of his letters, no copies of her responses appear to have survived, at least not at Yale, not in Brewster's official papers at the University of Maryland, and not in Brewster family papers.

On April 13, 1967, Carol Brewster and her son from her first marriage, Michael de Havenon, boarded an airplane and flew to Juarez, Mexico, where she was able to obtain an immediate divorce from Daniel Baugh Brewster. "We had to [go to Mexico] because [there] you didn't have to prove fault—you could get a no-fault divorce. At that time, it was something you couldn't have gotten in Maryland," de Havenon recalled. He said the two of them flew down, conducted their business, and flew back home. He described the divorce as one of mutual acceptance.[404] Carol retained custody of the two boys, Dan Jr., 11, and Gerry, 9.

The very next day, Brewster flew back to Ireland with the intention of marrying Anne as soon as possible and his office formally announced those plans on Saturday, April 15. But after he arrived in Ireland, Anne suffered a broken jaw and dislocated shoulder when the car she was driving across a farm field bounced into a ditch and she was thrown headfirst into the steering wheel.[405]

While Brewster waited in Ireland for his fiancée to recover, reporters began to gather outside the gates of Palmerstown House, Anne Bullitt Biddle's stud farm near the town of Naas, but the gate was too far away for them to even glimpse the two-story stone manor house. Members of the press complained that when they called the house to solicit information about the upcoming marriage, Anne's Spanish housekeeper would answer and say, "Mrs. Biddle no here. Senator no here. No speak English."[406] About the only time Danny and Anne escaped was to briefly attend the horse races at the nearby Curragh Racecourse. Photographers spotted Brewster with binoculars hanging from his neck and Anne with a race program in her gloved hand and a scarf over her hair.

Back in Maryland, political reporters began to speculate on the impact that Brewster's divorce and pending remarriage could have on his re-election chances. The *Baltimore News American* quoted one unnamed political observer as calling Brewster's decision to divorce his wife "the surest form of political suicide," yet another suggested that Marylanders had long since abandoned "that puritanical stage."[407]

Brewster returned to Washington, still unmarried. Asked when that might change, he told reporters they should ask his fiancée that question. "I went [to Ireland] once and it was smeared all over the papers," he complained. "I propose to stay right here. I'm going to stay on the job."[408] But two days later Anne arrived in the States and the two were finally married that evening, April 29, 1967. Both were forty-three years old. The wedding was a small, nighttime affair held at Windy Meadows Farm, Brewster's mother's home in Baltimore County. The groom's brother, Andre, stood as best man and the service was conducted by O. T. Gosnell, clerk of the Baltimore County Court. They said they would honeymoon later and that Brewster planned to return to the Senate on

Monday morning. Brewster's two sons, Dan Jr. and Gerry, were not invited to attend the wedding of their father and new stepmother at the home of their grandmother.[409]

"You could make a case—and this is pure conjecture on my part—that he married Anne Bullitt to try somehow to recreate an idyllic period in his life before drinking had taken control of it," said Michael de Havenon. "You could posit that. But who knows?"[410]

Walter Brewster, Danny's youngest brother, remained a lifelong fan of Carol Brewster, as did other friends and family. "She was a sweetheart. Everybody loved her. She was everything you could wish for. [Danny] lived with her just like they were husband and wife and finally married her because people told him if he wanted to run for the Senate he had to get married, and then he did. Then this other gal came along. Just took him away."[411] In a news brief about the breakup, *Time* magazine described Carol Brewster as a "notable campaign asset to her husband."[412]

Following their marriage, the newlyweds returned to Ireland to wind up affairs there. Brewster came back to the States first and used his time on the flight home to write not one but two more love letters to Anne. "We have left Shannon, and I am just sitting here thinking of you. My God, how I do love you," he wrote in a letter inscribed at the top, "Wednesday, Aboard Aer Lingus." After discussing plans to move his furniture into their new home on California Street in Washington, he wrote, "Darling, I already miss you something awful. I am just the luckiest guy in the world and will do everything possible to make you happy."[413] Then, in a second letter written during what Brewster described as an "absolutely endless" flight, the newly married Senator said the big mistake of his life was not to have reunited with Anne sooner. "I should have come straight to you the day the War ended—how I regret that I did not," he wrote.[414]

After their whirlwind romance and trans-Atlantic hopping between America and Ireland, the newly married Brewsters tried to find some normalcy and equilibrium in their lives, but it was not easy. Anne owned a West Highland terrier, Pie-Pie, which she adored, and she complained that Danny had somehow messed up plans to have the dog shipped to the States (the dog did finally arrive). She also must have expressed concern about his re-election prospects, because he replied to her, "There is no reason to worry about your husband. I believe the political situation is retrievable and know that I will be ok."[415] He had, after all, stood for election a dozen times and never lost. After they moved into their house in Washington, the detail-conscious Anne insisted on importing her own house painters from Ireland to help with the renovation.

Dick McIntosh still regularly drove the Senator to events, and he said that once Anne began to accompany them, the three of them shared many conversations. At some point, however, McIntosh thinks he must have offended Anne, because he suddenly was no longer asked to drive them.

"So, I didn't. But, long before that, I had concluded she was impossible—absolutely impossible. Incredibly headstrong, arrogant—perhaps very intelligent," McIntosh said years later. "I'd have a hard time coming up [with an example], but it was just more her manner. And she could really get him down. I remember one time they were in the car, and she said to him, something to the effect, 'You can create more tension than anybody I know.' And I thought to myself, 'He creates tension? What about you, lady?' She really did."[416]

Three weeks after their marriage, Anne for the first time went on the campaign trail, accompanying Dan to a routine re-election event before the Women's Suburban Democratic Club of Montgomery County. Perhaps not surprisingly, just two weeks later, on June 4, Brewster showed up at the important Jewish rally at the Pikesville Armory too intoxicated to speak. As Brewster's re-election challenges multiplied, and as his serious drinking problems were beginning to surface, some of his family, friends, and campaign staff began to worry that his sudden marriage to Anne Bullitt might turn out to be a disastrous rematch.

Records from that time demonstrate Anne's power over him. After they were married, Brewster drafted a last will and testament. It is undated, never went into effect, and later was superseded by another will, but it is a window into his thinking at the time. Under the will, almost everything he owned would have been left to Anne. Additionally, it requested a simple military funeral for Danny at Arlington National Cemetery and asked that three friends and employees receive $2,000 each: Ellen Turnbull Lynch, who for years was his personal secretary; Marcel LeMasson, his longtime horse trainer and farm manager; and John F. Sullivan, the top assistant on his Senate staff. As for his sons, he stated in the will that they were both "amply provided for in the two trusts established by their great, great grandparents." He therefore left Dan Jr. portraits of Danny's father and grandfather and a set of gold vest buttons and left to Gerry a set of pearl studs and a monogrammed military brush.[417]

In Anne Bullitt's previous three marriages, she had been childless, and it appears she wanted her fourth marriage to Danny Brewster to be the same. This desire likely led to an unfortunate agreement Danny made with her so that she would marry him.

In one of a series of desperate letters written to Anne in February 1970 after Brewster was committed to Irish hospitals for treatment of his alcoholism, he stated bluntly the agreement he had selfishly reached with Anne to help convince her to marry him. "When we were married, I knowingly gave up my sons," he said but added, "This does not mean that I do not care about them." He reminded her that he had inquired about them at Christmas but that she had not responded. He complained he had not seen his sons since June 1969 and added, "God only knows what effect all the bad publicity has had on these little boys."[418]

Brewster was the only one of Anne's husbands with the title of United States Senator. Brewster's Senate colleague, Joe Tydings, believed that was her primary reason for finally marrying him.

"She could have cared less about him," Tydings said in 2018, just a few months before his own death. "She liked the idea of being the wife of a US Senator, but she could care less about Danny Brewster."[419]

Chapter 14

DESCENT

Danny Brewster's ignominious descent began in earnest in 1964, a precipitous fall that worsened relentlessly year after year for more than a decade. He was weakened by political choices that backfired, by racism, by war, by riots, and by his distracting decision to divorce and remarry. His once bright future in public life was ended by two men he considered friends, one who remained his friend and the other a once loyal aide who later betrayed him. More than anything else, his inability to put down the bottle destroyed him.

Although his problems were already mounting, Brewster's fortunes tipped in May 1964. William S. "Billy" Townsend, manager of his '64 presidential primary campaign against Alabama segregationist George C. Wallace, jumped into his car to drive the twenty miles from Towson to Arbutus. The weight of Brewster's political future—and perhaps the fate of Lyndon Johnson's monumental civil rights legislation—was in his hands. Townsend's task was to shore up votes for his boss in the unexpectedly close race on his home turf in Baltimore County. The bitterly fought election against the Alabama governor, in which Brewster stood in as a surrogate for President Johnson, was just four days away.

But Townsend never made it to Arbutus because he suffered a heart attack en route. Townsend was a fellow Towson lawyer and frequent drinking buddy of Brewster's who had worked for him since 1958 and become head of his Senate staff. He survived the heart attack and later returned to public service, but he was never able to return as Brewster's chief Administrative Assistant. As a result, the workings of Brewster's staff unalterably changed.

With Townsend suddenly gone, Brewster gradually elevated another aide, John F. "Jack" Sullivan, to Administrative Assistant, a move that in just a matter of years would damage Brewster's life in ways no one could have imagined.

"Things changed in that office when Bill Townsend had his heart attack," remembered Bill Miller. "He had been very important. He was a very close friend of Danny's from congressional days. He was the balance in that office. And he was the complete confidant to Danny. There were differences that existed in the office between the legislative staff and primarily Jack [Sullivan], who wasn't a policy person at all. He was just into politics. And Bill Townsend was a very lovely person, very thoughtful person, very good with staff, and he really kept the balance in that office."[420]

Sullivan shared few of those qualities. He was a well-built, husky, six-foot-four-inch, former college basketball star who held multiple scoring records and was good enough to be drafted by the pros. Like Brewster, Sullivan had served in the Marine Corps, but he never faced the savage combat his boss endured. A good portion of Sullivan's military job was to play basketball on an all-service team in peacetime. He had short hair, was partial to cigars, had a my-way-or-the-highway approach, and was often described as gruff.

He had been one of Brewster's drivers but steadily rose in power—to staff assistant, then *top* assistant, campaign manager, political muscle, chief fund-raiser, friend, and, some other staffers believed, an enabler of the boss's drinking. The two were close enough that they occasionally spent nights at each other's houses. In the end, Jack Sullivan became Danny Brewster's Judas, but that came later.

"There was always tension in the office between those of us who were liberal and policy-oriented and Jack," said Miller, who at different times handled the Senator's legislative and press issues.[421]

Sullivan pitched in during the final days of the Wallace campaign, helping to borrow money needed to finance the race and to barely stave off an embarrassing defeat to Wallace in Baltimore County. Brewster won the election but ended up so bloodied he never fully recovered.

By opposing Wallace and supporting Johnson's civil rights legislation, Brewster alienated about half of Maryland's population, which—to Brewster's enduring surprise—vehemently and sometimes violently resisted desegregation. The white backlash to civil rights was a political reaction Brewster never saw coming. The thought of it offended his progressive, benevolent, educated outlook on life. He considered such attitudes racist and immoral.

Miller said that, even in liberal Montgomery County, the fear of white backlash was so great that the Brewster campaign could not convince a real estate company to donate space for use as a campaign office.[422]

Another portion of the populace, however, was unhappy with Brewster for the opposite reason, believing he had not pushed hard enough or fast enough to end discrimination and that his performance against the glib Alabama Governor was bland and lackluster. By the time that election was over, Brewster knew he was damaged goods and began to numb himself to that reality with alcohol.

That same year, Brewster suddenly had to worry about a new threat: being overshadowed by his new and younger Senate colleague, Joe Tydings. In the same election in which Brewster defeated Wallace, Tydings won a lopsided, upset victory over state Comptroller Louis L. Goldstein in the Democratic primary for Maryland's other US Senate seat. The favored Goldstein lost despite having the full backing of organized labor, the state's Governor and its heretofore dominant Democratic organization, and the state's incumbent Democratic Senator, Daniel B. Brewster. Tydings, a former federal prosecutor with a well-known name in Maryland politics (his adoptive father, Millard Tydings, had been a four-term United States Senator), represented a new "reform" wing of the Maryland Democratic Party that surprised and overwhelmed the Old Guard that was backing Goldstein. Tydings, with typical bravado, liked to describe his supporters as a separate party within the party. He received 279,564 votes to Goldstein's 155,086 and went on to easily beat the incumbent Republican Senator J. Glenn Beall Sr. in the fall general election.

With the sour taste of the Wallace campaign still fresh, Brewster began to have private doubts about staying in politics and whether he should run again in 1968. Now he also had to wonder what this shift in voter sentiment—the emergence of a reform wing of the party—would mean for him. The test came quickly enough in Maryland's crowded Democratic primary for governor in 1966. Eight candidates entered the race, but the marquee contest pitted Attorney General Thomas B. Finan, a native of Cumberland, friend of Brewster's, and prominent member of the established Democratic Party organization, against Carlton Sickles, Maryland's Congressman-at-Large and the latest darling of the reform wing of the party. In many ways, it looked like a repeat of the Goldstein-Tydings race of 1964—the party's Old Guard versus the party's young liberals, although Sickles lacked the flair for campaigning Tydings had.

Sickles was from the Washington suburb of Prince George's County and was the only Maryland member of the House elected statewide (Congressman-at-Large). He also was a longtime friend of Brewster's from their days together in the Maryland House of Delegates and later in Congress. Other candidates with name recognition were Clarence W. Miles, a Baltimore lawyer and community activist, and George P. Mahoney, the wealthy paving contractor who had become a perennial statewide candidate in Maryland, albeit a losing one.

Brewster's quandary was a simple but bald political calculation: Should he stay true to his colors by supporting the more moderate Finan, who was the favorite of the same entrenched Democratic organization that had backed Brewster throughout his political career, or should he acknowledge that times had changed and hew more closely to Tydings and the new and suddenly popular reform movement by shifting his support to the more liberal Sickles? Tydings was already trying to style himself as a reformer with national credentials through his friendship with the late President Kennedy's brother, Robert, then Senator from New York.

"Danny was very liberal in his legislative approach. That's one of the reasons he took Sickles," said Theodore G. "Ted" Venetoulis, a future Baltimore County executive who at the time was Sickles' chief of staff.[423] Others, however, doubted that was so. They saw Brewster's bend toward Sickles as both out of character and out of step with his legislative record. Maurice Wyatt, who later ran Brewster's constituent office in Baltimore, said he believed it was Sullivan who nudged Brewster into the Sickles camp because both Sullivan and Sickles were from Prince George's County.[424]

"I think he was afraid of [the reform movement]," Wyatt said. "I don't think Danny really embraced it. He was frightened by it. Keep in mind, this man just had his ass handed to him in that Wallace race."[425]

Steny Hoyer described the situation: "Danny is the senior Senator, but everybody knows he is suffering from this illness that is undermining his ability to be an effective representative. Joe [Tydings] is this bright and shiny knight in armor charging down the path and getting all this publicity. I am sure Danny resented that."[426]

As word circulated that Brewster and Tydings were considering backing Sickles, Herbert R. O'Conor Jr., the state banking commissioner and namesake son of a former Maryland governor, tried to talk the two Senators into not taking sides in the Democratic gubernatorial primary. The Brewster and O'Conor families were longtime friends and visitors at each other's homes and the pressure was not just political but personal.

"The only time I think they were apart politically was that my father was an adviser and somewhat of an organizer when Finan was running," recalled O'Conor's son, Herbert R. O'Conor III.[427]

Clarence Miles, who was aligned with the Baltimore business community, dismissed Sickles as "a captive of labor leaders." Other critics complained that Sickles and Tydings were too extreme, noting they were the only members of the Maryland congressional delegation willing to declare their support for President Johnson's too-hot-to-touch fair housing proposal then pending in Congress. That legislation would have prohibited homeowners from using race as a reason to deny the sale or rental of their real estate. (Brewster at first demurred, saying he had not yet had time to read the bill, although he noted that his strong civil rights record showed he had routinely opposed discrimination.[428])

Even though Congress would not decide the issue for another two years, it rapidly became a litmus test for candidates in Maryland's 1966 gubernatorial election. Mahoney, waging his seventh bid for statewide office, not only opposed the bill, he ran under the provocative segregationist banner "Your Home is Your Castle—Protect It." Miles also opposed the housing bill.

"Fresh in the minds of many politicians is the unexpectedly poor showing that Sen. Daniel B. Brewster made in his contest with Alabama Gov. George Wallace" in 1964, explained *Washington Post* reporter Alan L. Dessoff in an analysis of the effect the housing bill was having on the 1966 gubernatorial contest. "On the basis of Brewster's narrow victory, they are loath to go all-out for civil rights for fear that it would boomerang against them on election day."[429] Brewster actually defeated Wallace by more than ten percentage points, but the public impression was that he had done much worse or at least should have done much better.

In August, just before the Maryland gubernatorial primary, the housing bill passed the House of Representatives, 198-179, but only after it was watered down through an amendment proposed by Republican Congressman Charles McC. Mathias Jr. of Western Maryland, which substantially reduced the number of houses and apartments subject to the proposed law. Once in the Senate, the bill died as a result of a filibuster by Southern Democrats who continued to vote as a bloc against civil rights legislation.[17]

---

17. Johnson re-introduced the housing bill in 1967. An unrelated section of the bill involving a fairer way of selecting federal court juries was broken into separate legislation and given to a Judiciary subcommittee chaired by Tydings to handle, but the guts of the housing bill never got out of committee.

In 1968, Senator Walter Mondale, Democrat of Minnesota, teamed with Senator Edward Brooke, Republican of Massachusetts and the only African American in the Senate, to amend the Fair Housing Act into another civil rights bill then pending in Congress, and it passed the Senate on April 4. The bill was once again opposed by the Southerners. Of the sixty-four Democrats then in the Senate, only forty-two voted for the housing bill and only five—including Brewster and Tydings—were from states south of the Mason-Dixon line. Northern Republicans, led by Minority Leader Everett Dirksen of Illinois, provided the additional votes needed for passage.

Apart from the debate over the fair housing bill, the hot political question in Maryland was Tom Finan or Carlton Sickles. To the surprise of many, it was Brewster, not Tydings, who first came out publicly for Sickles—a switch of allegiances that reverberated in Maryland political circles. Brewster tried to avoid making enemies by saying, "I am 'for' Carlton Sickles and not against any other man."[430]

Bradford Jacobs, a political columnist for the *Baltimore Evening Sun*, succinctly summed up Brewster's decision: "Self-preservation was the motive," he said.[431]

"In his new pact with Mr. Sickles, the Senator seems to have hit upon an escape route from the threat of political stagnation," Jacobs opined. "The trouble lay with Mr. Brewster's political upbringing as an organization man—amiable to guidance from a series of factional bosses, grateful for their return boosts toward the top. The Senator found the up-escalator all too easy to ride." In 1964, Jacobs noted, Goldstein, the favored candidate of both Brewster's and the Democratic organization, was humiliated by Tydings, and Brewster himself "came out dangerously singed" from his race against Wallace. "As a result of 1964, he found himself lined up with a party faction of suddenly doubtful dominance and, worse, with his own prestige as a champion vote-getter in serious

---

Although the legislation likely would have died in the House, a shocking incident intervened. The same day the Senate passed the bill, Reverend Martin Luther King Jr. was assassinated in Memphis. In the immediate aftermath of King's death, dozens of American cities—including Baltimore and Washington—went up in flames as angry African Americans rioted. The politically instinctive Johnson seized on this emotional moment to press the House to pass the housing bill in King's memory, and it did so. On April 11, 1968, Johnson signed the Fair Housing Act of 1968 into law.

The Fair Housing Act would become the third of three major civil rights bills pushed through Congress by Johnson (following the Civil Rights Act of 1964 and the Voting Rights Act of 1965), but it may have been the most contentious. "A lot of [previous] civil rights [legislation] was about making the South behave and taking the teeth from George Wallace," Mondale explained. "This [legislation] came right to the neighborhoods across the country. This was civil rights getting personal."

Clarence Mitchell Jr., the famous Baltimore lobbyist for the National Association for the Advancement of Colored People who led the organization's civil rights effort, later reflected on Brewster's role on civil rights: "Dan was very good. He was not a person who gave extensive time to civil rights, per se, but he voted in favor of civil rights and was very sympathetic on these things."

Civil Rights Act of 1968, Wikipedia, https://en.wikipedia.org/wiki/Civil_Rights_Act_of_1968. Ernest B. Furgurson, "NAACP Chief Lobbyist: Mitchell Recalls Career as Civil Rights Advocate," *Baltimore Sun*, May 18, 1977.

question."[432]

Jacobs described Finan as "an old friend on whom the Brewster back is now turned," and said if the Attorney General were to win the September primary and be elected in November, it "would confront [Brewster] with a governor as unlikely to forgive as forget."[433]

But the September gubernatorial primary turned out even worse than that—worse than Brewster or Tydings could have imagined. Sickles didn't win, but neither did Finan; they split what could have been the state's decisive black vote. The narrow winner in the crowded, eight-man field was George P. Mahoney, with 30.2 percent of the vote to 29.8 percent for Sickles. Mahoney's margin over Sickles was 1,939 votes out of the 491,265 cast.

It became instantly clear that neither Brewster nor Tydings nor the reform wing of the party could support the segregationist Mahoney for Governor in the general election, even though he had become the official nominee of the Democratic Party. Instead, the two Senators and Sickles boycotted the race while liberal Democratic voters gravitated to the Republican column and voted to make Baltimore County Executive Spiro T. Agnew Maryland's next Governor. At that stage of his career, Agnew was seen as a moderate, having chaired Governor Nelson Rockefeller's campaign for President in Maryland. He swamped Mahoney, 455,318 to 373,543.[18] Mahoney would not forget the slight by his own party's leaders and vowed revenge.

"We supported Agnew over Mahoney [and] that was another thing that hurt [Brewster's re-election chances]," Miller remembered. "We had no idea that Agnew was what he was. He changed. Apparently, he was corrupt, which none of us knew. But his political shift came as a result of the riots (following the King assassination). He went with Nixon because of the shift."[434]

The Brewster/Tydings gambit had utterly failed. The two Senators could have remained neutral in the primary. Instead, driven by Tydings'

18. A third candidate, Baltimore Comptroller Hyman A. Pressman, ran as an independent and received 90,899 votes.

hubris and Brewster's political desperation, they fomented an intra-party war, produced the unwelcome specter of Mahoney as the party's standard bearer, and ultimately put Republican Spiro Agnew in the Governor's mansion in Annapolis. Their grasp for undisputed leadership of their party had not just come up short; it had weakened both of the Democratic incumbents. It was a debacle of the first order.

It is not a stretch to conclude, in retrospect, that the decision by Dan Brewster and Joe Tydings to endorse Carlton Sickles for Governor of Maryland in 1966 altered the course of American history. As a direct result, Spiro Agnew became Governor and then was selected by Richard Nixon to be Vice President, only later to be forced to resign due to his own misdeeds. That, in turn, led to the appointment of Michigan Congressman Gerald Ford to replace Agnew as Vice President. When Nixon was forced to resign as a result of the Watergate scandal, Ford became President—the only person to serve as both Vice President and President without being elected to either office by the Electoral College.[435]

Hoyer said he believes the period from the 1964 Wallace campaign through the gubernatorial campaign of 1966 was Brewster's "most politically difficult time"—a period that shook Brewster's self-confidence and caused him to increase his drinking. Even though Brewster was the senior Senator, Hoyer believes he felt overshadowed by Tydings, who had beaten the formidable Goldstein and was only too willing to show off his connections to the famous Kennedys.[436]

By the time Brewster began to ponder his own re-election, Hoyer said, he had quit thinking of himself as "the bright shiny star."[437]

The 1966 election did not alter the direction of Dan Brewster's political career as much as it reaffirmed its downward trajectory. The question now was whether he still had time—and the ability—to stop the fall. The Golden Boy of Maryland Politics no longer looked quite so invincible.

Chapter 15

REASON FOR CHANGE

In the wake of the '66 debacle, Daniel B. Brewster tried to re-invent himself.

With his own re-election now next on the state's political calendar, two years hence, he quickly sought to re-frame in voters' minds his approach to governance as more middle-of-the-road—what he called "an independent, moderate course through the problems facing us today."[438] As 1967 opened, Brewster's office began churning out a noticeable increase in press releases and began teaming with Tydings' office to produce a new line of joint releases. Brewster, said one newspaper, "is very conscious of the fact that Tydings got better publicity last year as a freshman."[439]

Brewster said he was fairly certain his Republican opponent in 1968 would be Eastern Shore Congressman Rogers C. B. Morton, but Baltimore County Congressman Clarence Long and other Democrats were also now eyeing the race. To those lusting for his job, the incumbent suddenly appeared vulnerable.

Knowing he needed to mend fences around the state, Brewster optimistically headed to the Lower Eastern Shore to meet with officials in conservative Wicomico County but got a sobering reception. The locals expressed unhappiness with his position on civil rights, castigated the "radical Supreme Court decisions" under Chief Justice Earl Warren, and listened skeptically as Brewster promised a "down-to-earth, middle of the road position on state and national affairs."[440]

Several days later, the Republican Agnew was sworn in as Governor on January 25, 1967, a fresh reminder to Democrats of the bollixed

'66 gubernatorial primary. Then Mahoney delivered another reminder by publicly pinning the blame for his—and the Democratic Party's—loss personally on Brewster, Tydings, and Sickles.[441] By then, however, Brewster was off to England as the US Senate's senior Democrat at the Ditchley conference outside London and his secret rendezvous with Anne Bullitt in Ireland. For the next several months, his Senate duties and his re-election campaign took a back seat to his head-over-heels obsession with divorcing his wife, Carol, and marrying Anne.

By the time newspapers began reporting that Dan and Carol Brewster had separated, other stories began to appear suggesting that Brewster's Republican opponent in 1968 might not be Rogers Morton after all but rather Brewster's friend and law school classmate Charles Mathias, by then a four-term congressman. Such articles also suggested that in heavily Democratic Maryland, a Republican could win only if the candidate was strong, if the Democrat was weak, and if a spoiler joined the race.

"Throw in a George Mahoney just for good measure," one local newspaper helpfully suggested.[442]

Hampered by drink and distracted by his renewed romance with Bullitt, Brewster had difficulty focusing. He would disappear for days at a time, miss or be late to appointments and appearances, and then, in the times he did show up, almost manically leap from one issue to another. Most of his constituents thought he had been happily married, then suddenly he was divorced and remarried. He had been consistent on policy issues throughout his career but now seemed scattered, in search of positions voters would embrace. At times he flipped from one issue to another, or from one side of an issue to another. For years, he styled himself as someone who considered each issue on its own merits, but then he uncharacteristically sided with the party's young reformers and then almost as quickly portrayed himself as a middle-of-the-road moderate.

To please environmentalists, he pursued measures to protect the Potomac River and C&O Canal, and he engineered a federal land swap that prevented development of the Glen Echo Amusement Park along the Potomac near Cabin John and turned it into a nonprofit arts park. He strongly backed Johnson's strategy in Vietnam, then publicly questioned it, and then almost immediately fell back in line with the administration policy. When young people protested his stance on Vietnam, rather than change his views, he countered by proposing to lower the voting age from twenty-one to eighteen.

To make up for insulting Maryland Jews by being too drunk to speak at the Jewish war bond rally in Pikesville in June 1967, Brewster flew off the very next month on a "fact finding trip" to Israel. There, he immediately called on the US to recognize Israel's right to unify the city of Jerusalem after East Jerusalem was seized during the just ended Six-Day War.[443] He also suggested sending the Israelis more arms, including selling them US-made F-4 Phantom jets.[444]

That same month he also backed Johnson's controversial nomination of Baltimore attorney Thurgood Marshall to become the first African American to sit on the US Supreme Court.

Following the assassinations of King and Robert Kennedy in 1968, Brewster co-sponsored gun registration legislation with Tydings, but almost as soon as he was confronted by rural voters in Hagerstown worried about losing their gun rights, he wavered. He said he opposed any tax on guns or gun registration and said any record keeping should be done only at the local level. Reporters noted that the parking lot where he spoke was full of cars sporting Wallace bumper stickers.[445]

"Danny ticked off a lot of people," said Maurice Wyatt, who, as Brewster's '68 campaign manager, was only too aware of the various factions Brewster had offended.[446]

Mac Mathias labeled Brewster "an ineffectual political weathervane, swinging with the changing winds of public opinion and Johnson administration policies, with no solid position to call his own." Brewster defended himself by saying he was demonstrating flexibility, not vacillation.[447]

"An accumulation of problems has beset Senator Brewster," conceded George S. Wills, head of the Young Democrats of Maryland.[448] His group began searching for an alternative big name candidate who could challenge Brewster in the party primary, perhaps state Senator and Brewster friend Harry R. Hughes or Thomas Hunter Lowe, conservative chair of Maryland's House Judiciary Committee, but neither joined the race.

Behind the scenes of the campaign, Brewster waged a more personal fight. He tried to control his drinking and, with it, his weight, by limiting his intake or going totally on the wagon. Then the effort would lapse, and his drinking would get out of hand again, a bad image for a high-profile public official seeking re-election. Herbert O'Conor III, the namesake son of one of Brewster's close friends and political supporters, said that by 1968, Brewster "was not a vigorous campaigner then. My mother arranged an event—a tea or something—for the Senator, and he failed to appear. I'm sure his alcoholism was at its peak."[449]

Brewster's youngest brother, Walter, recalled attending a campaign event in Westminster in front of a group of farmers he knew from throughout Carroll County. Danny showed up "about an hour and a half late and the room was just packed, and I was hoping he would just not show up. I was there, and I wish I was not there. He was totally drunk. He smiled and shook hands and started his speech, and it was gibberish. It was embarrassing; it was embarrassing! I was just devastated," Walter remembered decades later. "Oh, it was awful. I can't imagine it being any worse."[450]

Part of Brewster's problem was that he no longer was able to rely on Jack Sullivan's trusted guidance in the office. Senator Tydings said he came to believe the situation was actually worse than that—that Sullivan, who was Brewster's exclusive liaison to the Senate Post Office and Civil Service Committee, was somehow pocketing money, either through his official duties or through campaign fund-raising.

"Well, I can tell you from personal experience that Jack always carried a big wad of cash," said Miller, who worked on the staff with Sullivan. "He definitely had a lot of cash, but you don't know what the source was or what the use was."[451]

In Tydings' view, Sullivan "was a crook." "Sullivan was telling people who wanted a post office, he could arrange it with the chairman, and they would pay him some money," Tydings alleged. He said he (Tydings) and Richard Schifter, the prominent chairman of the Democratic Party organization in Montgomery County in suburban Washington, tried to convince Brewster to fire Sullivan. "We sat down with Danny and we said, 'Danny, this is what is happening and you have to get rid of this guy,'" Tydings said. "At this point in his life, Danny was drinking and Jack Sullivan was driving him around at night… and we were worried about Danny and his drinking and this Sullivan thing could explode in his face. We met with him once or twice and said, 'You've got to get rid of this guy,' and he agreed to do it, but he never did it."[452]

Tyler Abell, a Johnson aide who later became friends with Brewster after being appointed as Assistant Postmaster General for Facilities, said the day he met Sullivan, "I remember thinking that Sullivan was the wrong guy in the wrong place. I had an immediate instinct about him."[453]

Those internal problems, however, seemed overshadowed by the opposition to the Vietnam War throughout the country, which seemed to grow stronger with every passing month. Brewster's unbending support for the Johnson administration strategy alienated an increasing number of his longtime supporters. One night in October 1967, an antiwar protester vandalized Brewster's car as it was parked on a DC street, painting "End the War" across the trunk. Brewster complained it took him two hours to scrub off the paint, which made him late to an event in Baltimore honoring two naval reserve units.[454]

In January 1968, the North Vietnamese and Viet Cong unleashed their Tet offensive and more Americans began to question whether they were being told the truth about the war. As the American death toll climbed, many increasingly asked, "When is it going to end?" Unbowed, Brewster called for even more bombing. Mathias, who formally announced his candidacy for Brewster's Senate seat on February 11, said the bombing should stop.

With Johnson's presidency collapsing under the weight of the war, on March 16 Bobby Kennedy announced his intention to challenge the incumbent President of his own party. That bold decision was followed just two weeks later by an even more startling announcement: President Johnson informed a national TV audience that he would not run in the election that, at that point, was just seven months away. Brewster said when he heard Johnson's words as he watched the televised address, "I almost fell off my chair."[455] No Senator could have claimed to be more loyal to Johnson than Daniel B. Brewster of Maryland and no Senator probably depended more on the President's coattails for re-election.

"Danny was relying on Lyndon Johnson running back [for the Presidency]," said Wyatt. "He thought that once Lyndon Johnson was running back, he would have no problem winning re-election. When he didn't run back, that again cut the feet out from under Danny. After getting bitch-slapped by Wallace, now his big boy—who he went to take Wallace on for, who owed him big-time—disappears."[456]

One of Brewster's close Senate friends was Edward Kennedy of Massachusetts. They had lived next door to each other in Washington and both were members of the freshman Senate class of 1962. After LBJ withdrew, the leading Democratic candidates to replace him were Bobby Kennedy and Vice President Hubert H. Humphrey. Brewster quietly told Teddy Kennedy he would like to support his brother for President, and Ted relayed the message to Bobby. Brewster said Bobby called him to thank him and told him that when he got back from a campaign swing through California and Oregon, "We would get together and the two of us would head up the ticket in Maryland."[457]

"I wished him well and, of course, never saw him again," Brewster recalled.[458] The forty-four-year-old Brewster formally announced his own candidacy for re-election on June 3, 1968. Bobby Kennedy, just forty-two, was assassinated in Los Angeles the next day.

By then, it surely must have felt to Brewster as if anything that could go wrong had. Then, in mid-July, with Brewster and Anne living in Washington and his former wife, Carol, on an excursion in Europe, their sons' nanny, who was living at the Brewster's Worthington Farms, threw a party. The next morning, newspapers reported that the nude body of one of the party's guests, a twenty-six-year-old man, was found in the bottom of the backyard swimming pool behind the Brewster farmhouse, the apparent victim of an accidental drowning. The incident had nothing directly to do with Brewster, but it produced yet another embarrassing news story.

In the Capitol, meanwhile, Sullivan appeared to be gradually asserting more responsibility over the operations of Brewster's office—that he was becoming something of a surrogate Senator. White House records indicate that as early as 1966 and stretching through Brewster's final year in the Senate in 1968, Sullivan's name began to pop up almost as frequently as Brewster's for meetings with or inquiries to White House officials. Sullivan even bragged that he could sign Brewster's name so perfectly that it was almost impossible to tell whose signature it was.

As his problems mounted, Brewster's new wife became painfully aware he was in jeopardy of losing re-election and she began to assert herself in the campaign. "She was very opinionated that this should be done and how it should be done," Miller recalled.[459] Wyatt said one of the first things Anne did was to get rid of the beer refrigerator in Brewster's Senate office. Her goal, he said, was to try to keep him sober, at least through the end of the election.

"Anne gets involved and he's coming over [to Baltimore from Washington] and now I'm driving him," Wyatt remembered. "Anne is in the back seat and Danny is up front with me and he reaches into the glove compartment and whips out a bottle of Listerine—and he drinks it! He drinks it before we get to the next stop. And I say, 'Jesus, Danny, don't swallow that stuff. Let me pull over to the side so you can spit it out.' Anne looked at me and said, 'You've got to be kidding, aren't you?' I didn't know her that well. I said, 'That stuff will rot his stomach if he keeps swallowing it.' She says, 'Maurice, it has alcohol in it—he isn't going to spit it out.' That was my first clue not only at how bad [his drinking] was but also how much she knew about it."[460]

"She was strong as hell. Very attractive. And she was Danny's sweetheart, make no mistake about it. She was the first love of his life," Wyatt said. He also said that Anne "hated Sullivan. She knew that Sullivan was undermining him. And she determined to get rid of him. And she just cut him out of the campaign altogether."[461] After that, Wyatt, then only twenty-six, ran the Brewster re-election campaign, although by that point the ship had probably already taken on too much water.

"Jack Sullivan was not around in that campaign. He was in Washington, DC. She and I ran it. I'm not going to tell you he wasn't in Prince George's County doing this or doing that, but I think he knew he bit off more than he could chew with Anne," Wyatt said. With the arrival of Anne, "All of a sudden there was somebody more important to Danny than Jack, and Jack was very important to Danny because he kept everything afloat. Jack would tell him what he had to do."[462]

With both Johnson and Bobby Kennedy out of the presidential race, Humphrey became the favored candidate to win the nomination. To give Brewster's re-election a boost, President Johnson's political team picked him to deliver short opening remarks on national television at the August 1968 Democratic Convention in Chicago to publicly thank Mayor Richard Daley for hosting the event. But while Brewster was inside the convention hall reading his warmly worded speech off the teleprompter, television viewers at home were watching on split screen as Daley's Chicago police were outside the hall brutally beating anti-war protesters with billy clubs. "It was an unmitigated disaster," Brewster later said.[463]

His opponent, Mathias, was a legitimate, experienced, and thought-ful candidate who, after eight years in the House of Representatives, was popular in his mostly rural Western Maryland district. A resident of Frederick, he had lived at Fernwood, the Brewster family home, while both he and Brewster were in law school, and they were so close that Mathias became godfather to Brewster's first son, Dan Jr. Brewster became an usher in Mathias's wedding. Despite anything either of them said in this election, their friendship would last for the remainder of their lives. *Time* magazine described them both as liberals and said, "Both are for civil rights in a state that still clings to many Old South attitudes." It described Brewster as "relatively tough on law and order, while Mathias emphasizes the need to remedy the causes of social disorder."[464]

For months, Brewster refused to believe his old friend would try to unseat him and did not learn it was true until the day Mathias announced. "He was just stunned. I think he was really shocked," Miller remembered.[465] At some point, according to Brewster family lore, Mathias said to him, "Danny, somebody's going to beat you. It might as well be me."

Mathias's subtle but biting campaign slogan was Reason for Change, which captured a growing sentiment among the Maryland electorate. There suddenly seemed to be many reasons for change, not the least of which was Brewster's increasingly public struggle with alcoholism. Dr. Ross Z. Pierpont, a Baltimore physician who unsuccessfully challenged Brewster in that year's September 10 Democratic primary, criticized Brewster's failure to appear at scheduled events and publicly questioned whether the Senator was physically and mentally up to the job. "The health and ability of candidates to discharge their duties is very much the voters' business," Pierpont stated.[466]

Mathias made opposition to the Vietnam War the focus of his campaign, although Brewster complained for years afterward that Mathias never offered a cogent plan for how he would extricate the US from Southeast Asia. Mathias dismissed Brewster as "a mouthpiece" for Johnson and charged that his support for continued bombing of North Vietnam worked against any opportunity for a negotiated peace.

Vietnam "was a factor [in his re-election] because he lost a lot of liberals—and he had already lost the conservatives on civil rights," Miller said.[467]

An even bigger political problem for Brewster, however, was perennial Democratic candidate Mahoney, whose bitterness over Brewster's 1966 election snub prompted him to enter the 1968 Senate race as an independent. It was not that the maverick candidate had any chance of winning, but he had a good chance at siphoning away enough votes from Brewster that Mathias could win in a three-way race. By August, Brewster's own staff estimated that as much as 15 percent of the vote Brewster otherwise might expect was likely to go to Mahoney, either because of his views favoring segregation or as a protest for Brewster's decision not to support him in 1966.

Not long after Brewster and Mathias each easily won their party primaries on September 10 and began to turn their attention to the election's stretch run, Sullivan twice embarrassed Brewster through his mishandling of campaign fund-raising. Perhaps if Brewster's top aide had had more political experience, a more balanced demeanor, or was less controlling, or perhaps if Brewster himself had been more attentive to the nuts and bolts of his own campaign, he might have been spared.

Brewster, said Wyatt, "was by himself, babe. His good friends he grew up in politics with, Bobby Knatz and especially Townsend, the life was taken out of them, too. Sullivan got into all of Danny's relationships. He didn't want anybody near Danny but him."[468]

The first incident came when Sullivan arranged to have a letter soliciting campaign contributions mailed to maritime lobbyists who often had official business before the Senate Merchant Marine and Fisheries Subcommittee on which Brewster served. The letter, signed by Sullivan, was written on the stationery of a Hyattsville campaign organization called Housewives for Brewster, which listed as its treasurer Sullivan's wife, Patricia. Most troubling, the letter asked recipients to mail their checks (for $100-a-seat tickets to a fund-raising dinner with Brewster and Vice President Humphrey) directly to Brewster's Capitol Hill office.

Mathias called the letter "a clear misuse of Senatorial power and a violation of the public trust."[469]

"It won't be Little Red Riding Hood in a gingham apron opening envelopes at the 'Housewives' headquarters in Hyattsville. It will be the big bad wolf, sitting in Senator Brewster's own office on Capitol Hill.... Such a clumsy attempt to pressure an industry should not be tolerated," the Republican challenger said.[470] Brewster stated he was unaware of the letter in advance and agreed contributors should not have been asked to forward money directly to his Senate office. But, he explained, "I cannot control what my friends do."[471]

Two weeks later, Sullivan inadvertently smeared his boss's name a second time by releasing a campaign finance report that appeared to show that the Brewster campaign had been soliciting the Senator's staff and family members for nearly $30,000 in contributions. The donors listed in the report included Brewster himself and his wife, Anne; the Senator's sister and brother; his personal secretary, Ellen Lynch; Baltimore County aide Bobby Knatz; the father of another secretary in his office; Maurice Wyatt and even Wyatt's father, Joseph. One $1,000 contribution was listed as coming from Penny Bank, an office receptionist who was said to earn $5,000 a year. The report also showed $7,500 in donations from Housewives for Brewster, plus money from Patricia Sullivan, from her father in New York, and from her brother-in-law in Nevada. It even showed that the Sullivan's apparently precocious son, five-year-old Tim Sullivan, had contributed $1,000 to the re-election of Daniel B. Brewster.[472]

Brewster did not defend the report but said, "I have instructed anybody who works for me to be absolutely meticulous in money matters, and that if they are not, they'll be fired."[473]

With just two weeks to go before the election, the *Washington Post* followed with a critical editorial that stated that federal law prohibited members of Congress from directly or indirectly soliciting or receiving contributions for political purposes from employees and that to do so was punishable by a fine of not more than $5,000 or imprisonment for not more than three years, or both. It said Brewster's acknowledgment that "employees in his office 'all pitched in to help the boss' seems close to a confession that he has done what the law forbids."[474]

Because Brewster hated to ask people for money, he left the unsavory task of fund-raising almost completely to Sullivan, and he may have had minimal knowledge about who was donating to his campaign, how the money was being handled, or whether required reports were accurate. Months after the 1968 Senate election was over, newspapers revealed that the report Sullivan prepared that listed Brewster staff employees and family members as donors had been falsified—although it is not clear why—and that at least $14,000 of the money attributed to employees and relatives actually was raised legitimately at an October 1967 dinner in Baltimore sponsored by the AFL-CIO that featured an endorsement of Brewster by Vice President Humphrey. The event was commemorated with a photograph of Brewster and Humphrey, both in their tuxedos and smiling as they flanked Anne, who was wearing an eye-catching dress with zig-zag patterns across her shoulders and down the sleeves and a large black bow at the bodice.

Anne, profiled earlier in the campaign as part of a survey of candidates' wives, was described as "ebullient" and "equally at ease explaining her horse breeding business in Ireland to veterinary students and telling Maryland voters how her husband stands on gun legislation…Green eyed with longish dark hair, the picture of an Irish colleen…"[475]

Probably the most effective strategy Brewster employed in that 1968 campaign was to maximize political support through the influence he could exert as a member of the Senate Post Office and Civil Service Committee. This was a strategy he had been using throughout his six years in the Senate and it involved supporting pay raises, benefits, and better working conditions for postal employees, in particular, and government employees, in general, and pushing for construction, expansion, or renovation of local post office buildings in scores of Maryland towns and cities, small and large. Hardly a month passed by without a press release announcing an expansion of the post office in Cumberland, a new branch post office in Pikesville, or similar facilities in Frederick, Edgewood, Lonaconing, or elsewhere.

He also began awarding a Citation for Excellence to individual post offices—for Salisbury, Lusby, Cumberland, Brunswick, Olney, Silver Spring, Rockville, Jessup, Germantown, Boyds, and others. Almost every citation was accompanied by a picture of the local postmaster standing next to the state's senior Senator, which was then sent to, and usually printed in, the local newspaper.

Working with Sullivan, who understood the political power of labor unions, Brewster endeared himself to the various unions representing letter carriers and postal clerks as well as non-postal government unions.

Government employees were affected by and interested in the work of the Post Office and Civil Service Committee and its Subcommittee on Health Benefits and Life Insurance, which Brewster chaired. He and others in Congress pushed the Johnson administration for a pay raise for postal workers that conveniently went into effect July 1, 1968, just months before Brewster stood for re-election.

"In those days, government employees could only get raises if Congress passed a statute authorizing it," recalled Tyler Abell, the former Assistant Postmaster General. "And the [union of] Letter Carriers [was] always very successful getting that sort of legislation passed."[476]

Brewster's office announced that between 1963 and 1968, the Post Office Department had authorized ninety-eight new post office improvement projects in Baltimore and eighteen Maryland counties, almost all of them new construction.[477]

"That was good because in those days the post offices were the center of communities," said Miller, who handled both legislation and press relations for Brewster.[478]

Anne and Danny Brewster had their photograph snapped with Postmaster General Marvin Watson. And when Brewster had to cancel an appearance before the Auxiliary to the National Association of Postal Supervisors in Baltimore because he was called away to a hurriedly scheduled event with Humphrey, he dispatched his mother, Ottolie Cochran, to speak on his behalf. A briefing memo prepared for Mrs. Cochran said, "The Senator is very popular among postal workers. Has worked hard to better their lot. They realize this and are appreciative." The memo added that postal unions were responsible for making seven thousand phone calls on Brewster's behalf and stuffing campaign material into six thousand envelopes.[479]

Nine days before the election, Frank DeFilippo, the political reporter for the *Baltimore News American*, wrote a lengthy pre-election analysis that said despite all his problems—"notably his shift on the gun control issue, his slithering around the Vietnam war debate, and his campaign contribution list"—Brewster could still somehow win. "Brewster made an amazing political recovery and is now regarded by odds-maker[s] as a favorite to retain his seat," DeFilippo wrote.[480]

Vice President Humphrey and Senators Abraham Ribicoff of Connecticut, Edmund Muskie of Maine, and Teddy Kennedy of Massachusetts were among the big-name national figures who came to Maryland to stump for Brewster. Voters, however, agreed with Mathias that there was "reason for change." On November 5, Mathias unseated Daniel B. Brewster by a margin of 98,226 votes, taking 48 percent of the votes to Brewster's 39 percent. As predicted, Mahoney was the spoiler, winning 13 percent of the vote. If all of Mahoney's 148,467 votes had been combined with Brewster's 443,667, Brewster would have won, although who knows if that would have happened if Mahoney had not been in the race.

"Mahoney screwed things up for everybody every time he got involved in anything," said Senator Tydings, speaking from personal experience. In various elections over the years, Mahoney had opposed him, opposed his father, and opposed his mother.[481]

"George P. Mahoney probably wouldn't feel comfortable with the title of 'Mr. Republican,' but he has earned it," the *Washington Post* wrote in a post-election analysis. "The perennial Democratic candidate, who became an independent for one more fling this year, has done more than any other political figure to bring Maryland Republicans to prominence."[482]

Mathias himself conceded the point. "If it hadn't been for Mahoney, there might well have been Democratic loyalty and a Democrat might have prevailed," he said in later years. "I suspect most (votes) for George were Democrats—that was where his base was. He was sore at [Brewster]."[483]

The Mathias victory was impressive. The Republican won in twenty-one of Maryland's twenty-three counties (all but two rural Southern Maryland counties, Charles and St. Mary's) and clobbered Brewster in the populous Washington suburbs of Montgomery and Prince George's Counties. He even defeated Brewster in his home of Baltimore County by 35,602 votes.

Humphrey carried Maryland, but nationally he lost the presidency to Republican Richard Nixon and his surprise running mate and new right-wing attack dog, Maryland Governor Spiro Agnew.

Chapter 16

PALMERSTOWN HOUSE

Maurice Wyatt tells a story that seems to capture the post-election state of mind of both Anne and Danny Brewster.

Wyatt, the manager of Brewster's final campaign, said that in early spring 1969, several months after Brewster left the Senate, Anne was to host an evening dinner party in Washington. Brewster was at his mother's farm in Baltimore County after attending a local horse race but was so drunk his mother did not want him to drive himself home to Washington. She asked Wyatt, who was nearly twenty years Brewster's junior, if he would drive Danny home, saying, "I think he will get in the car with you—he likes you."[484]

Brewster refused at first but, with the help of two farmhands, was finally loaded into the car where he promptly nodded off and slept during the long trip into DC. By the time this was happening, Wyatt had landed a job on the Governor's staff and was driving an unmarked state police car, which he was nervous about taking into DC, especially with an unpredictable drunk in the front seat. Wyatt said he parked the car in front of the Brewsters' stately California Street house and went around the car to help Brewster up a couple steps and through an iron gate. At that point, Brewster—several inches taller and close to one hundred pounds heavier than Wyatt—pulled the young aide to the right side of the interior courtyard, where there was a handrail on the wall he could hold onto. The two stumbled together up a couple more steps and then turned left toward the front door. That's when Brewster announced, "You know, I haven't had a good fight in a long time," and without further warning powerfully slugged Wyatt in the shoulder, swinging so hard that Brewster fell down and Wyatt was knocked backwards and nearly off his feet. To keep from falling, Wyatt said he grabbed the front door knocker as he was going by and it rapped a couple times.[485]

"I come back to try to pick him up and as we both meet at the door, [Anne] opens the door. He says [to her], 'When I finish with him, you're next.' And with that, she has a derringer in her goddamn hand—a derringer in her goddamn hand! It comes out in her hand and she says, 'You son of a bitch, you get upstairs and you get sober before our guests come. You raise your hand to me and I'll blow your goddamn brains out!' All I said was, 'Goodbye.' True story. He was one strong son of a bitch."[486]

Brewster's loss came in his unlucky thirteenth election after twelve straight victories over eighteen years. It not only ended his political career but also did little for his new marriage to Anne Bullitt, suddenly the wife of a *former* United States Senator. At age forty-five, she was now on her fourth husband, none of whom seemed capable of measuring up to the standard set—at least in her mind—by her idolized late father, Ambassador William Christian Bullitt.

Not long after, Anne packed her belongings and returned to Palmerstown House, her Irish stud farm and estate in the emerald green, rolling horse country in County Kildare just west of Dublin. Danny stayed back in the States, opened a shell law office in Washington, and cast about for what to do next.

One of Brewster's allies during his '68 campaign had been Maryland House Speaker Marvin Mandel, who in that election year also served as chairman of the state Democratic Party. After Nixon and Agnew won, Agnew resigned his post as Governor after serving only two years so he could be sworn in as Vice President. There was no Lieutenant Governor in Maryland in those days, so Maryland's General Assembly selected one of its own—Speaker Mandel—to succeed Agnew as Governor. By March 1969, Brewster began showing up at Mandel's office in the Annapolis State House, apparently hoping to land the job as party chairman that the new Governor was vacating.

When asked why he was at the State House, Brewster, slightly embarrassed, replied that he just wanted "to be a worker in the vineyards of the party." But those who saw him in Annapolis in those days said he looked little like the remarkably handsome Senator from central casting that most Maryland voters had observed for nearly two decades.[487]

"Gone was the trim, youthful senator of 44 who had campaigned so strenuously through the long summer and unseasonably hot fall of 1968," wrote *Washington Post* reporter Peter A. Jay. "In his place, seven months after Rep. Charles McC. Mathias defeated him for the Senate seat, was an old man of 45, heavier than before with puffy, red-lined cheeks and the springy sureness gone from his step." Mandel, when asked about the appointment, said, "Anything could be possible," but Brewster never got the job. [488]

He tried to land a position in a law firm with Clark Clifford, the well-known establishment figure who had worked for Presidents Truman and Kennedy and was Lyndon Johnson's last defense secretary. But Clifford wrote back saying his firm, Clifford, Warnke, Glass, McIlwain & Finney, was not currently expanding.[489] Brewster also sent his resume to Robert D. Murphy, chairman of the board of Corning Glass International, but Murphy—without ever specifically mentioning the Nixon victory the previous November—replied, "I believe there is at this time sentiment that deserving Republicans enjoy a certain priority. I know you fully understand the problem."[490]

"He had nobody, brother," Wyatt explained. "Think about it. He had every reason in the world to enjoy life, and he was the loneliest son of a bitch you ever met in your life. He had nobody. Carol and the family were in Baltimore County. This guy is in DC rolling the dice with the big boys. That's no life. Booze was his life."[491]

By summer, the Brewsters sold their California Street home in Washington to the Brazilian government as a residence for their ambassador. Then, in mid-July, about nine months after he lost his Senate seat, Danny Brewster entertained an idea that people who knew him probably would have found unthinkable: selling Worthington Farms. It was more than just his home for the past fifteen years; it was also his farming and horse breeding operation and the site of the annual Maryland Hunt Cup, the premier steeplechase race within the horse country culture that had permeated his life since birth. But Brewster's marriage to Carol was over and she had moved to another house with their two boys. Anne had already fled the country for Ireland. He had quit riding, and drinking continued to interfere with his life. Now a new problem had surfaced: he was apparently under investigation by federal prosecutors in Baltimore who had convened a grand jury that, among an array of other subjects, was looking into Brewster's congressional financial records. As a result, on top of everything else, Brewster began to accumulate legal bills and needed money to pay them.

To initiate the sale, Brewster and his lawyers gathered at Snow Hill, the hilltop estate immediately across Tufton Avenue that looks down toward Worthington Farms. It was the home of Nancy "Nannie" Martin Black, widow of Bill Martin, who had originally sold Worthington Farms to the Brewster newlyweds in 1954. Nannie's new husband, Gary Black, was a descendant of the A. S. Abell family that founded and owned the *Baltimore Sun* and who was then chairman of the newspaper's board. Under the deed to the property, if Brewster decided to sell, his children had the right of first refusal, but in 1969 Dan Jr. was fourteen years old and Gerry was twelve. Obviously, neither boy was in a position to exercise his right of purchase, so the right reverted back to the Martin family and, more specifically, to one of Bill and Nannie Martin's four children, J. W. Y. "Duck" Martin and his wife, Glennie Reynolds Martin, who bought it.

Brewster moved to Ireland soon after, ostensibly to join Anne at Palmerstown House where she still managed a large stable of thoroughbred race horses, which grazed on tree-lined pastures reminiscent of the horse country in the Baltimore County valleys where Brewster had lived most of his life. Palmerstown is a large, handsome, historic two-story house, sturdily built of stone in a style described as "enlightened Queen Anne" architecture, with tall windows and an ornamental stone railing bordering the roof. The house was erected on the ancestral land of the family of Mayo in memory of the statesman Richard Southwell Bourke, who had been the sixth Earl of Mayo and fourth Viceroy of India. It was built at government expense in his honor in 1872 after he was assassinated while visiting a convict settlement in the Andaman Islands in the Bay of Bengal while serving as Viceroy. Above doorways at each end of the building are dedications to Bourke inscribed in the stone.

By the time Brewster arrived from America, his drinking was out of control. Danielle Brewster Oster, a daughter born years later to Brewster's third wife, said she was told by her father that when he arrived at Palmerstown, he considered himself an accomplished rider. But she said the people who ran Anne's stables saw "a fat Senator [who was] unfit" and put him on a strong horse that he could not control. "He couldn't hold the horse. It was like a big joke," she said.[492]

On August 26, 1969, following what one doctor later described as "an excessive intake of alcoholic beverages," Anne had Brewster committed to an Irish mental hospital where doctors concluded he was suffering from "confusion, disorientation and loss of memory."[493]

Embarrassed by his election loss, utterly estranged from Anne, out of touch with his former wife and his two boys, marooned in a country not his own, and mostly disconnected from other family or friends, Brewster would remain all but incarcerated in a series of Irish hospitals for the next seven months—from August 1969 through March 1970. The alcohol had taken a serious toll on his health, but his Irish doctors compounded the problem by treating him with tranquilizing drugs that nearly killed him and left him in an emotionless stupor for months.

Back home in Baltimore, the chief federal prosecutor for Maryland, US Attorney Stephen H. Sachs,[19] publicly confirmed that a special grand

---

19. Stephen H. Sachs was an Assistant US Attorney for Maryland from 1961 to 1964; US Attorney for Maryland from 1967 to 1970; elected Attorney General of Maryland in 1978 and reelected in 1982. He was an unsuccessful candidate to be the Democratic nominee for Governor of Maryland in 1986. During his public and private careers, he prosecuted in 1968 the Catonsville Nine protestors during the Vietnam War; represented FBI Director L. Patrick Gray during the Watergate scandal; and represented Dr. Elizabeth Morgan in a well-publicized international child custody case in 1989 and 1990. He died Jan. 12, 2022, at the age of 87.

jury was inquiring into possible violations of federal bribery laws by members of Congress and others. Among those whose names were implicated in the growing scandal were Brewster, Louisiana Senator Russell Long, and Victor Frenkil, head of a politically connected Maryland construction firm, Baltimore Contractors, Inc. The allegations being leaked to the press suggested Frenkil might have tried to bribe Brewster, Long, and perhaps others to help him recoup from the federal government an estimated $388,666 in cost overruns that Baltimore Contractors claimed to have incurred under a federal contract to build an underground parking garage for the Rayburn House Office Building.[494] Long, son of the legendary Louisiana Governor Huey Long, defended himself and said of his fellow Senator, "In my judgment, Dan Brewster is a scrupulously honest man."[495]

Interviewed in Baton Rouge, Louisiana, Long went further. He said the damning accusations came from "a former employee of Brewster's who had turned on his boss in an effort to protect himself from allegations of mishandling Brewster campaign funds." To anyone who knew Brewster or Brewster's staff, the clear implication from Long was that the allegations against the two US Senators emanated from Jack Sullivan, although Long never identified him by name.

Senator Long, the *Washington Post* reported, predicted that "at the end of the grand jury investigation it will be known that the man who made the allegation is a thief, trying to divert attention from his conduct and trying to confuse the issue by what he did with the money that went into his boss' campaign fund.

"This person cannot support charges he had made against me," Long said. "Whether he can support some of the charges against his boss, I don't know. That's a different thing."[496]

Stories about the grand jury's various inquiries began to leak. One suggested the panel was looking into whether Brewster or other members of Congress received illegal campaign contributions from the Seafarers' International Union. Another suggested he and as many as nine other members of Congress may have received contributions or other payments under the table in exchange for introducing individual pieces of legislation that would delay deportation of specific Chinese sailors who had jumped ship in the hope of remaining in the US. There was no question Brewster authored seventy-five such bills over a seven-month period, but he defended himself by saying he introduced the measures because it was impossible for his staff to investigate each Chinese sailor's case. His goal, he said, was to let the Senate Judiciary Committee staff conduct its own follow-up reviews. After the practice was questioned, an investigative committee headed by Senator John C. Stennis of Mississippi cleared Brewster and three other Senators of wrongdoing but said that the lawyers and lobbyists who brought the Chinese sailor cases to members of Congress should be investigated.

In early September 1969, the *New York Times* broke a story that the federal grand jury in Maryland was reviewing contributions made to Brewster's 1968 re-election campaign by Cyrus T. Anderson, the Washington lobbyist for the big Chicago mail-order firm Spiegel, Inc. Spiegel was interested in keeping postage rates low for third-class mail, such as advertising catalogs, and Brewster sat on the Post Office and Civil Service Committee that had jurisdiction over such matters. Anderson told the *Times* he "had arranged his personal contributions to Mr. Brewster's campaign through John F. Sullivan," adding that Sullivan, Brewster's exclusive staff liaison to the Post Office Committee, "handled all the financial transactions in the campaign."[497]

"I wanted to help a fellow who had carried the flag against George Wallace in the 1964 Maryland primary and who was up for re-election in 1968. There's nothing wrong with contributions—they're part of the political process," Anderson said when asked about the matter.[498]

The *Times* reported its attempts to contact Brewster failed because, it was told, he was "sailing off the coast of Ireland," when, in fact, he was hospitalized. The *Times* also said it could not reach Sullivan, whom it said, "is understood to have been a major source of information before the Grand Jury."[499]

There was a certain irony in Steve Sachs's pursuit of Danny Brewster.

Sachs had been appointed US Attorney for Maryland in 1967 largely through the efforts of Brewster's Senate colleague, Joe Tydings, although unquestionably with Brewster's acquiescence. Before being elected to the Senate, Tydings had also served as the chief federal prosecutor for Maryland and he had hired Sachs to be one of his office's Assistant US Attorneys. The two worked together and became close, making a name for themselves in an office that successfully prosecuted high-ranking elected officials, including convicting on savings and loan fraud charges two members of Congress—Democrats Thomas F. Johnson of Maryland and Frank W. Boykin of Alabama—as well as Brewster's old law partner, A. Gordon Boone, who at the time was Speaker of the Maryland House of Delegates. Just as Tydings had parlayed his reputation as US Attorney for a seat in the Senate, so Sachs harbored his own political ambitions. (He later was twice elected as Maryland's Attorney General and was an unsuccessful candidate for the state's Democratic gubernatorial nomination in 1986.) Sachs and Brewster had met a couple times, including a perfunctory lunch at the Valley Inn, a Baltimore County eatery, prior to Sachs's appointment being finalized, but otherwise they barely knew each other.

In Ireland, meanwhile, far from sailing off the coast, Brewster was struggling. Doctors cut back his drug treatments and he suffered a relapse. "I regret to say that the good progress which Mr. Brewster had manifested three weeks ago has not been maintained and that on the other hand he had a somewhat serious set-back," a Dublin doctor named John Dunne wrote to Anne at Palmerstown in November. "While I have hopes that he will eventually be restored to his normal health, I am of the opinion that this will not take place for a considerable time, some months at least."[500] So concerned were his physicians that Brewster was temporarily transferred to a different hospital to test whether he might have a brain tumor.

While suffering in this serious condition, Brewster, the World War II hero and onetime Golden Boy of Maryland Politics, received word on December 2, 1969, that he had been indicted a day earlier in Washington for allegedly soliciting and accepting $24,500 in bribes from Spiegel to influence his vote. A telegram arrived at Palmerstown Stud that said, "Associated Press would welcome your comments on federal indictment returned Monday. Stop. Appreciate you phone London at [phone number]—Associated Press."[501]

Anne delivered a statement to a *Baltimore Sun* reporter later that morning. "My husband is a patient undergoing tests in the neurosurgical unit of an Irish hospital. He is seriously ill. But he is most anxious to return to America to answer and refute the charges that have been brought against him, and will do so as soon as he is well enough."[502] She declined to identify the hospital or the nature of her husband's illness.

In November, Brewster's legal case was transferred from Baltimore to the federal court in Washington, although Sachs and two of his assistants were authorized to continue to serve as special prosecutors there. Brewster was to be arraigned on December 12, but because he was hospitalized, prosecutors agreed to a request by his lawyer, Norman P. Ramsey, for a thirty-day delay. Sachs questioned whether Brewster was really hospitalized or even in Ireland and said the Department of Justice would conduct its own investigation if Brewster did not appear within the thirty-day extension. Thomas A. Flannery, the US Attorney for Washington, DC, threatened to use the US extradition treaty with Ireland, if necessary. Cyrus Anderson and Spiegel, meanwhile, pleaded innocent.

By then, Brewster's doctors had discontinued the tranquilizing drugs and moved him to yet another Dublin area hospital. "He is moderately severely depressed and shows practically no emotional reaction to his present situation," concluded one of a number of different doctors who examined him.[503] Brewster's brother, Andre, briefly visited him and showed him a copy of the indictment.

An English doctor, K. Davison, examined Brewster and reported that Brewster told him that for the past two or three years—a third to a half of his term in the US Senate—he had been drinking huge amounts of alcohol virtually every day: "2 bottles of spirits, 5 bottles of wine, or 20 pints of beer a day." As a result, Davison said, Brewster experienced amnesia for most of his heaviest bouts of drinking and he said Anne had observed "a change of personality in that he is now dependent, apathetic, lacking in spontaneity and incisiveness."[504]

A few days before Christmas, Anne made a quick return trip to Washington to sort out a dispute over furnishings sold along with the California Street house. She briefly visited with Danny's other brother, Walter, left him some orchids as a Christmas present, and returned to Ireland. On Christmas Day, Anne brought her husband home to Palmerstown for the holiday but then returned him to the hospital.

"It gives me happiness and strength to think of you—thus I write this letter. It also helps put the awful loneliness out of my mind. Again, I thank you for Christmas day. It was wonderful to be at Palmerstown," Brewster wrote to her five days later. "I do miss you something terrible. I just wish there were some way I could show my love and thank you for all you have done."[505]

The boredom and monotony of his prolonged hospital confinement began to wear on him. A visit or a telephone call meant the world to Brewster, but Anne's calls were infrequent and her visits even more so. She telephoned him on New Year's Day, and the following day Brewster wrote her how happy that had made him and how it had cheered him up. "When you have been lonely and in the hospital as long as I have been, little things mean a lot. Please continue to give me a call from time to time." He had apparently discussed with Anne the need to write down anything he could remember about Sullivan and the dealings with Spiegel and the lobbyist Cy Anderson but said, "The trouble is that my knowledge is very limited and I had practically no contact with Anderson or Spiegel."[506]

In February, Brewster received a letter from his former wife, Carol, who told him how "desperately sorry" she was to hear he was so ill. "As for the charges that have been brought against you, the people with whom I have come in contact do not believe them to be true. Nor do I. I have explained this to the boys," she said of Dan Jr. and Gerry and then filled him in on the boys' grades, sports, travel, and other activities. "In your letter you mentioned good years and bad years we had together—mistakes made. I can only say the good brought happiness, the bad [brought] experience. Mistakes made yesterday should not be today's sorrow, but tomorrow's knowledge."[507]

Brewster also began to realize—possibly for the first time—that Sullivan had turned on him. This was a man he had hired, promoted, befriended, and trusted, but Brewster had never seen the potential treachery others in Brewster's orbit saw. Brewster trusted few people as much as he trusted Ellen Turnbull Lynch, his personal secretary for years and sister of his original law partner, John Grason Turnbull. Sometime around Christmas 1969, Brewster asked Lynch in a letter if she could imagine Sullivan turning against him.

"You ask if I can imagine Jack Sullivan is 'very much against' you. Of course I can, as can anyone who knows him," Lynch wrote him back. "It was a sorry day when he was pawned off on you, and in my opinion, and in the opinions of those who have spoken to me, he is the source of most of the difficulties. You were honest, guileless and trusting. I steered as clear of him as I could, as I felt he was not trustworthy from the start. I do want to reassure you that your friends are not oblivious to his character."[508]

What Brewster had no way of knowing at the time was that Sullivan and Sullivan's attorney, Herbert J. "Jack" Miller, a former head of the Criminal Division in the US Justice Department when Bobby Kennedy was Attorney General, had been secretly meeting with federal prosecutors since May 1969, including at least two meetings held in rooms at the International Hotel at Friendship International Airport (which, today, is known as Baltimore-Washington Thurgood Marshall International Airport). Sullivan by then was under suspicion of doing precisely what Senator Tydings had heard he was doing—selling at least one local post office job to a man with the unlikely name of Ronald Reagan in exchange for a $1,000 bribe. Miller's goal was to protect his client, so he negotiated with Sachs a request to a federal judge for a grant of immunity from prosecution in exchange for Sullivan's willingness to testify against his former friend and boss, US Senator Daniel B. Brewster.[20]

"Miller sold us Sullivan, to put it crudely," Sachs later admitted. "Dealing up was the way these cases were made. No matter how they came to you, you squeezed the little guy. We used to make jokes about an escutcheon in the office"—essentially, a coat of arms—"with faux Latin, 'Dealum Upem.'"[509]

Sachs said his office had begun to investigate payoffs related to the leasing of post offices. "We called post office employees to the Grand Jury and one of those guys said he got the job because he paid off Jack Sullivan. He dealt with Sullivan."[510]

Sullivan, under oath before the federal grand jury in Baltimore, was later asked why he had agreed to become a government witness. "I heard through the grapevine that Mr. Reagan had claimed he had paid a thousand-dollar payoff for his job and that the FBI or the United States Attorney's office was in the process of maybe indicting me or convicting me for selling jobs or the Senator selling jobs with me as his go-between," Sullivan testified. "I talked with my wife and we made a decision that—with five young children and I am 34 years of age—where are we going to go if we get indicted? We got a problem and then we thought that maybe the right thing to do was just to tell the Government what's been going on."[511]

Oblivious to all of this, Brewster reported to Anne from his hospital bed that he had written down everything he could remember about "the Spiegel, Anderson, Sullivan affair." Although the hospital where Brewster was confined was probably only a little more than an hour's drive from Palmerstown, Anne rarely made the trip. In January, she attributed her absence to having the flu. Brewster, meanwhile, seemed to be improving, saying on January 5, "I feel perfectly well and find it hard to believe that

---

20. During his long legal career, Herbert J. "Jack" Miller Jr. dealt with an array of famous people. As head of the Justice Department's Criminal Division, he successfully prosecuted Teamsters President Jimmy Hoffa as well as Bobby Baker, an aide and fixer for Lyndon Johnson in the Senate. Miller later represented former President Richard Nixon and brokered the pardon granted him by President Gerald Ford despite its implication of guilt. He also represented Senator Edward M. Kennedy, D-MA, after a woman drowned when his car plunged off a bridge on Chappaquiddick Island. Miller lived on a 200-acre farm in Boyds, MD, remained married to his wife for sixty-one years, and died in 2009 at the age of eighty-five.

I should be in the hospital." He said a mutual friend had visited the hospital and taken him for a drive through old Dublin to alleviate the boredom. "Do call me from time to time. It is wonderful to hear your voice and cheers me up greatly," he wrote his wife.[512]

One day about two weeks later he took a long walk from the hospital and, in his solitude, discovered a small road that led down to the sea and "a barren lonely beach where I stood and watched the water for a long time."[513] As he did so, he told Anne in a letter, the words of a poem by Alfred, Lord Tennyson that he had learned at St. Paul's School came back to him: "Break, break, break on thy cold gray shores, Oh sea; I wish that my heart could utter the thoughts that arise in me."[21]

"There's so much I would like to have done with you," he sadly wrote to Anne. "Remember when I gave you the little silver football at St. Paul's and the circular pin at Fernwood? In a way, this all seems like yesterday and yet so much has happened since then. We had a few really good days together, but somehow I was never able to make you happy. God, how I wish life would give me another chance, but the past is lost and today, the future seems less than bright. All I seem to have brought you, my love, is sadness and trouble. How sorry I am."[514]

As he reflected on his legal problems, Brewster seemed to find the situation unfathomable. "Through all my years in politics, I was always personally absolutely honest. I knew many who were not, and today I find myself in this mess. It seems inconceivable. I am really at rock bottom," he confided to Anne in a letter that clearly neither he nor she ever expected would be read by others or made public.[515]

In mid-January, Brewster's arraignment in federal court was postponed for a second time, which prompted Sachs to dispatch to Ireland an American neurologist from Columbia University, Dr. H. Houston Merritt, to determine how sick Brewster really was and report back. Merritt, accompanied by three other doctors, spent two days examining Brewster at St. Gabriel's Hospital in Cabinteely, southeast of Dublin,

---

21. "Break, Break, Break," a poem by Alfred, Lord Tennyson, written in 1835 and published in 1842. The words of the first stanza are, "Break, break, break, On thy cold gray stones, O Sea! And I would that my tongue could utter The thoughts that arise in me."

and studying his records, and then met with Anne. Merritt concluded Brewster did not have a brain tumor but was so ill that he may have suffered "organic brain damage."[516] As a result of his report, Brewster's trial was postponed indefinitely.

"I do not believe that in his present mental condition Mr. Brewster is competent to understand fully the charges against him or that he is able to assist his counsel in the effective preparation of his defense," Merritt wrote in his report. "He knows he is accused of accepting bribes but states that the money he accepted was given to aid his campaign for re-election and that he would like to return to the United States to clear his name."[517]

"The patient had been using alcohol in moderate or excessive amounts for some years. There had been some personality changes in the latter months of his tenure as a Senator with loss of initiative and blunting of emotional reactions," Dr. Merritt reported. "After his failure to achieve re-election, he apparently increased his [intake of] alcoholic beverages, mainly champagne and beer, but occasionally more potent alcoholic beverages in amount as great as 4/5 quart a day."[518]

Brewster's life at the hospital, Merritt said, "is a monotonous one. One day is the same as another. He sits in his room all day except for occasional walks around hospital grounds or the local neighborhood. He has no visitors except his physician. His wife had not visited between Christmas and the day of my visit because of a recent attack of 'flu.' He does not read newspapers or any of the many books which have been sent him by his wife. He listens to the television occasionally but does not keep up with current events. His business interests are carried on by his brothers and all legal matters are conducted by his wife."[519]

While Merritt was in Ireland examining Brewster, lawyers for Spiegel and its lobbyist, Anderson, were already in court in Washington making pre-trial motions, one of which publicly identified for the first time Jack Sullivan as the government's key witness. The Spiegel and Anderson attorneys emphasized that the only person other than Brewster and Anderson who was present for any conversations about any alleged bribe was Sullivan. That is, it was his word against theirs.[520]

At some point that winter, Brewster's youngest brother, Walter, was sent by the family to see how Danny was doing—"Did he still exist, or what?" Walter Brewster said.[521] He arrived at Palmerstown and had a late-night dinner with Anne in the house's large central hall. This fancy room featured double doors at one end, a grand staircase at the other framed by white Ionic columns, a fireplace off to one side, and a ceiling that opened to a large, circular rooftop skylight from which a chandelier hung at the level of the second-floor balcony that surrounded the rectangular room on all four sides. High on a wall just outside the central hall were sixteen curlicue bells arrayed in two lines, a remnant of the days when they were used to summon servants to various rooms throughout the house.

After dinner, Walter said, he was taken to a second-floor bedroom where, for some unknown reason, he believes he was locked in his room for the night. He rejoined Anne for breakfast but was told they would have to wait another day before they could see Danny. He said Anne was nice to him and he remembered being impressed by the large number of staff at the house and stud farm, including an in-house veterinarian and an in-house blacksmith. When he and Anne finally got to the hospital the following day, Walter said he was surprised that it was not a typical hospital but rather a "sanatorium… where crazy people are."[522]

"We were in just a little tiny room. It was Danny and Anne and I think two doctors," whom he said wore white smocks. "How are you?" Walter asked his big brother. "Fine," Danny replied in a monotone. "It was a very stilted conversation. I'm squirming just thinking about it. I was not comfortable. I don't think Anne and Danny spoke [and] I don't think she would have let me be in there without [her] being there." The next day Walter Brewster flew back to Maryland. "All I could come back and say is, 'I saw him. He talked. I think he was heavily sedated,' and that was all I could say about it."[523]

Despite his many problems—the loss of his Senate seat and the end of his political career, his prolonged hospitalization and health setbacks from alcoholism, and now his serious legal challenges in

Washington—Brewster's letters reveal his one overriding, almost uncontrollable obsession: his love for Anne Bullitt. He ended one missive to Anne, for example, by saying, "Thus we come to the only purpose to this letter, and that is to simply say, I absolutely adore you."[524]

"After all that has past, I know that you find it difficult to believe me when I say how much I care for you," he wrote to her on February 1. "Now don't laugh at me or throw this letter down—I do love you very much and miss you terribly.... One of the awful uncertainties of my life is not knowing where I stand with you. It has been ages since we talked." He concluded the love letter by saying, "I loved and lost in 1943 and life gave me another chance—God how I hope all is not lost.... Can't you just write or say that you still love me? This miserable business in America will pass, and there will be time for happiness. This letter is being written by a lonely and loving husband—give me a chance."[525]

Back in the States, however, Steve Sachs was doing his best to make the "miserable business in America" even worse for Brewster. In March, he asked the Department of Justice to allow him to let the federal grand jury indict Senators Brewster and Long, Louisiana Congressman Hale Boggs, and contractor Victor Frenkil in connection with the dispute over the cost overruns for building the underground garage for the Rayburn House Office Building. But the Justice Department refused to allow it, saying the case was weak because the charges were based exclusively on the testimony of a single witness, Jack Sullivan.

Sachs, decades later, said he believed the real reason the Justice Department refused to allow the indictments was that Attorney General John Mitchell did not want to charge two high-ranking members of Congress with whom the Nixon administration had to work. Long was chairman of the Senate Finance Committee and Boggs was the House Majority Whip. Sachs said he met personally with Mitchell in the Attorney General's office and can still remember him with his head in his hands, puffing his pipe and saying, essentially, "Steve, you're doing what you think is your job and I understand that and I respect that, but I've got a country to run. The chairman of the Senate Finance Committee and the Majority Whip in the House of Representatives are people we have to deal with, and Steve, you have to understand that."[526]

The grand jury became so unhappy with Mitchell's decision that it tried to force the issue by making an unorthodox "presentment" of the case it had developed—essentially, trying to make public the unsigned indictment—by delivering it to federal Judge Rozell Thomsen in Baltimore. By the time this happened, Sachs had resigned on June 1 to go into private practice and left the case to others. Thomsen refused to interfere with the Justice Department decision. Sachs's successor as US Attorney, George Beall, reviewed the proposed indictment and agreed with Sachs, but his renewed request to Attorney General Mitchell was likewise rebuffed. With that, the new set of proposed indictments against Brewster, Long, Boggs, and Frenkil finally died.[527]

As the dispute over the proposed indictments and the grand jury's presentment played out in court and the newspapers, the *Baltimore Sun* published a Sunday opinion piece that accused Attorney General Mitchell of blocking the prosecution of Southern legislators as part of the Nixon administration's broader "Southern Strategy."

"The uncontrolled discretion of the Justice Department to prosecute some but let others go free, without justification or explanation, when in both cases the grand jury has returned an indictment, may be an irresponsible erosion of the American doctrine of equality before the law," wrote Ronald M. Shapiro and Steven L. Barrett. "Although the congressmen in question are Democrats, their role as Southern political leaders would seem to make them an integral part of the Republican-Southern Democratic collation upon which the current administration builds its power base. For if prosecutions can be prevented, and grand jury findings can be buried, the public interest in honest and competent public service will be left unprotected."[528]

By then, Danny Brewster had finally been released from the hospital in Ireland and had flown home where he was briefly admitted for observation at the Johns Hopkins Hospital in Baltimore and given essentially a clean bill of health. "They tested me in every conceivable way and found absolutely nothing wrong," Brewster exuberantly wrote Anne on April 12.[529]

He felt good enough to attend the My Lady's Manor steeplechase race and reported that he "saw hundreds of my old acquaintances. All greeted me warmly. I was a little gun-shy at first, but everything went smoothly. No press, I am glad to report."[530]

His arrival home came just in time to participate in the pre-trial motions for his high-profile bribery case.

Chapter 17

SIX RUINOUS YEARS

From the December day in 1969 when he was indicted as he lingered alone in an Irish hospital, the criminal trials of Danny Brewster dragged on for six excruciating, ruinous years. They began when he was forty-six years old and ended when he was fifty-one. Related legal problems, in fact, continued even longer.

Nearly a full year after he was indicted, his case headed to the US Supreme Court to resolve a Constitutional challenge of whether Brewster could be prosecuted at all for a vote he had taken in his official capacity as a sitting member of Congress. The charges against him also brought into question whether the self-acknowledged alcoholic knew what was going on in his own office and in his own re-election campaign or whether he was blinded by his drinking to the improprieties of others—that he may not have seen it or understood it, even if he was in the room. While the ultimate responsibility for the actions of his high office rested with him, a reasonable case can be made that his drunkenness made it easy for others—such as his chief of staff and possibly federal prosecutors as well—to take advantage of him.

The charges against him begged the question of why the scion of a wealthy family, who had disclosed during his 1968 campaign that he was worth more than a million dollars and also was the beneficiary of a $1.4 million family trust, would debase himself and threaten his reputation and career for the comparative pittance of $24,500 in bribes spread over two years.

There was the further incongruity of observing this big, rich white guy—who as a young man had donned the brightly colored racing silks of a steeplechase rider, who as a Senator had risked his political future by supporting civil rights and standing against the segregationist George Wallace, and who had befriended two American Presidents, Kennedy and Johnson—standing trial in front of a panel of twelve African American women selected from the jury pool of the District of Columbia. Several potential jurors who were either male or white or both were excused after peremptory challenges from government and defense lawyers alike. There is little question that for a jury in a major criminal trial to be composed of twelve African American women was virtually unprecedented, then and now, but in this case even the six alternates chosen in case one or more of the jurors had to be replaced were also all African American women.[531]

"It would be neither racism nor snobbism if Danny Brewster finds a gentle irony in the phrase 'a jury of his peers,'" intoned *Baltimore Sun* opinion writer Theo Lippman Jr. "For there are probably no two worlds as different in America as that he comes from—exurban hunt country, top level politics, international society, old wealth, the best schools—and the 12 members of his jury represent—urban, black, low-paying jobs."[532]

As a member of the Senate Post Office and Civil Service Committee, Dan Brewster had spent virtually his entire Senate career vigorously supporting postal workers and advocating for low postal rates, which he believed would increase the volume of mail and thus make postal employees more necessary and therefore better paid. Yet he was charged with accepting bribes during the final two years of his six-year Senate term as if he suddenly had decided to demand payment before he would continue that support. Here was a Marine hero from World War II, who was wounded multiple times defending his country, who was elected and re-elected by his fellow citizens in a dozen elections, and who, during nearly two decades in the public eye, had earned a reputation for honesty and integrity, suddenly accused of accepting a payoff in exchange for his vote—all on the word of a single accuser, his former top aide, John F. Sullivan. Sullivan's own credibility and honesty was questioned by almost everyone with whom he had come into close contact. He was a man who had agreed to point his finger at Brewster only after being granted immunity from prosecution for his own wrongdoing.

"I never thought he was very trustworthy," W. Shepherdson Abell, who had served on Brewster's staff, said of Sullivan in a comment typical of what others who knew Sullivan said about him. "And I thought that when Danny was charged with stuff later on, it was Sullivan's doing."[533]

The highs and lows of Brewster's trial years were cruel. He happily saw the legal case against him quickly dismissed, only to watch as a helpless observer as it was reinstated by the nation's highest court. Then, following a trial that played out daily for nearly three weeks on the front pages of big city newspapers across the country, he was convicted, fined, and sentenced to serve years in prison. He walked out of the courtroom in disbelief with his shattered, sixteen-year-old son, Gerry, at his side. Then, after another long, agonizing wait and after resuming his embrace of alcohol, Brewster's case was thrown out a second time on appeal and it seemed like his nightmare was over. Yet, after all of that, after being thoroughly disgraced and drained of his wealth and some five years after being removed by voters from the Senate and no longer posing a political threat to anyone, the Republican administration in Washington decided to go after Danny Brewster one more time.

Over the course of his trials, among those who came to testify in his defense to speak of his honesty and integrity were his wife of thirteen years, whom he had divorced in 1967, the Republican who defeated him for his Senate seat in 1968, and Dan Brewster himself.

It was not until the spring of 1970, after he was released from the Johns Hopkins Hospital, that Brewster appeared for the first time in US District Court in Washington. On May 22, he declared he had "regained his health and [was] competent to prepare" for his trial. Four days later, he pleaded not guilty to the charges against him.[534]

In one pretrial skirmish, Brewster's lawyers tried to prevent the introduction of evidence based on documents they said Sullivan had stolen from Brewster's home in late May 1969. It later was revealed that during a June 24, 1969, meeting with prosecutors and FBI agents at a Friendship Airport motel, Sullivan's lawyer, Jack Miller, took US Attorney Stephen H. Sachs aside and the two of them briefly left the motel room so Miller could privately disclose to Sachs that Sullivan had entered Brewster's California Street house without Brewster's knowledge or permission and made copies of certain Brewster appointment diaries. In a filing with the court about three months later, government lawyers denied that any of their evidence was obtained unconstitutionally. "Miller was told not to give any such documents to any representatives of the government and, to this very day, no Government representative has ever seen the materials in question—not first hand, anyway," asserted Alan I. Baron, Sachs's deputy.[535]

Despite this incident and allegations against their primary witness, Sachs later said he found Sullivan to be trustworthy. "Oh, yeah. If he was lying, he gets an Academy Award."[536]

But Brewster's lawyers moved to have the case dismissed before the trial could begin because they said the government's allegations rested totally on the "uncorroborated testimony" of a single witness—Sullivan—who may himself have had "a hand in the till." They derided Sullivan as "possibly a thief, a gambler and a receiver of bribe money." William O. Bittman, attorney for Spiegel, said it was possible that some or all of the cash Spiegel donated to Brewster's re-election campaign ended up in Sullivan's pocket. Similarly, Sheldon Bernstein, attorney for the Spiegel lobbyist, Cyrus Anderson, said, "We submit [Sullivan] had his hand in the honey pot somewhere and when caught with honey on his hand, he decided to tell a story" that implicated Brewster, Spiegel, and Anderson.[537]

Baron countered by saying the trial was not about Sullivan's credibility but Brewster's and that of the other two defendants.[538] Both he and Sullivan's attorney, Miller, denied that Sullivan had agreed to cooperate in order to avoid prosecution himself. They dismissed suggestions that Sullivan had pocketed campaign money as nothing more than defense attorney "hunches."[539]

Brewster's lawyers hinted that they were considering two possible defense strategies. One would claim that even if the alleged bribe offers occurred, which they denied, Brewster could be excused from any criminal liability because his alcohol-induced mental disabilities, as documented in Ireland by Dr. Merritt, the court-appointed physician, may well have been present at the time of the alleged transactions. Brewster told his lawyers he wanted no part of this approach because he did not want to use his alcoholism as an excuse for his behavior, which he believed to have been honest.

The second strategy was more straightforward: simply to contend that as a Senator, Brewster could not be prosecuted under the US Constitution's Speech and Debate Clause, which his lawyers said protected members of Congress from prosecution for anything said on the floor of the House or Senate, including their votes.[22]

Baron, Sachs's deputy, argued before US District Judge George L. Hart Jr. that the Speech and Debate Clause was never intended to shield members of Congress who accepted bribes. "Your Honor, I refuse to believe that election to the Congress of the United States is the equivalent of a license to steal. I cannot believe that that is the message of the Speech and Debate Clause."[540]

"No one can doubt the validity of a policy which is intended to protect a Senator or Congressman from civil or criminal liability for his 'legislative acts,' and to the extent that the Speech and Debate Clause still affords that protection, I think it serves an extremely important service," Baron said. "But I submit… that the public has to have confidence in the integrity of the legislative process and that criminal sanctions for bribery, conflict of interest activities on the part of Congressmen, are necessary to protect the integrity of that process and that the Federal Judiciary is the appropriate forum in which to try any such cases."[541]

Judge Hart disagreed and quickly concluded that the Speech and Debate Clause "shields [Brewster] from any prosecution for alleged

---

22. The Speech and Debate Clause is found in the US Constitution, Article I, Section 6.1, and states that except for cases of treason, felony, or breach of peace, "for any Speech or Debate in either House they [i.e., Senators and Representatives] shall not be questioned in any other Place."

bribery to perform a legislative act" and dismissed the case. He based his decision "particularly" on his reading of a recent case involving Maryland Congressman Thomas F. Johnson, whose conviction in a savings and loan fraud case had been overturned by the US Supreme Court specifically due to the Speech and Debate Clause.

Congressman Johnson had been prosecuted, ironically enough, by Brewster's Senate colleague Joseph D. Tydings. At the time, Tydings was US Attorney for Maryland, Steve Sachs was one of his assistants, and the two of them received guidance on the Johnson case from Jack Miller, who then headed the Criminal Division of the US Justice Department. Sachs said that is when he and Miller—by now, Sullivan's lawyer— became chummy.

Congressman Johnson and three co-defendants were convicted in 1963 on eight counts each, including conspiracy to defraud the public of the fair and impartial services of House members. Johnson was sentenced to prison and fined. On appeal, however, the Supreme Court, in a 7-0 opinion in 1966, concluded that under the Constitution, only the House of Representatives could punish Johnson for his conduct on the floor of the House. By then, Tydings had been elected to the Senate and Sachs had become US Attorney, so Sachs tried Johnson a second time on all of the previous charges except the one having to do with a speech Johnson had given on the House floor. The former Congressman was convicted again and sent to prison.

Although Judge Hart said he was relying on the high court's verdict in the Johnson case, he urged an immediate appeal of his decision in the Brewster case to the US Supreme Court so it could rule on the application of the Speech and Debate Clause anew.[23] The difference, however, was that Brewster, unlike Johnson, was indicted under a bribery law revised in 1962, which expressly covered the behavior of members of Congress.[542]

Reporters, looking for comment from Brewster on the case dismissal,

23. The Speech and Debate Clause of the Constitution traces back to the English Bill of Rights, adopted in 1688 to protect members of Parliament from criminal or civil charges from a king who might want to punish them for their legislative actions.

described him as "in seclusion" at his mother's farm in Baltimore County. But, according to one story, "people familiar with the case [say] Brewster has again taken to drinking."[543]

That is when the waiting began. The Justice Department quickly asked the Supreme Court to review Judge Hart's October 10, 1970, decision to dismiss the case, but it wasn't until March 1971 that the high court agreed to review it and not until October 1971—a full year after Hart's decision—that the Justices actually heard oral arguments.

Brewster, stuck in seemingly interminable legal limbo, began to disintegrate. He was still married to Anne, but she was in Ireland and essentially out of his life. His two teenage boys were in separate schools and he had only limited contact with either. He had no job—his only income was from his trust—and his legal bills were draining him. He purchased a modest house on a wooded lot at the end of Longnecker Road in the horse country north of Glyndon and moved in with his old friend and former Administrative Assistant Billy Townsend, where the two men spent many of their days together drinking.

In January 1972, a Maryland state trooper saw Brewster's car weaving, pulled him over, and charged him with driving while intoxicated. Because he refused to take a breath test, his license was suspended for thirty days. Six weeks later he pleaded guilty to a lesser charge of driving while impaired and was fined $200.[544] Just two weeks after that, during a visit to Key West, Florida, he was charged with reckless driving and had to pay a fine of $275, plus $1,000 in attorney's fees.[545] In late June, Maryland State Police again arrested him, this time at one fifteen in the morning on the Baltimore Beltway where he was driving thirty-five miles per hour in a sixty mile-per-hour zone, and charged him with drunk driving. He admitted drinking four or five glasses of wine at a testimonial dinner followed by a glass of bourbon and water but again refused to take a breath test and later was found guilty and fined $220.[546]

While everyone waited for the Supreme Court to hear and decide Brewster's case, Jack Sullivan encountered his own new set of problems with the law. After Brewster left the Senate, Sullivan was hired to be the administrator of a national law fraternity, Delta Theta Phi. In July 1971, the muckraking journalist Jack Anderson broke a story that said the fraternity had discovered it had some $20,000 in unpaid bills. Sullivan and another fraternity official were summoned to meet with a high-ranking fraternity official in Chicago and were asked to bring with them Delta Theta Phi's financial books. When they got to Friendship Airport for the flight, however, they decided the books were too bulky and left them in Sullivan's car. When they returned from Chicago, the car had been stolen. It was found two days later, but a box of invoices had mysteriously disappeared. The fraternity immediately ordered an audit and suspended Sullivan from his job.[547]

Thirteen months later, a jury in Calvert County, Maryland, concluded that Sullivan had boosted his own pay by forging checks to take money from the fraternity and awarded Delta Theta Phi a $9,000 judgment against him.[548] Prince George's County prosecutors, meanwhile, filed criminal charges against Sullivan for misappropriating fraternity funds, and in January 1974, the former top aide to Senator Daniel B. Brewster pleaded guilty to diverting to himself as much as $46,878 by illegally drafting checks from the fraternity's treasury. A month later, Jack Sullivan was sentenced to two years in jail with all but six months suspended.[549] Unfortunately for Brewster, Sullivan's 1974 conviction came well after he testified against Brewster in court.

On June 29, 1972, about twenty months after Judge Hart dismissed Brewster's case, the US Supreme Court ruled, 6-3, that, in the words of Chief Justice Warren Burger, accepting an illegal bribe is "obviously, no part of the legislative process or function; it is not a legislative act. It is not, by any conceivable interpretation, an act performed as part of or even incidental to the role of a legislator." He added that, "There is no need for the government to show that [Brewster] fulfilled the alleged illegal bargain; acceptance of the bribe is the violation of the statute, not performance of the illegal promise."[550] (The dissenters, Justices William J. Brennan, Byron White, and William O. Douglas, said they believed Congress was the appropriate body to discipline Congressmen, not the courts.) The Supreme Court remanded Brewster's case to Judge Hart's courtroom for a new trial, which finally opened on October 30, 1972, in Washington, nearly three years after Brewster was originally indicted in 1969.

Sullivan, then thirty-seven and not yet in trouble for stealing money from the legal fraternity, took the stand on the trial's second day and testified that Brewster was paid $19,500 in cash and checks by Spiegel lobbyist Cy Anderson and, in return, Brewster promised to do all he could to help the Chicago mail-order firm, which opposed a Johnson administration proposal to raise third-class mail rates. Brewster opposed the increase on third-class mail rates in committee and on the floor but ultimately voted to support the bill after an effort to return the legislation to committee for new amendments failed.

During the trial, Anderson, a lobbyist who represented clients in addition to Spiegel, said he routinely kept $25,000 in cash in his office safe and gave thousands of dollars in cash to many Senators and Representatives, often in amounts that exceeded campaign limits. He called the practice widespread and "an integral part of the American political system."[551]

In those years, there was a certain level of cynicism—which some would say was well-deserved—that almost all politicians were crooked.

"I was sensitive to the idea that there was a lot of cash being passed around," recalled Frederic B. Hill, a reporter who covered the trial for the *Baltimore Sun*. "There was Watergate and then this zoning stuff and a lot of cash being given," he said, referring to then contemporaneous stories about cash payoffs being made by Maryland contractors to the Baltimore County executive in conjunction with zoning issues. It was this scandal that soon expanded to reveal that Vice President Spiro Agnew had been among those public officials who had accepted kickbacks, which led to his prosecution and resignation. Hill said that when he heard Spiegel lobbyist Cy Anderson "talk about $5,000 or $7,500, or whatever, being given to Sullivan in cash, rather than check, it had to add to the suspicion that it was bribery and not a campaign contribution."[552]

It was shown that it was Sullivan who decided to deposit the Spiegel donations into a heretofore secret fund called the DC Committee for Maryland Education. The committee, which had nothing whatever to do with Maryland education, had been set up in 1966 on the advice of Brewster's friend Senator Vance Hartke of Indiana precisely because campaign committees established in Washington, DC, were not required by law to report on or disclose who provided donations or how the money was spent. Hartke, then chairman of the Democratic Senatorial Campaign Committee, told Brewster that a number of US Senators had set up similar committees in DC for that reason. Brewster later admitted he liked the system because it allowed him to accept early contributions and make early campaign expenditures without having to formally, publicly, or prematurely announce his candidacy for re-election.

Norman Ramsey, Brewster's attorney, tried to show that most of the disputed contributions ended up in Sullivan's personal account, but on cross-examination Sullivan claimed he took the money only as reimbursement for campaign loans or expenses.

Brewster friends outside the courtroom who knew both men did not believe that story. "I don't think Danny would have taken a bribe," said former Assistant Postmaster General and Brewster friend Tyler Abell, "but Sullivan would have taken a bribe."[553]

To Brewster's astonishment, Sullivan also testified that he had no recollection of Brewster supporting lower postal rates even though Sullivan had been his primary staff to the Post Office and Civil Service Committee for six years. Brewster's support for postal workers was hard to dispute. He first began lobbying to build or expand post offices in Maryland when he was in the House of Representatives. As a Senator, he worked on pay raises and retirement benefits for postal workers, met with postal unions, and listened as private sector printers repeatedly urged him to do what he could to keep rates low for third-class mail, such as the mail-order catalogs and other advertisements they produced.

Brewster captured his position on third-class mail in a 1964 speech before an association of third-class mail users. "The Post Office

Department would find itself in far better shape if it leaned more upon the wisdom of people like yourselves, instead of trying to run you out of business through the imposition of extortionary [*sic*] postage rates," he told his audience. "The business users of the mail constitute an essential and extremely valuable segment of our economy. You are responsible for five million jobs. You are responsible for selling more than $30 billion worth of goods and services each year. And I am convinced that you pay at least your proper share of the cost of operating the postal service. I am not so convinced that this is true of those who have been your most persistent and bitter detractors."[554]

Without third-class mail, Brewster asserted, "The American economy would suffer substantial injury. The Postal Service itself would be far less efficient. You are pouring about $600 million into postal revenues every year, which would be almost completely lost if third class mail were destroyed or crippled. Thousands of postal employees would have to be removed from the roles and forced to join the ranks of the unemployed. Postal costs would rise so sharply that the price of first-class stamps would become prohibitive. And a quarter of a million small businessmen around the nation would be deprived of the most effective advertising tool they have—and one of the few advertising tools that they can afford to use."[555]

Over the years, Brewster regularly backed up this position with similarly worded letters to the editor defending so-called junk mail and through his votes to keep postal rates from rising. "The Post Office Department would practically collapse without third-class mail," he said in a Senate speech in 1967.[556] In January 1969, just as Brewster was about to leave the Senate for good, Postmaster General W. Marvin Watson, who had sometimes appeared at Brewster campaign events, presented him with a Distinguished Public Service Award "in grateful acknowledgment of services in the interest of a better postal system for the nation." A couple years before that, the National Association of Letter Carriers acknowledged the Senator's multi-faceted support for the postal industry by proclaiming him an unrivaled "Postal Champion."[557]

"I think I established myself as their spokesman and, gosh knows they certainly supported me," Brewster testified at his trial about postal workers.[558]

Sachs, the prosecutor, said he didn't buy it, arguing that Brewster's overt support for the Post Office "didn't come from Jehovah. You have to ask… was he born with a passion for lower postal rates, or does it come out of some initial arrangement with Spiegel?"[559]

Some trial testimony focused on the question of whether Sullivan, due to Brewster's struggles with alcoholism, had inserted himself as a surrogate Senator. Sullivan acknowledged that he could mimic Brewster's signature and signed Brewster's name to outbound office mail, but defense lawyers questioned whether he might also have signed Brewster's name to obtain campaign loans or make other deals without the Senator's knowledge. Sullivan maintained that he and Brewster split fund-raising chores, to which Brewster "winced in apparent disbelief at Sullivan's answer."[560] That claim did not even square with Sullivan's sworn grand jury testimony in which he said, "I was normally the only one in our operation that would contact anyone for money."[561] Years later, commenting on Sullivan's statement, Brewster explained, "I personally found fund-raising difficult, obnoxious and demeaning and only asked for [money from] friends on rare occasions."[562]

"Jack was always the one who handled money—political wheeling, dealing—and he handled the Post Office and Civil Service Committee, which was excluded from what the legislative assistants did," Bill Miller said. "It was that way from the start." One of Sullivan's political tasks, he said, was to help the Senator appoint people to be local postmasters.[563]

Miller had another reason to be suspicious of Sullivan. The first time Miller learned Brewster was under investigation came in early 1969 when Miller was subpoenaed to appear before the special grand jury in Baltimore. His first reaction, he said, was to call Sullivan to ask what this was all about. Sullivan told him, "'Gee, I don't know anything about that. After you go there, let me know what they say because this is the first I've heard of it.' That was obviously not true."[564]

The prosecution opened its case by calling to the stand bookkeepers who described the pattern of Spiegel contributions. Sullivan and a woman named Betsey Norton, however, were the prosecution's primary witnesses. Norton, who was said to have had an affair with lobbyist Cy Anderson, testified that she had been present when bribes that Spiegel was considering giving to Brewster were discussed by Anderson and Modie J. Spiegel, the mail-order firm's board chairman. Defense lawyers tried to discredit Norton by portraying her as Anderson's jilted and revengeful former lover.

The prosecution also tried to paint Brewster as someone in need of a bribe because he was close to personal financial ruin, but Brewster's own accountant disputed this claim. He testified to the Senator's wealth and implied he was rich enough that he had no need to solicit or accept bribes.

Then, on the eighth day of the trial, the defense attorneys called their star witness, Daniel B. Brewster, who defended himself on the stand for nearly five hours. Speaking in a clear, loud, and emphatic voice, Brewster acknowledged that Anderson had given money to his campaign but insisted they were contributions, not bribes. "My position was long established that I favored low cost mails and it seemed perfectly natural to me for a lobbyist for a company like Spiegel, that wanted to keep low rates, to make a contribution to my political campaign," Brewster testified in front of a packed courtroom that included his brother Andre and his son Gerry.[565]

On the stand, Brewster recounted his experiences as a Marine and his early years in politics and spoke candidly about his drinking problem. When asked about the bribery allegations made by Sullivan, he replied, "Rubbish, never!" He admitted that the DC Committee for Maryland Education was, in fact, just a political committee. "Education had no more to do with it than the price of eggs. It was just a name," he candidly said. He recalled Sullivan twice telling him about donations he received from Anderson and said each time he told his aide, "Good, take it down and deposit it in the account." He denied ever receiving an envelope with cash in it from Anderson and denied he ever gave Sullivan authority to withdraw money from the campaign account. Brewster said for years he had "completely trusted" Sullivan, even though "valued" staff members had warned him that Sullivan was "hurting me politically." He said Sullivan always convinced him that the other staffers were simply jealous.[566]

"Senator," Brewster's attorney, Norman Ramsey, asked him, "in your entire career in politics, have you ever agreed to sell your vote or to be influenced or affected for money?" Brewster replied, "Never in my entire career, Sir." Asked if he agreed to be influenced on his vote by Anderson or Spiegel, he said, "I never did."[567]

Under continued questioning from Ramsey clearly aimed at impugning Sullivan's truthfulness, Brewster said he now belatedly realized that some stories Sullivan had told him were simply not true. He said Sullivan had "bragged about" playing basketball on the 1960 US Olympic team in Rome that was led by Jerry West and Oscar Robertson and that he later played professionally for the New York Knickerbockers but that both of these stories turned out to be "absolute untruths."[568] While Sullivan never played with the Olympic team in Rome, it was true that he was one of twelve alternates for the Olympic team, chosen in case one of the players got sick or injured.[569] When he graduated from Mount St. Mary's College in Emmitsburg, Maryland, in 1957, he was drafted to play professionally by the Philadelphia Warriors of the National Basketball Association but instead went into the Marines and waited until 1961 before playing a single season with the Washington Tapers of the newly formed American Basketball League. Sullivan also stated in his official staff biography that he had been a member of the US Secret Service and, when he died in 2010, his obituary claimed he had been on duty for the Secret Service at the Kennedy compound in Hyannis Port, Massachusetts, on the same day in November 1963 that President Kennedy was assassinated in Dallas. In fact, according to Congressional staff records, Sullivan was employed full-time on Brewster's staff on that date. The US Secret Service responded to a Freedom of Information Act inquiry by saying it was "unable to identify records related" to Sullivan.[570]

A parade of character witnesses followed Brewster to the stand, starting with his former wife, Carol Brewster, who spoke of his honesty and reaffirmed his consistent support for low postal rates. Then the man who defeated him in 1968, his longtime friend, Republican Senator Charles McC. Mathias Jr., testified that he had no question about Brewster's "moral character" and attributed Brewster's political fall to the ravages of alcoholism.[571]

Other character witnesses included former Maryland Representative George H. Fallon who said, "I've known him for a long time [and] I can vouch for his honesty and integrity in any matter," and Ellery B. Woodworth, a legislative assistant on Brewster's staff, who testified that he and others on the staff considered Sullivan untrustworthy. That characterization was echoed by Ellen Turnbull Lynch, Brewster's personal secretary. General Edwin Warfield, Adjutant General of the Maryland National Guard and a friend of Brewster's since childhood, spoke of the former Senator's "lifelong reputation for honesty." Other defense witnesses characterized Sullivan as a man "who would rather lie than tell the truth."[572]

During the three-week trial, Brewster stayed at the Mayflower Hotel in Washington where he shared a suite with his son Gerry, who had taken a leave of absence from the Gilman School to attend the entire trial, and his son Dan Jr., who was in school in Rhode Island and therefore only able to attend part of the trial. On the Sunday night following the trial's second, pressure-filled week, Brewster and Gerry visited a cousin who lived in Georgetown, but Brewster was so upset he suddenly left the house. Gerry said he was sure his father was in search of a drink and he worried Brewster would be in no shape to be in court at nine the following morning. So the teenager followed his father for about ten blocks through the dark streets of Georgetown when, suddenly, his father turned back and said to him, "Son, don't follow me. Go back to [your cousin's]. I want to be alone."[573]

Gerry said he was devastated to be dismissed like that by his father, so he called Norman Ramsey to alert him that his father may be on a binge and might not make it to court in the morning. Ramsey replied, "Gerry, thanks for telling me. You go home and I'll take care of it." In the morning, Brewster had returned and was in court on time.[574]

By the time the case reached its end, Spiegel had separately pleaded guilty and been fined $20,000. Charges that Brewster had accepted $24,500 in bribes from Anderson had been reduced to an allegation that he accepted three different payments during 1967 totaling $14,500. Judge Hart, in his instructions to the jury, told them they could find both defendants guilty, one guilty and the other not guilty, or both not guilty. He also offered the jurors a new wrinkle, saying that instead of the charge of bribery, the jurors could consider a "lesser, included offense" against Brewster of accepting an unlawful gift or gratuity without corrupt intent, which he said would carry a lighter penalty. "The difference between the greater and lesser offenses is very fine," Judge Hart said, adding that the government did not have to show that an act was actually performed as a result of a bribe, only that an agreement had been made between the parties.[575]

"This offense," Hart said, referring to accepting an illegal gratuity, "differs from and is a lesser included offense of bribery, in that it is not necessary for the Government to prove as an element of the crime of soliciting, seeking, receiving, or agreeing to receive compensation for a gratuity that the defendant did so with corrupt intent to be influenced in the performance of his duty as a public official."[576]

The jury deliberated for four and a half hours on Thursday and another three hours on Friday, November 17, 1972, before announcing their verdict. The jury found Anderson guilty on three counts of giving bribes to Brewster yet convicted Brewster of three counts of the lesser charge of "accepting an illegal gratuity without corrupt intent." The jury also found Brewster innocent of the more serious crime of accepting bribes. No one at the time attempted to reconcile the two different outcomes and sentencing was postponed for three months.

Steve Sachs, the former prosecutor, acknowledged decades later the risks Brewster faced with a jury with such an unusual gender and racial makeup. "I think for black folks in the 'plantation' that was then DC, politicians didn't do them any good. It is not where I would have wanted to be tried. If I was Danny Brewster, I would have wanted to be tried as close to Towson as possible," Sachs said, referring to the Baltimore County seat where Brewster had practiced law.[577]

On leaving the courtroom with his son by his side, Brewster was advised by Ramsey not to say anything inflammatory with post-trial motions still pending. The former Senator simply said, "I'm bitterly disappointed" with the verdict and "this is not the end of the fight."[578] Ramsey said he would file motions for a new trial or, failing that, he would appeal the verdict.

On February 2, 1973, a cold and cloudy day in Washington, former United States Senator Daniel B. Brewster was sentenced to two to six years in prison and fined $30,000. Judge Hart said he was giving Brewster a stiffer sentence because he had "violated a trust placed in him by the people."[579] Spiegel lobbyist Cyrus T. Anderson, who had suffered a heart attack just days after he was convicted in November but nevertheless appeared in court, was sentenced to one and a half to four and a half years in jail for bribing Brewster and also fined $30,000.

Brewster appeared shaken. Prior to his sentence, he read in court a lengthy statement, which said, "Because of my abiding conviction that I have in no way been guilty of any wrongdoing, the verdict of the jury was to me both shocking and disappointing." He added, "I remain of the conviction that I have in no way violated the law and that I intend to take every step within my power to vindicate myself in this matter." Brewster said the government knew full well that many members of the House and Senate maintained fund-raising committees just like the DC Committee for Maryland Education but chose not to prosecute them. Likewise, he said, he could produce a list of twenty members of the Senate and House—"including some of the most respected members of Congress"—who had accepted campaign contributions from Spiegel, but none of them was charged. Brewster declined to share the list publicly, saying he had no desire to embarrass his former colleagues. "But I would argue that if I am guilty of anything, so are all these other men."[580]

This caught the new attention of an old enemy, President Richard M. Nixon. The day after Brewster was sentenced, Nixon—whose conniving voice can still be heard on an Oval Office tape recording now preserved for all time—secretly directed an aide named Charles W. Colson to seize on Brewster's post-conviction remarks and generate new investigations of any Democrat who accepted donations from Spiegel. Nixon made clear to Colson—who over the years performed so many dirty tricks for the President that he would earn the sobriquet "Nixon's Hatchet Man"[581]— that his only interest was to distract reporters, members of Congress, and the American people from the then expanding Watergate scandal that threatened and ultimately toppled his presidency. He specifically said he hoped such an investigation would somehow convince Special Watergate Committee Chairman Sam Ervin, a North Carolina Democrat, to back off his probe.

"Let me suggest another thing," Nixon is recorded saying, "this Brewster thing... runs a hell of a lot deeper and runs to a number of Democratic Senators.... What are we doing about having an investigation, calling in the Speaker, putting him under oath... and saying what other senator [is involved], going right down the list? What are we doing about that?" He directed Colson to get Attorney General Richard Kleindienst and the FBI involved. When Colson commented that not only had Democrats taken money from Spiegel but so had Republicans, Nixon shot back, "I don't give a shit if he was a Republican. I really don't." He made clear he was only interested in going after Democrats. He urged Colson to get investigations launched into Senators Vance Hartke of Indiana, Russell Long of Louisiana, and Joseph Montoya of New Mexico, among other Democrats.[582]

Years later, when Brewster was asked about Nixon, he said, "Of all the men I knew and served with in public life, I consider Richard Nixon the most devious, dishonest, untrustworthy, complicated man I ever had the misfortune to have to work with."[583]

In his pre-sentencing statement in court, Brewster also went after Sullivan, who had gone from chief of staff to chief accuser. He said his former Administrative Assistant had "made the wildest sort of unfounded accusations against innumerable public officials in a statement running over 125 pages in length, yet the prosecutor elected to treat as true charges made against me, although demonstrably false accusations against others… showed the essential nature of the man as an untruthful, self-serving individual."[584]

"Even though the essential evil of the man was known to them," Brewster said of the prosecution's view of Sullivan, "they shielded his wrongdoing and selected me from among the many he accused."[585]

Although Brewster had no way of knowing it at the time, he was only about halfway through his long legal ordeal. No matter how it would turn out, he now would be forever tainted. Gerry Brewster later described the day his father was convicted as "the most devastating day of my life. How could things get much worse?"[586]

In early 1975, before the final act of Danny Brewster's legal drama played out but after Sullivan had been convicted of stealing money from the fraternity that had employed him, *Baltimore Sun* columnist Peter A. Jay said this about the two men:

Sullivan, he said, was "an aggressive wheely-dealy heavy who ran the office when its Senator occupant was hitting the bottle, [and who] is seen by many of those close to the case as the real villain of the piece. That is fine as far as it goes. No one who knows Mr. Brewster thinks he is a thief. But he hired Jack Sullivan, and abdicated his responsibility to keep track of what was going on in his office. Nice guys fall as hard as knaves and reprobates, and probably harder."[587]

Part III

Resurrection:
Sobriety, Farming, Family, and Contentment

Chapter 18

ENOUGH

The central question in the criminal trial of former United States Senator Daniel B. Brewster was this: When is money given to an elected official considered a legal campaign contribution and when is it, instead, an illegal bribe? And, if a jury concludes that money given to a politician was not a bribe, how can it then distinguish between the acceptance of a bona fide campaign contribution and the acceptance of an "illegal gratuity without corrupt intent"?

Even before the verdict in Brewster's trial was handed down, Judge George L. Hart Jr. admitted that "Congress drew a dangerously thin line between illegal gifts and contributions." The federal judge twice said he agreed with Brewster's lawyer, Norman Ramsey, who said that the gratuity provision in the law "exposes every recipient of contributions to prosecution." Ramsey also claimed that if the government intended to prosecute Brewster under that "lesser" provision of accepting an illegal gratuity without corrupt intent, it should have included that charge in its original indictment but did not.[588]

"I think what you're saying, Mr. Ramsey, is that Congress should never have made a law of this nature. I couldn't agree with you more, but they did, and it's not for this court to make that judgment but to apply the law," Judge Hart said, even as he denied all motions for acquittal or a new trial.[589]

Newsweek magazine, in a news brief about Brewster's conviction, summarized the case by saying it could be reduced "to one key question: when is a gift really a bribe?"[590]

"This is all thin stuff," admitted Steve Sachs, Brewster's original prosecutor, whose personal knowledge of campaign finance law came from his two successful elections as Maryland's Attorney General and his unsuccessful race for Governor. "People make the argument that all campaign contributions are bribes. That's not so far-fetched."[591]

The Brewster case refocused the political world in Washington on the ambiguous nature of the nation's campaign finance laws. In an article entitled "The Fine Line Between Contributions and Bribes," *Washington Post* reporter Lawrence Meyer, who had covered the trial, noted that bankers, oil men, Teamsters, steelworkers, labor unions, dairy farmers, publishers, captains of industry, and many others regularly give money to the men and women who make the nation's laws. It is the way the process is set up to work.

"And, assuming they obey the campaign laws and other applicable legislation, make no deals and give or leave no impression that they expect something in return or that the money is a reward for something that has been done or will be done, the law says no wrong has been committed." That, he said, is why Judge Hart could tell the jurors that it was "entirely proper and legal if donors make contributions to legislators *in the hope* that they will continue to maintain general positions agreeable to the donor." Rightly or wrongly, the jury in the Brewster case, Meyer said, "decided something more than 'hope' was involved in Spiegel's payments to the Senator." Meyer went on to say that, "It seems self-evident that the whole point and purpose of making campaign contributions is to put people in office who are inclined to support the contributor's particular interest and to influence them to continue to support it"— precisely Brewster's explanation of why Spiegel contributed money to his campaign.[592]

The Brewster case, Meyer suggested, made it easier to imagine scrapping the existing system of financing political campaigns and replacing it with a system of publicly financed campaigns. "For the harmful effects of the present system are not, as some people imagine, merely the result of abuses by evil politicians who plot and conspire to work against the public interest for money. Rather, they involve ordinary men and women who hold elective offices and want to go on holding them, ordinary people who face temptation and find it occasionally irresistible."[593]

At the time this was going on, a man named Howard E. Shuman was serving as Legislative and Administrative Assistant to two of Brewster's Democratic contemporaries, Senators Paul Douglas of Illinois and William Proxmire of Wisconsin. Fourteen years after Brewster's conviction, Shuman, in a remarkable oral history recorded by the United States Senate Historical Office, singled out the Brewster case as one that "illustrates one of the dangers of working in the Senate. My point is that before you take a job up there, or shortly thereafter, you should have thought through how you would act in a series of difficult ethical situations."[594]

Shuman was familiar with the workings of the Post Office Committee, lobbyist Cy Anderson, and Spiegel's desire to keep postal rates low. "The Post Office Committee was virtually unanimous in the vote on this. They were all for Spiegel. Cy Anderson had given a Spiegel campaign contribution to Dan Brewster. His Administrative Assistant [a reference to Jack Sullivan] took the money and put it in his personal bank account and did not put it into the Senator's campaign fund. When this was found out, the AA claimed he had done this on behalf of the Senator, that it was a bribe to the Senator, and that he had not embezzled the funds. The prosecuting authorities, I think a bit zealous to get a big fish, indicted Brewster and indicted Cy Anderson for giving a bribe." He noted that, at the time, Brewster was "ill," a reference to his alcoholism.[595]

"I don't think there was a bribe. I think it was a legitimate campaign contribution. The vote wasn't needed, it was eight to one or eight to nothing in the committee. It was what I would call legal or 'honest graft,' rather than 'dishonest graft,' if there is a distinction. I say that because I think that legal campaign contributions are out of control. What I'm saying is that it was a questionable ethical act, but not necessarily an illegal act," Shuman said, adding, "I always believed that both Brewster and Cy Anderson were the victims of a man who had done wrong and then dumped on his superior."[596]

Three weeks after the conviction, the *Washington Post* somehow obtained a copy of Brewster's list of twenty Congressmen whom he said had received Spiegel contributions, which totaled about $160,000 between October 1964 and July 1968. Of thirty-four checks Spiegel issued during that period, twenty-one were deposited into DC-based campaign accounts similar to Brewster's DC Committee for Maryland Education but which listed no names of members or former members of Congress. Thirteen other checks went into DC committees linked to individual members or former members of Congress, including $30,000 to Indiana's Senator Vance Hartke.[597]

Fred Hill, the *Sun* reporter who covered the Brewster trial, noted that no Senators or Representatives were among the spectators, but said, "Members of Congress, past and present, must have followed the reports of the trial closely, and some surely must have sighed to themselves, 'There but for the grace of God go I.'"[598]

In late June 1973, Brewster's legal team, by then joined by premier Washington attorney Edward Bennett Williams, appealed his conviction to the US Court of Appeals for the DC Circuit, arguing that Judge Hart had erred when he instructed the jury that instead of the bribery charge for which Brewster had been indicted, they could instead consider the lesser offense of accepting an illegal gratuity without corrupt intent—essentially giving the jury an eleventh-hour opportunity to strike a compromise between rendering a guilty verdict on the serious charge of bribery or finding Brewster innocent and setting him free.

Brewster's legal appeal also said Judge Hart failed to provide adequate guidance to the jury that would have permitted them to distinguish between legal and illegal contributions. "Political contributions to candidates for public office and elected office-holders are and always have been an accepted—indeed, a vital—part of the American political system," Brewster's appeal stated. "Every politician solicits and accepts contributions on the basis of past performance in office and promises of future performance."[599]

"In any event, it is plainly a denial of due process to convict a defendant of a crime with which he was never charged and which there is no evidence to support," Brewster's appeal asserted.[600]

By then—and far away from the accusations against him unfolding in the Washington, DC, courthouse—Brewster discovered that his luck was not all bad. He managed to purchase his mother's beautiful Baltimore County farm, Windy Meadows. His mother, Ottolie Cochran, had shifted to a smaller house in 1970 and, at the time, sold the farm to Brewster's sister, Frances, and her husband, Crompton "Tommy" Smith. Now they, too, had decided to move. As a five-time winner of the Maryland Hunt Cup steeplechase race, Tommy Smith was a local celebrity, but by 1973 he was facing the same debilitating problem with drink that afflicted Brewster and other members of Brewster's family. Frances and Tommy said they would sell the farm for what they had put into it—about $370,000—and, to keep it in the family, they invited Frances's siblings to draw from a deck of playing cards to determine which of them would buy it. High card would win. On the day the new buyer was to be selected, Danny was represented by one of his lawyers, Thomas J. S. Waxter.

"Well, Danny was so drunk he couldn't be there, and Tom Waxter stood in for Danny," remembered Brewster's youngest brother, Walter. He said their sister, Catherine Brewster Jackson, "drew something like the 2 of clubs and I drew the 5 of spades and Danny—or Waxter—got the 7 of something and Danny got the right to buy it."[601]

Over time, Windy Meadows turned out to be a great place for Brewster to live, but in 1973 he found himself dwelling on his problems alone, again waiting for the courts to decide his fate, and again turning to alcohol. Family members remember visiting him and sometimes finding him almost in a booze-induced trance, sometimes sitting in his Marine skivvies and sometimes brandishing the Colt .45 both he and his father had carried in separate world wars.

Gerry Brewster said he cannot recall the precise date, but he remembered driving out to Windy Meadows during those years and pouring all of his father's liquor, beer, and wine down the drain. He said his father might go through five bottles of wine or a case of Budweiser in a single day. "He drank an incredible amount of Bud in cans—that he would chug it down and then crunch the can. I remember Bud as being his smell." The son said his father would pop the breath mints Altoids "morning, noon and night to cover up the smell." For a time while he was still in school at Gilman and later at Princeton, Gerry admitted, he probably drank more than he should have and—like his father—would cover up the smell by sucking on Altoids. "We developed a vocabulary—if you took two Altoids, they were 'Dual-Toids.' If you ran out, you had a 'Toid-Void.'"[602]

In an undated, handwritten letter to his father during those difficult times, the teenager bluntly said, "I was very discouraged to hear that you were drinking again. I guess after the Drunk Farm you were physically sober, but maybe you weren't mentally prepared to stay sober. I don't understand why if you know drinking is bad for you and you know that drinking is ruining your life, you don't stop. I guess you're, as they say, addicted to it. But it seems to me that if you realize your problem, you could stop. I would hope that you could be a man enough to do this for yourself and for others. I and others have so much faith in you, can't you for once make us proud to have that faith? We never leave you and we're always by your side. So, it will constantly be up to you as to when you want to sober up."[603]

In a sad reply, Brewster wrote his son, "Dear Gerry—All I can say is that I am sorry. When a man is drinking, his thoughts are irrational. This is no excuse—just what happens. Someday, you will understand."[604]

In March 1974, Edward Bennett Williams argued before the federal appellate court that Brewster had been unfairly convicted, saying the jury at his trial had acquitted him of bribery, the only crime with which he had been charged, and that he had been denied due process by being convicted of a lesser offense for which he was never charged.[605] Five months later, on August 2, 1974, a three-judge panel of the US Court of Appeals agreed, overturning the conviction and saying that although Judge Hart "strove manfully and judicially to make these fine distinctions for the jury," he had failed to do so.

"We think the whole of it is indigestible," wrote Judge Malcolm R. Wilkey in the unanimous, forty-one-page opinion. "A defendant is entitled to more than a jury room compromise. He is entitled to have his guilt or innocence voted up or down on the clearest possible lines of distinction." He added, "No politician who knows the identity and business interests of his campaign contributors is ever completely devoid of knowledge as to the inspiration behind the donation."[24] Federal prosecutors were left with the choice of whether to appeal the case to the entire nine-member Court of Appeals, appeal it to the US Supreme Court, retry it, or dismiss it.[606]

Brewster, who hoped his ordeal was finally over, told a *Post* reporter, "This is one of the few calls from the press that I haven't minded taking." He said he was trying to straighten out his life, trying to get back into shape, trying to ride horses every morning, and trying to quit drinking. He said with the cloud over his head, he had not been practicing law but hoped to start again. But he said he had no intention of running for public office again and even asked the reporter not to address him by the title "Senator.[607]

"I was a harassed man," but he added that he now had more perspective and inner calm. "Somehow, I'm a much better person. I'm no longer confined by the shackles of ambition."[608] In a separate interview, he admitted, "It's no fun to be convinced of your innocence. After you spent a lifetime in public service to be proud of your record and then to be indicted by the government you fought for on the battlefield." While he spoke, his brother, Andre, arrived with a copy of the appellate court decision, which Brewster had yet to read. The accusations, he said, had "played merry hell" with his life.[609]

Seven days later, Richard Nixon resigned as President to avoid being impeached for crimes related to the Watergate scandal. President Gerald Ford gave him a full pardon the following month.

---

24. Joining Wilkey in the unanimous decision were Judges Edward A. Tamm and Spottswood Robinson. Source: Timothy Robinson, "US Court Overturns Brewster's Conviction," *Washington Post*, Aug. 3, 1974.

Nixon may have been gone, but the Nixon Justice Department that originally indicted Brewster was still there and on January 3, 1975, just over six years after Brewster was originally indicted, government lawyers announced that they would try him yet again in the spring.

"Once the government charges somebody, it is very hard to convince them that it is a mistake," acknowledged Alan Baron, who was the deputy prosecutor against Brewster when his case began in 1969.[610]

Brewster immediately re-hired Edward Bennett Williams to handle the case. In a letter to Williams, along with a $4,000 retainer, Brewster said he knew that Williams did not really know him personally, so he was enclosing a copy of a school paper Gerry Brewster had written about his father's 1964 race against George Wallace, which he said was "well done" and "does give you some insight into my personality and philosophy."[611]

Williams began negotiating with prosecutors to avoid another trial. Despite Brewster's bravado and claims of cutting out drinking, he was still in bad shape and the prospect of yet another trial was almost too much to bear. He was broken, both spiritually and financially. Williams negotiated a plea deal that this time really would end his legal problems, but the stubborn Marine insisted he had done nothing wrong and refused to accept any deal that implied he had. Finally, bowing to days of relentless pressure from his son, his minister, and his closest friends, Danny Brewster reluctantly agreed to end his long legal nightmare by pleading no contest to a single misdemeanor charge of accepting an illegal gratuity without corrupt intent.

On June 25, 1975, Brewster was back before Judge Hart for the final time. He pleaded *nolo contendere*—a plea that is not an admission of guilt but rather means he will not continue to contest the one remaining charge against him. The judge, however, said, "You cannot leave this court unwhipped by justice" and fined him $10,000.[612] In exchange, the government dropped the remaining two counts of accepting unlawful gratuities without corrupt intent.

"I think it is time in this case to cry, 'Enough,'" Judge Hart said.[613]

Despite his plea, Brewster told the court flatly, "I did not accept a bribe. A jury in this very court acquitted me of the charge of bribery. I gave nothing in return for the contribution. I made no bargain whatsoever, and the jury so found. I also did not put the contribution to any personal use. The money was spent for routine office and political purposes. Despite the connotations that may be derived from the gratuity statute, I do not believe that the acceptance of a political contribution from a supporter is a corrupt act."[614]

He added, "This case has dragged on for six years. I have already been through two appeals and one trial. That litigation has taken a heavy toll on my family, friends, and my supporters and on me. No one can bear the burdens of the criminal process for so many years without being depleted in human as well as material resources."[615]

Brewster's friends and longtime political associates—House Speaker Nancy Pelosi, House Majority Leader Steny Hoyer, former Maryland Governor Harry R. Hughes, former US Senator Joseph D. Tydings, and veterans of Brewster's staff—used different words to describe Brewster's legal ordeal, but agreed he was an honest man who had been set up by an unscrupulous aide.

"Anybody familiar with Danny knew that Danny didn't take the money. He didn't need it," said former Governor Hughes, a close friend of Brewster's since their days in the Maryland General Assembly. "Everybody felt it was his aide, Sullivan, who later turned out to be no good."[616]

"He relied too much on other people. He put his trust in them and gave them responsibility and they took advantage of him," Ellen Turnbull Lynch, his personal secretary, said in a 1980 interview. "He is a fine man with too much honesty and integrity to do what he was accused of doing."[617]

Paul Mark Sandler, now a Baltimore attorney who in the 1960s was an intern and driver in Brewster's office, said in his view, "Sullivan abused his authority and power, or took some bribes or something of that nature, and was caught and blamed it on the Senator. That's what I think. Let me say this: as a young man who encountered the Senator in many different facets, it would surprise me if he did anything that was dishonest or corrupt because of the nature of his character and personality."[618]

For his part, Steve Sachs—the former US Attorney who convened the special grand jury that originally indicted Brewster and led the initial prosecution in the case—never abandoned the belief that he had done the right thing by pursuing Brewster and asserted that the case's conclusion proved he was right.

"The toughest decision to make was actual responsibility of [Brewster], given the shape he was in," Sachs said. To not prosecute him, "I would have had to conclude he was an un-functioning robot—at the whim of his [Administrative Assistant]—which some expected. Nobody said he was a stumbling drunk.... We concluded he knew and chose to look the other way. Did he know what Jack Sullivan did in his name? I believe he did know."[619]

"I believed he was guilty of bribery then and I believe he was guilty of bribery now," Sachs said years later, after he had been elected as Maryland's Attorney General, even though Brewster had been found innocent of the charge of bribery.[620]

Sachs said that Norman Ramsey, Brewster's attorney, "believed everything Danny Brewster was charged with was arranged by Sullivan. Sure, Danny was in his cups. But he was the Senator. It is hard to say he gets a pass because of [the actions of] his [Administrative Assistant]."[621]

Maurice Wyatt, who ran Brewster's Baltimore office and later directed his 1968 re-election campaign, said he doubted that is what Sachs really believes deep down. "I know Steve well enough that I think he knows the overreach with Danny Brewster—that Danny was set up. He was a drunkard, and Sullivan was setting him up, and [Sachs] was just too ambitious to say, 'This isn't fair.'"[622]

Bill Miller, who worked on Brewster's Senate staff for the entire six-year term, said, "Steve Sachs was out to make a name for himself with this kind of [case]. I thought that was fairly obvious."[623]

Former US Senator Joe Tydings, who originally hired Sachs to be a federal prosecutor, was instrumental in getting him appointed as US

Attorney, and remained a close friend throughout Tydings' long life, said a few months before he died, "The allegation [against Brewster] could have been wrong. When US Attorneys start going, they throw around a lot of stuff. So Steve Sachs was not infallible, any more than I was."[624]

Brewster simply moved on.

"I gave up. I simply quit," he said of his acceptance of the plea deal. "I had gone through years of pure hell and I was sick and tired of fighting. My health was broken, my career was gone, and I had spent a small fortune in legal fees. I had to call an end to it."[625]

"I wish now I had stayed and fought another round and cleared my name. I didn't. But I still consider myself totally innocent of the charge. I may have been careless about some things, but there was nothing illegal or corrupt in what I did… I never benefited personally."[626]

Chapter 19

SAME MAN BUT A CHANGED MAN

Before he enlisted in the Marine Corps and went off to fight in World War II, young Danny Brewster was a Princeton man. So was Danny's father, as was Danny's next youngest brother, Andre. So it was with a heightened level of family pride and tradition that Danny's son Gerry informed his father in the spring of 1975, prior to graduating from the Gilman School, that he, too, had been accepted at Princeton.

This bit of good news came just weeks before Danny accepted the plea deal that brought an end to his prolonged criminal case. "I am very proud of you both because of your work at Gilman and because of your admission to Princeton," Brewster wrote in a letter to Gerry, who by then had moved away from home and was living with the family of a friend named Peter Parker. "I am sorry that I have not been of more help to you and that my many problems have caused you concern. You have, in fact, helped me far more than I have helped you. I am most grateful."[627]

Thinking that his dad would enjoy a nostalgic return visit to Princeton, Gerry asked his father to drive him to school that fall. Brewster readily agreed. But on the day Gerry showed up at Windy Meadows farm to load his belongings into his father's old station wagon for the trip to New Jersey, he discovered his father unshaven, incoherent, and drunk in bed. At the last moment, Gerry—both embarrassed and distraught by his father's condition—was forced to ask Peter Parker's mother, Gail, to drive him to Princeton and arranged with another Baltimore County family with a daughter headed to Princeton to strap some of his furniture on the roof of their car.[628]

By then, even Brewster's neighbors in the Worthington Valley were worrying about his drinking and his health and began calling Brewster's two brothers, Andre and Walter, pleading with them to do something to help Danny. "They were always on my back, saying we'd have Danny's blood on our hands if we didn't do something about his drinking," Walter recalled.[629]

Around the time Gerry went off to Princeton by himself, Andre and Walter drove out to Windy Meadows to see if they could convince their brother to seek professional help with his alcoholism. When they arrived, they found Danny in his V-neck undershirt and boxers, drunk and lying on a sofa. "We must have talked to him until about eight thirty or so, or even later—an hour or so, and finally Andre said, 'I'm not going to have your blood on my hands—I'm going to have you committed tomorrow,'" Walter remembered but said they were getting nowhere with Danny. He and Andre returned to Andre's house and Walter said, "Andre, let me have one more shot at him," and the youngest brother returned to Windy Meadows.[630]

Walter said that when they had left Danny, the door at Windy Meadows had been unlocked, so when he returned and it seemed to be jammed, he put his shoulder into the door only to realize that Danny had fastened the chain lock. "Well, all the molding up the side and across the top came crashing down. He was on the telephone—who he was talking to, I don't know… he said, 'They're breaking in here! They're breaking in here! They're breaking into my house—I've got to go!' So the molding from around the door was on the floor and I had to step over it. This was probably nine o'clock." Walter said when they resumed the conversation, "He was over on the sofa stretched out and I was over in a chair, and I talked to him and talked to him and talked to him. I said this is not fair to your immediate family, it is not fair to your brothers and sisters, and you're giving us all a hard time. All I want to do is take you up to Hiddenbrook," referring to a treatment center for alcoholics in Harford County about an hour or so northeast of Windy Meadows. "That's when I started believing in the good Lord." Walter remembered raising his voice and almost shouting to his older brother, "I don't know what you want—but you've got to help! For the last time, will you go to Hiddenbrook?' He said yes."[631]

Walter said he found Danny's suitcase, packed it with some clothes, and convinced Danny to get into Walter's car. By the time they arrived at Hiddenbrook, he said it was about two in the morning. He was surprised to see a group of staff congregating on the building's front porch at that hour, but he said they swarmed Danny like a "homecoming party. They were all over him like a wet blanket."[632]

The treatment didn't take right away. Brewster left Hiddenbrook, returned, fell off the wagon a second time, then returned again before he finally began to experience results.

At some point during that rough period, the same motivations that had driven Danny Brewster to become a staunch advocate for civil rights led him into a difficult confrontation with some of his longtime friends and associates at the exclusive Green Spring Valley Hunt Club, a club that dates to the late 1800s and at which Brewster and his extended family had been members for generations. The issue was whether a close friend of Brewster's, Jerold Hoffberger, owner of the National Brewing Company and the Baltimore Orioles baseball team, would be permitted to join the club or be denied membership because he was Jewish. Jews were still targets of discrimination in certain circles in the mid-1970s. At the time, the Hunt Club was divided into two parts: a lower club, which featured tennis, swimming, and golf around a classic old clubhouse, and an upper club that provided stables for horses and was devoted primarily to riding and fox hunting. Hoffberger, who was one of the most prominent Democratic political fund-raisers in Maryland and a staunch supporter of Brewster's career in public office, was also a rider and he kept his horses at the upper club. Because the two clubs were, at that time, under the same governance, the lower club had to approve new members for the upper club. But when Danny Brewster proposed Jerry Hoffberger, the nomination was blackballed by lower club members.

Hoffberger died in 1999, but his son, Richard, clearly remembers the incident. He said his father wasn't so much shocked by the discrimination—there was too much of it then, Richard said, and still too much of it today. But he said, "There was an appreciation of what Danny and his family tried to do."[633]

Brewster reacted to the rejection by going on a bender, becoming so incapacitated he was forced to ask his brother, Walter, to deliver the bad news to Hoffberger in person. "And Jerry Hoffberger was the most fantastic gentleman," Walter recalled. "He said he knew it was very difficult for me to be carrying a message from my brother to him."[634] When this scenario was repeated a second time with the rejection of another prominent applicant who was a friend of Walter's and also happened to be Jewish, in protest Walter permanently resigned from the lower club where he had been a board member and where his wife was a regular on the tennis courts. Eventually, because of these membership disputes, the upper and lower clubs split and the upper club began admitting Jewish members, followed soon thereafter by the lower club.

"One of the proudest things I've ever done," Walter said years later of his decision to resign on principle.[635]

Danny, meanwhile, returned to Hiddenbrook and finally edged toward sobriety. The catalyst for his cure came from an unlikely source: his chance meeting while sharing kitchen duty with another recovering alcoholic, a blonde from Arnold, Maryland, and self-described "partier" named Judy Aarsand. Originally from Huntington, West Virginia, and a former cheerleader at Davis & Elkins College, Judy was thirty-four when they met, some seventeen years younger than Brewster, and looked even younger than her age. She was also married and the mother of two teenagers. Brewster was smitten by her and she soon reciprocated. They began playing bridge together in the evenings and seeing each other constantly.

Judy said that before they were actually introduced, she was at a lecture when "somebody at my table... said, 'See that man over there?' and he was across the room, 'That's Senator Brewster.' And I said, 'Senator

Brewster?' I knew nothing about politics nor cared about it." She said she later learned that Danny had slipped into the Hiddenbrook office to see if he could determine from her records how old she was. "I thought that was always funny—that he didn't want to step on any toes by my being too young."[636]

Judy's first marriage was in West Virginia at age nineteen to an immigrant named Knut Aarsand, whose family had fled Norway just before the Nazis invaded at the start of World War II. After graduating from Marshall University, Knut became an officer in the Marine Corps and his young family lived at Camp Lejeune and Quantico. After he got out, he started a stock brokerage firm in Northern Virginia but then moved near Annapolis, Maryland, and lived the boom-and-bust life of an entrepreneur. Their children, Krista and Kurt, attended a private school in a majestic, twenty-two-room riverside mansion named Wroxeter-on-the-Severn (which, as it turns out, was built by Danny Brewster's great uncle, Edwin Pugh Baugh in 1909). Knut and Judy loved to go to dances and to parties and on trips to the Caribbean. They owned a thirty-six-foot Pearson sailboat on which they entertained and took voyages from Annapolis to other East Coast ports such as Nantucket and Martha's Vineyard.

"Dad was an absolute go-getter, a total entrepreneur, and loved a good party. So they had fun," remembered their daughter, Krista Aarsand Bedford. "Their twenties were a time of fun and change and rise—and then the fall by the time they were thirty," she said, referring to a stock market decline coupled with the forced closing of her father's brokerage business. "That was sort of what started Mom's drinking," she said. It all came to a head one night when her parents had such a loud argument that Kurt and Krista felt compelled to summon a neighbor. By the next day, their mother had left. Their father took the two of them out to dinner and announced, "Your mom has an illness. It is called alcoholism and we're taking her to a place where she can get help. It is not her fault, and we need to be supportive.'... And that is pretty much what I remember: medical and matter-of-fact," Krista said.[637]

After that, they talked with their mother by phone but didn't really see her for about two or three months until she and a man they had not met before drove to Annapolis to pick them up and go to the movies. Krista said her first impression of Danny Brewster was that he was "an old man." They went to a theater to see the movie *American Graffiti* but shortly after it started, Danny stepped out for some popcorn and never returned. When the movie ended, they found him seated in the lobby reading the *Baltimore News American* and the *Baltimore Sun*. "And we were, 'My god, Mom, who is this guy?' It was just so odd, not only was he old, he was boring. So that was my first memory of him."[638] The fact that Brewster had been a US Senator meant almost nothing to the young teenagers, although they readily admit that their view changed as they got older and understood what a rare distinction being elected to the Senate was.

Most treatment centers discourage their recovering alcoholics from dating each other because it increases the likelihood that if one of them falls off the wagon, they both will. But by November 1975, before she was even divorced, Judy Aarsand moved into Windy Meadows with Danny Brewster. (By then, Brewster and Anne Bullitt had been divorced for three years.)

There are different stories about precisely how Brewster convinced Knut Aarsand to divorce Judy (one story, from the widow of Brewster's best friend, Crocker Nevin, suggests Danny wrote Knut a large check to convince him to go away quietly[639]), but the story Judy tells—and which Knut's memoirs seem to confirm, according to Krista—is that she and Danny were planning to fly to Haiti so she could get a quickie divorce there when Danny suddenly suggested, "Why don't we just send your ex-husband, or your future ex-husband?" Judy said Knut "jumped at the chance" and took his new girlfriend with him to Haiti and obtained the divorce.[640]

It was around that time that Krista said they were all sitting in the Windy Meadows kitchen "when Danny said, 'Kids, I think you should call me Danny, not Mr. Brewster.' 'OK, Mr. Brewster.' It wasn't very long before he said, 'Kids, your mother and I are going to marry.' That was it. It was quite a surprise."[641]

On June 9, 1976, Judy Aarsand became Danny Brewster's third—and final—wife in a civil ceremony at the courthouse in Towson where Danny had practiced law in the years after the war. John Grason Turnbull, his old friend and law partner who, by then, was a Maryland judge, showed up in his judicial robe to witness the marriage. Afterward, they received a blessing at Brewster's church and then hosted a small reception at Windy Meadows farm.

Danny often drove his stepchildren to school, but one morning not long after the wedding, Krista recalled, Judy also came along. She said she and Kurt were seated in the back seat when Danny said, "Kids, what would you think about having a little brother or sister?" Krista said she and Kurt looked at each other and replied dismissively, "We're good," which prompted Danny and Judy to look at each other and announce, "We're not really asking you. We're going to have a baby."[642]

Judy and Danny's first child, Danielle, was born about nine months to the day after they were wed.

"I'm thinking, 'Oh my gosh! This man has been in treatment three times, what on earth would convince my mother to hook up with some guy who had been in treatment?'" Krista Bedford recalled thinking a few years later. "We're taught things [during treatment for alcoholism] like, 'stick with the winners,' or 'don't make any major decisions in the first year of your sobriety,' so here's Mom's life: first year of sobriety after she goes into treatment, she has an affair, she leaves her husband and children, she gets married, and she gets pregnant, all within ten months."[643]

Yet, for the first time in a long time, Danny Brewster was both sober and happy—the same man but a changed man. "It was a far, far different life than what we were accustomed to," Kurt Aarsand said. "But as time progressed, the 'old' factor kind of went away because Danny was pretty active. He worked on the farm all day and rode horses, mucked stalls; he was just pretty active. I think I kind of lost that 'old man' feeling about him."[644]

But Danny did have a problem: he felt like he was broke. "My finances are in disarray because of not working for seven years, terrible legal expenses, running a losing farm operation and alcoholism. I can end the legal expenses in a year, stop the alcoholism now, go back to work if I am not disbarred, and hopefully hold onto the farm," he said in a letter to his son Gerry.[645]

Even though his trial was finally over, his legal problems were not. The Internal Revenue Service was auditing his taxes and the state's Attorney Grievance Commission was considering whether to revoke his license to practice law. The first bit of good news came when the IRS concluded, after looking at his income tax returns, that the $4,500 he had accepted as a campaign contribution—the so-called unlawful gratuity [accepted] without corrupt intent—was actually what Brewster had all along claimed it was, a political contribution accepted for that purpose and used to cover legitimate political expenses.

In September 1976, the Attorney Grievance Commission focused on the question of whether Brewster's *nolo contendere* plea constituted a "crime involving moral turpitude," a legal term that means "an act of baseness, vileness, or depravity in the private and social duties which a man owes his fellow men or to society in general."[646] The legal brief filed on Brewster's behalf by attorney Richard W. Emory recounted Brewster's torturous legal road, noted he had "self-suspended" from the practice of law for nearly seven years, and said he pleaded no contest only "under the most extenuating circumstances of health… [and] out of fear that the stress and trauma of a second trial not only endangered his health but seriously threatened the loss of his life."[647]

"There is not one scintilla of evidence of fraud or deceit on his part," the brief said. "Not only has Mr. Brewster been acquitted of bribery and corruption charges, he has not even been accused by the Internal Revenue Service of fraud and deceit in the receipt and disbursement of the money received from Spiegel, Inc."[648]

It took the Maryland court system another year of deliberations before Maryland's highest court, the Court of Appeals, on June 21, 1977, finally dismissed the Attorney Grievance Commission's petition and thus refused to disbar Brewster after concluding that his conviction was "not a crime involving moral turpitude."[649] Brewster, vacationing in Bermuda, got the news by phone.

This time, Danny Brewster's legal problems really were over. His long and torturous descent—through an alcoholic haze, his impetuous divorce from Carol, the unrealized love from his marriage to Anne Bullitt, and the political mistakes of his final Senate years—had finally bottomed out. But it had cost him dearly, including his seat in the Senate and what had once been considered a promising political future. It is impossible to calculate the exact cost, either in terms of his finances or what it did to his spirit and feelings of self-worth, but he surely expended all the money he had made throughout his career in public office, his law practice, and more defending himself. Although he had inherited two trusts, the Daniel Baugh Trust and the Elizabeth Wills Baugh Trust, he had never been entitled to the principal of either, only the income they generated. He had divorced his first wife, Carol, to marry Anne, but after alienating her, they, too, were divorced in Haiti in 1972. He had been forced by both finances and marital circumstances to sell Worthington Farms and only by—literally—the luck of the draw was he able to buy Windy Meadows Farm, and then only by taking out a mortgage.

"Danny didn't have a job for much of his life. Give him some credit for his job as a congressman and a senator, but there wasn't much before that or after that," said his friend and companion, Charlie Fenwick, who helped run a horse stable with him in Danny's later years.[650]

Money, or the lack of it, became a fairly regular source of conflict between Brewster and his son Gerry. At one point, Brewster mailed Gerry his monthly child-support check but asked him to hold off a few weeks before cashing it, admitting, "I am a little broke right now."[651] Yet despite Brewster's woe-is-me complaining about his finances, he managed to help all of his children attend private schools and colleges and had enough extra to have a full-time housekeeper and a full-time farm hand, Krista Bedford said, not to mention his investments in race horses.[652] He was "broke" perhaps only by comparison to the standards of wealth with which he had been raised.

From time to time, newspapers would print reminders of Brewster's trials and tribulations, which he surely found hurtful. Immediately after his plea deal was made public, the *Baltimore News American* ran a story with a headline that read, "Brewster's Let Off With $10,000 Fine," as if Brewster had paid no other price during his six years of misery over an alleged crime he fervently insisted he never committed.[653] Mike Lane, the *Baltimore Evening Sun* cartoonist, drew a cartoon for the paper's editorial page that depicted all of the Maryland politicians who had gotten in trouble with the law in recent years—Vice President Spiro Agnew, County Executives Dale Anderson and Joe Alton, Congressman Tom Johnson and Senator Daniel Brewster—gathering together to telephone Governor Marvin Mandel, who was by then also under federal investigation, jointly saying, "Congratulations, Marvin!"[654] In a snide little month-by-month "Year in Review" column in the *Baltimore Sun* just before New Year's, under the month of June it said, "Former Senator Dan Brewster recited the Maryland motto, *nolo contendere*, in a DC court."[655] To this day, news stories that mention Brewster regularly and erroneously report that he was once found guilty of bribery.

In a bit of black humor, Gerry Brewster would sometimes jokingly say, "But he ended up as one of the few members of Congress certified to be noncorrupt by a jury of his peers!" Gerry, however, would confess, "It was all personally devastating." He said his father would remark, "I've devoted my life fighting for my country in war, serving my country in peace, and to have my country come after me for something I did not do was one of the most difficult things I've ever encountered in my life."[656]

Yet the new Brewster who emerged from the horrors of war, the cocoon of public service, the embarrassment of criminal prosecution, and the ravages of alcoholism no longer seemed bothered by any of this nor bitter about the way he had been treated, said Danielle Brewster Oster, his first daughter with Judy.

"He was perfect," she said of the father she still idolizes. "He had a presence about him. People were drawn to him. One thing I really admired about him is that he did not give a shit what people thought of him. He did what he wanted to do; he said what he wanted to say; he was honest. I care too much about what people think of me, but he didn't. He was just himself. His family was the most important thing to him as we were growing up. He loved his family. He did not get too emotional—in fact, he would get annoyed with me and say, 'Danielle, you get too emotional.'"[657]

In late 1978, the man who ousted Brewster from public office, US Senator Charles McC. Mathias Jr., tried to wipe the slate clean for his lifelong friend. Mathias, a Republican, petitioned the US Department of Justice to get President Jimmy Carter, a Democrat, to pardon Brewster. "I have seen [Brewster] at frequent intervals during the past three years and have also seen his wife and his sons. From my observation, and from information from the family, it is apparent that he has subjected himself to rigid self-examination and self-discipline. He has turned his problems as an alcoholic into an asset by using his experience to counsel other alcoholics at Veterans Administration hospitals and other clinics. He leads an active, busy and useful life with every evidence of full rehabilitation. I strongly recommend that a pardon be granted."[658]

The Mathias petition for pardon included a half dozen affidavits attesting to Brewster's character, including from judges, a priest, a leader of the Maryland State Fair, a psychiatrist, and the alcoholism coordinator for a Veterans Hospital in Baltimore. John E. Raine Jr., a Circuit Court judge in Baltimore County who said he had known Brewster intimately for thirty years, said, "He had serious problems with alcohol during his incumbency as US Senator. I attribute his legal difficulties solely to the alcoholism and I believe him to be completely honest and of good moral character."[659] Unfortunately for Brewster, nothing ever came of the bid to gain a pardon and the effort was finally dropped.

Brewster no longer seemed to care about such things. He was too busy raising horses and cattle, playing with his two dogs, building fences on his farm, and spending hours seated high on a large tractor mowing the 150-acre farm's big fields. Kurt and Krista, Judy's two teenage children, moved in with them and transferred to the private McDonogh School nearby (the tuition for which was paid for, at least in part, by their father, Knut). They soon got into farm life, helping to raise cattle and mucking out horse stalls. Brewster rented out stall space in his barn to others with horses and tried to ride every day himself, and in season he once again participated in local fox hunts. "My biggest problem has always been weight," the 185-pound Brewster complained, evidence that the "problems" that worried him now were much different than they had been when he was in jeopardy of going to prison, was too drunk to function, was trying to win re-election, or was looking for ways America could win the war in Vietnam.[660]

Walter Brewster recalled one evening after he and his older brother had gone to a Bible class together when, upon leaving, Danny turned to him and said out of the blue, "You owe me $158.56." Walter replied, "What's that for?" and Danny said, "You broke that door down [at Windy Meadows the night we went to Hiddenbrook] and I had to get a carpenter in there." Walter said, "Well, you owe me $358.56 for driving you up there." Walter said the subject never came up again.[661]

"Danny was basically a farm boy," Norman Lauenstein said with a laugh. Lauenstein, who served sixteen years on the Baltimore County Council, including four times as chairman, and who knew Brewster through local politics for years, said, "He would wear those old clothes he had and an old floppy hat, and he'd get on his tractor and then pick the kids up and take them to school. So, this old, dilapidated farmer would tie up traffic, stop, let the kids off at the school, and go back to his stable. He was as happy as a pig in mud."[662]

Brewster, interviewed in late 1977, explained, "My life is rewarding, fulfilling and I am far happier than I was at the time I was a friend of the President, assistant majority leader of the US Senate and chairman of the Maryland delegation to two National Democratic Conventions. I have totally withdrawn from all political activity for now and the future, but I'm not bitter about my experiences in politics."[663]

Chapter 20

REDEMPTION

"About a decade ago," journalist Robert Timberg wrote in the *Baltimore Evening Sun* in March 1977, "US Senator Daniel B. Brewster looked down into his political grave, saw a bottle at the bottom and leaped in after it. The politician was buried in that hole. The man apparently survived the fall."[664]

Timberg, who died in 2016, was a Marine Corps veteran severely wounded in Vietnam, but who, after multiple surgeries, gradually rebuilt his shattered life to become a top-notch reporter. He likely had a special empathy for the long, hard road Danny Brewster had traveled—both the depth of the valleys Brewster had slogged through and the relative heights to which he once again managed to climb.

Timberg was not talking about the rebirth of Dan Brewster the Senator; he was describing the redemption of Dan Brewster the person—how someone so utterly ruined could somehow find his soul again. In the late 1970s, Brewster finally faced up to his alcoholism, described it for what it was, took responsibility for his actions, publicly acknowledged the pain and problems he had caused others, and demonstrated a heartfelt willingness to help those afflicted with the same disease.

"A person must admit his powerlessness over alcohol and that his life has become unmanageable and then try to do something about it," Brewster said, adding that he had stopped drinking at least three times, only to relapse twice before he finally righted his ship. "The periods of sobriety would be longer, my dedication to sobriety became greater. I also had a great deal of informal contact with other sufferers."[665]

A new Brewster emerged, one with no hint of personal political ambition, a man no longer infatuated by power or the powerful, a new father who for the first time in his life wanted to make time for his wife and family. He doted on his daughter, Danielle. He and his new wife, Judy, lived quietly, happily on their farm. Together, they joined Alcoholics Anonymous, and he agreed to chair the Governor's Advisory Council on Alcoholism and began looking for ways to help those who were ruining their lives with drink just as he had done not too many years before.

He drove to the State House in Annapolis, where two decades earlier he had served in the House of Delegates, to use his own shameful example to convince lawmakers of the need to raise the tax on alcoholic beverages from $1.50 a gallon to $1.70 so the proceeds could be used to finance rehabilitation programs for alcoholics. He acknowledged in front of the state Senate's budget committee—which still included members who had been among his drinking buddies in the 1950s—that he had "nearly died of alcoholism."[666]

"I didn't know it at the time. And if I had known it, I probably wouldn't have had the courage to admit it," he testified, adding, "It is hard to know when you cross the line" between social drinking and alcoholism. "It did impair my effectiveness.... I would have been a better Senator if I hadn't been drinking."[667]

State legislators marveled at Brewster's bravery for being so candid in such a public setting. "I'm particularly happy you had the guts to come here today," remarked Senator Julian L. Lapides of Baltimore. "I'm very touched, and I believe the whole committee is touched." Senator Meyer Emanuel of Prince George's County said he had been wavering on the alcohol tax bill until he heard Brewster testify but was now convinced he had to support it. "Here was a guy who had everything in the palm of his hand and then threw it away," Emanuel said in amazement after the hearing. "It took courage for him to come back today."[668] Despite Brewster's efforts, the General Assembly eventually voted down the proposed tax increase.

In the summer of 1977, Brewster's handsome image, with his now silver hair neatly combed to one side, landed on the cover of a magazine that had nothing to do with politics: the *Maryland State Medical Journal*. In a piece entitled "Phoenix—The Rise, Fall and Resurrection of Sen. Daniel Brewster," the fifty-three-year-old delivered a remarkably blunt interview about the agony of alcoholism, the difficulty of stopping, the pain it causes family and friends, and the failure—as he saw it—of the medical profession to adequately help those suffering from the disease. He revealed how close it had pushed him to suicide.[669]

Brewster said he first began drinking at age fifteen or sixteen and increased his drinking over the years, including regular social drinking while serving in the Maryland General Assembly and Congress. He conceded what his colleagues and family already knew, that in the mid-1960s, probably starting with his ugly presidential primary campaign against George Wallace in 1964, the amount of his drinking increased until it was out of control. He acknowledged that drinking impaired his performance as a Senator, made him miss meetings and appearances, and almost certainly led to both of his divorces.[670]

"I really wanted to stop—but I thought I could control it, not knowing that control was impossible for an alcoholic," he told *Medical Journal* interviewer Blaine Taylor. Asked if he realized that others knew he was an alcoholic, Brewster said, "In all cases of alcoholism, the disease is usually apparent to friends and family and outsiders before it is obvious to the person who is afflicted." He said some friends and family attempted to warn him yet remained overprotective, a "well-meaningness (that) in nearly all cases was totally counterproductive."[671]

Brewster saved his heaviest criticism for the medical care he received at the time, saying, "Generally speaking, I do not believe that the American medical profession as a whole understands alcoholism." He was especially critical of physicians using drugs such as Librium, Valium, Tuinal, or other narcotics and tranquilizers. "In my judgment, the use of all of these drugs—in nearly all cases—does no good in treating the active alcoholic and, in most cases, does very real harm." For the first time, Brewster talked publicly about the treatment he received in Ireland, saying he had become intoxicated and that a "well-meaning person"—probably Anne Bullitt Brewster—called a doctor, who administered a powerful sedative directly into his bloodstream in an effort to put him to sleep. When the doctor arrived, Brewster said, he was conscious, not ill, and not experiencing withdrawals. But because the high level of alcohol already in his system interacted with the sedative, he said, "I nearly died, was unconscious for several days and had complete amnesia for nearly a week!" Then, during his recovery, he said he was kept heavily sedated and had no idea what sort of drugs were being administered. When a new doctor took over, the drugs were withdrawn, and then he went through episodes of drug withdrawal. On top of it all, one doctor concluded he may have suffered brain damage, an embarrassing misdiagnosis that somehow found its way into the newspapers just as he was facing bribery charges in the US courts.[672]

"Knowing what I know now, I accuse the medical profession of callous indifference and of being 'pill-slingers' just to get the troublesome alcoholic out of their office and off their necks," Brewster concluded. "A prescription for Valium may be written in a few seconds, whereas an explanation of alcoholism will be difficult and lengthy." If the medical profession would recognize alcoholism as the disease it is and treat it accordingly, he said, that could be a game-changer for struggling alcoholics. "My advice to doctors is 'Tell a drunk he's a drunk,' and then explain carefully and fully all the known facts about alcoholism."[673]

Unlike articles in many medical journals, the Brewster interview generated a higher-than-normal demand and copies were widely circulated. In addition to being sent to doctors and hospitals throughout Maryland, copies were distributed to medical societies and hospitals in other states and circulated on Capitol Hill. Local newspapers did not re-run it, but it was such an honest discussion of a serious issue that they assigned reporters to write fresh stories about Brewster and his views. Among those who read the interview was Brewster's friend, Senator Mathias, who wrote the *Medical Journal* to say, "Not only does the interview demonstrate the devastating effects of the human tragedy of alcoholism, but it provides an insight into the character of a courageous and honorable man. Danny Brewster's long and tortured journey through the dark night of alcoholism, and the selfless efforts he is now making to help others debilitated by this insidious and addictive disease, stand as examples of the best that is in us all."[674]

Brewster went back on the road, but his latest campaign focused not on himself but on helping alcoholics recover. For ten to fifteen hours a week, he would speak candidly about his experiences as an alcoholic: before the Eastern Shore Council on Alcoholism meeting in Easton, before a group gathered at Hood College in Frederick, and in interviews with various local newspapers and publications, even including the *Maryland Horse* magazine. At an Alcoholics Anonymous meeting in the mid-1970s, Brewster met a kindred soul in Francis X. Kelly, another recovering alcoholic from Baltimore County, who in 1978 would be elected to the first of three terms in the Maryland Senate.

Helping others recover, Kelly said, was right in line with the last step of the "Twelve Steps of Alcoholics Anonymous."[675] "Well, you know the twelfth step is that to keep [your sobriety], you've got to give it away. When they say somebody is 'twelfth-stepping somebody,' it also means they are helping somebody." Danny, he added, "was always open to helping somebody else. And I think the fact that he and Judy were married, as a couple they helped people."[676]

John Howard, who was a young man when he joined Brewster's law firm in Towson, admitted that in later years he had his own three-year battle with alcoholism and that Danny and Judy Brewster together helped him recover. "So I spent some time with him back then. He was a big help. But he helped a lot of people."[677]

Brewster's stepdaughter, Krista Bedford, said she also struggled with excessive drinking in her late teens, but that by then Danny had married her mother and had become her "go-to guy." "When I had a problem, I went to him because he was very neutral, unemotional.... When I was having a difficult problem with alcohol, it was Danny whom I called. I said, 'I'm having a rough time, can you come talk to me?' He said, 'I'll be there in twenty minutes.' He showed up at this apartment I was living in and he said, 'What seems to be the problem?' and I said, 'I think I have a drinking problem.' He said, 'Oh, thank God. I was afraid you were going to tell me you were pregnant!'" She said he started asking questions about her drinking and ended up referring her to an alcoholism counselor he knew and that "was the start of my recovery."[678]

The bulk of Brewster's time, however, was spent on the farm, developing horses for the area's races and fox hunts, raising cattle, and playing tennis with Judy a couple times a week. Although he and Judy entertained regularly, they never served alcohol at their house. Liza Nevin, the widow of Crocker Nevin, one of Brewster's classmates at the St. Paul's School and a lifelong friend, recalled with a laugh their clandestine efforts to have a drink while they visited the dry Brewster household. Once, she said, they put vodka in their baby's bottle, only to have it accidentally served to their infant daughter, Jennie Nevin.[679]

Brewster, for the first time in a long time, was just having fun. In April 1978, the fifty-four-year-old former United States Senator pulled on a cherry red turtleneck with a white sash diagonally across the front, white nylon jodhpurs, and a white helmet, and saddled a horse named Jay's Trouble to compete in the My Lady's Manor, the steeplechase race he had won thirty years before. Competing against some riders who were not even born when he last competed, Brewster finished last, four lengths behind the second-place finisher among the three horses that finished the race. A picture from the day shows him smiling broadly as his horse jumped a four-rail timber fence. Afterward, he received the largest ovation from the crowd of about two thousand.

Brewster was so transparent about his past that he agreed to help his son Gerry, then a junior at Princeton, with his 221-page senior thesis that ultimately would be entitled *Daniel Baugh Brewster: The Triumphs and Tragedies of a Maryland Politician*. Despite having had a rocky and often distant relationship with his father, the younger Brewster found in his father's political life a rich trove of material for various school projects over the years. As a senior at Gilman, Gerry Brewster and a classmate, J.

Reiley McDonald, wrote a senior term paper on Danny Brewster's race against George Wallace entitled *The 1964 Maryland Democratic Primary: A Study in Personalities and Politics*. The younger Brewster then reprised that piece for a politics class at Princeton, writing *Wallace: The Man and the Movement, 1956-1976*. He also wrote a paper for a 1977 history class called *The Gulf of Tonkin Affair of 1964* about the legislation that made possible the unlimited escalation of the Vietnam War. And, as a junior at Princeton, he delved into the legal distinctions regarding political contributions that were raised at his father's bribery case in a paper called *The Case of United States v. Brewster*.

"I know you are very wary about my writing on such a subject," Gerry wrote to his father, trying to sell him on the senior thesis idea. But, he said, "The material is there. There is no better senior thesis topic for me! My approach is to be scholarly and academic—not emotional and biased!—I want to do a factual biography." He added, "I know the good and the bad, Dad—so don't worry I'll find something you would rather not have me know about—I'm sure I have heard it. I only hope that your feelings about this are not too negative. I have been working toward this since my first Brewster paper on 1964, then I have subsequently done papers on Tonkin, Alcoholism, Wallace, and researched US v. Brewster."[680]

His father approved of the project and later wrote, "Keep me posted on the progress with the senior thesis. I want to assist when possible. Be objective and truthful—there is no need to worry about my feelings. My mistakes are legion."[681]

By the end of the 1970s, newspapers and magazines in Baltimore and Washington began writing glowing feature stories about Danny Brewster and his new "sober life." In one he said he did not miss the Senate. "No. No more than I miss the Marines. I think about it sometimes, I remember it all right. But I don't miss it. Life goes on. As a young man, I was forever thinking of tomorrow. Then, with my defeat and illness, I thought only of the past. Idealism turned into ambition which turned into alcoholism." He said he now preferred simpler things—working in his garden, jogging, canning beans and tomatoes with Judy, attending cattle auctions. "It took a long time to ruin what seemed a promising career, and it takes a long time to rebuild a life," adding, as if it wasn't obvious, "I'm a happy man."[682]

On April 17, 1979, Judy Brewster gave birth to twins, Jennilie and Dana. That made Danny the father of five—Dan Jr. and Gerry from his first marriage to Carol and Danielle, Jennilie, and Dana with Judy—plus he was stepfather to four—Carol's sons, Michael and Andre de Havenon, and Judy and Knut Aarsand's children, Kurt and Krista.

Two days after the twins were born, Gerry completed his thesis, dedicating it "To the children of public figures everywhere," a subtle acknowledgment of the difficulties the children of frequently absent or distracted public officials are often forced to endure. Gerry also informed his father that after graduation from Princeton he planned to take a job on the staff of Senator Mathias, the Republican who had defeated his father in 1968. Brewster wrote his son back to say, "The Mathias job makes sense to me. Capitol Hill is a most interesting place and Mac is a good Senator. You have my best wishes."[683]

Gerry Brewster's various school papers seem to reveal a son's admiration and adulation for a father who rose to become a United States Senator and a friend of Presidents, yet his private correspondence also shows a son who wanted his father's attention but rarely got it. Despite what probably appeared to outsiders as a level of comity between father and son, Brewster's second son sometimes privately aired a lifetime of grievances to his father in long, pained, handwritten letters. Every attribute of the elder Brewster's happy new life with Judy and their family stood in bitter contrast to the lonely feelings of abandonment Gerry felt from an upbringing largely overseen by foreign-born nannies and absentee parents.

"I have always been bitterly disappointed in you as a father. You know this and will be the first to admit that you weren't only a terrible father, but you were a non-existent one," Gerry wrote to his father in one scorching letter, undated but probably written in late 1978. "This hurt a lot as a kid growing up. I only saw you fighting with Mom, Dan and I and that's most of all of my recollections." The letter went on in a similar vein for fourteen anger-filled pages, but ended by saying, "I do not want a war. I do want to be able to get along with you and with Judy and with everyone else.... For my part, I seek peace and hope for civil relations and mutual respect.... I hope you react to this letter positively as it comes in hopes for a better relationship. You are my father and I do need your support to help me to become a better person."[684]

Brewster replied to his son, saying, "I have received and carefully read your long letter. The depth of your anger amazes me. I had no idea you so thoroughly disliked me. Obviously, I am hurt and disappointed." Rather than reply point-by-point to Gerry's "bill of complaint," as Brewster called it, he invited his son to Christmas dinner or any other dinner he might choose and said, "I am ready to discuss any matter with you in person."[685] In the file drawers that contain the Brewster family papers, however, is the son's original letter on long yellow legal paper onto which the elder Brewster underlined sections, numbered others, and wrote notes in the margins such as "thanks," "sorry," "wrong," "no," "explain," "tell story," "go to hell," "proud," "thanks to grandma/trust/my expenses," and "will continue to do so."[686]

In a separate letter to Gerry less than a week later, Brewster said, "Sincerely hope all is well with you. Keep that temper under control— perhaps you say things at times that you do not fully understand or mean."[687]

As he got older, Danny Brewster tried to make up for the mistakes of his life and to apologize to the people he had hurt. Judy Brewster, in an interview for a cover story in the *Baltimore Sun Magazine* about Brewster and his new life, said he used to wake up and think, "Oh, God, another day," but now he wakes up and says, "Thank God for another day."[688]

"Life is so much more meaningful to him. The first time around, he was so busy he had no time for his family," she said, perhaps not realizing how her happiness would appear to the children of his first marriage. "Now he knows what's important and nothing is so important in our lives that we can't drop it for our children. He's a fantastic husband and father, a gentle man, a caring man, and if he hadn't been to the depths, I don't think he would be where he is today." To which the then twenty-two-year-old Gerry Brewster, in the same article, replied, "I respect my father for his ability to overcome his problems, but I'm disappointed in him as a father. I think to a certain degree he is disappointed in himself and would like a second shot, but he's aware my brother and I are grown men now and he can't undo what he did in the past."[689]

Danny gradually got involved in other endeavors. He chaired the state's Korean War Memorial Commission and served as a member of a state Commission on Port Efficiency. He chaired the board of the Franklin Square Hospital in Baltimore County and helped orchestrate its merger with Union Memorial Hospital, which eventually grew into the even larger MedStar Hospital System. When the AIDS epidemic broke out, Governor William Donald Schaefer needed someone to chair a new state Commission on AIDS, but no one would do it. Danny agreed to take it on but said he would need a budget and staff, and he got both. Brewster also served on the state Greenways Commission, helping to protect natural habitat from development, and also on the board of the national group Former Members of Congress—a recognition that his former colleagues appreciated a man who had the strength and character to rebuild his life.

At a small gathering in September 1992 at Captain Harvey's Restaurant on Reisterstown Road, for years a favorite hangout for Baltimore County Democrats, the local Fourth District Democratic Club named Daniel B. Brewster its Citizen of the Year.[690] The accolade surely passed unnoticed by everyone outside of a tight political circle in the county, yet it also was a measure of how far Brewster had come since his defeat, his alcoholism, and his trial to redeem his good name.

Through his hospital work, Brewster became personal friends with an administrator named Mike Merson. Together, they oversaw the hiring of hospital managers and staff as well as several hospital mergers. Merson said he came to depend on Brewster's judgment of the character of others and his clear, honest way of dealing with hospital issues. "It must have been his military and senatorial background. Where he had learned all of these things, I'm not sure, but they were the most straightforward, easiest to relate to, easy to understand, rule set of how you worked together," Merson said.[691]

The day Merson retired, the two of them went into business together buying and racing thoroughbreds. At first, while their horses were winning enough to keep their costs under control, they had fun. Together, they invested $50,000 in a horse named Western Halo, but he failed miserably during his first race on a dirt track. So, Merson said, their trainer suggested they run him on a grass track, and the horse took off. Soon, others were trying to buy Western Halo for as much as $200,000, but Merson said they were having too much fun racing him to sell. He said when they would show up at a track, "Dan knew so many people in every dimension. Wherever he went, people would just come out of nowhere and they all wanted to just shake his hand, and they all called him 'Senator,' even at the racetrack. Tired jockeys would be there hanging out, and they'd come up to him, and say, 'Senator, how are things going?'" Merson recalled.[692] He said he and Brewster and their wives would travel to races in various parts of the country and had a great time together.

Brewster also separately owned other horses, including a steady winner named Rolling Cart. Trained by Mary Eppler, Rolling Cart ran in seventy-four races between 1987 and 1994 and won eighteen, finished second in seventeen, and third in eleven—win, place, or show in more than half his races. His total winnings were nearly $330,000.[693]

Merson said when he and Brewster were alone together talking, Danny sometimes admitted some of the regrets in his life, such as blindly supporting the war in Vietnam. He said he reflected on the missed opportunity of his life with Anne at the Palmerstown stud farm, telling Merson she had "'one of the greatest stables of horses.' He said, 'If I wasn't such a drunk, there should have been nothing else in my life that would have been more satisfying.'" He said Brewster harbored a particular grudge against the physicians who sedated and almost killed him in 1969. "He was very bitter that those people who treated him medically, that they never 'fessed up," Merson said.[694]

Judy Brewster said Danny sometimes mused over why his aide, Jack Sullivan, betrayed him. "He always hoped that maybe Jack Sullivan, before he died, would tell the truth," Judy said.[695]

Brewster always thought—erroneously, as it turns out—that he was on Richard Nixon's infamous "enemies list" of people the President considered political foes. There is no question that Nixon's Justice Department pursued Brewster relentlessly and did so at Nixon's explicit direction, even if he wasn't listed as an enemy. So, in his later years, Brewster seemed to get some satisfaction that Nixon was hounded from office and Attorney General John Mitchell and other high-ranking officials from Nixon's White House all went to jail, but Danny Brewster did not.

"He talked about it and was adamant that he was not found guilty, that he pled no contest. It is brutal. It was not fair," said his daughter Danielle Brewster Oster. "You know, he didn't lie. If he had done something wrong, he would have admitted it. He admitted all his faults. He openly admitted all the shit he did that was wrong, with no hesitation. He was an open book that way. If he did something wrong, he would have told us. He would have admitted to it."[696]

"If he did do something wrong," she said, thinking about the possible effects of his alcoholism, "he didn't know it."[697]

Chapter 21

NO TIME FOR BITTERNESS

The line of fancy cars, the Porsches and Mercedes and BMWs, rolled up the long driveway at the McDonogh School to pick up students after classes when Danny Brewster's stepdaughter, Krista, said she started to hear the rattle of her stepfather's old pickup truck coming from way down the lane. Fresh from the cattle auction in Westminster, Brewster noisily came to a stop in front of the posh private school, looking a bit like old Henry Fonda in his faded khaki clothes and floppy hat and with four or five young steers crowded in the truck bed.

"Oh, God," an embarrassed Krista remembers saying to her stepfather, "can't you just pick us up without the cattle in the back?"[698]

To Krista's classmates, Brewster looked like some old farmer or perhaps just the farmhand, or maybe he was Krista's grandfather. Brewster couldn't care less what others thought. He was a man content with himself, with his suddenly large family, with his beautiful farm, with his new, quiet, stable life. He had found that illusive quality in life: equilibrium. Finally.

"Sure, he was a US Senator and a war hero, but what I really know is he was a simple man who worked the farm and spent time with his family. And he just had an amazing presence about him. Sadly, I don't think I'll ever meet anyone like him in my life," said his youngest son, Dana Brewster.[699]

Brewster would rise each day and quietly read the morning newspapers cover to cover. On Sunday mornings, he'd watch the political talk shows on TV. Most of the rest of the time was spent on the endless chores around the farm or activities with Judy and their children. Sometimes he'd pop into the kitchen to escape the midday heat, grab a Ball jar filled with home-grown tomatoes off the shelf, unscrew the lid, slurp down the contents, and then go back to work. He rarely talked about the important people he had met when he was in politics or his war experiences, although he did keep on a shelf in his study the helmet with the bullet holes front and back he had worn when he was ambushed on Okinawa. "He wasn't one to brag about anything or talk about his accomplishments," Dana said.[700] He wasn't quite taciturn, but he had become a man of few words.

All his children have vivid memories of how tough he was. Both Danielle and Jennilie remember that on frigid mornings before driving the kids to school, Danny would sometimes use his fingernails to scrape the ice off the windshield. Kurt Aarsand recalls finding Danny in the kitchen—the morning after Danny broke his arm in a riding accident— cutting off his cast with a handsaw. Kurt also tells of Danny getting flipped from his horse onto the top of a wood rail jump and seriously injuring his back but getting back aboard the horse to ride it home. That likely explains why, when Danielle fell from her horse and got kicked in the head, her father's reaction was—once she regained her senses—to put her back in the saddle.

Dana Brewster said his father always gave his kids a lot of freedom on the farm, and that when Dana was about four or five years old, he asked if he could climb the ladder to the hayloft in the barn. Danny said fine, but when Dana reached the top, he momentarily let go with both hands and immediately fell backward about fifteen feet toward the barn floor. "He wasn't actually looking, but he turned the corner and reached out with his arms just in time and caught me perfectly. All I remember is balling and crying by the time I hit his arms," Dana recalled. "That would have been game over."[701]

When he was ten, Dana was helping his dad take a mare and a foal out to the field. Danny asked which one he wanted to lead, and Dana picked the foal because he was small and cute. He also was untrained.

Dana said he still doesn't know exactly how it happened, but the next thing he knew he was crouched down with his hands on his knees and blood pouring from his face onto the dirt trail. The foal had kicked him in the face and shattered his jaw. "Dad came up and took his dirty handkerchief out of his pocket and said, 'Put this on your chin and go sit in the tack room while I go get the horse.' So I put the handkerchief on my chin, stumbled into the tack room, dad put the horse out in the field and came back and got me. Only someone who had gone through the war and seen some pretty ugly stuff would not be phased by that." Dana said he was driven to the emergency room, was in intensive care for three days, and had his mouth wired shut for over a month. The only bright part of this story is that Danny later named that foal Dana's Jawbreaker, although he didn't turn out to be a very successful racehorse.[702]

By the time Dana turned thirteen, he was playing quarterback on a school football team and after school would often practice his passing in the back yard with Danny, who would run patterns as his son's sixty-nine-year-old wide receiver. As Danny jogged through a down-and-out pattern, Dana's pass went just off his fingertips and Danny sprawled on the ground. "I held my hands up like, 'This was awesome. You were so close,' only to find out he wasn't diving—he had snapped his Achilles tendon." His father, Dana said, limped into the house and sat in his chair for a long time debating whether he needed to go to the hospital or whether it would heal if he just gave it some rest. "He was a tough as nails guy. He might have been in pain for a while and not said a word."[703] As it turned out, his father had completely severed his Achilles tendon and surgeons had to reattach it.

"We were in the barn one day when a horse kicked him in the knee—knocked him up against the wall," leaving a massive bruise that lasted for weeks, his eldest daughter, Danielle recalled. "He just rubbed it and kept going."[704] In his later years, Brewster also battled multiple cancers and, for a while at least, appeared to have beaten them.

Charlie Fenwick, his neighbor who rented horse stalls from Danny at Windy Meadows Farm, said the two of them would spend hours in the barn every day and developed a close friendship, even though Danny was twenty-four years older. One of the more unpleasant chores around the farm each fall was to castrate the new bull calves that were not going to be used for breeding. Fenwick said that one year after the castration, Danny had put the entrails into a pot to be used later to feed his dogs, but he left the pot outside and the contents froze. Before going up to the barn one morning to pick up his newspaper and check on things, Fenwick said, Danny put the pot on the kitchen stove and turned on the heat to thaw them. But he ran into Charlie and the two started talking. Suddenly, Fenwick recalled, the phone in the barn rang. Judy was calling. Danny answered it, hung up and yelled "Jesus Christ," jumped in his truck, and raced back to the house. The pot had not only boiled over but essentially exploded its contents onto the kitchen ceiling and walls. Fenwick said Brewster somehow explained away the mess to Judy but that the true story of what was in that pot was not disclosed until Fenwick told the tale at Brewster's eightieth birthday party in 2003.[705] Judy Brewster said she did not remember the incident, "but that sounds like something Danny would do."[706]

Brewster put the turbulence of his past life behind him. He intently avoided conflict, hoping everyone would just get along. "We never fought. He never raised his voice," his daughter Danielle said.[707] Her younger brother, Dana, said his father's steady calm extended to his relationship with Judy. "I never saw them fight or squabble of any kind," he said. "He was done with conflict and maybe she didn't want to fight either."[708]

"My father was very cool," Jennilie Brewster said. "What I mean by that, people noticed right away he was very comfortable with who he was—comfortable in his body, very present. He managed to come off as both tough and warm. I think people liked to be in his sphere. I know I certainly liked being in the room with him."[709]

Danielle focused on riding; Jennilie turned to writing and art; and Dana became a musician. The kids in his new family said their father was always there—a far cry from the experience Gerry Brewster relates from growing up as a child of Brewster's first marriage to Carol. "He was never there," Gerry said, although he also admitted that in the last decades of his life, his father tried to make amends with those he had hurt.

Danny and his daughter Danielle developed a special bond. To this day, she tears up when talking about him and carries with her small reminders of his life, including a piece of the T-shirt he wore the day he died. She admits to even consulting mediums to try to connect with her father. Much of their relationship revolved around horses and learning to ride and eventually learning to race. Carrying on a long family tradition, Danielle started with pony races, then competed at the My Lady's Manor and Grand National race meets, and finally rode in the Maryland Hunt Cup. "Most parents would get nervous if their kids were riding in a race, but he was never like that. He was never worried about my physical safety in that sense," Danielle said.[710]

Danielle says that she and Charlie Fenwick, for whom she has worked for years, were about to take a horse ride with her father one day when one of them suggested he replace the soft floppy hat that he favored with a hard-hat helmet, to which Danny replied, "The Japs didn't kill me; cancer didn't kill me; booze didn't kill me; three wives didn't kill me; I'll be damned if this horse is going to kill me."[711]

Gerry Brewster tells a similar story about his father driving his car into a parking lot and passing a car driven by his former wife Carol. The two stopped and rolled down their windows and Carol inquired how he was doing. "Well, Carol, I'm a survivor," Brewster replied. "I survived the Japs; I survived booze; I survived the federal government; I survived cancer." To which Carol quickly retorted, "Well, Danny, I'm a survivor too. I survived you."[712] Yet, in 1989, when Brewster's mother, Ottolie, died at the age of eighty-six, Carol was quick to write him a lovely condolence note saying she was "very fond of her and I will miss her very much."[713]

In some ways, Gerry Brewster has spent portions of his life trying to replicate, if not emulate, the successes of his father's life. They rode in the same steeplechase races, attended Princeton and became lawyers, served as head of the Maryland State Fair, and were elected to the Maryland

House of Delegates where they served on the Judiciary Committee, and in 1994, Gerry tried to win his father's former seat in House of Representatives. The seat had been held most recently by Republican Helen Delich Bentley who gave it up to run for Governor. Robert Ehrlich was nominated by Republicans to take her place and Gerry Brewster by the Democrats. Bobby Ehrlich and Gerry Brewster had traveled similar roads to get to this election: both were from Baltimore County, they had been in the same graduating classes at Gilman and Princeton, and then they both were elected to the Maryland House of Delegates where they served on the Judiciary Committee.

During the campaign, the entire Brewster family worked hard for Gerry's election. Danny Brewster toured the county pounding in thousands of lawn signs on Gerry's behalf, as he had when Gerry first ran for the House of Delegates. Senator Mac Mathias, Danny's friend and Gerry's former boss, was the honorary co-chair of both Gerry's House of Delegates and congressional campaign committees even though Mathias was a Republican and Gerry was a Democrat.

Danny's friend Mike Merson said it was obvious to him that Danny "had a great desire to see Gerry succeed on the political stage. Great, great desire. But he also knew, and expressed to me, that he didn't have confidence that Gerry had the toughness, or meanness or whatever—the fire in the belly—and he didn't really know if his pushing was the right thing or not. He was incredibly fond of Gerry—beyond the ambition that he had for Gerry."[714]

Despite Gerry's best efforts, 1994 was the year of US House Speaker Newt Gingrich's "Contract for America," which propelled a Republican tidal wave that swept the country. Ehrlich won handily. "When I lost, he was supportive," Gerry said of his father. "He said, 'You did your best. I know what it's like to lose an election. You'll be back. There will be another day. You'll be back.'" But Gerry admitted years later that he already knew he wouldn't be back, that there would not be another day, and that in a way he was relieved. While winning his father's old seat would have had a redemptive quality, Gerry Brewster admitted that after observing his father's political career and working himself as a county prosecutor, on the staff of a county executive, on the staff of a US Senator, and as a Maryland state Delegate, he had already soured on the idea of holding higher elective office. As he absorbed the defeat, he said, he realized he wanted to move in a completely new direction—his own direction. He decided he was more interested in trying his hand at education and soon became a Baltimore County public school teacher, first at Chesapeake High School in Essex and then at Towson High School. (As a teacher, Gerry Brewster became a friend to and supporter of one of his most talented students, a swimmer named Michael Phelps, who would go on to Olympic glory.)

Several months after the election, Danielle said she and her father were leaving a horse race and Danny was carrying her heavy tack bag to her white Subaru. He told her to "pop the trunk" so he could throw it in. Danielle said she hadn't opened the trunk for months and when she did, it was full of Bob Ehrlich signs that she and her friends had stolen from along county roads in middle-of-the-night efforts to help Gerry win the election. "They had been there for months, and I had forgotten they were in there," she recounted. "And we all looked at each other and I was like, 'Whoops!' My dad just looked at me and [loudly whispered] 'Good girl!'"[715]

When invited, the elder Brewster became peripherally involved in politics. At the request of a young state legislator from Prince George's County named James Rosapepe, Brewster teamed up once again with his former United States Senate colleague Joe Tydings to co-chair the short-lived 1988 Maryland presidential campaign of Illinois Senator Paul Simon. Rosapepe recalled, "People's reaction was very much, 'He's a serious guy who has done serious things in politics and government. And he had problems and overcame them.'"[716]

Brewster also helped James T. Smith, a former member of the Baltimore County Council and later a judge, run for Baltimore County Executive in 2002 and often accompanied Smith to campaign events. "His presence with me was noted by everybody in the group I was speaking to, so he brought me great credibility," Smith recounted, saying none of Brewster's previous problems seemed to have affected his reputation, at least not locally. "For one thing, he had a hell of a presence. He was handsome, tall, distinguished, and he was very nice to people. What I saw of him was his phase of humility. I don't mean he was groveling at all. He was very unassuming, which made him even more attractive to the people when he was with them. It made him more attractive to them because he was so accomplished—yes, he had his problems—but he had done mighty things that most people can't do, including making his way through alcoholism. That became an asset in terms of the regard people had for him. It certainly was an asset in my eyes, because I admired him greatly for conquering, or getting through, his alcoholism and maintaining his sobriety."[717]

Smith recalled that Danny wore a sports coat at all his events and that he often would take an unassuming seat in the back until Smith would introduce him. "I'd work the room, shaking hands, and he'd make his presence known and everybody knew he had come."[718] People often remarked that when Brewster was speaking with them, they had his whole attention—his eyes were not looking over the person's shoulder as if in search of someone else to talk to.

As Brewster aged and his children got a bit older, there were some bumps in the road. He regularly worried about his finances, halfway joking that he didn't know which would run out first, his money or his health. His relationship with his sons from his first marriage ran hot and cold. Alcoholism and even drug problems arose, if only temporarily, with some of his offspring. Even Judy from time to time slipped into old habits. Danny himself took the dangerous risk of having a drink, but only rarely, his children said. At Christmas, the family would always visit the home of Ellen Turnbull Lynch, Brewster's longtime personal secretary, and they said they would almost always find their dad with a twinkle in his eye hovering near the punchbowl sampling Ellen's spiked eggnog. And Brewster almost always hoisted a drink on the birthday of the US Marine Corps as a way of honoring the men he had fought with and who had died by his side.

For the most part, his life remained happy. In the summer of 2003, when Danielle married Laurence Oster, it was a glorious day for Danny Brewster. With about 375 people attending the wedding reception at Windy Meadows, Danielle said her dad sat at a table and lined up four flutes of champagne, which over the course of the evening he drank in celebration. She remembered him calling Jennilie over to announce, "Well, Jenny, I'm going to light the fuse."[719]

Danny and his new son-in-law, Laurence, became friends and even invested in cattle futures together, although not altogether successfully. Danny also helped Danielle and Laurence move four separate times. "He had a kind smile, disarming presence, and no agenda," Laurence Oster said. "For me, the man was truly inspiring, and not for all that he accomplished but for what he was able to overcome. He was a genuine person of true character, modesty, and humility."[720]

Later that year, Brewster turned eighty, and Danielle recalled that that was about the time he began to show his age. The world around him had changed. The fighting on Okinawa was now nearly sixty years in his past. Wickcliffe, the Tudor-style castle that had been home to his grandparents, had been housing a prep school for Catholic girls for just as long. Palmerstown House, Anne Bullitt's stud farm in Ireland, had been sold and converted into a PGA-caliber eighteen-hole golf course. Baltimore, a robust city of 950,000 in 1950 when Danny was young, had lost a third of its population, was beset by crime and drug problems, and was on financial life support. The 9/11 terrorist attacks in New York City and Washington, DC, had rocked the country just two years before.

"The sad part of his life was that alcoholism brought him low when he could have been very high," said Steny Hoyer. "Not because he was a great intellectual—he was not. But he was very popular with his colleagues and he could have been a real Senate leader. He had good instincts. He was smart, well educated." Hoyer continued, "I don't know if I learned this from Brewster, but he was an example of it: I try to be nice to everybody and I think Brewster tried to be nice to everybody. He didn't demean people. Even though he was of privilege, he had been in the Marines. I'm sure he relied on his life being saved by guys who didn't have privilege, and his manifestation of that, he tried to be thoughtful and nice to everybody he came to deal with."[721]

Judge John Grason Turnbull, Brewster's original law partner and political mentor, interviewed for Gerry Brewster's Princeton thesis, said of Danny, "There was no question of a bad reputation—I never knew him to take a nickel. He never fudged around.... I get hot under the collar—I feel he got a terrible bum rap. He made a lot of serious and stupid mistakes [but] at no time was he dishonest or dishonorable, of that I am positive."[722]

House Speaker Nancy Pelosi said the legal problems Brewster faced later in his life "just didn't ring true to me, that just isn't who he[was]. He was a person of integrity. That was why I was suspicious of how [the alleged bribery] could have ever happened.... In other words, if that one thing happened it would have been such an aberration, and that should have spoken to his integrity. I just never lost any respect for him for that because it just didn't sound like something he would be doing."[723]

Danny's lifelong friend C. A. Porter Hopkins added, "I would say he was the product of a wonderful education and strong family who had participated in the building of America, who served wonderfully in the war, and let John Barleycorn get a hold of him once he had started his political career." He noted that Danny's recovery in later life was less well known to the general public. "People see the build-up, see what happens to him, but then they lose interest in whether he came out of it or not."[724]

Herbert R. O'Conor III, whose family were friends with the Brewsters for decades, said, "I believe you can hear [in] the tone of my voice that [Danny Brewster] was a genuine person. He was a warm person. I certainly felt he was a man of his word. He was certainly honorable. That's why I was puzzled by his criminal difficulties and followed it closely. It was a real education for me as a young law student. I put him in the corner of someone who was unfairly prosecuted. There was a similar sentiment among [other] Towson lawyers."[725]

Richard Hoffberger, whose late father Jerold Hoffberger was a key financial supporter of Brewster's political career, summed it up by saying, "The conventional wisdom at the time was that anybody who knew Danny Brewster knew he wouldn't steal any money. He might be caught at the local bar, but he wouldn't take anybody's money. He wouldn't know how to do it."[726]

In March 2007, Danny Brewster was back in the news briefly one last time after he attended a luncheon at the Maryland Club in Baltimore with US Senators Benjamin L. Cardin and Barbara A. Mikulski and former US Senators Joseph D. Tydings, Paul Sarbanes, and Charles McC. Mathias Jr.—all of Maryland. The common denominator of the group: they were all opposed to what they saw as the disastrous US war in Iraq.

By that summer, however, Brewster's cancer had returned and his health declined. In July, he and Judy moved from their beloved farm, Windy Meadows, to a comfortable house on Chittenden Lane a short distance from the Green Spring Valley Hunt Club. Danny was hospitalized but then brought home just as his children began to arrive from New York and elsewhere. Friends stopped by with food. Family slept where they could but took turns monitoring his health and managing his pain relief. Dana, who years before had written a song called "Windy Meadows," strummed it on the guitar. Daniel Baugh Brewster died in his own bed at home, surrounded by his family, on August 19, 2007. He was eighty-three.

The day before Brewster died, Anne Bullitt Brewster died in Ireland. She, too, was eighty-three. A week later, Judy Brewster suffered a pulmonary embolism and briefly appeared close to death herself. The joke was, said her daughter, Krista Bedford, "God, Danny died and he's taking all his wives with him!" Carol Leiper Brewster died in 2010 at age ninety-two.

After Danny's death, Judy remarked, "We may as well not have any service because no one is going to come—most of his friends have died," to which one of their children replied, "I don't think you know, Mom."[727] Brewster's funeral at St. Thomas' Episcopal Church in Owings Mills was so large that an overflow crowd had to watch the service on remote TV screens set up in the large Parish hall. The service was attended by Governors, Senators, Congressmen, former members of his staff, his extended family, friends, and farmers, who eulogized him for living a life courageously, if imperfectly, and praised him for demonstrating his bravery yet again by overcoming his alcoholism.

Family friend and LBJ confidant Tyler Abell observed, "He went sailing up, sailing down, caught himself, and sailed back up again."[728]

In 1980, Brewster and his family were interviewed for a cover story in the *Baltimore Sun Magazine* that was later entitled "A New Life." In it, he reflected on his old life.

"I used to be bitter about it. I resented people and I thought I had been badly used. But I don't anymore. I don't have time for that. I'm at peace with the world." Gesturing to Judy, he said, "This is my life—Judy and the children—and I can say, unequivocally, that I have never been happier. I've had a fascinating, interesting, rewarding life. There have been some successes and some disasters and I'm happy I had the experiences I had, but they pale next to what I have today. Life couldn't be better."[729]

Acknowledgments

I have been blessed by having the same "first reader" for every manuscript I have written—my patient wife, Priscilla Cummings. An author herself, she read every word of this manuscript before anyone else saw it, identifying areas that were confusing or slow but also highlighting those she found more interesting or exciting. Her genre is children's books, so she brought an unbiased eye to the task. Such honest help is what every writer needs.

This would not have even become a project were it not for Senator Daniel Baugh Brewster's second son, Gerry Leiper Brewster, who knew his late father's story probably better than anyone and knew it was worth telling. To Gerry's lasting credit, he insisted from the start that I try to tell about his father's ups and downs as truthfully as possible, not only his achievements as a war hero, as a successful elected official, and as a civil rights leader but also the agony brought to him and his family by his alcoholism, his broken marriages, and his bribery trial.

Gerry opened to me the Brewster family papers—file drawers full of family letters, official correspondence from Presidents and Senators, photographs, old news clips, and family heirlooms from Baugh Fertilizer Company brochures to the Croix de Guerre awarded to Danny's father in the First World War. I was privileged to read Danny Brewster's handwritten war diary written between engagements in the South Pacific and Gerry's own papers, including achingly personal letters between him and his father, Gerry's thoroughly researched Princeton thesis on his father's political career, and other school papers Gerry wrote about his father's political life over the years. After a full day of research, Gerry and I would often enjoy a glass (or two) of wine together and discuss what I had found, how I interpreted it, and how he sometimes saw the same facts differently. Stories or family relationships I couldn't quite understand,

Gerry would explain. He never imposed his views on me but always gave me his views to consider. We developed a genuine friendship, which I have every expectation will continue.

I am also indebted to Danny Brewster's extended family—his third wife, Judy Lynn Brewster, their three children, Danielle, Jennilie, and Dana, and Judy's children from an earlier marriage, Kurt Aarsand and Krista Bedford. All were interviewed; all were helpful; all were captivated by Daniel B. Brewster. Their embrace of Danny's life was as if they were still wrapping their arms around him.

Michael de Havenon, the son of Danny Brewster's first wife, Carol, from a previous marriage, gave me a thoughtful, sensitive interview about Brewster's life, his marriage to Carol, and Danny's highs and lows.

Michael Shultz, an old friend from our days together as reporters at the *Baltimore Sun* (and over the years, as shipmates on many a Chesapeake Bay sailing trip) volunteered to read and edit the entire manuscript. Mike is a great editor. He knocked out excessive words (particularly adverbs!), asked clarifying questions, suggested rewriting some sections, and generally cleaned up my first draft. My thanks to Mike for his help.

I also received expert editorial advice from The Writers Ally, including thoughtful and comprehensive copy editing by Julie Haase.

Throughout the project, I received help from Gerry's assistant, Shannon Sheetz, who dug through and transcribed the scratchy recordings of old Richard Nixon White House tapes, created a Brewster family tree to help readers understand Danny Brewster's notable family lineage, researched Brewster's World War II military decorations, dug out obscure footnote citations, and then helped scan and organize more than four hundred Brewster family photographs that we considered for this book. He was assisted in this latter effort by another young man, Jeff Sanchez, who turned many faded or otherwise murky photographs into crisper versions suitable for publication. Shannon, in particular, was a constant help.

I did more than fifty interviews for this book, but two, in particular, stand out for me. They were with former Maryland Governor Harry R.

Hughes and former Maryland US Senator Joseph D. Tydings, both of whom were eager to talk about their friend, Danny Brewster, at a time when both knew they were in the final months of their own lives.

I got an unexpected window on the vicious fighting Brewster encountered on Okinawa from Daniel Perskie of Northfield, New Jersey, whose father in 1945 led a desperate attack against embedded Japanese troops and managed to save Brewster and what was left of his ambushed platoon. My thanks also to Steve Passman, a Florida man who sent me materials from his late father, Ben, who was saved at one juncture on Okinawa when Brewster and Perskie together separated burning munitions from an ammo dump that otherwise would have exploded.

On beautiful, windswept, pony-dotted Assateague Island, National Park Service rangers Liz Davis and Bill Huslander spent most of a day with me explaining the history of the Assateague National Seashore, which Brewster's legislation created. Among the artifacts they showed me were plat books from the 1950s for a proposed development that would have almost covered the barrier island with houses and roads.

Towson, Maryland, historian Blaine Taylor talked to me about two of the most intriguing interviews Danny Brewster gave during his lifetime. One was his candid interview with Taylor for the *Maryland State Medical Journal* about dealing with the ravages of alcoholism; the other, an interview with Taylor for *Vietnam* magazine in which Brewster revealed belated regrets over his blind support for the war in Vietnam. Blaine, himself a Vietnam War veteran, also provided me with many documents related to these and other episodes in Brewster's life. Sadly, Blaine Taylor passed away in 2021 at age seventy-four.

Much of the research on political biographies is done at or through libraries. Brewster's official papers are at the Hornbake Library on the campus of the University of Maryland where Elizabeth Novara, Emily Flint, and other librarians helped me find the boxes of materials I needed to see. Priscilla and I jointly researched the William Christian Bullitt papers at Yale University's Sterling Memorial Library in New Haven, Connecticut where we uncovered details of Brewster's hospitalization in

Ireland as well as love letters he wrote to Bullitt's daughter, Anne. We were helped in that effort by librarian Michael Frost, who later dug out additional materials for me when I doubt he was supposed to do so.

The staff at the Maryland Legislative Library helped me research the long history of Jim Crow laws in Maryland as well as the more recent fight for civil rights within the Maryland General Assembly.

My thanks to David Levesque, the archivist at Ohrstrom Library at the St. Paul's School in Concord, New Hampshire, not only for the excellent tour he gave me of the school but also for lessons about the school's history as well as research he provided on Danny Brewster's years as a student there.

Tyler Abell, a friend of and former aide to President Johnson, also became a close friend of Danny Brewster and the Brewster family. Tyler was interviewed for this book and became such an advocate for it that he sometimes shared the draft with his former Johnson administration colleagues. It was Tyler who nudged Brian McNerney of the Lyndon Baines Johnson Library in Austin, Texas, to provide me with copies of White House documents showing some of the close relationship between Brewster and LBJ.

Laura Booze of the alumni office at the Foxcroft School in Middleburg, Virginia, provided some background material on Anne Bullitt's years as a student there. And the rich database of old newspapers provided by the Baltimore County Public Library System allowed me to research old issues of the *Baltimore Sun, Washington Post, Washington Star, Baltimore News American*, and other papers from the comfort of my home.

Chelsea Crow of Palmerstown House in County Kildare, Ireland, arranged for Priscilla and me to tour the manor house and grounds once owned by Anne Bullitt. She also provided me with a history of the estate.

Finally, I want to thank my friend, Jan Eliassen, who discussed this biography with me before the first chapter was written and helped me think about the stresses on some members of the Greatest Generation when they returned from war. Smart, handsome, and successful Danny Brewster surely would have denied the connection, but it is hard to examine his turbulent life without seeing the probable link between the savage, prolonged war he fought in the South Pacific and his later alcoholism and symptoms of post-traumatic stress disorder. As Jan said to me, that was the "dark side" for far too many of the Greatest Generation.

About the Author

John W. Frece spent about half of his career as a newspaper and wire service reporter and half working for the state and federal government. Knowledgeable about Maryland political history, he has written three previous books, including co-writing the autobiographies of former Maryland Governor Harry R. Hughes and former Maryland U.S. Senator Joseph D. Tydings. Drawing from his experience as a gubernatorial aide, Frece also wrote an insider's view of the political machinations behind Maryland's controversial land use policy known as smart growth.

Frece is a former reporter and Maryland State House Bureau Chief for the *Baltimore Sun* (1984-1995) and *United Press International* (1978-1984). He also covered the Virginia General Assembly in Richmond for UPI and was an editor, reporter and photographer for the *Reston Times*, a weekly newspaper in Fairfax County, Va. He later worked on the staff of Maryland Governor Parris N. Glendening, at a University of Maryland smart growth research center, and as director of the smart growth office within the US Environmental Protection Agency during the first five years of the Obama administration.

Frece is married to the children's book author, Priscilla Cummings, and they have two grown children, Will and Hannah, two grandsons, and two cats. Frece graduated from the College of William & Mary in Virginia in 1969 and was honorably discharged as a lieutenant in the U.S. Army in 1971.

His other books include:
- **"MY LIFE IN PROGRESSIVE POLITICS: AGAINST THE GRAIN,"** by former U.S. Senator Joseph D. Tydings with John W. Frece, Foreword by Joe Biden, Texas A&M University Press, May 2018.

- "SPRAWL AND POLITICS: THE STORY OF SMART GROWTH IN MARYLAND," by John W. Frece, State University of New York Press, 2008.

- "MY UNEXPECTED JOURNEY: THE AUTOBIOGRAPHY OF GOVERNOR HARRY ROE HUGHES," by Governor Harry Roe Hughes with John W. Frece, The History Press, August 2006

Endnotes

Prologue

1. Chris Hutchins, interview with the author, Jan. 31, 2019.

Chapter 1

2. Sgt. George R. Voigt (a Marine Corps combat correspondent who formerly worked for the *Los Angeles Daily News*), summary of the ambush of L Company, 4th Marine Regiment, 6th Marine Division, on Okinawa, April 20, 1945, 1, found in March 2019 in the personal papers of M. Daniel Perskie of Northfield, NJ.
3. Daniel B. Brewster, handwritten war diary, Nov. 19, 1943, to Aug. 18, 1945, Brewster family papers, 27.
4. Brewster, Daniel B., war diary, 29.
5. Blaine Taylor, "Steep Typhoon at Okinawa," Warfare History Network, accessed Oct. 13, 2017, http://warfarehistorynetwork.com/daily/steep-typhoon-at-okinawa/print/
6. Michael H. Rogers, ed., *Answering Their Country's Call: Marylanders in World War II*, feature on Daniel B. Brewster, Glyndon, Md., Sixth Marine Division, The Johns Hopkins University Press, Baltimore, Md., Nov. 5, 2002.
7. Sgt. George R. Voigt, US Marine Corps correspondent, "L Company," April 20, 1945, 4.
8. Voigt, summary, 4.
9. Voigt, summary, 4.
10. Brewster, Daniel B., war diary, 30.
11. Voigt, summary, 4–5.
12. Brewster, Daniel B., war diary, 30.
13. Brewster, Daniel B., war diary, 30.
14. M. Daniel Perskie (son of US Marine Corps Lt. Marvin D. Perskie, L Company Executive Officer), interview with the author, March 10, 2019.
15. Brewster, Daniel B., war diary, 30.
16. Voigt, summary, 5.
17. Perskie, interview.
18. Voigt, summary, 6.
19. Brewster, Daniel B., war diary, 30.
20. "The Drive Up Ishikawa," Chapter 7, *History of the Sixth Marine Division*, edited by Revan G. Cass, The Battery Press, Nashville, Tenn., 51–53.
21. Brewster, Daniel B., war diary, 31.
22. Laura Homan Lacey, *Stay Off the Skyline: The Sixth Marine Division in Okinawa*, Potomac Books, University of Nebraska Press, Lincoln, Neb., 2005, 2.
23. Lacey, *Stay Off the Skyline*, 2.
24. Lacey, *Stay Off the Skyline*, 2.
25. E. B. Sledge, *With the Old Breed*, Presidio Press, Random House, Inc., New York, 1981, 118.
26. Brewster, Daniel B., war diary, 24.

Chapter 2

27. Walter W. Brewster (youngest brother of Daniel B. Brewster), interview with the author, April 5, 2018.
28. Brewster, Walter W., interview.

29. Daniel B. Brewster, "The President's Speech," *Horae Scholasticeae* LXXV, no. 1 (Oct. 6, 1941): 2, St. Paul's School archives, Concord, NH.

30. Brewster, Walter W., interview.

31. Samantha Kymmell, *Wickcliffe: A History*, 2010, picture copyright 2010 by Maryvale Preparatory School.

32. US Census records, 1920 and 1930.

33. *Baugh's Farmers' Almanac and Reference Book* (Baugh & Sons Co, 1913), 1, Brewster family papers.

34. Society Column, *Baltimore Evening Sun*, June 28, 1920, downloaded March 18, 2019, https://www.newspapers.com/image/368054756

35. "Du Pont Heiress in S.F. after Trip to Hawaii; Honeymooning Pair Arrive on Lurline," *San Francisco Examiner*, Dec. 23, 1937, downloaded March 18, 2019, https://www.newspapers.com/image/legacy/458067771/

36. This paragraph, Francis N. Iglehart, *Recollections of an Occasional Attorney* (Baltimore: American Literary Press, Inc., 2004), 16–18.

37. Azam Ansari, MD, Barry J. Maron, MD, and Daniel G. Berntson, MD, "Drug-Induced Toxic Myocarditis," *Texas Heart Institute Journal* (2003), https://www.ncbi.nlm.nih.gov/pmc/?term=toxic+myocarditis

38. Gerry L. Brewster to Daniel B. Brewster, Andre Brewster, Walter Brewster, Frances Cochran, and Daniel B. Brewster Jr., March 10, 2004, Brewster family papers.

Chapter 3

39. DeCourcy "Dick" McIntosh (US Senate staffer for Sen. Daniel B. Brewster), interview with the author, March 1, 2019.

40. This and the previous quote, Norman B. Nash to Mrs. William F. Cochran Jr. (a.k.a. Ottolie Brewster and later as Ottolie Cochran, mother of Daniel B. Brewster), June 14, 1941, Brewster family papers.

41. David Levesque (archivist, St. Paul's School, Concord, NH), interview with the author, Oct. 9, 2019.

42. Nash to Cochran.

43. St. Paul's School, President's Medal commendation to Daniel B. Brewster, June 12, 1942, Brewster family papers.

44. Laura Homan Lacey, *Stay Off the Skyline: The Sixth Marine Division in Okinawa*, Potomac Books, University of Nebraska Press, Lincoln, NE., 2005), 23.

45. Daniel B. Brewster, handwritten war diary, Nov. 19, 1943, to Aug. 18, 1945, Brewster family papers, 14.

46. Vesta Kelling, "Capital's Inner Circle Honoring Anne Bullitt," *Baltimore Evening Sun,* June 12, 1941.

47. Liam Collins, *The Dark Side of Celebrity: Irish Courtroom Scandals of the Rich and Famous* (Dublin, Ireland: Mentor Books, Ltd., 2009), 154.

48. Collins, *Dark Side of Celebrity*, 154.

49. Anne Bullitt to William Bullitt, William C. Bullitt papers, Manuscripts and Archives, MS 112, series I, box 13, folder 266, Sterling Memorial Library, Yale University.

50. "Forever Little Anne Bullitt," *The Daily Mail* (London), Jan. 31, 1999.

51. Kelling, "Capital's Inner Circle."

52. Kelling, "Capital's Inner Circle."

53. Kerri Gonzalez (assistant librarian/archivist, The Foxcroft School, Middleburg, VA), interview with the author, Nov. 29, 2018.

54. Nancy Randolph, "Anne Bullitt's Party to Be Big Blowout," *Daily News*, June 19, 1941.

55. Kelling, "Capital's Inner Circle."

56. This paragraph, Nancy Randolph, "Anne Bullitt's Party."

57. Anne Bullitt to William Bullitt.

58. Brewster, Daniel B., war diary, 8.

59. Brewster, Daniel B., war diary, 8.

60. Brewster, Daniel B., war diary, 8.

61. Brewster, Daniel B., war diary, 9.

62. Brewster, Daniel B., war diary, 10.

63. This and the previous paragraph, Ottolie Cochran to Lt. Daniel B. Brewster, Nov. 10, 1943, Brewster family papers.

64. Brewster, Daniel B., war diary, 10.

65. Brewster, Daniel B., war diary, 10.

66. Brewster, Daniel B., war diary, 10–11.

67. Brewster, Daniel B., war diary, 11.

68. Brewster, Daniel B., war diary, 12.

69. Brewster, Daniel B., war diary, 12–13.

70. Brewster, Daniel B., war diary, 13.

71. Brewster, Daniel B., war diary, 14.

Chapter 4

72. 1st Lt. Daniel B. Brewster (Sr.) to Elizabeth Baugh Brewster, Oct. 12, 1918, "Letters from Lieutenant Daniel Baugh Brewster, USMC," 1918–1919, Brewster family papers.

73. Daniel B. Brewster, handwritten war diary, Nov. 19, 1943, to Aug. 18, 1945, Brewster family papers, 17.

74. 2nd Lt. Daniel B. Brewster (Sr.) to Benjamin Harris Brewster Jr., May 14, 1918, "Letters from Lieutenant Daniel Baugh Brewster, USMC," 1918–1919, Brewster family papers.

75. Order of the Army to 2nd Lt. Daniel B. Brewster of the 76th Company of the 6th Marine Regiment, Croix de Guerre citation, Order N-11768 "D" of Nov. 20, 1918, Brewster family papers.

76. This and the previous, 1st Lt. Daniel B. Brewster (Sr.) to Elizabeth Baugh Brewster, Oct. 19, 1918, "Letters from Lieutenant Daniel Baugh Brewster, USMC," 1918–1919, Brewster family papers.

77. 1st Lt. Daniel B. Brewster (Sr.) to Elizabeth Baugh Brewster, Nov. 4, 1918, "Letters from Lieutenant Daniel Baugh Brewster, USMC," 1918–1919, Brewster family papers.

78. Brewster, Daniel B., war diary, 16–17.

79. E. B. Sledge, *With the Old Breed* (New York: Presidio Press, Random House, Inc., 1981), 18.

80. Sledge, *With the Old Breed*, 5.

81. Brewster, Daniel B., war diary, 15.

82. Brewster, Daniel B., war diary, 15.

83. Brewster, Daniel B., war diary, 17.

84. Brewster, Daniel B., war diary, 19.

85. This and the two quotes above it, General Lemuel C. Shepherd Jr., USMC (retired), interview by Benis M. Frank and Colonel Robert D. Heinl Jr., July 27 and Aug. 4, 1966, in Warrenton, VA, for the Marine Corps Oral History Collection, Historical Division, Headquarters, US Marine Corps, Washington, DC, 34.

86. Brewster, Daniel B., war diary, 21.

87. Sledge, *With the Old Breed*, 130.

88. Dana Brewster (son of Daniel B. and Judy Brewster), interview with the author, Feb. 20, 2019.

89. Brewster, Daniel B., war diary, 21-22.

90. Brewster, Daniel B., war diary, 22.

91. Brewster, Daniel B., war diary, 32.

92. This and the two previous quotes, Brewster, Daniel B., war diary, 34.

93. Shepherd, interview, 34.

94. Blaine Taylor, "Steel Typhoon at Okinawa," Warfare History Network, accessed Oct. 13, 2017, 3, http://warfarehistorynetwork.com/daily/steep-typhoon-at-okinawa/print/

95. Taylor, "Steel Typhoon," 7.

96. Laura Homan Lacey, *Stay Off the Skyline: The Sixth Marine Division in Okinawa*, Potomac Books, University of Nebraska Press, Lincoln, NE, 2005), 172.

97. Taylor, "Steel Typhoon," 10.

98. Lacey, *Stay Off the Skyline*, 128.

99. Bernard G. Passman (Delray Beach, Florida) to M. Daniel Perskie (son of L Company Lt. Marvin D. Perskie), undated, found in March 2019 in the personal papers of M. Daniel Perskie of Northfield, NJ.

100. Passman to Perskie.

101. This and preceding paragraph, Passman to Perskie.

102. Brewster, Daniel B., war diary, 35.

103. Brewster, Daniel B., war diary, 35.

104. Taylor, "Steel Typhoon," 10.

105. Sledge, *With the Old Breed*, 266.

106. Brewster, Daniel B., war diary, 39.

107. Sledge, *With the Old Breed*, 217.

108. Brewster, Daniel B., war diary, 40.

109. Taylor, "Steel Typhoon," 8.

110. Liz F. Kay and Frederick N. Rasmussen, "Senator, War Hero Backed Civil Rights," *Baltimore Sun*, Aug. 21, 2007.

111. From official US Marine Corps photograph of US Marine Corps Reserve Colonel Daniel Baugh Brewster dated Mar. 9, 1967, which shows Brewster in uniform with his decorations on display; and cross-checked with US Marine Corps Ribbon Chart and Award Criteria for Marine Corps Awards, at https://www.mcieast.marines.mil/portals/33/documents/adjutant/usmc%20 ribbon%20chart.docx

112. Brewster, Daniel B., war diary, 45.

113. Brewster, Daniel B., war diary, 24.

Chapter 5

114. Daniel B. Brewster, handwritten war diary, Nov. 19, 1943, to Aug. 18, 1945, Brewster family papers, 45.

115. Brewster, Daniel B., war diary, 23.

116. Brewster, Daniel B., war diary, 5.

117. Brewster, Daniel B., war diary, 4.

118. Brewster, Daniel B., war diary, this and previous quotes, 16.

119. Brewster, Daniel B., war diary, 17.

120. Brewster, Daniel B., war diary, 16.

121. Walter W. Brewster (youngest brother of Daniel B. Brewster), interview with the author, April 5, 2018.

122. Brewster, Walter W., interview with author, April 5, 2018.

123. Brewster, Walter W., interview with author, April 5, 2018.

124. Brewster, Walter W., interview.

125. Brewster, Walter W., interview.

126. Brewster, Walter W., interview.

127. John F. Lewis, "He Who Runs May Ride," *Baltimore Sun*, April 23, 1950.

128. Charlie Fenwick (Baltimore County horseman and neighbor of Daniel B. Brewster), interview with the author, June 18, 2018.

129. Fenwick, interview.

130. Fenwick, interview.

131. John Howard (attorney at Turnbull, Brewster, et al. law firm), interview with the author, July 15, 2019.

132. Gerry L. Brewster (youngest son of Daniel B. and Carol Brewster), interview with the author, May 10, 2019.

133. Brewster, Walter W., interview

134. Michael de Havenon (son of Carol Brewster, stepson of Daniel B. Brewster), interview with the author, Dec. 4, 2018.

135. De Havenon, interview.

136. Gerry L. Brewster, interview with the author, June 7, 2019.

137. Brewster, Gerry L., interview, June 7, 2019.

138. "Island Heights Girls Sail Sloop Like Old Baymen, Father Boasts," *Asbury Park (NJ) Press*,

July 19, 1930.

139. Brewster, Walter W., interview.

140. Brewster, Walter W., interview.

141. Brewster, Walter W., interview.

142. Sue Cronk, "Carol Brewster Asking Voters for Justice," *Washington Post*, May 13, 1964.

143. "Marylander of Promise," *Maryland Report* 4, no. 25 (Aug. 4, 1955): 3.

Chapter 6

144. Joyce Pocklington, "Brewster: Thoroughbred with a Love for the People," *Washington Post*, undated, Brewster family papers.

145. Harry R. Hughes (Governor of Maryland, 1979–87, and friend of Daniel B. Brewster), interview with the author, Nov. 15, 2018.

146. "Meet Your County Officials, Daniel B. Brewster, House of Delegates," unidentified newspaper, 1954, Brewster family papers.

147. Lawrence W. Efford, "Proposed Dog Law is Taken for Airing," *Baltimore Evening Sun*, June 12, 1957.

148. Paul Moore, "New Man on an Old Job: Brewster on Tight Schedule: Goal? Best Congressman," *Baltimore Evening Sun*, Jan. 29, 1959, 29.

149. Gerry L. Brewster (youngest son of Daniel B. and Carol Brewster), interview with the author, March 8, 2018.

150. "Looking Forward to '54 Congressional Election," *Jeffersonian*, Nov. 13, 1953.

151. "Brewster Announces Candidacy in County Congressional Race Here," *Union News*, June 21, 1957.

152. Greater Towson Junior Chamber of Commerce, recommendation submitted to US Junior Chamber of Commerce, Sept. 20, 1957.

153. John Grason Turnbull, interview by Gerry L. Brewster, April 2, 1979, for his Princeton thesis, "Daniel Baugh Brewster: The Triumphs and Tragedies of a Maryland Politician," April 18, 1979, Brewster family papers.

154. Daniel B. Brewster, interviews by Gerry L. Brewster, Nov. 24, 1974, Nov. 27, 1974, March 11, 1979, May 5, 1977, and March 15, 1979, for his Princeton thesis, "Daniel Baugh Brewster: The Triumphs and Tragedies of a Maryland Politician," April 18, 1979, Brewster family papers, 34-35.

155. Peter Aiello, "Congressional Candidate," letter to the editor, *Baltimore Evening Sun*, July 18, 1958.

156. James P. S. Devereux, interview by Gerry L. Brewster, March 11, 1979, for his Princeton thesis, "Daniel Baugh Brewster: The Triumphs and Tragedies of a Maryland Politician," April 18, 1979, Brewster family papers, 39.

157. "Symington Irked by Poster" *Baltimore News-Post*, Oct. 1, 1958.

158. "Some Revealing Questions and Answers on… Why I Should Vote for Daniel B. Brewster," political ad, Daniel B. Brewster papers, series 10, box 1, Hornbake Library, University of Maryland, College Park, MD.

159. Laurence W. Efford, *Baltimore Evening Sun*, Jun. 20, 1957.

160. Nelson Rightmyer, letter to the editor, *Baltimore Sun*, Oct. 26, 1958.

161. *Eastern Enterprise*, Oct. 30, 1958, and *Union News*, Oct. 31, 1958, Brewster family papers.

162. "The Coming Election," *Union News*, Oct. 31, 1958.

163. Endorsement, *Baltimore Sun*, Oct 27, 1958.

164. Endorsement, *Baltimore News American*, Nov. 6, 1960, handwritten in Brewster family files.

165. Paul Moore, "New Man On an Old Job: Brewster on Tight Schedule: Goal? Best Congressman," *Baltimore Evening Sun*, Jan. 29, 1959.

166. Dee Hardie, "Wife of Congressman Stays Busy All the Day," *Baltimore News-Post*, Sept. 2, 1960.

167. "Combat Troops Wasted, Rep. Brewster Declares," *Baltimore News-Post*, June 2, 1959.

168. Pres. John F. Kennedy, "Remarks of Senator John F. Kennedy, Towson Shopping Center, Towson, MD," American Presidency Project, Sept. 16, 1960, https://www.presidency.ucsb.edu/node/274739.

169. Charles Whiteford, "Brewster, Lee, Hughes, Lacy, State Ticket is Proposed," *Baltimore Sun*, July 19, 1961.

170. Governor Harry Roe Hughes with John W. Frece, *My Unexpected Journey: The Autobiography of Governor Harry Roe Hughes* (Charleston, SC: History Press, 2006), 59.

Chapter 7

171. Theodore G. "Ted" Venetoulis (former Baltimore County Executive), interview with the author, Oct. 1, 2019.

172. Charles Whiteford, "Lee Tries to Link Brewster with Savings and Loan Issue," *Baltimore Sun*, Apr. 18, 1962, https://www.newspapers.com/clip/108688720/savings-and-loan-clip/

173. "Brewster Hits Lee's Jab as 'Low Road,'" *Baltimore Evening Sun*, March 23, 1962.

174. "Grady, Brewster Attack Pollock," unknown newspaper, undated, Brewster family papers.

175. "The State Elections," editorial, *County Papers*, May 3, 1962.

176. "Postscript on the Election: Six are Enough," *Baltimore Sun*, May 1962.

177. "Golden Boy of Maryland Politics," *Bethesda (MD) Tribune*, July 13, 1962.

178. Marie Smith, "She Runs the Farm as He Runs for the Senate," *Washington Post*, Aug 19, 1962.

179. Baroness Stackelberg, "Washington Datebook: Brewster's Vivacious Wife Should Be Political Asset," *Baltimore News-Post*, Aug. 29, 1962.

180. Smith, "She Runs the Farm."

181. Smith, "She Runs the Farm."

182. Marie Smith, "She Runs the Farm as He Runs for the Senate," *Washington Post*, Aug 19, 1962, F-1

183. DeCourcy "Dick" McIntosh (US Senate staffer for Sen. Daniel B. Brewster), interview with the author, March 1, 2019.

184. McIntosh, interview.

185. Charles Whiteford, "Thousands See, Hear President," *Baltimore Sun*, Oct. 11, 1962.

186. Pres. John F. Kennedy, "Remarks in Baltimore at the Fifth Regiment Armory," American Presidency Project, Oct. 10, 1962, https://www.presidency.ucsb.edu/node/236006.

187. Whiteford, "Thousands See, Hear President."

188. Frank A. DeFilippo, "America Hasn't Shed a Tear in 50 Years for a President," Nov. 18, 2013, Splicetoday.com, https://www.Splicetoday.com/politics-and-media/America-hasn-t-shed-a-tear-in-50-years-for-a-president

189. "Other State Contests," editorial endorsements, *Baltimore Evening Sun*, Oct 30, 1962.

190. Editorial endorsement, *Baltimore Sun*, October 1962.

191. Vice Pres. Lyndon B. Johnson to Sen.-elect Daniel B. Brewster, Nov. 12, 1962, Brewster family papers.

192. Paul B. "Red" Fay Jr. to Sen. Daniel B. Brewster, Christmas card, Dec. 1962, Brewster family papers.

193. Nancy Pelosi (former Brewster staffer, Speaker of the House of Representatives), interview with the author, May 11, 2019.

194. Pelosi, interview.

195. Robert A. Manekin (former Brewster office intern), interview with the author, May 7, 2018.

196. Steny Hoyer (former Brewster staffer, House Majority Leader), interview with the author, July 18, 2019.

Chapter 8

197. Barbara Arthur, Margaret Carter, Kathy Krzystan, Mary MacDonald, Joan Perry, Richard Rheiner, Patricia Ritchie, and Dana Thompcon, editors, *Under the Dome: The Maryland General Assembly in the 20th Century* (Annapolis, MD: Maryland Department of Legislative Services, 2001), 204–205.

198. *Under the Dome*, 201.

199. Ida A. Brudnick and Jennifer E. Manning, *African American Members of the United States Congress: 1970-2018*, Congressional Research Service, updated Dec. 28, 2018, 7–8. file:///G:/

My%20Drive/Books/Danny%20Brewster/Civil%20Rights/african-americans%20in%20the%20 military%20-%20WWII%20Museum.pdf .

200. Joseph D. Tydings, interview with the author, Feb. 4, 2014.

201. US Census records, 1920 and 1930.

202. Walter W. Brewster (youngest brother of Daniel B. Brewster), interview with the author, April 5, 2018.

203. Bernard C. Nalty, "The Right to Fight: African-American Marines in World War II," History and Museums Division, Headquarters, US Marine Corps, Washington, DC, 1995, https:// www.nps.gov/parkhistory/online_books/npswapa/extcontent/usmc/pcn-190-003132-00/sec14. htm.

204. Nalty, "The Right to Fight." https://www.nationalww2museum.org/sites/default/ files/2017-07/african-americans.pdf

205. Nalty, "The Right to Fight."

206. "African Americans in World War II: Fighting for a Double Victory," National WWII Museum, https://www.nationalww2museum.org/sites/default/files/2017-07/african-americans.pdf

207. Nalty, "The Right to Fight."

208. Brewster, Walter W., interview.

209. Francis N. Iglehart, *Recollections of an Occasional Attorney* (Baltimore: American Literary Press, Inc., 2004), 25–27.

210. Gerry L. Brewster (youngest son of Daniel B. and Carol Brewster), interview with the author, Nov. 13, 2019.

211. Iglehart, *Recollections*, 25–27.

212. Brewster, Walter W., interview.

213. Gerry L. Brewster, interview with the author, Nov. 14, 2017.

214. Michael de Havenon (son of Carol Brewster, stepson of Daniel B. Brewster), interview with the author, Dec. 4, 2018.

215. Charles McC. Mathias Jr., interview by Gerry L. Brewster for his Princeton thesis, "Daniel Baugh Brewster: The Triumphs and Tragedies of a Maryland Politician," April 18, 1979, Brewster family papers, Mar. 22, 1979.

216. Hubert H. Humphrey, "Speech on Civil Rights" (Democratic National Convention, Philadelphia, PA, July 14, 1948), Minnesota Historical Society, http://www2.mnhs.org/library/ findaids/00442/pdfa/00442-00187.pdf.

217. Exec. Order No. 9981 (July 26, 1948), promulgated by Pres. Harry S. Truman.

218. Gerry L. Brewster, interview by Clarence Mitchell IV, the *C4 And Bryan Nehman Show,* WBAL (Baltimore), March 6, 2020.

219. Daniel B. Brewster, "The President's Speech," *Horae Scholasticeae* LXXV, no. 1 (Oct. 6, 1941): 1, St. Paul's School archives, Concord, NH.

220. Brewster, Daniel B., "The President's Speech," 2.

221. Brewster, Daniel B., "The President's Speech," 2.

Chapter 9

222. Laura Homan Lacey, *Stay Off the Skyline: The Sixth Marine Division in Okinawa*, Potomac Books, University of Nebraska Press, Lincoln, NE, 2005), x–xi.

223. Gerry L. Brewster and J. Reiley McDonald, "The 1964 Maryland Democratic Primary: A Study in Personalities and Politics," senior term paper, The Gilman School, Baltimore, Dec. 2, 1974, 3, Brewster family papers.

224. Medgar Evers, Wikipedia, https://en.wikipedia.org/wiki/Medgar_Evers.

225. Rev. Martin Luther King Jr., "I Have a Dream," Aug. 28, 1963, Martin Luther King Jr. Research and Education Institute, Stanford University, https://kinginstitute.stanford.edu/king-papers/documents/i-have-dream-address-delivered-march-washington-jobs-and-freedom.

226. Charles Whiteford, "Cambridge Talk Urged by Brewster," *Baltimore Sun,* Oct. 15, 1963.

227. Robert A. Caro, *The Passage of Power: The Years of Lyndon Johnson* (New York: Vintage Books, 2013), 9.

228. "President Lyndon B. Johnson's Address to a Joint Session of Congress, November 27, 1963," Center for Legislative Archives, National Archives, http://www.archives.gov/legislative/

features/civil-rights-1964/lbj-address.html.

229. Katharine Rasmers of Baltimore to Sen. Daniel B. Brewster, Feb. 20, 1964, Daniel B. Brewster papers, series 1, box 11, Civil Rights Feb. 1964, Hornbake Library, University of Maryland, College Park, MD.

230. William M. Werber (civil rights opponent, Werber Insurance Agency, Washington, DC) to Sen. Daniel B. Brewster, Jan. 24, 1964, Daniel B. Brewster papers, series 1, box 11, Civil Rights, Hornbake Library, University of Maryland, College Park, MD.

231. Werber to Brewster, March 18, 1964, Daniel B. Brewster papers, series 1, box 12, Civil Rights, Hornbake Library, University of Maryland, College Park, MD.

232. Brewster to Werber, March 21, 1964, Daniel B. Brewster papers, series 1, box 12, Civil Rights, Hornbake Library, University of Maryland, College Park, MD.

233. Philip James Bunch of Hyattsville, MD, to Sen. Daniel B. Brewster, March 6, 1964, Daniel B. Brewster papers, series 1, box 11, Civil Rights March 1964, Hornbake Library, University of Maryland, College Park, MD.

234. Sen. Daniel B. Brewster to Philip James Bunch, March 16, 1964, Daniel B. Brewster papers, series 1, box 11, Civil Rights March 1964, Hornbake Library, University of Maryland, College Park, MD.

235. Adolph F. Sckow of Bethesda, MD, to Sen. Daniel B. Brewster, March 17, 1964, Daniel B. Brewster papers, series 1, box 11, Civil Rights March 1964, Hornbake Library, University of Maryland, College Park, MD.

236. Mr. and Mrs. Harald Rausch of Kensington, MD, to Sen. Daniel B. Brewster, Jan. 14, 1964, Daniel B. Brewster papers, series 1, box 11, Civil Rights Dec. 1963–Jan. 1964, Hornbake Library, University of Maryland, College Park, MD.

237. Sen. Daniel B. Brewster to Juanita Jackson Mitchell (president of the Maryland State Conference NAACP Branches), March 2, 1964, Daniel B. Brewster papers, series 1, box 11, March 1964 (2), Hornbake Library, University of Maryland, College Park, MD.

238. Thomas V. Mike Miller Jr. (former Maryland Senate President), interview with the author, July 24, 2019.

239. Daniel B. Brewster, interview by Gerry L. Brewster, Nov. 27, 1974, for his senior term paper at the Gilman School, "The 1964 Maryland Democratic Presidential Primary: A Study in Personalities and Politics," by Gerry L. Brewster and J. Reiley McDonald, Brewster family papers.

240. Herb Thompson, Associated Press, "Brewster Files to Block Wallace," *Salisbury (MD) Times*, March 17, 1964.

241. William Townsend, interview by Gerry L. Brewster, Nov. 28, 1974, for his senior term paper at the Gilman School, "The 1964 Maryland Democratic Presidential Primary: A Study in Personalities and Politics," by Gerry L. Brewster and J. Reiley McDonald, Brewster family papers.

242. John F. Sullivan, Federal Grand Jury empaneled in Baltimore, Md., Apr. 1, 1969, grand jury testimony, Feb. 12, 1970, 55–56.

243. "Phone Calls Threaten Sen. Brewster, Wife, Unless He Withdraws," *Baltimore News American*, March 18, 1964.

244. Brewster, Daniel B., interview, Nov. 27, 1974.

245. "Brewster at the Bridge," *Baltimore Evening Sun*, April 11, 1964.

246. Townsend, interview.

247. Steny Hoyer (former Brewster staffer, House Majority Leader), interview with the author, July 18, 2019.

248. This and the previous paragraph, Townsend, interview.

249. Civil Rights Act of 1964, Wikipedia, https://en.wikipedia.org/wiki/Civil_Rights_Act_of_1964.

250. Nancy Pelosi (former Brewster staffer, Speaker of the House of Representatives), interview with the author, May 11, 2019.

251. Sen. Daniel B. Brewster, April 20, 1964 (statement, AFL-CIO Committee on Political Education, Baltimore).

252. Bill Miller (aide to Sen. Daniel B. Brewster), interview with the author, July 11, 2018.

253. "Brewster Hit in 'Hate' Mail," *Baltimore Sun*, April 17, 1964.

254. "Uninvited Guest," *Time*, May 22, 1964, https://content.time.com/time/subscriber/arti-

cle/0,33009,871094,00.html

255. John J. Synon, *George Wallace: Profile of a Presidential Candidate* (Kilmarnock, VA: Ms, Inc., 1968), 94–95.

256. George Bowen, Associated Press, "Kennedy Urges Vote for Senator," *Hagerstown (MD) Mail*

257. Richard H. Levine, "Winner's Atmosphere Slow to Appear in Brewster Camp," *Baltimore Sun*, May 19, 1964.

258. This and the previous quote, Cong. Rec. S11464 (May 20, 1964) (speech by Sen. William Proxmire, D-WI).

259. Joseph Hearst, "Senate Cloture Hopes Rise as Rights Backers Explain Changes," *Philadelphia Inquirer*, May 20, 1964.

260. Barry Williams (former Baltimore County Public Schools principal), interview with the author, Jan. 28, 2020.

261. Joseph D. Tydings, interviews by Gerry L. Brewster, Nov. 27 and 28, 1974, for his Princeton thesis, "Daniel Baugh Brewster: The Triumphs and Tragedies of a Maryland Politician," April 18, 1979, Brewster family papers.

262. Theodore H. White, *The Making of the President 1964* (New York: New American Press, 1965), 281.

263. "Brewster Edges Wallace," *The South Bend Tribune*, South Bend, Ind., May 20, 1964, 1.

264. Associated Press, "Strong Anti-Rights Vote Given Wallace," *Pensacola Journal*, May 20, 1964.

265. V. J. Hughes Sr. of Baltimore to Sen. Daniel B. Brewster, June 8, 1964, Daniel B. Brewster papers, series 1, book 12, Civil Rights May 1964–July 1966, Hornbake Library, University of Maryland, College Park, MD.

266. Robert D. Douglass of Baltimore to Sen. Daniel B. Brewster, June 11, 1964, Daniel B. Brewster papers, series 1, book 12, Civil Rights May 1964–July 1966, Hornbake Library, University of Maryland, College Park, MD.

267. Carroll E. Stewart to Sen. Daniel B. Brewster, June 15, 1964, Daniel B. Brewster papers, series 1, book 12, Civil Rights May 1964–July 1966, Hornbake Library, University of Maryland, College Park, MD.

268. Frederic Kelly, "Daniel Brewster Savors His Turn-Around Life," *Baltimore Sun Magazine*, June 29, 1980.

269. Hoyer, interview.

270. Rev. Martin Luther King Jr. to Sen. Daniel B. Brewster, June 24, 1964, Daniel B. Brewster papers, series 1, book 12, Civil Rights May 1964–July 1966, Hornbake Library, University of Maryland, College Park, MD.

271. Harry R. Hughes (Governor of Maryland, 1979–87, and friend of Daniel B. Brewster), interview with the author, Feb. 22, 2004.

272. Joseph D. Tydings (former Maryland US Senator), interview with the author, May 15, 2018.

273. Tydings, interview, Nov. 27 and 28, 1974.

Chapter 10

274. *Plat Guide and Manual: Ocean Beach of Assateague Island, Maryland*, in files of the National Park Service, US Department of the Interior, Assateague Island National Seashore, Berlin, MD.

275. Dean Kotlowski, "The Last Lonely Shore: Nature, Man, and the Making of Assateague Island National Seashore," *Maryland Historical Magazine* 99, no. 2 (Summer 2004): 174.

276. Kotlowski, "Last Lonely Shore," 172.

277. Kotlowski, "Last Lonely Shore," 175.

278. Sen. Daniel B. Brewster, speech, 13th Annual Governors' Conference and Middle Atlantic District Recreation and Park Conference, Lord Baltimore Hotel, May 10, 1964).

279. South Ocean Beach price list, effective Sept. 15, 1954, from the transcript of hearings on Senate bills 20 and 1121, before the Subcommittee on Parks and Recreation of the Committee on Interior and Insular Affairs, United States Senate, March 17, 18, 19, 22, 1965, US Government Printing Office, 215.

280. Bill Miller (aide to Sen. Daniel B. Brewster), interview with the author, July 11, 2018.

281. Kotlowski, "Last Lonely Shore," 189.

282. Sen. Daniel B. Brewster, testimony, from the transcript of hearings on Senate bills 20 and 1121, before the Subcommittee on Parks and Recreation of the Committee on Interior and Insular Affairs, United States Senate, March 17, 18, 19, 22, 1965, US Government Printing Office, 13.

283. C. A. Porter Hopkins, testimony, from the transcript of hearings on Senate bills 20 and 1121, before the Subcommittee on Parks and Recreation of the Committee on Interior and Insular Affairs, United States Senate, March 17, 18, 19, 22, 1965, US Government Printing Office, 81.

284. C. A. Porter Hopkins (friend of Daniel B. Brewster, former member of Maryland General Assembly, and lifelong conservationist), interview with the author, Aug. 5, 2019.

285. Fred C. Lewis, testimony, from the transcript of hearings on Senate bills 20 and 1121, before the Subcommittee on Parks and Recreation of the Committee on Interior and Insular Affairs, United States Senate, March 17, 18, 19, 22, 1965, US Government Printing Office, 109.

286. William R. Perl, testimony, from the transcript of hearings on Senate bills 20 and 1121, before the Subcommittee on Parks and Recreation of the Committee on Interior and Insular Affairs, United States Senate, March 17, 18, 19, 22, 1965, US Government Printing Office, 318.

287. Letters from Senator Daniel B. Brewster and Representative Rogers C. B. Morton, respectively, stating their opposition to federal takeover of Assateague Island, introduced by Wallace M. Smith, attorney for Ocean Beach, from the transcript of hearings on Senate bills 20 and 1121, before the Subcommittee on Parks and Recreation of the Committee on Interior and Insular Affairs, United States Senate, March 17, 18, 19, 22, 1965, US Government Printing Office, 199.

288. Sen. Alan Bible (subcommittee chairman), remarks made on the record, from the transcript of hearings on Senate bills 20 and 1121, before the Subcommittee on Parks and Recreation of the Committee on Interior and Insular Affairs, United States Senate, March 17, 18, 19, 22, 1965, US Government Printing Office, 319–320.

289. Miller, Bill, interview, July 11, 2018.

290. Joseph W. Fehrer Jr. (son of Joseph W. Fehrer Sr., former Interior Department employee), interview with the author, Aug. 23, 2019.

291. Liz Davis (National Park Service ranger), interview with the author, Aug. 15, 2019.

292. Bill Huslander (National Park Service ranger), interview with the author, Aug. 15, 2019.

293. Huslander, interview.

Chapter 11

294. United States Marine Corps, https://www.usna.edu/MarineCorps/index.php#:~:text=COME%20LEAD,fatigue%20and%20scrutiny%20%E2%80%94%20Marines%20win.

295. Daniel B. Brewster, statement, July 7, 1962, Brewster family papers.

296. Tom Kelleher (former employee of Sen. Daniel B. Brewster), interview with the author, May 24, 2019.

297. 110 Cong. Rec. 18403 (1964) (statement of Sen. Daniel B. Brewster).

298. 110 Cong. Rec. 18403–18404 (1964).

299. 110 Cong. Rec. 18403–18404 (1964).

300. 110 Cong. Rec. 18403–18404 (1964).

301. Gulf of Tonkin Resolution, Pub. L. No. 88-408.

302. Sen. Wayne Morse, Gulf of Tonkin debate, *Congressional Record*. August 6-7, 1964. pp18132-33. 18406-7. 18458-59, and 18470-71.

303. Daniel B. Brewster, interviews by Gerry L. Brewster, May 5, 1977, for his Princeton thesis, "Daniel Baugh Brewster: The Triumphs and Tragedies of a Maryland Politician," April 18, 1979, Brewster family papers.

304. Nancy Pelosi (former Brewster staffer, Speaker of the House of Representatives), interview with the author, May 11, 2019.

305. Mrs. John S. Webb of Greenbelt, MD, to Sen. Daniel B. Brewster, Jan. 1, 1964, Daniel B. Brewster papers, series 1, box 63, Viet Nam Jan.–March 1965, Hornbake Library, University of Maryland, College Park, MD.

306. Dr. George J. Cohen of Silver Spring, MD, to Sen. Daniel B. Brewster, Dec. 19, 1964,

Daniel B. Brewster papers, series 1, box 63, Viet Nam Jan.–March 1965, Hornbake Library, University of Maryland, College Park, MD.

307. Lorraine Claggett and Maurine Parker (the Third Haven Meeting, Religious Society of Friends [Quakers]) to Sen. Daniel B. Brewster, Jan. 6, 1965, Daniel B. Brewster papers, series 1, box 63, Viet Nam Jan.–March 1965, Hornbake Library, University of Maryland, College Park, MD.

308. Lawrence O'Brien (congressional assistant to the president) to Sen. Daniel B. Brewster, April 12, 1965, Lyndon B. Johnson Library, Austin, TX.

309. Jack Valenti (special assistant to the president) to Sen. Daniel B. Brewster, May 26, 1965, White House Central Files, Lyndon B. Johnson Library, Austin, TX.

310. W. Shepherdson Abell (former legislative assistant to Daniel B. Brewster), interview with the author, Aug. 19, 2019.

311. Blaine Taylor, "A Senator Looks Back," *Vietnam*, Aug. 1999, 27.

312. Bill Miller (aide to Sen. Daniel B. Brewster), interview with the author, July 24, 2019.

313. PFC John Bambacus (Marine serving in Da Nang, South Vietnam; later college professor and member Maryland General Assembly) to Sen. Daniel B. Brewster, Oct. 25, 1965, Bambacus family papers.

314. Sen. Daniel B. Brewster to PFC John Bambacus, Nov. 1, 1965, Daniel B. Brewster papers, accession 7, series 1, box 63, Hornbake Library, University of Maryland, College Park, MD.

315. Charles H. Page of Baltimore to Sen. Daniel B. Brewster, Oct. 14, 1965, Daniel B. Brewster papers, accession 7, series 1, box 63, Hornbake Library, University of Maryland, College Park, MD.

316. Mrs. Henry Kates Jr. of Mitchellville, MD, to Sen. Daniel B. Brewster, Feb. 7, 1968, Daniel B. Brewster papers, accession 7, series 1, box 64, Hornbake Library, University of Maryland, College Park, MD.

317. Milton Hoffman of Greenbelt, MD, to Sen. Daniel B. Brewster, Oct. 19, 1965, Daniel B. Brewster papers, accession 7, series 1, box 63, Hornbake Library, University of Maryland, College Park, MD.

318. Brewster to Hoffman, Nov. 9, 1965, Daniel B. Brewster papers, series 1, box 63, Viet Nam Jan.–March 1965, Hornbake Library, University of Maryland, College Park, MD.

319. Charles McC. Mathias Jr., interview by Gerry L. Brewster, March 22, 1979, for his Princeton thesis, "Daniel Baugh Brewster: The Triumphs and Tragedies of a Maryland Politician," April 18, 1979, Brewster family papers.

320. Don Maclean, "Senators Secretly Snickering at What Brewster Did to Morse," *Baltimore News American,* July 25, 1965.

321. "Two Senators Draw Praise for Amity," *Washington Post,* July 17, 1965.

322. Gerry L. Brewster (youngest son of Daniel B. and Carol Brewster), interview with the author, Dec. 27, 2019.

323. Sen. Daniel B. Brewster, address to the annual convention of the Disabled American Veterans, New Orleans, LA, Aug. 5, 1965.

324. Brewster, Daniel B., address to DAV.

325. Tyler Abell (former aide to President Johnson, Brewster family friend), interview with the author, Oct. 24, 2018.

326. Abell, Tyler, interview.

327. Peter J. Kumpa, "US Proud of Marines in Vietnam, Brewster Says," *Baltimore Sun,* Oct. 12, 1965.

328. Carl Schoettler, "One Man's Okinawa: 'Worst Day of My Life,' Brewster Says," *Baltimore Evening Sun*, Aug. 30, 1985.

329. Charles V. Flowers, "Senator Has Viet Report," *Baltimore Sun*, Oct. 17, 1965.

330. Taylor, "A Senator Looks Back," 23.

331. This and the previous paragraph, "From the People," a *Radio Press International* panel program moderated by Charles Langston with panelists Herb Brubaker (*RPI* Washington Bureau Chief) and Joe Stern (*Baltimore Sun* Washington Bureau), Nov. 1965, Washington, DC.

332. "From the People."

333. Daniel B. Brewster, Associated Press, "Brewster Backs Viet Fighting" (speech, first model

legislature of the Maryland Junior Chamber of Commerce, Maryland State House, Annapolis, MD, Nov. 18, 1966).

334. 112 Cong. Rec., 3981, Feb. 24, 1966, (speech by Sen. Daniel B. Brewster).

335. James MacNees, "Brewster Again Backs Viet Policy," *Baltimore Sun*, Oct. 25, 1967.

336. MacNees, "Brewster Again Backs."

337. "Brewster Backs LBJ Viet Stand," unknown newspaper, Oct. 25, 1967, Daniel B. Brewster papers, series 10, Hornbake Library, University of Maryland, College Park, MD.

338. Lillian R. Sonberg of Abingdon, MD, to Sen. Daniel B. Brewster, June 19, 1968, Daniel B. Brewster papers, accession 7, series 1, box 64, Hornbake Library, University of Maryland, College Park, MD.

339. Bill Miller (aide to Sen. Daniel B. Brewster), interview with the author, July 11, 2018.

340. Miller, Bill, interview, July 11, 2018.

341. "1957-1975: The Vietnam War," libcom.org, https://libcom.org/article/1957-1975-vietnam-war.

342. Taylor, "A Senator Looks Back," 23.

343. Taylor, "A Senator Looks Back," 23–24.

344. Mike Merson (hospital administrator and friend of Daniel B. Brewster), interview with the author, Feb. 28, 2019.

345. Taylor, "A Senator Looks Back," 25.

346. Taylor, "A Senator Looks Back," 28.

Chapter 12

347. Judy Brewster (third wife of Daniel B. Brewster), interview with the author, Nov. 23, 2018.

348. Frederic Kelly, "Daniel Brewster Savors His Turn-Around Life," *Baltimore Sun Magazine*, June 29, 1980.

349. John Howard (attorney at Turnbull, Brewster, et al. law firm), interview with the author, July 15, 2019.

350. C. A. Porter Hopkins (friend of Daniel B. Brewster, former member of Maryland General Assembly, and lifelong conservationist), interview with the author, Aug. 5, 2019.

351. Gerry L. Brewster (youngest son of Daniel B. and Carol Brewster), interview with the author, Nov. 14, 2017.

352. Michael de Havenon (son of Carol Brewster, stepson of Daniel B. Brewster), interview with the author, Dec. 4, 2018.

353. Steny Hoyer (former Brewster staffer, House Majority Leader), interview with the author, July 18, 2019.

354. DeCourcy "Dick" McIntosh (US Senate staffer for Sen. Daniel B. Brewster), interview with the author, March 1, 2019.

355. McIntosh, interview.

356. Maurice Wyatt (former campaign manager for Daniel B. Brewster), interview with the author, July 29, 2019.

357. W. Shepherdson Abell (former legislative assistant to Daniel B. Brewster), interview with the author, Aug. 19, 2019.

358. Abell, W. Shepherdson, interview.

359. Charles Whiteford, "Brewster Assails Wallace, Urges Vote of 'Conscience,'" *Baltimore Sun*, May 13, 1964; and, Arnold R. Isaacs, "U. of M. Students Hear Wallace: Governor Greeted by Jeers, Cheers and Rebel Yells," *Baltimore Sun,* May 13, 1964.

360. Michael Olesker (former *Baltimore Sun* reporter), interview with the author, Nov. 8, 2019.

361. Bill Miller (aide to Sen. Daniel B. Brewster), interview with the author, July 11, 2018.

362. Abell, W. Shepherdson, interview.

363. Miller, Bill, interview, July 11, 2018.

364. Wyatt, interview.

365. Miller, Bill, interview, July 11, 2018.

366. Brief, *Washington Post,* July 30, 1964.

367. Carol Brewster, interview by Gerry L. Brewster, March 11, 1979, for his Princeton thesis, "Daniel Baugh Brewster: The Triumphs and Tragedies of a Maryland Politician," April 18, 1979,

Brewster family papers.

368. Sen. Daniel B. Brewster, introduction of Pres. Lyndon B. Johnson (5th Regiment Armory, Baltimore, Oct. 24, 1964), transcription by Shannon Sheetz.

369. Harry C. McPherson Jr. to Pres. Lyndon B. Johnson, memorandum, Feb. 18, 1966, White House Central Files, Lyndon B. Johnson Library, Austin, Texas.

370. Steve Bennett, *Baltimore Sun*, June 6, 1967.

371. Frank DeFilippo, "Brewster Silent at Israel Fete," *Baltimore News American,* June 6, 1967.

372. "A Correction and Apology," *Baltimore Sun*, June 7, 1967.

373. Blaine Taylor, "Phoenix: The Rise, Fall and Resurrection of Sen. Daniel Brewster," *Maryland State Medical Journal* (July 1977): 39.

374. Taylor, "Phoenix," 39.

375. "Genetics of Alcohol Use Disorder," National Institute of Alcohol Abuse and Alcoholism, https://www.niaaa.nih.gov/alcohols-effects-health/alcohol-use-disorder/genetics-alcohol-use-disorder.

376. "Alcohol Addiction and Genetics, Addiction Center, https://www.addictioncenter.com/alcohol/genetics-of-alcoholism/#:~:text=Some%20who%20have%20inherited%20genes,whether%20someone%20will%20develop%

377. "Dual Diagnosis: Post Traumatic Stress Disorder and Addiction," Foundations Recovery Network, https://www.foundationsrecoverynetwork.com/mean-dual-diagnosis/

378. Laura Homan Lacey, *Stay Off the Skyline: The Sixth Marine Division in Okinawa,* Potomac Books, University of Nebraska Press, Lincoln, NE, 2005), 2 and 125–129.

379. E. B. Sledge, *With the Old Breed* (New York: Presidio Press, Random House, Inc., 1981), 264.

380. Daniel B. Brewster, handwritten war diary, Nov. 19, 1943, to Aug. 18, 1945, Brewster family papers, 41.

381. Kurt Aarsand (son of Judy Brewster, stepson of Daniel B. Brewster), interview with the author, March 13, 2020.

382. M. Daniel Perskie (son of Lt. Marvin D. Perskie, Marine Corps L Company Executive Officer), interview with the author, March 10, 2019.

383. Francis N. Iglehart, *Recollections of an Occasional Attorney* (Baltimore: American Literary Press, Inc., 2004), 22.

384. Jennilie Brewster (daughter of Daniel B. and Judy Brewster), interview with the author, Dec. 7, 2018.

385. Brewster, Jennilie, interview.

386. Danielle Brewster Oster (daughter of Daniel B. and Judy Brewster), interview with the author, March 1, 2019.

387. Abell, W. Shepherdson, interview.

388. Abell, W. Shepherdson, interview.

Chapter 13

389. *History of Palmerstown Estate*, provided by Chelsea Crowe, Palmerstown Estate, Sept. 11, 2019.

390. Daniel B. Brewster, handwritten war diary, Nov. 19, 1943, to Aug. 18, 1945, Brewster family papers, 13–14.

391. Joseph D. Tydings (former Maryland US Senator), interview with the author, May 15, 2018.

392. Tydings, interview, May 15, 2018.

393. "Sen. Brewster and Wife Part," *Baltimore News American*, March 23, 1967.

394. Steny Hoyer (former Brewster staffer, House Majority Leader), interview with the author, July 18, 2019.

395. DeCourcy "Dick" McIntosh (US Senate staffer and driver for Sen. Daniel B. Brewster), interview with the author, March 1, 2019.

396. Bill Miller (aide to Sen. Daniel B. Brewster), interview with the author, July 11, 2018.

397. Miller, Bill, interview, July 11, 2018.

398. John Grason Turnbull, interview by Gerry L. Brewster, April 2, 1979, for his Princeton

thesis, "Daniel Baugh Brewster: The Triumphs and Tragedies of a Maryland Politician," April 18, 1979, Brewster family papers.

399. Daniel B. Brewster to Anne Bullitt Biddle, William C. Bullitt papers, group 112, series VI, box 212, folder 239, Sterling Memorial Library, Yale University.

400. Brewster to Biddle, April 18, 1979.

401. Brewster to Biddle, April 18, 1979.

402. Brewster to Biddle, undated, William C. Bullitt papers, group 112, series VI, box 213, Folder 253, Sterling Memorial Library, Yale University.

403. Brewster to Biddle, William C. Bullitt papers, group 112, series VI, box 213, Folder 253, Sterling Memorial Library, Yale University.

404. Michael de Havenon, (son of Carol Brewster, stepson of Daniel B. Brewster), interview with the author, Dec. 4, 2018.

405. "Fiancée Injured, Brewster Says," unknown newspaper, undated, Daniel B. Brewster papers, series 10, Hornbake Library, University of Maryland, College Park, MD.

406. Muriel Bowen, "Sen. Brewster Has Irish Jigging," *Washington Post, Times Herald,* April 22, 1967.

407. Frank DeFilippo, "Brewster Divorce Impact Assessed," *Baltimore News American*, April 17, 1967.

408. "Brewster to Stay on the Job; Marriage to Anne Biddle in Future," *Washington Post,* April 27, 1967.

409. Jean R. Hailey, "Brewster Weds Anne Biddle," *Washington Post,* April 30, 1967.

410. De Havenon, interview.

411. Walter W. Brewster (youngest brother of Daniel B. Brewster), interview with the author, April 5, 2018.

412. "Milestones," *Time*, April 21, 1967, https://content.time.com/time/subscriber/article/0,33009,843633,00.html

413. Daniel B. Brewster to Anne Bullitt Brewster, undated, William C. Bullitt papers, group 112, series VI, box 213, folder 253, Sterling Memorial Library, Yale University.

414. Brewster to Bullitt Brewster, William C. Bullitt papers, group 112, series VI, box 213, folder 253.

415. Brewster to Bullitt Brewster, William C. Bullitt papers, group 112, series VI, box 213, folder 253.

416. McIntosh, interview.

417. Daniel B. Brewster, undated will, William C. Bullitt papers, group 112, series VI, box 213, folder 253, Sterling Memorial Library, Yale University.

418. Daniel B. Brewster to Anne Bullitt Brewster, Feb. 19, 1970, William C. Bullitt papers, group 112, series VI, box 212, folder 251, Sterling Memorial Library, Yale University.

419. Tydings, interview, May 15, 2018.

Chapter 14

420. Bill Miller (aide to Sen. Daniel B. Brewster), interview with the author, July 11, 2018.

421. Miller, Bill, interview, July 11, 2018.

422. Miller, Bill, interview, July 11, 2018.

423. Theodore G. "Ted" Venetoulis (former Baltimore County Executive), interview with the author, Oct. 1, 2019.

424. Maurice Wyatt (former campaign manager for Daniel B. Brewster), interview with the author, July 29, 2019.

425. Wyatt, interview.

426. Steny Hoyer (former Brewster staffer, House Majority Leader), interview with the author, July 18, 2019.

427. Herbert R. O'Conor III (grandson of the former Governor of Maryland), interview with the author, Oct. 22, 2019.

428. Charles V. Flowers, "Tydings, Sickles Backs Rights Bill," *Baltimore Sun*, May 1, 1966.

429. Alan L. Dessoff, "Rights Issue Plagues Md. Candidates," *Washington Post, Times Herald,* June 10, 1966.

430. Frank DeFilippo, "Brewster to Support Sickles for Governor: Senator Enters Tydings Camp," *Baltimore News American*, May 16, 1966.

431. Bradford Jacobs, "Next, Senator Brewster," *Baltimore Evening Sun*, April 7, 1967.

432. Bradford Jacobs, "Mr. Brewster's Switch," *Baltimore Evening Sun*, May 17, 1966.

433. Jacobs, "Mr. Brewster's Switch."

434. Miller, Bill, interview, July 11, 2018.

435. Gerald Ford, Wikipedia, https://en.wikipedia.org/wiki/Gerald_Ford.

436. Hoyer, interview.

437. Hoyer, interview.

Chapter 15

438. Sen. Daniel B. Brewster, "From the Capitol: Sen. Dan Brewster Reports," newsletter, 1966.

439. Shirley Elder, "Maryland Senators Off to Fast Start for 90th Congress," *Washington Star*, Jan. 8, 1967.

440. "Brewster Finds Wicomico Is Hot and Cold on '68," *Baltimore Sun*, Jan. 11, 1967.

441. "Mahoney Blames Brewster, Tydings, Sickles for Defeat," *Baltimore Sun*, Feb. 2, 1967.

442. "This and That," *Central Maryland News*, March 1967.

443. "Sen. Brewster Says America Should Recognize Unification of Jerusalem," Jewish Telegraphic Agency, Archive, July 7, 1967, https://www.jta.org/1967/07/07/archive/sen-brewster-says-america-should-recognize-unification-of-jerusalem.

444. "Sen. Brewster Urges US Sell 50 Phantom Jets to Israelis," *Baltimore News American*, Jan. 7, 1968.

445. Phil Ebersole, "Brewster Campaigns in Hagerstown, Encounters Backlash on Gun Laws," *Daily Mail* (Hagerstown, MD), July 16, 1968.

446. Maurice Wyatt (former campaign manager for Daniel B. Brewster), interview with the author, July 29, 2019.

447. Peter A. Jay, "Brewster Voting Record Is a Hot Campaign Issue: Brewster Defends His Votes," *Washington Post, Times Herald*, Oct. 10, 1968.

448. Jerome Kelly, "Democrat Calls Brewster Seat 'Vulnerable,'" *Baltimore Evening Sun*, April 21, 1967.

449. Herbert R. O'Conor III (grandson of former Governor of Maryland), interview with the author, Oct. 22, 2019.

450. Walter W. Brewster (youngest brother of Daniel B. Brewster), interview with the author, April 5, 2018.

451. Bill Miller (aide to Sen. Daniel B. Brewster), interview with the author, July 11, 2018.

452. Joseph D. Tydings (former Maryland US Senator), interview with the author, May 15, 2018.

453. Tyler Abell (former aide to President Johnson, Brewster family friend), interview with the author, Oct. 24, 2018.

454. "War Foes Daub Brewster's Car," unknown newspaper, Oct. 21, 1967, Daniel B. Brewster papers, series 10, Hornbake Library, University of Maryland, College Park, MD.

455. Blaine Taylor, "A Senator Looks Back," *Vietnam*, Aug. 1999, 23.

456. Wyatt, interview.

457. Taylor, "A Senator Looks Back," 22–28.

458. Taylor, "A Senator Looks Back," 22–28.

459. Miller, Bill, interview, July 11, 2018.

460. Wyatt, interview.

461. Wyatt, interview.

462. Wyatt, interview.

463. Taylor, "A Senator Looks Back," 22–28.

464. "Maryland," *Time*, Nov. 1, 1968, https://content.time.com/time/subscriber/article/0,33009,839582-2,00.html

465. Miller, Bill, interview, July 11, 2018

466. "Pierpont Sets Full Schedule, Scores Brewster Absences," *Baltimore Sun*, Aug. 21, 1968.

467. Miller, Bill, interview, July 11, 2018.

468. Wyatt, interview.

469. "Brewster 'Unaware' of Funds Letter," *Washington Post*, Oct. 11, 1968.

470. Peter A. Jay, "Mathias Criticizes Brewster Fund-Raising Letter," *Washington Post, Times Herald*, Oct. 10, 1968.

471. "Brewster 'Unaware,'" Oct. 11, 1968.

472. Richard Homan and Willard Clopton, "Brewster Helpers, Relatives Chip in $30,000 to Campaign," *Washington Post, Times Herald*, Oct. 23, 1968.

473. Homan and Clopton, "Brewster Helpers."

474. "Brewster's Campaign Funds," editorial, *Washington Post*, Oct. 24, 1968.

475. Elizabeth Shelton, "The Busy Life of a Candidate's Wife: Maryland Senatorial Race: Mrs. Brewster," *Washington Post, Times Herald*, Oct. 13, 1968.

476. Abell, Tyler, interview.

477. Brewster 1968 Campaign, "Brewster Reports 98 New Postal Projects for Maryland Since 1963; $32.9 Million in New Construction; Improved Postal Facilities and Service are Results," press release, Nov. 1, 1968, Brewster family papers.

478. Miller, Bill, interview, July 11, 2018.

479. Memorandum for Mrs. Ottolie Cochran about 10th Anniversary Luncheon of the Auxiliary to the National Association of Postal Supervisors (Governor's Club, Eutaw Street, Baltimore, Saturday, Oct. 19, 1968), memo undated and author unidentified, Brewster family papers.

480. Frank DeFilippo, "The Senate Race: Mathias' Early Lead Threatened by Brewster's Late Surge," *Baltimore News American*, Oct. 27, 1968.

481. Tydings, interview, May 15, 2018.

482. Richard Homan, "The GOP Loves You, George P. Mahoney," *Washington Post*, Nov. 26, 1968.

483. Charles McC. Mathias Jr., interview by Gerry L. Brewster, March 22, 1979, for his Princeton thesis, "Daniel Baugh Brewster: The Triumphs and Tragedies of a Maryland Politician," April 18, 1979, Brewster family files.

Chapter 16

484. Maurice Wyatt (former campaign manager for Daniel B. Brewster), interview with the author, July 29, 2019.

485. Wyatt, interview.

486. Wyatt, interview.

487. Associated Press, "Brewster May Seek Position of Party Chief," *Washington Post*, May 29, 1969.

488. Peter A. Jay, "Brewster's Image Eroded by Time," *Washington Post*, Aug. 31, 1969.

489. Clark M. Clifford to Sen. Daniel B. Brewster, May 20, 1969, Brewster family files.

490. Robert D. Murphy to Sen. Daniel B. Brewster, June 2, 1969, Brewster family files.

491. Wyatt, interview.

492. Danielle Brewster Oster (daughter of Daniel B. and Judy Brewster), interview with the author, March 1, 2019.

493. Peter Osnos, "Brewster Collapse Reported: 'Severe Mental' State Is Cited by Examiner," *Washington Post*, Feb. 25, 1970.

494. "Grand Jury Probes Brewster and Long in Garage Contract," *Washington Star*, Aug. 30, 1969.

495. "Bribery Charges Denied," *Washington Post*, Aug. 30, 1969.

496. Leonard Downie Jr. and John Hanrahan, "FBI Probes Funds Given to Brewster: Review Ordered on Garage," *Washington Post*, Aug. 31, 1969.

497. "Brewster Funds Believed Studied: Jury Apparently Reviewing Campaign Gifts in 1968," *New York Times*, Sept. 1, 1969.

498. "Brewster Funds Believed Studied," *New York Times*.

499. "Brewster Funds Believed Studied," *New York Times*.

500. Professor John Dunne, MD, Dublin, to Anne Bullitt Brewster, Nov. 10, 1969, William C. Bullitt papers, group 112, series VI, box 212, folder 242, Sterling Memorial Library, Yale University, regarding Daniel B. Brewster.

501. Associated Press to Daniel B. Brewster, telegram, William C. Bullitt papers, group 112, series VI, box 213, folder 253, Sterling Memorial Library, Yale University.

502. Anne Bullitt Brewster to the *Baltimore Sun*, statement, William C. Bullitt papers, group 112, series VI, Sterling Memorial Library, Yale University.

503. Dr. H. Houston Merritt, MD, *Report on Mr. Daniel B. Brewster, Examined Jan. 25 and 26, 1970*, William C. Bullitt papers, group 112, series VI, box 213, folder 253, Sterling Memorial Library, Yale University.

504. K. Davison, MB, report on Daniel B. Brewster, William C. Bullitt papers, group 112, series VI, box 212, folder 242, Sterling Memorial Library, Yale University.

505. Daniel B. Brewster to Anne Bullitt Brewster, Dec. 30, 1969, William C. Bullitt papers, group 112, series VI, Sterling Memorial Library, Yale University.

506. Daniel B. Brewster to Anne Bullitt Brewster, Jan. 5, 1970, William C. Bullitt papers, group 112, series VI, box 212, folder 251, Sterling Memorial Library, Yale University.

507. Carol Brewster to Daniel B. Brewster, Feb. 13, 1970, Brewster family papers.

508. Ellen Turnbull Lynch to Daniel B. Brewster, April 18, 1979, Brewster family papers, in reply to a Dec. 26, 1969, letter from Brewster to Lynch, based on notes collected by Gerry L. Brewster for his Princeton thesis, "Daniel Baugh Brewster: The Triumphs and Tragedies of a Maryland Politician."

509. Stephen H. Sachs (former US Attorney), interview with the author, July 5, 2018.

510. Stephen H. Sachs, interview by Gerry L. Brewster, March 12, 1979, for his Princeton thesis, "Daniel Baugh Brewster: The Triumphs and Tragedies of a Maryland Politician," April 18, 1979, Brewster family papers.

511. John F. Sullivan, Federal Grand Jury empaneled in Baltimore, Md., Apr. 1, 1969, grand jury testimony, Feb. 10, 1970.

Feb. 10, 1970, 72, Brewster family papers.

512. Brewster to Bullitt Brewster, this and previous quotes, Jan. 5, 1970.

513. Brewster to Bullitt Brewster, Jan. 24, 1970.

514. Daniel B. Brewster to Anne Bullitt Brewster, Jan. 24, 1970, William C. Bullitt papers, group 112, series VI, box 212, folder 251, Sterling Memorial Library, Yale University.

515. Brewster to Bullitt Brewster, Jan. 24, 1970.

516. Houston, *Report on Mr. Daniel B. Brewster.*

517. Houston, *Report on Mr. Daniel B. Brewster.*

518. Houston, *Report on Mr. Daniel B. Brewster.*

519. Houston, *Report on Mr. Daniel B. Brewster.*

520. Osnos, "Brewster Collapse Reported."

521. Walter W. Brewster (youngest brother of Daniel B. Brewster), interview with the author, April 5, 2018.

522. Brewster, Walter W., interview.

523. Brewster, Walter W., interview.

524. Brewster to Bullitt Brewster, Jan. 24, 1970.

525. Daniel B. Brewster to Anne Bullitt Brewster, Feb. 1, 1970, William C. Bullitt papers, group 112, series VI, box 212, folder 251, Sterling Memorial Library, Yale University.

526. Sachs, interview, July 5, 2018.

527. Thomas B. Edsall, "The Man Who Came to Dinner," *Baltimore Sun,* Nov. 10, 1974.

528. Ronald M. Shapiro and Steven L. Barrett, "Grand Jury Needs Power to Override Attorney General," *Baltimore Sun,* June 8, 1970.

529. Daniel B. Brewster to Anne Bullitt Brewster, April 12, 1970, William C. Bullitt papers, group 112, series VI, box 212, folder 251, Sterling Memorial Library, Yale University.

530. Brewster to Bullitt Brewster, April 12, 1970.

Chapter 17

531. "Brewster Trial Begins in Capital," *New York Times*, Oct. 31, 1972.

532. Theo Lippman Jr., "The Story of Danny Brewster," *Baltimore Sun*, Dec. 4, 1972.

533. W. Shepherdson Abell (former legislative assistant to Daniel B. Brewster), interview with the author, Aug. 19, 2019.

534. Peter Osnos, "Brewster Recovers; Hearing Set Monday," *Washington Post, Times Herald*, May 22, 1970.

535. Alan I. Baron to Hon. George L. Hart Jr., Oct. 8, 1970, US District Court for the District of Columbia, US Court House, Washington, DC.

536. Stephen H. Sachs (former US Attorney), interview with the author, July 5, 2018.

537. Martha Angle, "Sen. Brewster Defense Raps Key Witness," *Washington Star*, Aug. 29, 1970.

538. Angle, "Sen. Brewster Defense.".

539. John Hanrahan, "Brewster Witness Scathed: Lawyers Try to Belittle His Credibility," *Washington Post*, Aug. 29, 1970.

540. United States of America v. Daniel B. Brewster, Cyrus T. Anderson, and Spiegel, Inc., transcript of hearings on motions before Judge George L. Hart Jr. (Oct. 9, 1970), 24.

541. US v. Brewster et al., transcript.

542. Patrick Young, "US to Appeal Decision in Bribe Case: 'License to Steal' Ruling Raises Key Issues on Legislators' Immunity," *National Observer* 9, no. 42 (Oct. 19, 1970).

543. "1968 Brewster Defeat Sent Him to Seclusion," *Washington Post*, Oct. 10, 1970.

544. "Ex-Senator Is Fined on Driving Charge," *Washington Post*, March 11, 1972.

545. Invoice from Shutts & Bowen, attorneys-at-law, Key West, FL, March 17, 1972, Brewster family papers.

546. Joy Aschenbach, "Brewster Again Convicted of Driving While Impaired," *Washington Star and Daily News*, July 28, 1972.

547. Jack Anderson, "Witness Caught Up in Fiscal Scandal," Washington Merry-Go-Round, *The Sedalia (MO) Democrat*, July 12, 1971.

548. Frederic B. Hill, "Brewster Witness Must Pay Fraternity," *Baltimore Sun*, Aug. 10, 1973.

549. "Brewster Witness Gets Fraud Term," *Baltimore Sun*, Feb. 16, 1974.

550. US v. Brewster, 408 US 501 (1972).

551. Frederic B. Hill, "Brewster Guilty of Taking Gifts from Lobbyist," *Baltimore Sun*, Nov. 18, 1972.

552. Frederic B. Hill (former *Baltimore Sun* reporter), interview with the author, April 19, 2019.

553. Tyler Abell (former aide to President Johnson, Brewster family friend), interview with the author, Oct. 24, 2018.

554. Sen. Daniel B. Brewster (speech, Third Class Mail Users Association, New York City, Oct. 16, 1964).

555. Brewster, Daniel B., Third Class Mail Users Assoc.

556. Cong. Rec. S (April 3, 1967) (speech by Sen. Daniel B. Brewster, "Third Class Mail"), https://www.congress.gov/bound-congressional-record/1967/04/03/senate-section?p=0

557. John Morrow, "Senator Daniel B. Brewster: Postal Champion," *Oriole*, President's Column, 2–3 (official publication of Oriole Branch 176, National Association Letter Carriers), Daniel B. Brewster papers, series 10, box 1, Hornbake Library, University of Maryland, College Park, MD.

558. Lawrence Meyer, "Brewster Denies He Ever Sold Vote," *Washington Post*, Nov. 10, 1972.

559. Sachs, interview, July 5, 2018.

560. Lawrence Meyer, "Brewster Accuser Attacked," *Washington Post*, Nov. 2, 1972.

561. John F. Sullivan, Federal Grand Jury empaneled in Baltimore, Md., Apr. 1, 1969, grand jury testimony, Feb. 12, 1970. 3.

562. Daniel B. Brewster, interview by Gerry L. Brewster, March 11, 1979, for his Princeton thesis, "Daniel Baugh Brewster: The Triumphs and Tragedies of a Maryland Politician," April 18, 1979, Brewster family papers.

563. Bill Miller (aide to Sen. Daniel B. Brewster), interview with the author, July 11, 2018.

564. Miller, Bill, interview, July 11, 2018.

565. Frederic B. Hill, "Brewster Takes Stand, Denies Allegations," *Baltimore Sun*, Nov. 10, 1972.

566. This paragraph, Hill, "Brewster Takes Stand."

567. Hill, "Brewster Takes Stand."

568. Meyer, "Brewster Denies."

569. United Press International, "Robertson, West Head US Olympic Basketball," *Washington Post, Times Herald*, April 4, 1960.

570. Reply to the author's Freedom of Information Act request, Freedom of Information Act &

Privacy Act Program, United States Secret Service, Washington, DC, July 3, 2019.

571. Lawrence Meyer, "Brewster Finances Argued," *Washington Post*, Nov. 9, 1972, C-1.

572. This paragraph, Lawrence Meyer, "Brewster Finances Argued," *Washington Post*, Nov. 9, 1972.

573. Gerry L. Brewster (youngest son of Daniel B. and Carol Brewster), interview with the author, March 8, 2018.

574. Brewster, Gerry L., interview, March 8, 2018.

575. Frederic B. Hill, "Jury Gets Brewster Bribery Case, Reaches No Verdict After 4 Hours," *Baltimore Sun,* Nov. 17, 1972.

576. Norman P. Ramsey and Edward Bennett Williams, Brief of Appellant Brewster, United States Court of Appeals for the District of Columbia Circuit, No. 73-1304, June 29, 1973.

577. Sachs, interview, July 5, 2018.

578. Lawrence Meyer, "Brewster Convicted on Bribery Counts," *Washington Post,* Nov. 18, 1972.

579. James P. Day, "Brewster Given Jail Sentence of 2-to-6 Years, Fined $30,000," *Baltimore Evening Sun*, Feb. 2, 1973, A-1.

580. Lawrence Meyer, "Brewster Gets 6-Year Term, $30,000 Fine," *Washington Post*, Daniel B. Brewster statement prior to sentencing, Feb. 3, 1973, A-1.

581. "Nixon Hatchet Man: Call It What You Will. Chuck Colson Handles the President's Dirty Work," *Wall Street Journal,* Oct. 15, 1971.

582. Stanley I. Kutler, ed., *Abuse of Power: The New Nixon Tapes*, (Phoenix Books, 1997), Feb. 3, 1973 conversation between President Richard M. Nixon and Charles W. Colson, 205.

583. Blaine Taylor, "A Senator Looks Back," *Vietnam*, Aug. 1999, 23–28.

584. Meyer, "Brewster Gets 6-Year Term."

585. Meyer, "Brewster Gets 6-Year Term."

586. Brewster, Gerry L., interview, March 8, 2018.

587. Peter A. Jay, "Md. Has Comforting Bipartisan Corruption," *Baltimore Sun,* Jan. 8, 1975.

Chapter 18

588. This paragraph, Frederic B. Hill, "Post-Trial Motions in Brewster Case Denied by Judge," *Baltimore Sun*, Jan. 27, 1973.

589. Hill, "Post-Trial Motions."

590. "Trials: Just a Gratuity," *Newsweek*, July 27, 1972, 26.

591. Stephen H. Sachs (former US Attorney), interview with the author, July 5, 2018.

592. Lawrence Meyer, "The Fine Line Between Contributions and Bribes," *Washington Post,* March 15, 1973.

593. Meyer, "The Fine Line."

594. Howard E. Shuman, interview by Donald A. Ritchie, Oct. 9, 1987, Shuman, 1936-1990, papers collection at the University of Illinois archives.

595. Shuman, interview.

596. Shuman, interview.

597. John Hanrahan, "Was Brewster Lone Recipient of Spiegel Bribes, Payoffs?" *Washington Post* news service, *Miami Herald,* Feb. 25, 1973.

598. Frederic B. Hill, "Brewster Unlucky, Not Unusual," *Baltimore Sun,* Nov. 1972.

599. Brief of Appellant Daniel B. Brewster, United States Court of Appeals for the District of Columbia Circuit, No. 73-1304 (US v. Cyrus T. Anderson) and No. 73-1305 (US v. Daniel B. Brewster), June 29, 1973, 21–23.

600. Appellant Daniel B. Brewster, brief, 16.

601. Walter W. Brewster (youngest brother of Daniel B. Brewster), interview with the author, April 5, 2018.

602. Gerry L. Brewster (son of Daniel B. and Carol Brewster), interview with the author, Oct. 3, 2018.

603. Gerry L. Brewster to Daniel B. Brewster, undated but probably written in 1974, Brewster family papers.

604. Daniel B. Brewster to Gerry L. Brewster, Sept. 18, 1974, Brewster family papers.

605. George Hanst, "Brewster's Attorney Seeks Overturn of Conviction," *Baltimore Evening Sun,*

March 5, 1974.

606. This paragraph and the previous quote, Timothy Robinson, "US Court Overturns Brewster's Conviction," *Washington Post,* Aug. 3, 1974.

607. Douglas Watson, "Happy on His Farm; Brewster: Confident of Exoneration," *Washington Post,* Aug. 3, 1974.

608. Watson, "Happy on His Farm."

609. Tracie Rozhon, "Brewster's 'On Road to Final Vindication,'" *Baltimore Sun,* Aug 3, 1974.

610. Alan I. Baron (former Deputy US Attorney), interview with the author, July 17, 2018.

611. Daniel B. Brewster to Edward Bennett Williams, Jan. 8, 1975, Williams, Connolly & Califano, Washington, DC.

612. Associated Press, "Ex-Senator Brewster Pleads No Contest; Is Fined," *New York Times*, June 26, 1975.

613. Associated Press, "Ex-Senator Brewster Pleads No Contest; Is Fined," *New York Times*, June 26, 1975.

614. Daniel B. Brewster, statement to the court before imposition of sentence, United States v. Brewster, June 25, 1975.

615. Brewster, Daniel B., statement prior to sentencing.

616. Harry R. Hughes (Governor of Maryland, 1979–87, and friend of Daniel B. Brewster), interview with the author, Feb. 22, 2004.

617. Frederic Kelly, "Daniel Brewster Savors His Turn-Around Life," *Baltimore Sun Magazine*, June 29, 1980.

618. Paul Mark Sandler (former intern and driver for Daniel B. Brewster), interview with the author, July 12, 2018.

619. Sachs, interview, April 18, 1979.

620. Sachs, interview, April 18, 1979.

621. Stephen H. Sachs (former US Attorney), interview with the author, May 10, 2018.

622. Maurice Wyatt (former campaign manager for Daniel B. Brewster), interview with the author, July 29, 2019.

623. Bill Miller (aide to Sen. Daniel B. Brewster), interview with the author, July 11, 2018.

624. Joseph D. Tydings (former Maryland US Senator), interview with the author, May 15, 2018.

625. Kelly, "Daniel Brewster Savors."

626. Kelly, "Daniel Brewster Savors."

Chapter 19

627. Daniel B. Brewster to Gerry L. Brewster, June 8, 1975, Brewster family papers.

628. Gerry L. Brewster (youngest son of Daniel B. and Carol Brewster), interview with the author, June 19, 2018.

629. Walter W. Brewster (youngest brother of Daniel B. Brewster), interview with the author, April 5, 2018.

630. Brewster, Walter W., interview, April 5, 2018.

631. Brewster, Walter W., interview, April 5, 2018.

632. Brewster, Walter W., interview, April 5, 2018.

633. Richard Hoffberger (son of Daniel B. Brewster friend and supporter Jerold Hoffberger), interview with the author, July 1, 2020.

634. Walter W. Brewster legislative and administrative assistant to Senators Paul Douglas and William Proxmire, 1955-1982, interview with the author, July 30, 2019.

635. Brewster, Walter W., interview, July 30, 2019.

636. Judy Brewster (third wife of Daniel B. Brewster), interview with the author, Nov. 23, 2018

637. Krista Aarsand Bedford (daughter of Judy Brewster, stepdaughter of Daniel B. Brewster), interview with the author, March 10, 2020.

638. Bedford, interview.

639. Liza Nevin (wife of Daniel B. Brewster's best friend Crocker Nevin), interview with the author, March 26, 2019.

640. Brewster, Judy, interview, Nov. 23, 2018.

641. Bedford, interview.

642. Bedford, interview.

643. Bedford, interview.

644. Kurt Aarsand (son of Judy Brewster, stepson of Daniel B. Brewster), interview with the author, March 13, 2020.

645. Daniel B. Brewster to Gerry L. Brewster, Sept. 20, 1975, Brewster family papers.

646. Richard W. Emory, attorney for Brewster, brief in the case of Attorney Grievance Commission of Maryland v. Daniel B. Brewster, Misc. Docket, No. 7, September Term, 1976, No. 1861 – Miscellaneous.

647. Richard W. Emory, brief for Respondent Daniel B. Brewster, Attorney Grievance Commission of Maryland v. Daniel B. Brewster, Misc. Docket, No. 7, Sept. Term, 1976, No. 1861— Miscellaneous.

648. Emory, brief.

649. J. Smith, C. J. Murphy dissents, opinion, Attorney Grievance Commission of Maryland v. Daniel B. Brewster, Court of Appeals of Maryland, Misc. Docket (Subtitle BV), No. 7, Sept. Term, 1976, filed June 21, 1977.

650. Charlie Fenwick (Baltimore County horseman and neighbor of Daniel B. Brewster), interview with the author, June 18, 2018.

651. Daniel B. Brewster to Gerry L. Brewster, March 29, 1976, Brewster family papers.

652. Bedford, interview.

653. "Brewster's Let Off with $10,000 Fine," *Baltimore News American*, June 26, 1975.

654. Mike Lane, editorial cartoon, *Baltimore Evening Sun*, Nov. 25, 1975.

655. "Year in Review," *Baltimore Sun,* Dec. 29, 1975.

656. Gerry L. Brewster (youngest son of Daniel B. and Carol Brewster), interview with the author, March 28, 2018.

657. Brewster Oster, interview, March 1, 2019.

658. US Sen. Charles McC. Mathias Jr. to the president of the United States, "Petition for Pardon after Completion of Sentence," Oct. 30, 1978.

659. Mathias to the President of the United States, petition.

660. Lucy Acton, "Brewster Is Happy on Farm," *The Maryland Horse*, Vol. 43, No. 13, December 1977, 44-47.

661. Brewster, Walter W., interview, April 5, 2018.

662. Norman Lauenstein (former Baltimore County Councilman), interview with the author, Sept. 30, 2019.

663. Lucy Acton, "Brewster is Happy on Farm," *Maryland Horse* 43, no. 13 (Dec. 1977): 44–47.

Chapter 20

664. Robert Timberg, "Brewster Confesses to his 'Devastation'—Alcoholism," *Baltimore Evening Sun,* March 18, 1977.

665. Timberg, "Brewster Confesses."

666. Barbara Palmer, "Ex-Senator Brewster Admits Alcoholism," *Washington Star,* March 18, 1977.

667. Palmer, "Ex-Senator Brewster."

668. Donald Kimelman, "Brewster Backs Alcoholism Bill," *Baltimore Sun,* March 18, 1977.

669. Blaine Taylor, "Phoenix: The Rise, Fall and Resurrection of Sen. Daniel Brewster," *Maryland State Medical Journal* (July 1977): 35–47.

670. Taylor, "Phoenix," 38.

671. Taylor, "Phoenix," 39.

672. Taylor, "Phoenix," 44–45.

673. Taylor, "Phoenix," 45.

674. Sen. Charles McC. Mathias Jr., "The Open Forum," letter to the editor, *Maryland State Medical Journal* (Oct. 1977): 8.

675. "The 12 Steps of AA," Alcoholics Anonymous of Great Britain and English Speaking Continental Europe, https://www.alcoholics-anonymous.org.uk/about-aa/the-12-steps-of-aa.

676. Francis X. Kelly (former Maryland state Senator), interview with the author, Dec. 20, 2018.

677. John Howard (attorney at Turnbull, Brewster, et al. law firm), interview with the author, July 15, 2019.

678. Krista Aarsand Bedford (daughter of Judy Brewster, stepdaughter of Daniel B. Brewster), interview with the author, March 10, 2020.

679. Liza Nevin (wife of Daniel B. Brewster's best friend Crocker Nevin), interview with the author, March 26, 2019.

680. Liza Nevin, interview with author, Mar. 26, 2019.

681. Daniel B. Brewster to Gerry L. Brewster, Sept. 15, 1978, Brewster family papers.

682. Michael Kernan, "The Fall and Rise of Dan Brewster: Life Close to the Land," *Washington Post,* Aug. 24, 1978.

683. Daniel B. Brewster to Gerry L. Brewster, May 1, 1979, Brewster family papers.

684. Gerry L. Brewster to Daniel B. Brewster, undated but probably written in mid-Nov. 1978, Brewster family papers.

685. Daniel B. Brewster to Gerry L. Brewster, Nov. 26, 1978, Brewster family papers.

686. Gerry L. Brewster to Daniel B. Brewster, undated but probably written in mid-Nov. 1978, Brewster family papers.

687. Daniel B. Brewster to Gerry L. Brewster, Nov. 30, 1978, Brewster family papers.

688. Frederic Kelly, "Daniel Brewster Savors His Turn-Around Life," *Baltimore Sun Magazine,* June 29, 1980.

689. Kelly, "Daniel Brewster Savors."

690. "Citizen of the Year" award, 4th District Democratic Club, state senator Janice Piccinini chair, Sept. 30, 1992, Brewster family papers.

691. Mike Merson (hospital administrator and friend of Daniel B. Brewster), interview with the author, Feb. 28, 2019.

692. Merson, interview.

693. Thoroughbred Database, Pedigree Online, https://www.pedigreequery.com/rolling+cart.

694. Merson, interview.

695. Judy Brewster (third wife of Daniel B. Brewster), interview with the author, Nov. 23, 2018.

696. Danielle Brewster Oster (daughter of Daniel B. and Judy Brewster), interview with the author, March 1, 2019.

697. Brewster Oster, interview, March 1, 2019.

Chapter 21

698. Krista Aarsand Bedford (daughter of Judy Brewster, stepdaughter of Daniel B. Brewster), interview with the author, March 10, 2020.

699. Dana Brewster (son of Daniel B. and Judy Brewster), interview with the author, Feb. 20, 2019.

700. Brewster, Dana, interview.

701. Brewster, Dana, interview.

702. Brewster, Dana, interview.

703. Brewster, Dana, interview.

704. Danielle Brewster Oster (daughter of Daniel B. and Judy Brewster), interview with the author, Feb. 2, 2018.

705. Charlie Fenwick (Baltimore County horseman and neighbor of Daniel B. Brewster), interview with the author, June 18, 2018.

706. Judy Brewster (third wife of Daniel B. Brewster), interview with the author, Dec. 7, 2018.

707. Danielle Brewster Oster (daughter of Daniel B. and Judy Brewster), interview with the author, March 1, 2019.

708. Brewster, Dana, interview.

709. Jennilie Brewster (daughter of Daniel B. and Judy Brewster), interview with the author, Dec. 7, 2018.

710. Brewster Oster, interview, March 1, 2019.

711. Brewster Oster, interview, March 1, 2019.

712. Gerry L. Brewster (youngest son of Daniel B. and Carol Brewster), interview with the author, Feb. 14, 2018.

713. Carol Brewster to Daniel B. Brewster, Sept. 19, 1989, Brewster family papers.

714. Mike Merson, interview with the author, Feb. 28, 2019.

715. Brewster Oster, interview, Feb. 2, 2018.

716. James Rosapepe (former member of the Maryland General Assembly and former Ambassador to Romania), interview with the author, Dec. 9, 2018.

717. James T. Smith (former Baltimore County Executive), interview with the author, July 8, 2019.

718. Smith, James T., interview.

719. Brewster Oster, interview, March 1, 2019.

720. Laurence Oster (husband of Danielle Brewster Oster), interview with the author, Feb. 18, 2020.

721. Steny Hoyer (former Brewster staffer, House Majority Leader), interview with the author, July 18, 2019.

722. John Grason Turnbull, interview by Gerry L. Brewster, April 2, 1979, for his Princeton thesis, "Daniel Baugh Brewster: The Triumphs and Tragedies of a Maryland Politician," April 18, 1979, Brewster family papers.

723. Nancy Pelosi (former Brewster staffer, Speaker of the House of Representatives), interview with the author, May 11, 2019.

724. C. A. Porter Hopkins (friend of Daniel B. Brewster, former member of Maryland General Assembly, and lifelong conservationist), interview with the author, Aug. 5, 2019.

725. Herbert R. O'Conor III (grandson of a former Governor of Maryland), interview with the author, Oct. 22, 2019.

726. Richard Hoffberger (son of Daniel B. Brewster friend and supporter Jerold Hoffberger), interview with the author, July 1, 2020.

727. Judy Brewster, interview with author, Nov. 23, 2018.

728. Tyler Abell (former aide to President Johnson, Brewster family friend), interview with the author, Oct. 24, 2018.

729. Frederic Kelly, "Daniel Baugh Brewster: A New Life," *Baltimore Sun Magazine,* June 29, 1980.

Index

353

Birmingham, Michael J. "Iron Mike", 85
Bittman, William O., 254
Black, Gary, 236
Black, Nancy Martin "Nannie", 68, 236
Blair, Francis Preston, 83
Blair, Montgomery, 83
Boggs, Hale, 248-49
Bolte, Charles, 100
Boone, A. Gordon, 63, 73, 76, 85-86, 240
Bourke, Richard Southwell, 237
Boykin, Frank W., 240
Brennan, William J., 258
Brewster, Andre Walker, viii, 21
Brewster, Andre Walker II, viii, 28, 32, 58-59, 155, 160, 178, 203, 241, 263, 279, 285-86
Brewster, Benjamin Harris, viii, 20
Brewster, Benjamin Harris Jr., viii, 26, 62
Brewster, Benjamin Harris III, viii, 27
Brewster, Carol Leiper, viii, 22-23, 65-69, 74, 78-81, 88, 90-92, 101, 118, 148, 158-59, 162,
    173, 184-85, 189, 198, 200-02, 204, 218, 222, 235-36, 242, 265, 293, 304, 313, 319, 322;
    divorce, Juarez, Mexico, 148, 200-03; marriages, 65; running Worthington Farms, 69, 80, 185
Brewster, Dana Franklin, viii, 179, 180, 304, 309-12, 319, 322
Brewster, Daniel Baugh Sr., viii, 26-29, 43, 62, 155
Brewster, Daniel Baugh Jr., viii, 28, 74, 78, 88, 162, 202-03, 206, 224, 236, 242, 265, 304
Brewster, Elder William, 26
Brewster, Elizabeth Baugh, viii, 26
Brewster, Gerry L., iv, viii, 5-6, 20, 29, 62, 64, 66-67, 74, 78, 88, 101, 144, 162, 179, 180, 185,
    202-03, 206, 236, 242, 253, 263, 265, 269, 277-78, 280, 285-86, 292-94, 302-06, 312-25,
    318, 321-22
Brewster, Jennilie B., viii, 179-80, 194, 304, 310, 312, 317, 322
Brewster, Judy Aarsand, viii, 179-80, 193, 288-91, 294, 296, 298, 301-02, 304-05, 308, 310,
    312, 316, 319-20, 322; divorce from Knut Aarsand in Haiti, 290; Hiddenbrook, 279; Windy
    Meadows Farm, 6, 179, 180, 203, 277, 285-87, 290-91, 293, 296, 311, 317, 319
Brewster, Nathanial, viii, 21
Brewster, Walter Wickes, ix, 19-21, 28, 59-60, 62, 64, 67-68, 100-01, 155, 160, 178, 204, 220,
    242, 246-47, 277, 286-88, 296
bribery trial, 237-50, 251-69, 273-83; appellate appeal, 278-79; Attorney Grievance Commis-
    sion decision, 292-93; character witnesses, 265; 1969 grand jury indictment, 240-41; federal
    trial, 241, 245, 251-69, 273-83; immunity for John F. Sullivan, 243-44, 252-53; IRS ruling,
    292; jurors offered compromise charge, 276; Nixon administration involvement, 268, 279-80,
    308; nolo contendere plea, 280, 292, 294; pardon request, 295; sentencing, 253, 266-67;
    Spiegel and Cyrus Anderson, 239, 241-42, 244, 246, 254, 259-60, 263-64, 266-68, 274-76;
    third class mail rates, 239, 252, 259-63, 265, 275; U.S. Supreme Court 1972 ruling on
    Speech and Debate Clause, 255-56
Brooke, Edward, 96, 212
Brown, Edmund G. "Jerry", 121
Bryant, Louise, 34, 36-37, 156
Buckner, Simon Bolivar Jr., 49, 51
Bullitt, Anne Moen, viii, 34-41, 45-47, 148-49, 156, 175, 177, 197-206, 218, 222-24, 227-29,
    233-34, 236-37, 240-42, 244-45, 247-49, 257, 290, 293, 300, 307, 317, 319, 324; coming
    out party, 36-37; engagement in 1943, 38-40; her adoring father, 34-37; licensed in Ireland as
    horse trainer, 177, 198; marriage to Brewster in 1967, 202-04; Palmerstown Stud, 198, 236;
    reunited with Brewster in 1967, 198-99
Bullitt, John C., 34
Bullitt, William Christian, viii, 34-38, 40, 46-47, 58, 156, 198, 234
Bunch, Philip James, 110

354

Burger, Warren, 258
Burton, Bill, 133
Butler, John Marshall, 81, 87
Camp Kieve, 28-29, 58
Cardin, Benjamin L., 319
Caro, Robert, 108
Carroll, Charles, 24
Carter, Cliff, 112
Carter, Jimmy, 121, 295
Carvel, Elbert N., 88, 165
Caso, Anthony, 12-13
Celler, Emanuel, 108
Church, Frank, 118
civil rights, i, 2, 101-04, 105-23, 142, 145, 187, 207, 209, 212-13, 224, 252, 287, 321, 324;
    Civil Rights Act of 1964, 2, 128, 151, 169, 213; constituent letters for and against, 122-23,
    109-11, 116-17; integration of the armed forces, 98-101; Jim Crow laws, 95-104, 106, 324;
    Martin Luther King Jr. support, 122
Clark, Joe, 202
Clifford, Clark, 235
Clinton, Bill, 121
Cochran, Ottolie Hobart Wickes Brewster, viii, 23-24, 27-28, 32, 37-38, 58-60, 155, 178, 183,
    229, 277, 313
Cochran, William C. Jr., ix, 58
Cohen, George J., 139
colleges, universities, and private schools; Ambler College, 69; Brillantmont International School,
    69; Bryn Mawr, 21; Foxcroft School, 21, 35-37, 324; Garrison Forest, 21; Gilman School, 20,
    29, 43, 58-59, 92, 95, 265, 278, 285, 302, 314; Goucher College, 144; Harvard University,
    20-21, 33, 91; Johns Hopkins University, 63; McDonogh School, 296, 309; Princeton Uni-
    versity, 20, 27, 31, 33, 38, 40, 43, 58, 63, 77, 84, 101, 278, 285-86, 302-03, 313-14, 318,
    321; Roland Park Country School, 31; Shipley School, 69; St. Paul's School, 20-21, 31-33,
    40, 47, 57-58, 84, 95, 104, 157, 159, 183, 245, 302, 324; University of Maryland, 92, 109,
    187, 197, 202, 323, 327; University of Maryland Law School, 63; Wroxeter-on-the-Severn,
    289; Yale University, 20, 33-34, 39, 46-47, 202, 323
Colson, Charles W., 268
Cox, Archibald, 32
Crothers, Austin L., 95-96
Culver, Charles, 85
Culver, Donald B. "Squeaky", 64, 68
Dale, Nelson C., 10-14
D'Alesandro, Thomas III, 1, 176, 179
Davis, Liz, 133, 323, 328
Davison, K., 241
de Havenon, Andre, viii, 65-66
de Havenon, Gaston, 65
de Havenon, Michael, viii, 65-66, 101, 185, 202, 204
DeFillipo, Frank, 191, 229-30
Denckla, Polly Leiper, 66-67
Dessoff, Alan, 191, 212
Devereux, James P. S., 74-76
Dilweg, Diane, 91
Dilweg, LaVern, 91
Dirksen, Everett, 106, 119, 144, 212
Douglas, Paul, 11, 275
Douglas, William O., 258
Doyle, Paddy, 49, 53

Drinker, Ernesta, 35
Dukakis, Michael, 121
Duke, Angie Biddle, 32
Dunne, John, 240
Eastland, James O., 108-09
Ehrlich, Robert, 314-15
Eisenhower, Dwight D., 102, 136, 149
Eisenstaedt, Alfred, 65
Emanuel, Meyer, 298
Emory, Richard W., 86, 201, 292
Eppler, Mary, 307
Ervin, Samuel, 176, 268
estates; Ditchley Park, 198-200, 217; Fernwood, 28-29, 58-59, 64, 97, 101, 224; Mar-a-La-
    go, 37; Sagamore Farm, 69; Scrooby Manor, 26-28; Snow Hill Farm, 22, 60, 64, 68, 236;
    Wickcliffe, 24-28, 59, 97, 101, 156, 184, 317; Windy Meadows Farm, 6, 179-80, 203, 277,
    285-87, 290-91, 293, 296, 311, 317, 319; Worthington Farms, 22, 60, 64, 68-69, 78-79,
    112, 162 171, 185, 222, 235-36, 293; Younglands, 23
Evers, Medgar, 106, 325
Fallon, George H., 265
Farley, James A., 36
Fay, Paul D. "Red", 91
Fehrer, Joseph W. Jr., 133
Fehrer, Joseph W. Sr., 133
Fenwick, Charlie, 61-62, 293, 311-1
Finan, Thomas B., 81, 112, 210-14
Fitzgerald, F. Scott, 27, 32
Flannery, Thomas A., 241
Flowers, Charles, 19
Fonda, Henry, 309
Ford, Gerald, 215, 244, 279
Forrestal, James, 40
Frankfurter, Felix, 36
Franklin, Benjamin, viii, 20-21
Frenkil, Victor, 238, 248-49
Frick, Henry Clay, 77
Frick, Martha Howard, 77
Friedel, Samuel, 127
Fulbright, J. William, 137-38
Gingrich, Newt, 314
Goldstein, Louis L., 81, 114, 120, 127-28, 131, 133, 163, 168, 176, 209-10, 213, 215
Goldwater, Barry, 137
Gorky, Arshile, 65
Gosnell, O. T., 203
Green, William, 126-27
Green Spring Valley Hunt Club, 38, 183, 287, 319
Gruening, Ernest, 138
Hargrove, John R., 97
Hart, George L. Jr., 255-60, 266-68, 273-74, 276, 278, 280
Hart, Philip A., 190
Hartke, Vance, 189, 260, 268, 276
Hearst, William Randolph, 32
Hedahl, Everett A., 11, 13-14
Hill, Frederic B., 259
Hitler, Adolph, 36, 150
Hobart, Byron Frank Jr., ix, 23-24

Hochmuth, B. A., 52

Hocker, George, 81

Hoffberger, Jerold, 86, 202, 287-88, 319

Hoffberger, Richard, 288, 319

Hoffman, Milton, 143

Holcomb, Thomas, 98

Hopkins, C. A. Porter, 131, 133, 184, 318

horse races and tracks; Daniel Baugh Brewster Memorial, 62; Curragh Racecourse, 203; Grand
National, 22, 60, 313; John Rush Streett Memorial, 60; Maryland Hunt Cup, 22, 24, 44, 60-
62, 67, 69, 159, 236, 277, 313; My Lady's Manor, 22, 60, 178, 250, 302, 313; Pimlico Race
Course, 63, 69; Preakness Stakes, 69; White Marsh Valley Hunt, 66

horses, 21-22, 43, 59-64, 67-69, 178, 198, 302, 307, 310-13; Bachelor's Double, 60-61; Clifton's Dan, 60, 66, 159; Curwick Tim, 60; Dana's Jawbreaker, 311; Dunlora, 60; Jay's Trouble,
178, 302; Milesian, 198; Ned's Flying, 67; Rolling Cart, 307; Seabiscuit, 69; Sindon, 198;
War Admiral, 69; Western Halo, 307

hospitals; Franklin Square Hospital, 306; Hiddenbrook, 386-90, 296; MedStar Hospital System,
306; St. Gabriel's Hospital, 245; Union Memorial Hospital, 22

Howard, John, 63, 184, 301

Hoyer, Steny, i, 1, 92-93, 115, 164, 185, 200, 211, 281, 317

Hughes, Patricia, 81

Hughes, V. J., 121

Hughes, Harry R., 72, 81-82, 123, 179, 220, 281, 322, 327-28

Humphrey, Hubert H., 101-02, 119, 121, 151, 175, 177, 222, 224, 226, 228-31

Huslander, Bill, 134, 323

Hutchins, Chris, 5

Hutton, E. F., 37

Hutton, Nedenia "Deenie", 37

Iglehart, Francis N. "Ike", 28, 100-01, 194

Inouye, Daniel, 118, 190

Ireland, 9, 148, 177, 198-205, 218, 228, 236, 239, 240-42, 245-46, 249, 255, 257, 299, 317,
319, 324; Curragh Racecourse, 203; Irish hospitals, 237-245; Palmerstown House and Stud
Farm, 177, 198, 203, 233-250, 307, 317, 324

Jackson, Andrew, 83

Jackson, Catherine Brewster, viii, 178, 277

Jackson, Henry M. "Scoop", 132

Jacobs, Bradford, 213

Jay, Peter A., 235, 269

Jefferson, Thomas, 104

Johnson, "Lady Bird", 173

Johnson, Lyndon Baines, i, 2, 6, 90-91, 103, 107-08, 111-15, 117-19, 122, 129, 132, 134, 137-
40, 143, 145-46, 148-51, 164-65, 167, 169, 170, 173, 187, 189-90, 207, 209, 211-13, 219,
221-22, 224-25, 229, 235, 244, 252, 259, 324

Johnson, Thomas F., 240, 256, 294

Jones, Adrienne, 119

Kahl, Chris, 183

Keaton, Diane, 35

Kelleher, Tom, 137

Kelly, Francis X., 301

Kennedy, Edward M., 118, 174, 222, 230, 244

Kennedy, Jacqueline Bouvier, 39, 79

Kennedy, John F., iv, 2, 32, 39, 79-81, 89-91, 103, 106-08, 121, 126, 136-37, 149, 150, 161,
162, 163, 164, 165, 187, 210, 215, 235, 252, 264

Kennedy, John F. Jr., 90

Kennedy, Robert, F., 119, 148, 166, 173-74, 176, 197, 210, 215, 219, 221-22, 224, 243

Kerry, John, 32

257-59, 269; Post Office and Civil Service Committee, 220; running Senate staff, 208, 223; Townsend's heart attack, 112-13, 207-08; Wallace campaign, 113

Apprentice
House Press
Loyola University Maryland

Apprentice House is the country's only campus-based, student-staffed book publishing company. Directed by professors and industry professionals, it is a nonprofit activity of the Communication Department at Loyola University Maryland.

Using state-of-the-art technology and an experiential learning model of education, Apprentice House publishes books in untraditional ways. This dual responsibility as publishers and educators creates an unprecedented collaborative environment among faculty and students, while teaching tomorrow's editors, designers, and marketers.

Eclectic and provocative, Apprentice House titles intend to entertain as well as spark dialogue on a variety of topics. Financial contributions to sustain the press's work are welcomed. Contributions are tax deductible to the fullest extent allowed by the IRS.

To learn more about Apprentice House books or to obtain submission guidelines, please visit www.apprenticehouse.com.

Apprentice House
Communication Department
Loyola University Maryland
4501 N. Charles Street
Baltimore, MD 21210
410-617-5265
info@apprenticehouse.com • www.apprenticehouse.com